Mastering JSP Custom Tags and Tag Libraries

James Goodwill

Wiley Computer Publishing

John Wiley & Sons, Inc.

NEW YORK • CHICHESTER • WEINHEIM • BRISBANE • SINGAPORE • TORONTO

Publisher: Robert Ipsen
Editor: Robert M. Elliott
Managing Editor: John Atkins
Book Packaging: Ryan Publishing Group, Inc.
Copyeditors: Tiffany Taylor and Kim Cofer
Proofreader: Nancy Sixsmith
Page Layout: Gina Rexrode
Technical Editor: Avery Regier

This book is printed on acid-free paper. ∞

Published by John Wiley & Sons, Inc.

Published simultaneously in Canada.

Library of Congress Cataloging-in-Publication Data:

ISBN: 0-471-21303-9

Printed in the United States of America.

10 9 8 7 6 5 4 3 2 1

To my girls Christy, Abby, and Emma

Contents

Acknowledgments

I would like to begin this text by thanking the people who made this book what it is today. They are the people who took my words and shaped them into something that I hope will help you use and develop JSP custom tag libraries to their fullest. Of these people, I would like to explicitly thank Tim Ryan, Avery Regier, and Tiffany Taylor. They all contributed considerably to what I hope is a successful book. On a closer note, I would like to thank everyone at my company, Virtuas Solutions, LLC, for their support while I was completing this text. The entire, "UNREAL" staff contributed by picking up my assignments when my plate was too full.

Finally, the most important contributors to this book are my wife Christy, and our daughters Abby and Emma. They are the ones who really sacrificed during the development of this text. They are the ones who deserve the credit for this book. Without their support, this text would be a collection of words that make very little sense.

About the Author

James Goodwill is the co-founder and Chief Technology Officer of Virtuas Solutions, LLC, located in Denver, Colorado. With more than 10 years of experience, James leads Virtuas' Senior Internet Architects in the development of cutting-edge tools designed for J2EE e-business acceleration. Virtuas' products includes the tag libraries Jtag and Jtag Wireless, and a MVC framework called Web Application Model (WAM), which was architected and designed by Mr. Goodwill.

In addition to his professional experience, James is the author of the bestselling Java titles *Developing Java Servlets*, *Pure JavaServer Pages*, and *Apache Jakarta-Tomcat.* James is also a regular columnist on the Java community Web site, OnJava.com.

More information about James, his work, and his previous publications can be found on his company's Web site at http://www.virtuas.com.

Introduction

I have been working with server-side Web technologies for many years, and have seen both the good and the bad. I have been most impressed with the Java server-side technologies, namely servlets, EJBs, JSPs, and of course JSP custom tags.

Throughout this time, I have designed and developed many Web applications using all of these technologies, and although there is varying opinion as to what the best combination of EJB, servlets, and JSPs is, it is strictly up to you, the application developer, as to what that solution is. There are some people that would have you believe that custom tags are meant only as a presentation mechanism. In a large enterprise application, this may be true, but at the same time this depends solely on the project and staff involved. There may be times when your staff and project requirements fit a complete JSP/custom tag solution. This is by no means a bad thing. It is simply the nature of the project. The most common of these times is when you have to develop a Web application quickly with limited resources.

The goal of this text is to give you a thorough understanding of JSP custom tags, rich code examples that demonstrate how to use specific tags, the architectural knowledge to develop your own tags and tag libraries, and the foundation needed to determine where custom tags fit into your Web application.

One of the main reasons custom tags exist is to take care of some of the perceived problems with JSPs, namely complicated scriptlet code that has become too difficult to modify and maintain. These circumstances really allow custom tags to show off their usefulness. This book demonstrates how you can encapsulate complex business logic into reusable tags that are both simple to use and maintain.

To get the full benefit from the topics covered in this text, you should have a working knowledge of the Java language and be familiar with Web technologies, including the request/response model. This text provides you with a brief introduction to servlets and JSPs, but does not cover some of the more advanced topics related to these technologies.

If you would like more information about programming with servlets and JSP, please see my other books covering these technologies: *Developing Java Servlets* or *Pure JSP*.

Organization of the Book

This book is both a tutorial and a reference, divided into three distinct sections. It begins by describing the process of developing JSP custom tags and tag libraries. It then moves on to the two reference sections, which describe both Apache's Jakarta Taglibs project and Sun's new JSP Standard Tag Libraries (JSTL).

Part I is a tutorial for developing JSP custom tags and custom tag libraries. It begins by introducing JSP custom tags and Java Web applications. It describes the process needed when configuring your own Web application environment—detailed instructions are provided for installing and configuring Jakarta-Tomcat. This section of the book also provides a brief introduction to both servlet and JSP technologies. It then goes on to discuss the actual development of the different types of JSP custom tags, including simple custom tags, tags that process their bodies, iteration tags, and cooperating tags.

Part II is a code-intensive reference for Apache's Jakarta Taglib project. Apache has led the way in developing Java open source solutions, and its Jakarta Taglib collection of custom tag libraries is indispensable to Java Web application developers. This section begins by describing the Jakarta Taglibs project including how you obtain and install the taglibs archive. Jakarta Taglibs is an ongoing project; some tags are mature, while others are new and still in beta. This book discusses the most relevant, useful, and polished tag libraries included in the Jakarta Taglibs project. The goal of this book is not to be simply exhaustive, but to focus on real-world solutions for developing Java Web applications.

Part III is a code-intensive reference for Sun's new JSP Standard Tag Library (JSTL) project (also known as JSR 052). The JSTL was developed through the Java Community Process, but the product itself is hosted on Apache's Jakarta Taglibs site. This section of the book begins by describing the goals of the JSTL project, where to obtain the product, and how to install the JSTL archive. It then continues by describing the tag libraries included in the project. At the time of this writing, the JSTL is in Early Access 3. This book takes the same approach to covering JSTL as Jakarta Taglibs. I focus on the most relevant and useful aspects of JSTL: the core tags, SQL tags, and the new expression language (EL) support.

Part IV is an appendix that lists the Tag Library APIs.

Source Code and More Information

You can find all the source code and examples used in this book at the following link: http://www.wiley.com/compbooks/goodwill.

As with any book project, there will be items that I have not discussed but are of interest to individual readers. If you run across such an issue or just have a question, please feel free to contact me at *books@virtuas.com*. Please be sure to place the text "custom tags" in the subject line. I hope you enjoy this title and get much use out of its words.

Thanks,

James Goodwill, III

CHAPTER

1

Introducing JSP Custom Tags and Web Applications

In this chapter, we begin our JSP custom tag discussions. Our goal will be to get a solid overall picture of the components used in a tag library solution. We will start by describing Web applications, which act as the container for custom tags. We then move on to defining custom tags and the steps required when packaging them into libraries. At the end of this chapter, you should have an understanding of what a tag library is and how tag library solutions are assembled.

Web Applications

To understand the role of a custom tag library, you need to have an understanding of Java Web applications. The Java Servlet Specification 2.2 introduced the concept of a *Web application*. According to this specification, "A Web Application is a collection of servlets, html pages, classes, and other resources that can be bundled and run on multiple containers from multiple vendors." Essentially, a Web application is a collection of one or more Web components that have been packaged together for the purpose of creating a complete application that can be easily distributed and deployed into the Web layer of an enterprise application. The following list contains the common components that can be packaged in a Web application:

- Servlets
- JSPs
- JSP custom tag libraries
- Utility classes

- Static documents, including HTML, images, JavaScript, and so on
- Meta information describing the Web application

Directory Structure

All Web applications are packed into a common directory structure. This directory structure is the container that holds the components of a Web application. The first step in creating a Web application is creating this structure. Table 1.1 lists the directories for a sample Web application named *wiley*, and describes what each directory should contain. Each directory will be created from the <SERVER_ROOT> of the Servlet/JSP container. An example of a <SERVER_ROOT> using Tomcat 4 would be D:\Jakarta Tomcat 4.0\webapps\.

Table 1.1 Web Application Directory Structure

DIRECTORY	CONTAINS
/wiley	All JSP and HTML files. This is the root directory of the Web application.
/wiley/WEB-INF	All resources related to the application that are not in the document root of the application. Your Web application deployment descriptor is located in this directory. Note that the WEB-INF directory is not part of the public document. No files contained in this directory can be served directly to a client.
/wiley/WEB-INF/classes	Servlet and utility classes.
/wiley/WEB-INF/lib	Java Archive (JAR) files that the Web application depends on. You will use this directory to store your custom tag libraries after they have been packaged. You will also use this directory to hold your tag library descriptors (TLDs). We discuss custom tag libraries and TLDs later in the chapter.

NOTE **Web applications allow classes to be stored in both the /WEB-INF/classes and /WEB-INF/lib directories. The class loader will load classes from the /classes directory first, followed by the JARs in the /lib directory. If you have duplicate classes in both the /classes and /lib directories, the classes in the /classes directory will take precedence.**

Web Application Deployment Descriptor

The backbone of any Web application is its deployment descriptor, which describes all the components in the Web application. The Web application deployment descriptor is an XML file named web.xml that is located in the /<SERVER_ROOT>/*application-*

name/WEB-INF/ directory. For the Web application wiley, the web.xml file would be located in the /<SERVER_ROOT>/wiley/WEB-INF/ directory. The information that can be described in the deployment descriptor includes the following elements:

- ServletContext init parameters
- Localized content
- Session configuration
- Servlet/JSP definitions
- Servlet/JSP mappings
- Tag library references
- Mime type mappings
- Welcome file list
- Error pages
- Security Realm Configurations

The following code snippet shows an example deployment descriptor that defines a tag library. We will examine the taglib element in much more detail later in this text:

```
<?xml version="1.0" encoding="ISO-8859-1"?>

<!DOCTYPE web-app PUBLIC
  '-//Sun Microsystems, Inc.//DTD Web Application 2.3//EN'
  'http://java.sun.com/j2ee/dtds/web-app_2_3.dtd'>

<web-app>

  <taglib>
    <taglib-uri>
      /customtags
    </taglib-uri>
    <taglib-location>
      /WEB-INF/lib/customtags.tld
    </taglib-location>
  </taglib>

</web-app>
```

Creating and Packaging a Web Application

Now that we have a good understanding of what makes a Web application, let's go through the physical steps required when creating and packaging a Web application. Each of the required steps are covered in the following list:

1. Decide upon a unique name that identifies your Web application. This name will be used as part of the Web application URI and as the packaging name.
2. Create the directory structure that we discussed in the previous section, "Directory Structure," substituting the name of your Web application for the previously mentioned wiley Web application name.

3. Create an empty web.xml file, and copy this file to the */webappname/*WEB-INF/ directory. An example empty web.xml file is the following:

```
<?xml version="1.0" encoding="ISO-8859-1"?>

<!DOCTYPE web-app PUBLIC
  '-//Sun Microsystems, Inc.//DTD Web Application 2.3//EN'
  'http://java.sun.com/j2ee/dtds/web-app_2_3.dtd'>

<web-app>

</web-app>
```

4. Move all of your Web application components, JSPs, servlets, and so on into the appropriate directories mentioned earlier.
5. Modify the web.xml, if necessary.

That is it. You now have a complete Web application. At this point, you can decide upon your application deployment mechanism. The simplest form of deployment is to move your entire Web application directory structure in to a JSP/servlet container. If you use the Tomcat 4 container, then you would move your directory structure into the following directory:

```
<TOMCAT_HOME>/webapps/
```

The second method of deployment involves packaging your Web application in an archive file. To do this, you use the standard packaging format for a Web application, which is a Web ARchive (WAR) file. A *WAR file* is simply a JAR file with the extension .war as opposed to .jar. You can create a WAR file by using Java's archiving tool jar. To create a WAR file, you simply need to change to the root directory of your Web application, and type the following command:

```
jar cvf webappname.war .
```

For instance, the command jar cvf wiley.war . will produce an archive file named wiley.war that contains the entire wiley Web application. Now you can deploy your Web application by distributing this file.

What Are JSP Custom Tags?

JavaServer Pages (JSP) custom tags encapsulate functional and/or business logic that can be reused inside a JSP. They give you the ability to insert Extensible Markup Language (XML) style tags representing complex business logic into a JSP without having the JSP code itself become overly complicated. The basic composition of a custom tag includes an XML tag with optional tag attributes and an optional tag body. Some of the characteristics that define custom tags are listed here:

- Custom tags have access to all the implicit JSP objects. We will discuss each of these objects in Chapter 4, "JSP Overview and Architecture."
- Custom tags can be dynamically configured using tag attributes.

- Custom tags can communicate with each other through either nesting or shared objects.
- Custom tags render complex business logic into a simple XML syntax.

To illustrate the power of using custom tags, the code snippet in Listing 1.1 shows an example JSP containing two custom tags used to perform a SQL query and iterate over the results. As you examine this JSP, you should notice the bolded text. These sections represent the custom tags that will perform the query and iterate over the results. The tag code used here is obviously much less complicated than the Java code that would be used to actually perform the same logic:

```
<%@ taglib uri="/dbexample" prefix="sql" %>

<html>
<head>
  <title>Custom Tags Demo</title>
  <meta http-equiv="Content-Type" content="text/html;
charset=iso-8859-1">
</head>

<body bgcolor="#FFFFFF">

<sql:sqlQuery driver="sun.jdbc.odbc.JdbcOdbcDriver"
           url="Jdbc:Odbc:contacts"
           resultId="results"
           scope="page">
SELECT * FROM CONTACTS
</sql:sqlQuery>

<table border="1" width="500">
  <tr>
    <th>Username</th><th>First Name</th><th>Last Name</th>
  </tr>
  <sql:sqlIterator resultId="results" scope="page">

  <tr>

    <td><sql:getColumn column="username" /></td>
    <td><sql:getColumn column="firstname" /></td>
    <td><sql:getColumn column="lastname" /></td>

  </tr>

  </sql:sqlIterator>
</table>

</body>
</html>
```

Listing 1.1 JSP containing two custom tags to perform SQL queries and iterate over the results.

This simple XML notation is possible because the Java code that actually implements this complex logic is abstracted into a Java class called a *tag handler*. Every custom tag has a tag handler. Three types of tag handlers are available: tag handlers without bodies (simple tags), tag handlers with bodies, and iteration tag handlers. We will focus on each of these throughout the remainder of this book.

Custom Tag Libraries

Custom tags are usually grouped together into libraries called, plainly enough, custom tag libraries. A *custom tag library* is composed of one or more custom tag handlers with a Tag Library Descriptor (TLD). A *TLD* is an XML file that defines each tag handler in a tag library. All tag handlers are required to have an entry in the TLD.

The steps involved when you're creating and deploying a custom tag library are part of a well-defined process. This process can be broken down into the following steps.

1. Create one or more tag handlers containing the logic to be executed when a tag is encountered. The following code shows a simple tag handler:

```
import java.io.IOException;

import javax.servlet.jsp.tagext.Tag;
import javax.servlet.jsp.PageContext;
import javax.servlet.jsp.JspWriter;
import javax.servlet.jsp.JspException;

import javax.servlet.jsp.tagext.TagSupport;

public class SimpleTag extends TagSupport {

  public int doStartTag()
    throws javax.servlet.jsp.JspException {

    // Get a JspWriter from the PageContext
    JspWriter out = pageContext.getOut();

    try {

      out.print("Hello from a simple JSP.");
    }
    catch (IOException e) {

      throw new JspException("IOException thrown:" +
        e.getMessage());
    }

    return Tag.EVAL_BODY_INCLUDE;
  }
}
```

NOTE **For now, you can ignore the details of this tag handler and its TLD. We will describe these details in subsequent chapters.**

2. This tag simply writes the string *Hello from a simple JSP.* to the client browser that made the request to the JSP referencing this tag handler.

   Describe this tag handler. To do this, you must create a TLD that defines this tag handler. The TLD used to describe this tag handler can be found in the following code snippet:

```
<?xml version="1.0" encoding="ISO-8859-1" ?>
<!DOCTYPE taglib
  PUBLIC "-//Sun Microsystems, Inc.//DTD JSP Tag Library 1.1//EN"
  "http://java.sun.com/j2ee/dtds/web-jsptaglibrary_1_1.dtd">

<!-- a tag library descriptor -->

<taglib>
  <tlibversion>1.0</tlibversion>
  <jspversion>1.2</jspversion>
  <shortname>chapter1</shortname>

  <tag>
    <name>simple</name>
    <tagclass>SimpleTag</tagclass>
    <bodycontent>JSP</bodycontent>
    <info>Just a Simple Tag Example</info>
  </tag>
</taglib>
```

   As you can see, this snippet defines a single tag that can be referenced in a JSP using the name *simple*. It defines the tag handler named SimpleTag that will be executed with every occurrence of the simple tag.

3. Publish this tag library to a Web application so that it can be used by a JSP. To do this, you need to add an entry to the Web application's web.xml file. The entry to deploy this library is as follows:

```
<?xml version="1.0" encoding="ISO-8859-1"?>

<!DOCTYPE web-app PUBLIC
  '-//Sun Microsystems, Inc.//DTD Web Application 2.3//EN'
  'http://java.sun.com/j2ee/dtds/web-app_2_3.dtd'>

<web-app>

<taglib>
  <taglib-uri>/chapter1</taglib-uri>
  <taglib-location>
    /WEB-INF/lib/chapter1.tld
```

```
    </taglib-location>
  </taglib>

</web-app>
```

This entry in the web.xml file tells the Web application two things. First, it defines a URI, using the <taglib-uri> subelement. The URI represents a unique key that the Web application can use to look up this tag library. Second, the entry defines the location of the TLD representing this tag library, using the <taglib-location> subelement.

4. Add a tag to a JSP that references the SimpleTag handler. An example JSP containing a reference to the simple tag is listed here:

```
<%@ taglib uri="/chapter1" prefix="chp1" %>

<html>
<head>
  <title>Custom Tag Example</title>
</head>

<body bgcolor="#FFFFFF">

<chp1:simple/>

</body>
</html>
```

Two elements in this JSP are used to reference the SimpleTag handler. The first is the taglib directive. A *taglib directive* is a JSP directive that tells the Web application container which tag libraries this JSP will use and what prefix each of these tags will be referenced by. The second element is the actual tag element. This element represents the SimpleTag handler that is referenced by the URI /chapter1. The output of this JSP would be an HTML page containing the text *Hello from a simple JSP.*

After you have examined these four components, you will see that there is a link between each of them, starting with simple.jsp. This link is shown in Figure 1.1.

The container uses these links to determine which tag handler should be executed when a particular tag is encountered. The steps performed by the Web application container when it encounters a reference to the simple tag are as follows:

1. The Web application container encounters the tag <chp1:simple /> and parses out the prefix *chp1* and the tag name *simple.*
2. The container then looks in the list of taglib directives referenced in this JSP for a prefix attribute with a value of *chp1*.
3. Once it finds a matching taglib directive, the container gets the value of the taglib uri attribute. In this case, the uri attribute has a value of */chapter1*. The container looks in the Web application's web.xml file for a <taglib> element that has a <taglib-uri> equal to /chapter1.

4. Once the container finds the matching <taglib-uri>, it gets the location of the tag library's TLD from the <taglib-location> subelement. In this case, the TLD is in a file named chapter1.tld located in the /WEB-INF/lib/ directory of the Web application.
5. The container then looks in TLD for a <tag> named simple. When the container finds the matching <tag> element, it has completed its search and has all the values it needs to execute the appropriate tag handler, which in this case is the class SimpleTag.

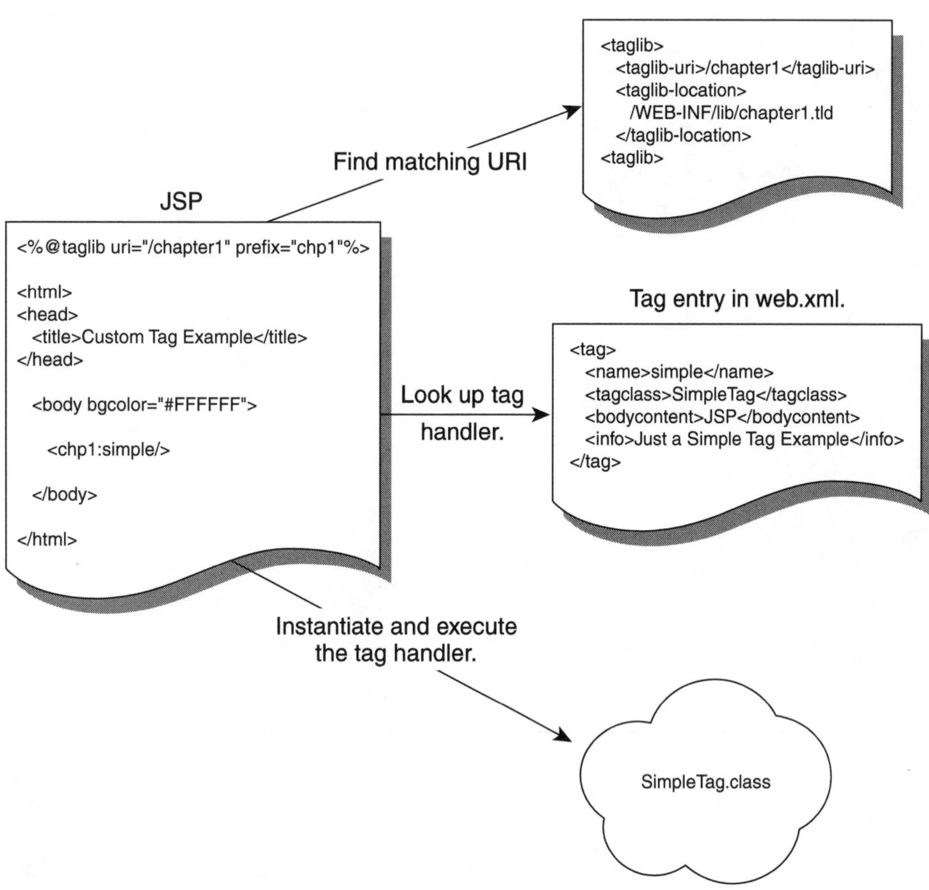

Figure 1.1 Link between custom tag components.

Summary

In this chapter, we began our custom tag coverage. We started by describing Java Web applications, which act as the container for custom tag libraries. We then went on to describe custom tags and custom tag libraries and their components. We concluded by describing the steps the container completes when it encounters a custom tag while processing a JSP. In the next chapter, we will explain how to install and configure the Tomcat JSP/servlet container, and develop a custom tag application that shows the power of custom tag libraries.

CHAPTER

2

Configuring and Testing the Web Application Environment

In this chapter, you will configure the Web application environment that you will use throughout the rest of this text. We will start by describing the steps involved in installing and configuring the Jakarta-Tomcat Web application container, which will be our container of choice for all our examples. We will then move on to creating and deploying an example Web application using the Jakarta Taglibs Project.

Apache Jakarta-Tomcat Project

The Tomcat server is an open source, Java-based Web application container that was created to run servlet and JavaServer Page (JSP) Web applications. It has become the reference implementation for both the servlet and JSP specifications. You will be using Tomcat 4 for all the examples in this book.

Before you get started with the installation and configuration of Tomcat, you need to make sure you have the items listed in Table 2.1.

Table 2.1 Tomcat Installation Requirements

COMPONENT	LOCATION
Jakarta-Tomcat 4	http://jakarta.apache.org/
JDK 1.3 Standard Edition	http://java.sun.com/j2se/1.3/

Installing and Configuring Tomcat

You will be installing Tomcat as a stand-alone server on both the Linux and Windows NT/2000 operating systems. Before you can begin the Tomcat installation, you need to install the JDK, following the installation instructions included with the JDK archive.

Installing Tomcat on Linux

The installation is much simpler on a Linux than a Windows machine. Follow these steps:

1. Set the JAVA_HOME environment variable. To do this under Linux, find your shell in Table 2.2 and type the matching command. You will need to replace */jdk1.3* with the root location of your JDK installation.

Table 2.2 Java Environment Settings

SHELL	COMMAND
bash	JAVA_HOME=*/jdk1.3*
tcsh	setenv JAVA_HOME */jdk1.3*

2. Extract the Tomcat server to a directory of your local disk. The directory you choose will become the <TOMCAT_HOME> directory. For this installation, we will assume that Tomcat will be installed to /JakartaTomcat4.0.
3. Set the <TOMCAT_HOME> environment variable. To do this under Linux, find your shell in Table 2.3, and type the matching command. You will need to replace the value */JakartaTomcat4.0* with the location of your Tomcat installation.

Table 2.3 Tomcat Environment Settings

SHELL	COMMAND
bash	TOMCAT_HOME=*/JakartaTomcat4.0*
tcsh	setenv TOMCAT_HOME */JakartaTomcat4.0*

This is all there is to it. If you are not interested in the Windows installation, you can move on to "Testing Your Tomcat Installation."

Installing Tomcat on Windows 2000/NT

To install Tomcat on Windows, you need to first extract the Tomcat server to a temporary directory. The default Tomcat archive does not contain an installation program; therefore, extracting the Tomcat archive is equivalent to installation. Again, you are installing to drive D:, which will make the TOMCAT_HOME directory D:\Jakarta Tomcat 4.0.

NOTE **You can install Tomcat 4 using a Windows installation program. This installation program will install Tomcat as a Windows NT/2000 service.**

After you have extracted Tomcat, the next step is setting the JAVA_HOME and TOMCAT_HOME environment variables. These variables are used to compile JSPs and run Tomcat, respectively. To do this under NT/2000, perform the following steps:

1. Open the NT/2000 Control Panel.
2. Start the NT/2000 System application and select the Advanced tab.
3. Click the Environment Variables button. You will see a screen similar to Figure 2.1.

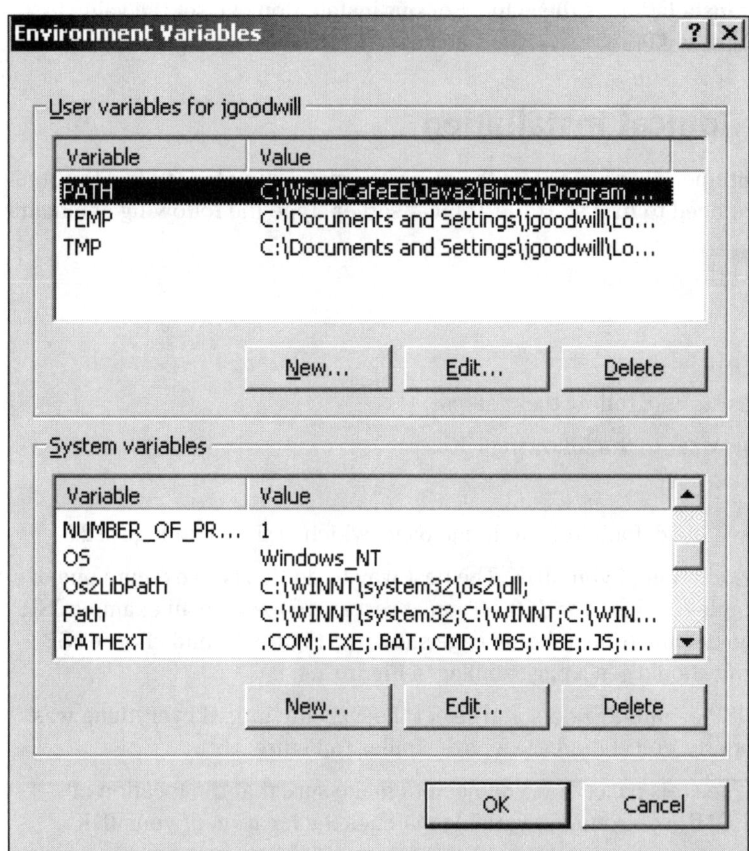

Figure 2.1 Environment Variables dialog box.

4. Click the New button in the System Variables section of the Environment Variables dialog box. Add a variable named JAVA_HOME, and set its value to the location of your JDK installation. Figure 2.2 shows the settings associated with our installation.

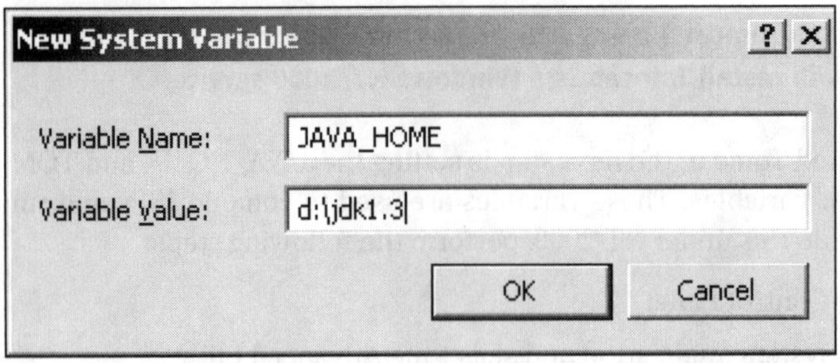

Figure 2.2 JAVA_HOME environment settings for our installation.

5. Repeat Step 4 using TOMCAT_HOME for the variable name and the location of your Tomcat installation as the value. For our installation, we set the value to D:\Jakarta Tomcat 4.0.

Testing Your Tomcat Installation

Before you can continue, you need to test the steps you just completed. To test the Tomcat installation, you need to first start the Tomcat server. Type the following command for Windows:

```
<TOMCAT_HOME>\bin\startup.bat
```

or Linux:

```
<TOMCAT_HOME>/bin/startup.sh
```

Once Tomcat has started, follow these steps:

1. Open your browser to the following URL:

```
http://localhost:8080
```

   You should see the default Tomcat home page, which is shown in Figure 2.3.

2. Verify the installation of your JDK. The best way to do this is to execute one of the JSP examples provided with the Tomcat server. To execute an example JSP, start from the default Tomcat home page shown in Figure 2.3 and choose JSP Examples. You should see a page similar to Figure 2.4.
3. Choose the JSP example Snoop, and select the Execute link. If everything was installed properly, you should see a page similar to Figure 2.5.
4. If you do not see this page, then you need to make sure that the location of your JAVA_HOME environment variable matches the location of your JDK installation.

An Example Custom Tag Web Application

Now that your Web application container is installed, you will develop and deploy a simple contact management Web application using the Jakarta Taglibs Projects. The purpose of this exercise is to give you a foundation in the practical application and use of

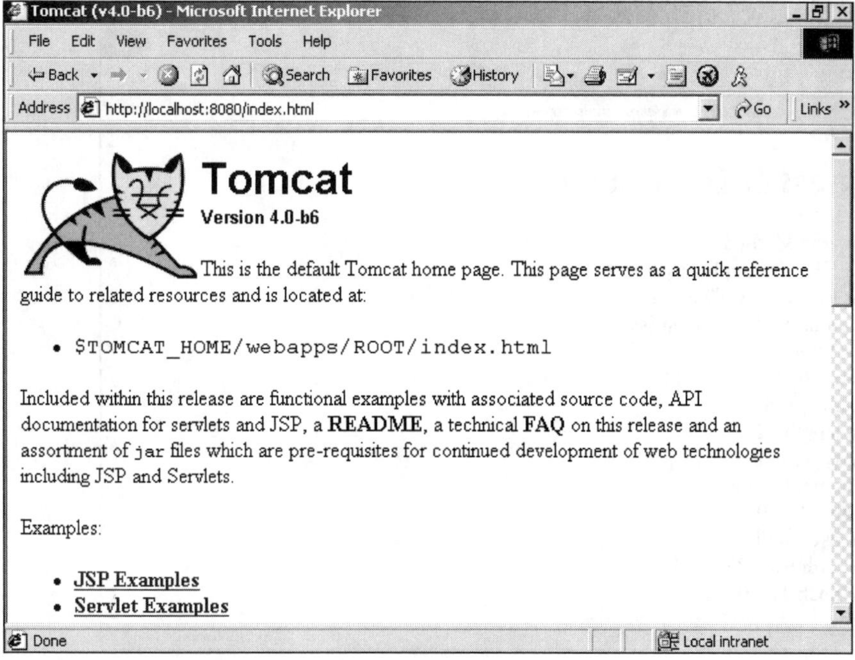

Figure 2.3 Default Tomcat home page.

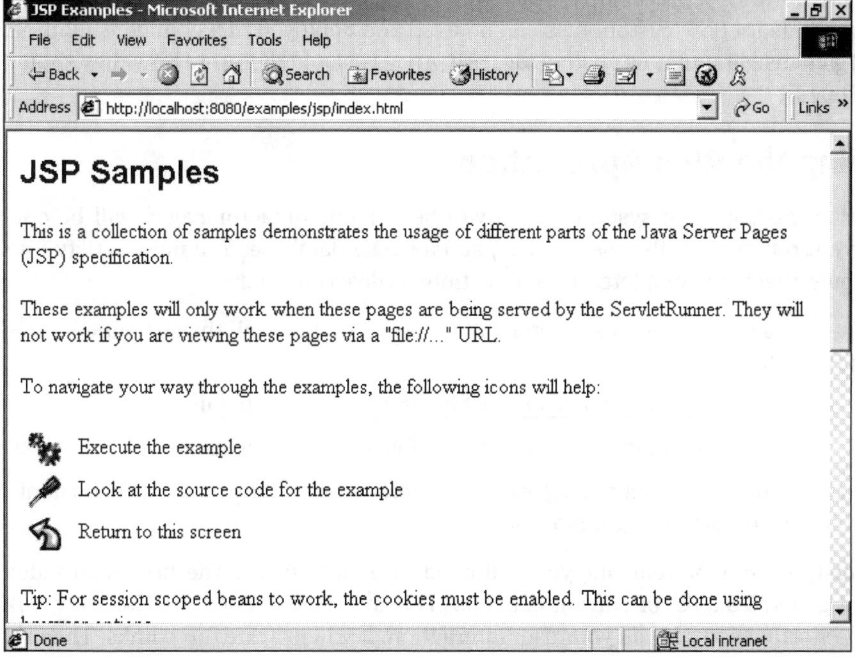

Figure 2.4 JSP Samples page.

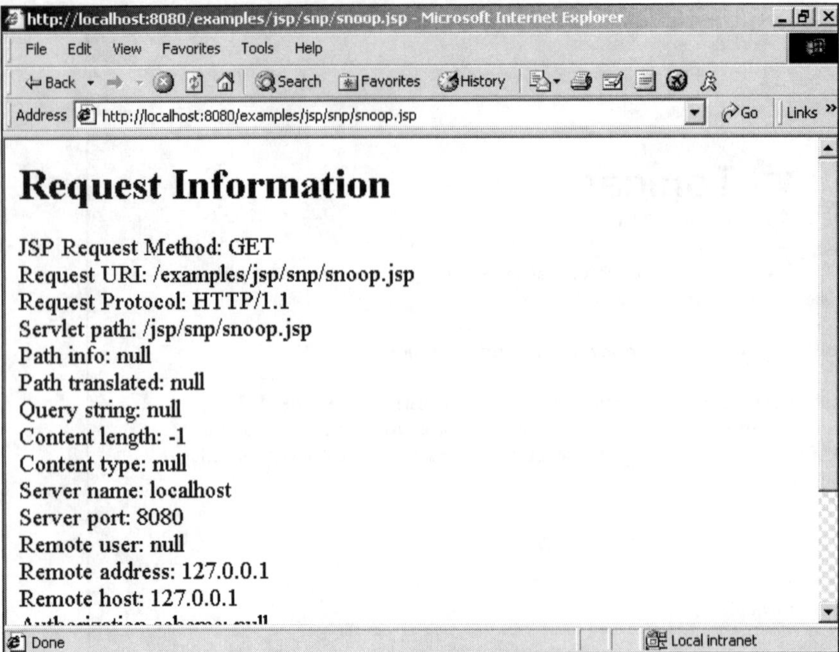

Figure 2.5 Results of executing the Snoop JSP.

custom tag libraries. By developing this Web application using only JSPs and custom tags, you will learn how custom tags can be used and deployed in a complete solution. You will gain insight into how custom tags are processed and therefore how they should be developed.

Defining the Web Application

The contact management system, which will be named contactmanager, will be constructed entirely from JSPs, custom tags, and a single database. You must satisfy four basic requirements to complete this application, as described here:

1. The contact manager must contain a homepage that lists all the current contacts in the database.
2. The user of the contact manager must be able to edit a listed user.
3. The user of the contact manager must be able to add a new user.
4. The user of the contact manager must be able to launch the default email client from the contact manager interface.

To satisfy these requirements, you will need three interfaces. The first is an index page that generates a list of current contacts. This interface, named the List View, will act as the starting point for all your user interaction. It will provide three links: The first lets the user select a current contact they would like to edit, the second lets the user send an email to a current contact, and the third lets the user add a new contact.

The second interface will be displayed when the user selects a user to edit from the List View. This interface, named the Edit View, will populate an HTML form with a selected contact's information. The information can then be edited and the database updated with the changes.

The last interface will be displayed when the user selects the Add link from the List View. This interface, named the Add View, will contain an empty HTML form with the possible attributes for a contact. Once the contact's information has been entered, the new values will be inserted into the database.

Creating the Web Application Directory Structure

You now need to create the directory structure that will hold your Web application. You will use the name of your Web application, contactmanager, as the root directory of this structure; therefore your directory structure will be laid out as described in Table 2.4.

Table 2.4 Contact Manager Directory Structure

DIRECTORY	CONTAINS
/contactmanager	All your JSP views and their associated images
/contactmanager/WEB-INF	The web.xml file for the contactmanager Web application
/contactmanager/WEB-INF/classes	All the class files for your tag handlers
/contactmanager/WEB-INF/lib	The JAR file and TLD for the Jakarta Taglib that you will be using in this application

NOTE **All the directories in Table 2.4 are assumed to be relative to the <TOMCAT_HOME>webapps/ directory described in the previous section.**

To make this structure complete, you also need a default web.xml file. Listing 2.1 contains an empty web.xml file that you can use in this application. You should create this file, and move it to the /contactmanager/WEB-INF directory.

```
<?xml version="1.0" encoding="ISO-8859-1"?>

<!DOCTYPE web-app PUBLIC
   '-//Sun Microsystems, Inc.//DTD Web Application 2.3//EN'
   'http://java.sun.com/j2ee/dtds/web-app_2_3.dtd'>

<web-app>

</web-app>
```

Listing 2.1 An empty web.xml file.

Creating the Contact Manager Database

The database you will use in this example application consists of a single table named contacts, which contains all the contact information used in this application. You will create this database in both Microsoft Access and the open source database MySQL. The structure of this table is described in Table 2.5.

Table 2.5 Contacts Table Structure

COLUMN	DESCRIPTION
username	A unique key identifying the contact. It is a varchar(10).
firstname	The string representation of the contact's first name. It is a varchar(30).
lastname	The string representation of the contact's last name. It is a varchar(30).
title	The string representation of the contact's job title. It is a varchar(30).
phone	The string representation of the contact's phone number. It is a varchar(30).
email	The string representation of the contact's email address. It is a varchar(30).

The data that populate this table can be found in Table 2.6.

Table 2.6 Contents of the contacts Table

USER NAME	FIRST NAME	LAST NAME	TITLE	PHONE	EMAIL
abrickey	Art	Brickey	President	(303) 555-1214	abrickey@anywhere.com
tharris	Todd	Harris	Sales Associate	(206) 555-9482	tharris@anywhere.com
sriley	Sean	Riley	VP of Sales	(206) 555-3412	sriley@anywhere.com
jgoodwill	James	Goodwill	CTO	(303) 555-1214	jgoodwill@anywhere.com
tgray	Tim	Gray	Waterboy	(303) 555-9876	tgray@anywhere.com

NOTE **Although you can use any Java Database Connectivity (JDBC)-compliant database with this example, I am including a Microsoft Access database with the source for this book. You can download all the code for this book at www.wiley.com/compbooks/goodwill.**

Creating and Configuring a MySQL Database

To create the contacts database in MySQL, you need to download and install the MySQL server, which you can find at www.mysql.com. You should also download the latest JDBC driver for MySQL, which you can find at the same Web site.

After you have installed MySQL, complete the following steps to create and configure the contacts database:

1. Start the mysql client found in the <MYSQL_HOME>/bin/ directory.
2. Create the database, which will be explicitly named contacts, by executing the following command:

```
create database contacts;
```

3. Select the newly created database using the following command:

```
use contacts;
```

4. Create the contacts table using the following commands:

```
create table contacts
(
  username varchar(10) not null primary key,
  firstname varchar(30),
  lastname varchar(30),
  title varchar(30),
  phone varchar(30),
  email varchar(30) not null);
```

5. Insert the data into the contacts table by executing the following commands:

```
insert into contacts
  values("abrickey",
         "Art",
         "Brickey",
         "President",
         "(303) 555-1214",
         "abrickey@anywhere.com");
insert into contacts
  values("tharris",
         "Todd",
         "Harris",
         "Sales Associate",
         "(206) 555-9482",
         "tharris@anywhere.com");
insert into contacts
  values("sriley",
         "Sean",
         "Riley",
         "VP of Sales",
         "(206) 555-3412",
         "sriley@anywhere.com");
insert into contacts
  values("jgoodwill",
         "James",
```

```
                  "Goodwill",
                  "CTO",
                  "(303) 555-1214",
                  "jgoodwill@anywhere.com");
    insert into contacts
      values("tgray",
                  "Tim",
                  "Gray",
                  "Waterboy",
                  "(303) 555-9876",
                  "tgray@anywhere.com");
```

6. Copy the MySQL JDBC driver into the <TOMCAT_HOME>lib/ directory.

You now have a MySQL database of contacts.

Creating and Configuring a Microsoft Access Database

Microsoft Access uses a single file to represent a database; therefore, you can simply use the contacts.mdb file included with this text's source code instead of going through the steps normally required to create a contacts database.

Although you do not have to create the contacts database, you will need to set up an ODBC data source that can be referenced by the JDBC-ODBC bridge. The following steps describe the process of setting up a new data source:

1. Open the Windows NT/2000 Control Panel.
2. Double-click on the Administrative Tools icon.
3. Double-click on the Data Sources (ODBC) icon, and select the System DSN tab; see Figure 2.6.
4. Click the Add button to open the Create New Data Source dialog box (see Figure 2.7).
5. Select Microsoft Access Drive, and click Finish. You should see a window similar to Figure 2.8.
6. Enter “contacts” in the Data Source Name edit box.
7. Click the Select button, and navigate to the location of the contacts.mdb file, which was packaged with the text's source code. Click OK for all remaining actions.

You now have an ODBC data source that contains your database of contacts.

Acquiring and Installing the Taglibs

In this example, you will use a set of custom tags from the Jakarta Taglibs project: the DBTags tag library. You can find it on the Jakarta Project Web site at the following URL:

```
http://jakarta.apache.org/taglibs/binarydist.html
```

You will have to download the entire collection of libraries and then extract the archive to a directory on your local system. Once you have the archive extracted, find the files dbtags.jar and dbtags.tld. Both files should be in the /jakarta-taglibs/dbtag

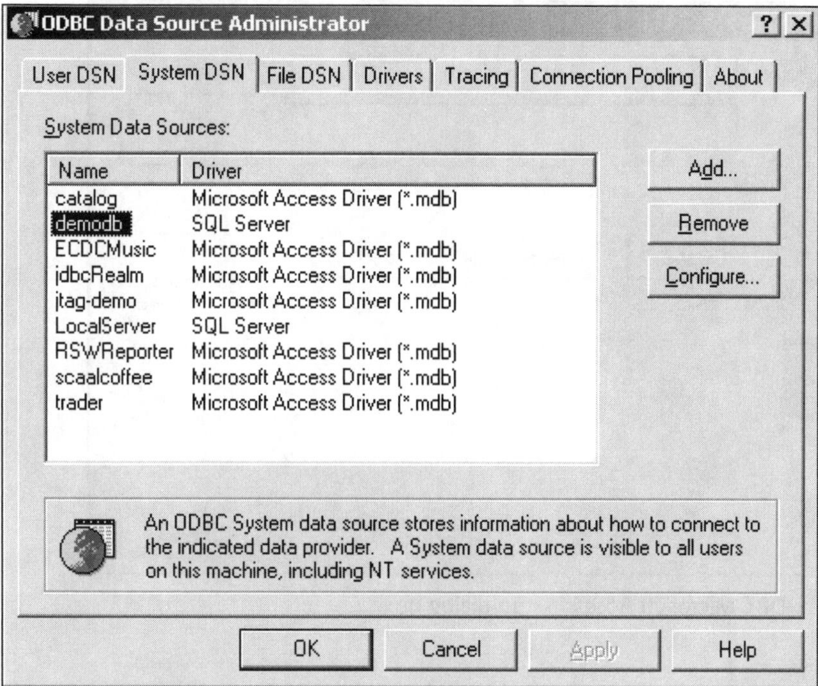

Figure 2.6 ODBC Data Source Administrator.

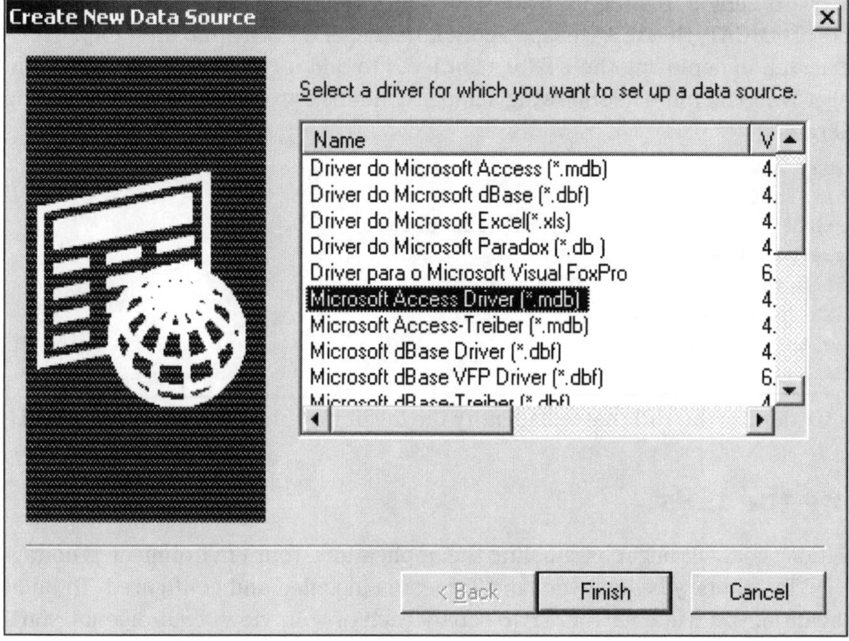

Figure 2.7 Create New Data Source dialog box.

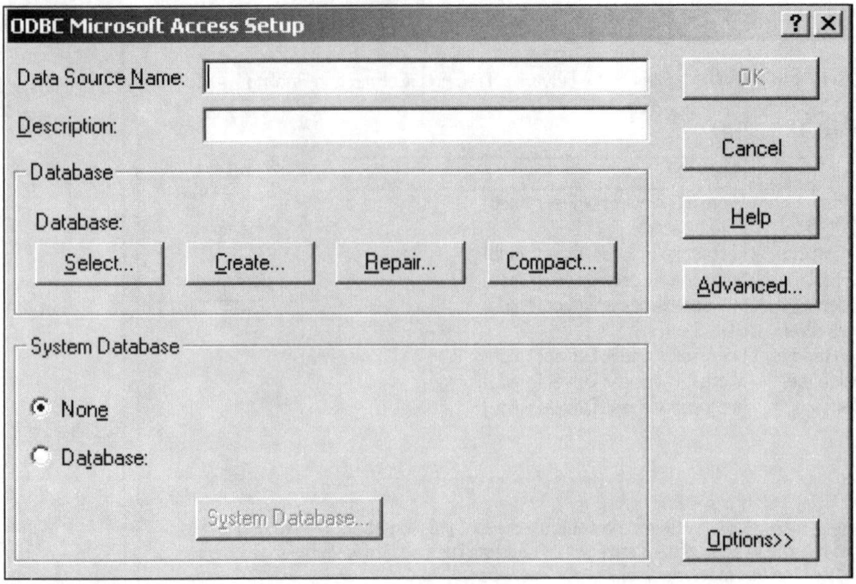

Figure 2.8 ODBC Microsoft Access Setup dialog box.

directory of the extracted archive. These files contain the tag handlers and the TLD, respectively. To deploy this tag library to the contactmanager application, copy both files to the <TOMCAT_HOME>/webapps/contactmanagerWEB-INF/lib directory.

The final step in deploying the DBTags library is to add a <taglib> entry to the contactmanager web.xml file. The following snippet contains the <taglib> entry describing this tag library:

```
<taglib>
  <taglib-uri>
    http://jakarta.apache.org/taglibs/dbtags
  </taglib-uri>
  <taglib-location>
    /WEB-INF/dbtags.tld
  </taglib-location>
</taglib>
```

This entry defines the URI that will identify the tag library and the location of its TLD.

Creating the JSPs

In this section, you will begin assembling the application. Your environment is configured, the DBTags library is deployed, and Tomcat is installed and configured. To build your application, you will create a JSP to satisfy each of your view requirements, starting with the List View, which is represented by the JSP index.jsp. This JSP can be found in Listing 2.2.

NOTE **Each JSP begins with the same taglib directive. This directive states that the tag library you are using is represented by a URI that points to the DBTags tag library. It also states that all tags from the DBTags library should be prefixed with the string *sql*.**

```
<%@ taglib
  uri="http://jakarta.apache.org/taglibs/dbtags"
  prefix="sql" %>

<html>
<head>
<title>Contacts Web Application</title>
<meta http-equiv="Content-Type" content="text/html;
charset=iso-8859-1">
</head>

<!-- open a database connection -->
<sql:connection id="conn">
  <sql:url>Jdbc:Odbc:contacts</sql:url>
  <sql:driver>sun.jdbc.odbc.JdbcOdbcDriver</sql:driver>
</sql:connection>

<body bgcolor="#FFFFFF">
<table width="100%" border="0" height="534" cellspacing="0">
  <tr bgcolor="#36566E">
    <td height="68" width="48%">
      <div align="left">
        <img src="images/hp_logo_wiley.gif" width="220"
          height="74">
      </div>
    </td>
  </tr>
    <td valign="top" align="right" height="68" width="52%">
      <font size="-1" face="arial">
      <a href="new.jsp">Add New Contact</a>
      </font>
    </td>

  <tr valign="top">

    <td width="100%" colspan="2" align="center">
      <!-- open a database query -->
```

Listing 2.2 index.jsp JSP. *(continues)*

```
        <table width="100%" border="0">

        <!-- Perform the Query -->
        <sql:statement id="stmt" conn="conn">
          <sql:query>
            select * from contacts
          </sql:query>

          <!-- iterate over the results of the query -->
          <sql:resultSet id="rset">
            <tr>
              <td>
                <a href="edit.jsp?username=<sql:getColumn
                position="1"/>">
                <sql:getColumn position="2"/></a>
              </td>
              <td><sql:getColumn position="3"/></td>
              <td><sql:getColumn position="4"/></td>
              <td><sql:getColumn position="5"/></td>
              <td><a href="mailto:
                <sql:getColumn position="6"/>">email</a>
              </td>
            </tr>
          </sql:resultSet>
        </sql:statement>
        </table>

      </td>
    </tr>
  </table>
  </body>
  </html>
```

Listing 2.2 index.jsp JSP. *(continued)*

This JSP builds the list of all the current contacts from the *contacts* database, and displays them in an HTML table. This JSP also contains links allowing you to edit a current contact, email a current contact, and create a new contact. When the container evaluates this JSP, it processes it as follows:

1. The container first encounters the connection tag. The connection tag establishes a JDBC connection to a database. It has a single attribute id, which represents the JDBC connection that will be used later in this JSP. The connection tag also has two children, a url tag and a driver tag. These two tags map directly to the JDBC URL and driver attributes of a standard JDBC connection. The values of these child tags state that you are connecting to the contacts database using the JDBC-ODBC bridge driver. If you are using MySQL, you should substitute

the following code snippet for the connection tag entries throughout this example. You should also replace the values for *user* and *password* with the appropriate values for your database instance:

```
<%-- open a database connection --%>
<sql:connection id="conn">
  <sql:url>jdbc:mysql://localhost/contacts?
   user=username;password=password</sql:url>
  <sql:driver>org.gjt.mm.mysql.Driver</sql:driver>
</sql:connection>
```

2. The next tag encountered by the container is statement. The statement tag is the parent to your database interaction tags. This instance states that it will use the conn object from the previously evaluated connection tag in the evaluation of its body.
3. The container then evaluates the body of the statement tag, encountering the query tag first. The query tag is a very simple tag that performs the SQL query contained in its body, using the database referenced by the conn object.
4. The container next encounters the second child of the statement tag, which is the resultSet tag. The resultSet tag iterates over its body, once for every row in the ResultSet returned by the query tag.
5. The body of the resultSet contains an HTML table row that, when evaluated, will contain the results from the query tag. These results are displayed using the getColumn tag, which takes a single attribute representing the table column to be displayed.

The next JSP, edit.jsp, represents the Edit View. This view is displayed when someone selects a contact to be edited. The contents of this JSP are shown in Listing 2.3.

```
<%@ taglib
  uri="http://jakarta.apache.org/taglibs/dbtags"
  prefix="sql" %>

<html>
<head>
<title>Contacts Web Application</title>
<meta http-equiv="Content-Type" content="text/html;
charset=iso-8859-1">
</head>

<body bgcolor="#FFFFFF">
<table width="100%" border="0" height="534" cellspacing="0">
  <tr bgcolor="#36566E">
    <td height="68" width="48%">
      <div align="left">
```

Listing 2.3 edit.jsp JSP. *(continues)*

```
        <a href="index.jsp">
          <img border="0" src="images/hp_logo_wiley.gif"
            width="220" height="74">
        </a>
      </div>
    </td>
  </tr>
    <td valign="top" align="right" height="68" width="52%">
    <font size="-1" face="arial">
      <a href="new.jsp">Add New Contact</a>
    </font>
    </td>
  <tr>
    </tr>

  <tr valign="top">

    <td width="100%" colspan="2" align="center">

    <!-- open a database connection -->
    <sql:connection id="conn">
      <sql:url>Jdbc:Odbc:contacts</sql:url>
      <sql:driver>sun.jdbc.odbc.JdbcOdbcDriver</sql:driver>
    </sql:connection>

    <!-- perform a database query -->
    <table width="100%" border="0">

    <sql:statement id="stmt" conn="conn">
      <sql:query>
        select *
          from contacts

          where username =
          '<%=request.getParameter("username") %>'
      </sql:query>

      <!-- iterate over the results of the query --%>
      <sql:resultSet id="rset">

      <table width="100%" border="0">
        <form method="get" action="commit.jsp">
          <input type="hidden" name="username"
            value="<%=request.getParameter("username") %>">
```

Listing 2.3 edit.jsp JSP. *(continues)*

```
<table width="75%" border="0" cellspacing="0">
<tr>
  <td>
    First:
  </td>
  <td>
    <input type="text" name="firstName"
      value="<sql:getColumn position="2 "/>">
  </td>
  <td>
    Last:
  </td>
  <td>
    <input type="text" name="lastName"
      value="<sql:getColumn position="3"/>">
  </td>
</tr>
<tr>
  <td>
    Title:
  </td>
  <td>
    <input size="30" type="text" name="title"
      value="<sql:getColumn position="4"/>">
  </td>
  <td>
    Phone:
  </td>
  <td>
    <input type="text" name="phone"
      value="<sql:getColumn position="5"/>">
  </td>
</tr>
<tr>
  <td>
    Email:
  </td>
  <td>
    <input size="30" type="text" name="email"
      value="<sql:getColumn position="6"/>">
  </td>
</tr>
<tr valign="bottom" align="right">
  <td colspan="4"><input type="submit" name="Submit"
```

Listing 2.3 edit.jsp JSP. *(continues)*

```
                value="Submit"></td>
            </tr>
            </table>
          </form>
        </table>
      </sql:resultSet>
    </sql:statement>

      </td>
    </tr>
  </table>
  </body>
  </html>
```

Listing 2.3 edit.jsp JSP. *(continued)*

This JSP creates an HTML form that is pre-populated with the values of the contact selected from the List View. It allows you to change these values and update the database with these changes. When the container evaluates this JSP, it processes as follows:

1. The container first encounters the connection tag. This connection tag has the same attribute values and children as the connection instance of the List View.
2. The next tag encountered by the container is statement. This instance states that it will use the conn object from the previously evaluated connection tag in the evaluation of its body.
3. The container then evaluates the body of the statement tag, encountering the query tag first. The body of this query tag is a little different from the one contained in the List View. It contains a SQL statement that is built using a JSP expression. This expression gets the username from the request. The username was selected from the List View. Otherwise, it performs exactly as the query tag in the List View.
4. The container next encounters the second child of the statement tag, which is the resultSet tag. The resultSet tag will evaluate its body only because the result of the query tag should contain only one row.
5. The body of the resultSet contains a single HTML form that is pre-populated using the getColumn tag. The action of this form is a JSP named commit.jsp, with the username included in a hidden input.

The next JSP, new.jsp, represents the Add View. This view is displayed when someone selects the Add New Contact link from any of your JSPs. The contents of this JSP are shown in Listing 2.4.

```
<html>
<head>
<title>Contacts Web Application</title>
<meta http-equiv="Content-Type" content="text/html;
charset=iso-8859-1">
</head>

<body bgcolor="#FFFFFF">
<table width="100%" border="0" height="534" cellspacing="0">
  <tr bgcolor="#36566E">
    <td height="68" width="48%">
      <div align="left">
        <a href="index.jsp">
          <img border="0"
            src="images/hp_logo_wiley.gif"
            width="220" height="74">
        </a>
      </div>
    </td>
  </tr>
    <td valign="top" align="right" height="68" width="52%">
    <font size="-1" face="arial">
      <a href="new.jsp">Add New Contact</a>
    </font>
    </td>
  <tr>
     </tr>

  <tr valign="top">

    <td width="100%" colspan="2" align="center">

      <table width="100%" border="0">

      <table width="100%" border="0">
        <form method="get" action="commit.jsp">
          <table width="75%" border="0" cellspacing="0">
          <tr>
            <td>First:</td><td><input type="text"
              name="firstName"></td>
            <td>Last:</td><td><input type="text"
              name="lastName"></td>
          </tr>
          <tr>
```

Listing 2.4 new.jsp JSP. *(continues)*

```
            <td>Title:</td><td><input size="30" type="text"
              name="title"></td>
            <td>Phone:</td><td><input type="text"
              name="phone"></td>
          </tr>
          <tr>
            <td>Email:</td><td><input size="30" type="text"
              name="email"></td>
          </tr>
          <tr valign="bottom" align="right">
            <td colspan="4"><input type="submit" name="Submit"
              value="Submit"></td>
          </tr>
          </table>
        </form>
      </table>

    </td>
  </tr>
</table>
</body>
</html>
```

Listing 2.4 new.jsp JSP. *(continued)*

This JSP creates an HTML form that is exactly the same as the edit.jsp, except that it is not pre-populated with the values of the contact selected from the List View. It allows you to add a completely new contact. This JSP contains no custom tags and could just as easily have been simple HTML. The only thing that you should note is that its action, like that of edit.jsp, points to the commit.jsp, but does not include a username. This is the case because this form builds a new user.

The final JSP, commit.jsp, does not represent any one of your defined views. It is used strictly to update the database. The contents of this JSP are shown in Listing 2.5.

```
<%@ taglib
  uri="http://jakarta.apache.org/taglibs/dbtags"
  prefix="sql" %>

<!-- open a database connection -->
<sql:connection id="conn">
  <sql:url>Jdbc:Odbc:contacts</sql:url>
  <sql:driver>sun.jdbc.odbc.JdbcOdbcDriver</sql:driver>
</sql:connection>
```

Listing 2.5 commit.jsp JSP. *(continues)*

```
<%

  String username= request.getParameter("username");
  String firstName = request.getParameter("firstName");
  String lastName = request.getParameter("lastName");
  String title = request.getParameter("title");
  String phone = request.getParameter("phone");
  String email = request.getParameter("email");

  StringBuffer queryString = new StringBuffer();

  if ( username == null ) {

    int index = email.indexOf('@');
    username = email.substring(0, index);

    queryString.append("insert into contacts ");
    queryString.append("values('" + username + "', ");
    queryString.append("'" + firstName + "', ");
    queryString.append("'" + lastName + "', ");
    queryString.append("'" + title + "', ");
    queryString.append("'" + phone + "', ");
    queryString.append("'" + email + "')");
  }
  else {

    queryString.append("update contacts set ");
    queryString.append("firstname='" + firstName + "', ");
    queryString.append("lastname='" + lastName + "', ");
    queryString.append("title='" + title+ "', ");
    queryString.append("phone='" + phone + "', ");
    queryString.append("email='" + email + "' ");
    queryString.append("where username='" + username + "'");
  }

%>

  <!-- execute a database query -->
  <sql:statement id="stmt" conn="conn">

    <!-- set the SQL query -->
    <sql:query>
      <%= queryString.toString() %>
```

Listing 2.5 commit.jsp JSP. *(continues)*

```
    </sql:query>
    <sql:execute/>

  </sql:statement>

<jsp:forward page="index.jsp" />
```

Listing 2.5 commit.jsp JSP. *(continued)*

The commit.jsp JSP is used to perform your database update and insert transactions. No presentation is associated with this JSP. When the container evaluates this JSP, it processes as follows:

1. The container first encounters the connection tag. This connection instance, again, has the same attribute values and children as the connection instance from your prior views.
2. The next section evaluated is a scriptlet section. This section creates a SQL string that that is an update if the username is on the request, or an insert if username is *null*. The created SQL statement is stored in a reference named queryString.
3. After the scriptlet has created the appropriate SQL statement, the container encounters a statement tag that contains a sql tag, which executes the SQL statement stored in the queryString variable.
4. This JSP finishes its processing by using the JSP forward standard action, which forwards the request back to the List View, where the changes should be displayed.

To deploy these JSPs, you simply need to copy them to the <TOMCAT_HOME> webapps/contactmanager/ directory.

Using the Application

Now it is time to use the contactmanager application. To do this, restart Tomcat, and open your browser to the following URL:

```
http://localhost:8080/contactmanager/
```

The browser will display the index.jsp page, which represents your List View. This view, which is displayed in Figure 2.9, contains the current list of contacts.

Now you will edit one of your contacts. To do this, select one of the contact names found in the leftmost column of the contacts table. For this example, we have selected the contact Sean; doing so executes a get request to the edit.jsp page with the username of the selected contact. Figure 2.10 shows the results of this selection.

This JSP generates an HTML form with the selected contact's values pre-populated in the form's input attributes. To edit the contact, change the value of the Title input to *King of the World*, and click Submit. Doing so executes a get request to the commit.jsp with the username of the edited contact as part of the request. The results of this submission are shown in Figure 2.11.

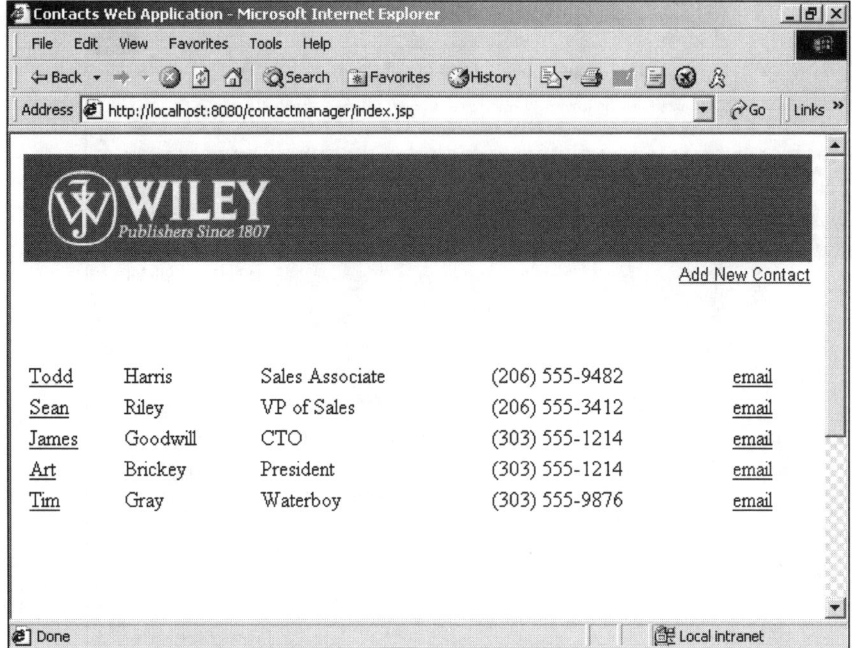

Figure 2.9 Output of index.jsp.

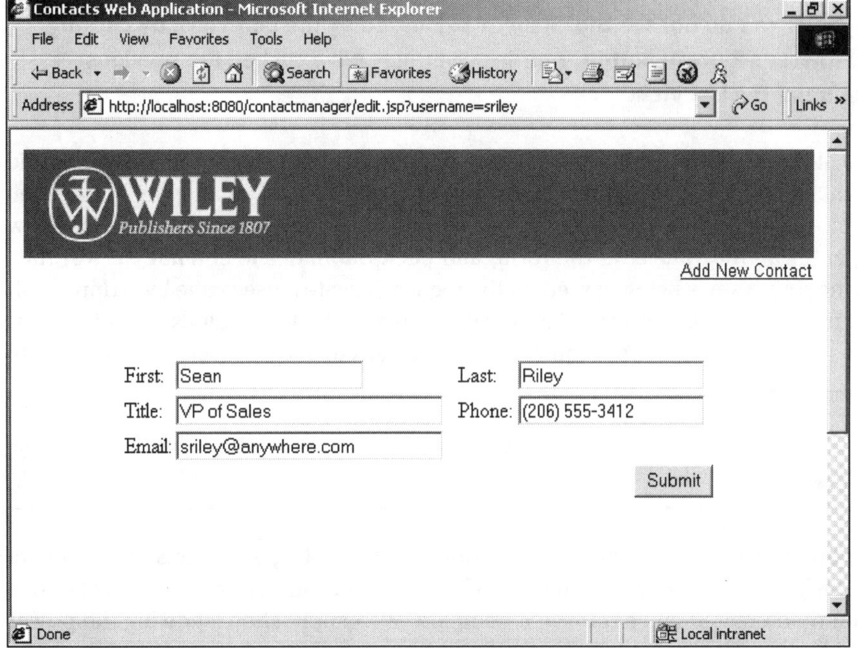

Figure 2.10 Output of edit.jsp.

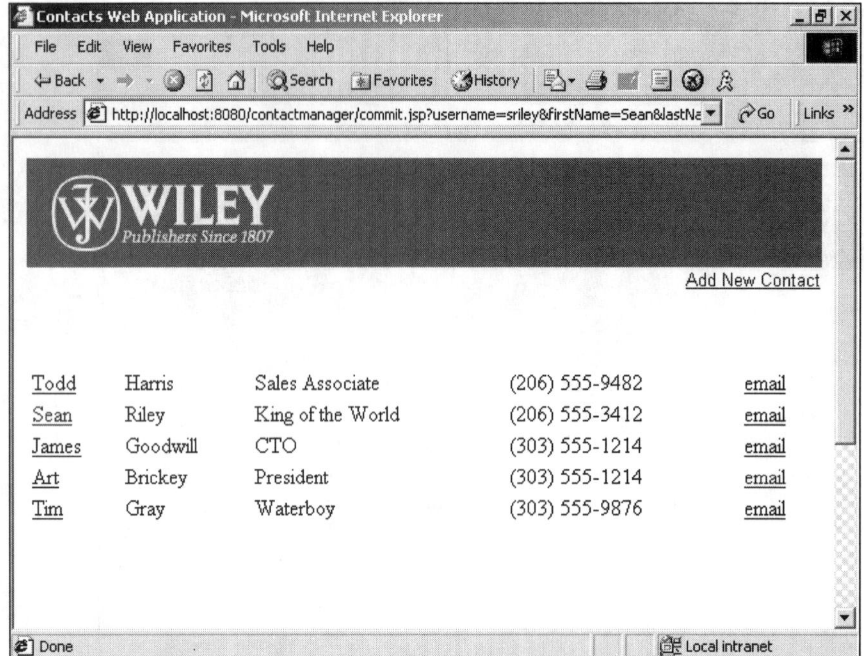

Figure 2.11 Output of commit.jsp.

NOTE **If you do not see the changes submitted by the Edit View, try clicking your browser's Refresh button. Your browser may have cached the previous execution of the List View.**

The final step that you will perform using the Contact Manager application is to add a new contact. To do so, click the Add New Contact link found on all your JSPs. When you select this link, you will be presented with an empty contact form. To add a new contact, enter all the values on the form, and click Submit. The commit.jsp will then retrieve the form values being passed on the request, create a username by stripping off the beginning of the contact's email address, and insert the form values using the username as the unique key. After the contact is inserted, the request is sent back to index.jsp.

Summary

In this chapter, we covered quite a bit of information. We began by installing and configuring the Tomcat JSP/servlet container, which you will use throughout the rest of this book. You then created and deployed a complete Web application, showing the power of custom tag libraries, using only four JSPs and one tag library. In the next chapter, we will discuss the Java servlet architecture.

CHAPTER

3

Java Servlet Overview and Architecture

This chapter will:

- Describe the Java servlet architecture
- Define the servlet life cycle
- Demonstrate how to create a simple Java servlet
- Discuss the servlet context and its relationship with its Web application
- Explain the process of retrieving form data using a servlet

Java Servlet Architecture

A *Java servlet* is a platform-independent Web application component that is hosted in a JSP/servlet container. Servlets cooperate with Web clients by means of a request/response model managed by a JSP/servlet container. Figure 3.1 graphically depicts the execution of a Java servlet.

Two packages make up the servlet architecture: javax.servlet and javax.servlet.http. The javax.servlet package contains the generic interfaces and classes that all servlets implement and extend. The second, javax.servlet.http, contains all servlet classes that are HTTP protocol-specific. An example is a simple servlet that responds using HTML.

At the heart of this architecture is the interface javax.servlet.Servlet, which is the base class for all servlets. The Servlet interface defines five methods. The three most important are init(), which initializes a servlet; service(), which receives and responds to client requests; and destroy(), which performs cleanup. These are the servlet life-cycle methods. A subsequent section describes these life cycle methods.

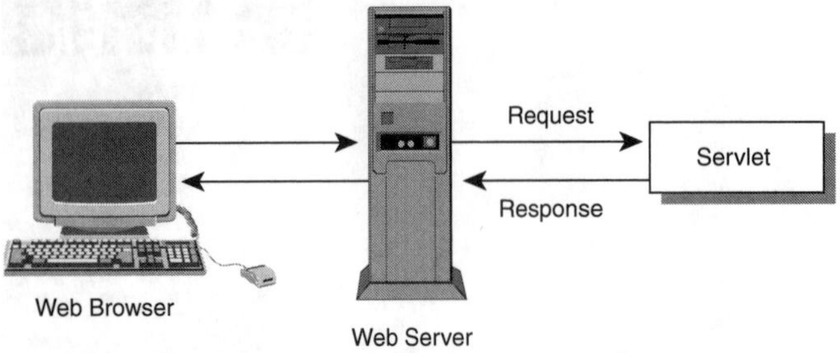

Figure 3.1 Execution of a Java servlet.

All servlets must implement the Servlet interface, either directly or through inheritance. Figure 3.2 is an object model that gives a very high-level view of the servlet framework.

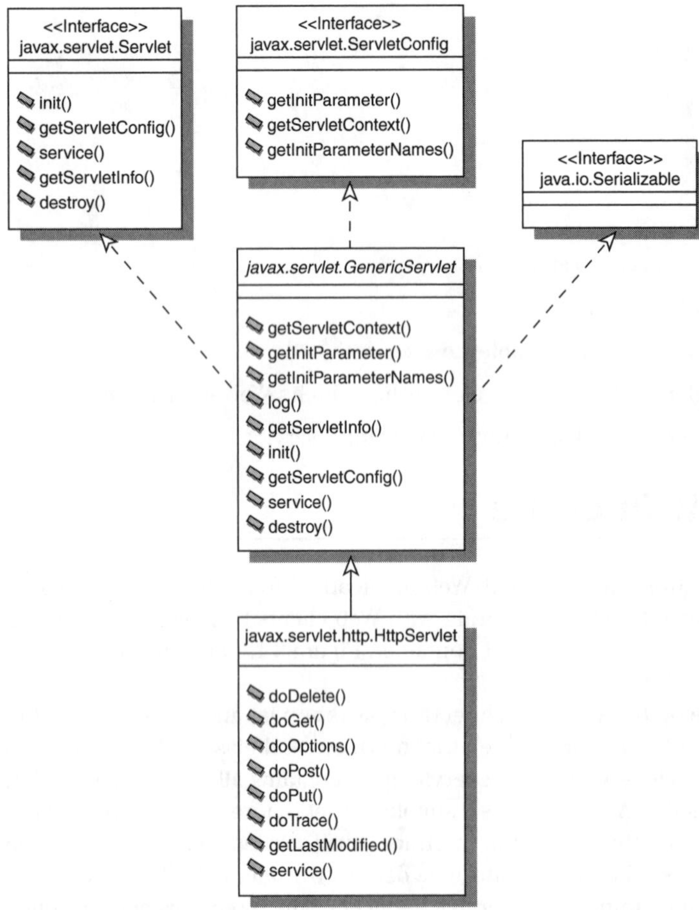

Figure 3.2 A simple object model showing the servlet framework.

GenericServlet and HttpServlet Classes

The two main classes in the servlet architecture are GenericServlet and HttpServlet. The HttpServlet class is extended from GenericServlet, which in turn implements the Servlet interface. When developing your own servlets, you will most likely extend one of these two classes.

When extending the GenericServlet class, you must implement the service() method. The GenericServlet.service() method is defined as an abstract method to force you to follow this framework. The service() method prototype is defined as follows:

```
public abstract void service(ServletRequest request,
  ServletResponse response) throws ServletException,
IOException;
```

The two parameters passed to the service() method are ServletRequest and Servlet Response objects. The ServletRequest object holds the information that is being sent to the servlet, and the ServletResponse object holds the data you want to send back to the client.

In contrast with the GenericServlet, when you extend HttpServlet, you usually don't implement the service() method. The HttpServlet class has already implemented the service() method for you. The following prototype contains the HttpServlet.service() method signature:

```
protected void service(HttpServletRequest request,
  HttpServletResponse response)
  throws ServletException, IOException;
```

When the HttpServlet.service() method is invoked, it reads the method type stored in the request and determines which HTTP-specific methods to invoke based on this value. You should override these methods. If the method type is GET, it will call doGet(). If the method type is POST, it will call doPost(). Five other method types are associated with the service() method, but we will focus on doGet() and doPost().

You may have noticed the different request/response types in the service() method signature of the HttpServlet as opposed to the GenericServlet class. The HttpServletRequest and HttpServletResponse classes are just extensions of ServletRequest and ServletResponse with HTTP-specific information stored in them.

Life Cycle of a Servlet

The life cycle of a Java servlet follows a very logical sequence. The javax.servlet.Servlet interface declares the life-cycle methods init(), service(), and destroy(). This sequence is described in the following simple three-step process:

1. A servlet is loaded and initialized using the init() method. This method is called when a servlet is pre-loaded or upon the first request to this servlet.
2. The servlet services zero or more requests. The servlet services requests using the service() method.
3. The servlet is destroyed and garbage collected when the Web application containing the servlet shuts down. The destroy() method is called upon shutdown.

init()

The servlet's life begins in the init() method, which is called immediately after the servlet is instantiated. This method is called only once. The init() method should be used to create and initialize the resources that it will use while handling requests. The init() method's signature is defined as follows:

```
public void init(ServletConfig config) throws ServletException;
```

The init() method takes a ServletConfig object as a parameter. This reference should be stored in a member variable, so that it can be used later. A common way of doing this is to have the init() method call super.init(), passing it the ServletConfig object.

The init() method also declares that it can throw a ServletException. If, for some reason, the servlet cannot initialize the resources necessary to handle requests, it should throw a ServletException with an error message signifying the problem.

service()

The service() method services all requests received from a client using a simple request/response pattern. The service() method's signature is as follows:

```
public void service(ServletRequest req, ServletResponse res)
 throws ServletException, IOException;
```

The service() method takes two parameters: a ServletRequest object, which contains information about the service request and encapsulates information provided by the client; and a ServletResponse object, which contains the information returned to the client.

This method usually isn't implemented directly, unless you extend the GenericServlet abstract class. The most common implementation of the service() method is in the HttpServlet class. The HttpServlet class implements the Servlet interface by extending GenericServlet. Its service() method supports standard HTTP/1.1 requests by determining the request type and calling the appropriate method.

destroy()

The destroy() method signifies the end of a servlet's life. When a Web application is shut down, the servlet's destroy() method is called. All resources created in the init() method should be cleaned up in destroy(). The signature of destroy() is shown in the following code snippet:

```
public void destroy();
```

A Simple Servlet

Now that you have a basic understanding of what a servlet is and how it works, this section explains how to build a very simple servlet. The servlet will service a request and respond by outputting the address of the client. After we have examined the source for this servlet, we will look at the steps involved in compiling and installing it. Listing 3.1 contains the source code for this example.

```
package chapter3;

import javax.servlet.*;
import javax.servlet.http.*;
import java.io.*;
import java.util.*;

public class SimpleServlet extends HttpServlet {

  public void init(ServletConfig config)
    throws ServletException {

    // Always pass the ServletConfig object to the super class
    super.init(config);
  }

  //Process the HTTP Get request
  public void doGet(HttpServletRequest request,
    HttpServletResponse response)
    throws ServletException, IOException {

    doPost(request, response);
  }

  //Process the HTTP Post request
  public void doPost(HttpServletRequest request,
    HttpServletResponse response)
    throws ServletException, IOException {

    response.setContentType("text/html");
    PrintWriter out = response.getWriter();

    out.println("<html>");
    out.println("<head><title>Simple Servlet</title></head>");
    out.println("<body>");

    // Outputs the address of the calling client
    out.println("Your address is " + request.getRemoteAddr()
      + "\n");

    out.println("</body></html>");
    out.close();
  }
}
```

Listing 3.1 SimpleServlet.java.

Let's examine each of SimpleServlet's integral parts, including where the servlet fits into the servlet framework, the methods that the servlet implements, and the objects being used by the servlet. The following three methods are overridden in the Simple-Servlet:

- init()
- doGet()
- doPost()

Let's look at each of these methods in more detail.

init()

The SimpleServlet first defines a very straightforward implementation of the init() method. It takes the ServletConfig object that it is passed, and passes it to its parent's init() method, which stores the object for later use. The code that performs this action follows:

```
super.init(config);
```

NOTE **GenericServlet is the SimpleServlet's parent, and actually holds on to the ServletConfig object.**

Notice that this implementation of the init() method does not create any resources. For this reason, the SimpleServlet does not implement a destroy() method.

doGet() and doPost()

All the business logic is performed in the SimpleServlet's doGet() and doPost() methods. In this case, doGet()simply calls the doPost() method. The doGet() method will be executed only when a GET request is sent to the container. If a POST request is received, then doPost()will service the request.

Both doGet() and doPost() receive HttpServletRequest and HttpServletResponse objects as parameters. The HttpServletRequest contains information sent from the client, and the HttpServletResponse contains the information that will be sent back to the client.

The first executed line of the doPost() method sets the content type of the response that will be sent back to the client. This is done using the following code snippet:

```
response.setContentType("text/html");
```

This method sets the content type for the response. This response property can be set only once, and you must set it prior to writing to a Writer or an OutputStream. In this example, the response type is set to "text/html."

Next, doPost() gets a PrintWriter by calling the ServletResponses's getWriter() method. The PrintWriter lets you write to the stream that will be sent in the client response. Everything written to the PrintWriter will be displayed in the client browser. This step is completed in the following line of code:

```
PrintWriter out = response.getWriter();
```

Once you have a reference to an object that will let you write text back to the client, you can use this object to write a message to the client. This message includes the HTML that will format the response for presentation in the client's browser. The next few lines of code show how this is done:

```
out.println("<html>");
out.println("<head><title>Simple Servlet</title></head>");
out.println("<body>");

// Outputs the address of the calling client
out.println("Your address is " + request.getRemoteAddr()
  + "\n");
```

The SimpleServlet uses a clear-cut method of sending HTML to a client. It simply passes to the PrintWriter's println() method the HTML text to be included in the response, and closes the stream. You may have a question about the following few lines:

```
// Outputs the address of the calling client
out.println("Your address is " + request.getRemoteAddr()
  + "\n");
```

This section of code takes advantage of information sent by the client. It calls the HttpServletRequest's getRemoteAddr() method, which returns the address of the calling client. The HttpServletRequest object holds a great deal of HTTP protocol-specific information about the client. To learn more about the HttpServletRequest or HttpServlet Response object, visit the Sun Web site:

```
http://java.sun.com/products/servlet/
```

Building and Deploying the SimpleServlet

To see the SimpleServlet in action, you need to first create a Web application that will host this servlet, and then compile and deploy this servlet to the created Web application. These steps are as follows:

1. Create a Web application named customstags using the steps described in Chapter 1, "Introducing JSP Custom Tags and Web Applications."
2. Add the servlet.jar file to your classpath. This file should be in the <TOMCAT_HOME>/common/lib/ directory.
3. Compile the source for the SimpleServlet.
4. Copy the resulting class file to the <TOMCAT_HOME>webapps/customtags/WEB-INF/classes/chapter3/ directory. The /chapter3 reference is appended because of the package name.

Once you have completed these steps, you can execute the SimpleServlet and see the results. To do so, start Tomcat and open your browser to the following URL:

```
http://localhost:8080/customtags/servlet/chapter3.SimpleServlet
```

You should see an image similar to Figure 3.3.

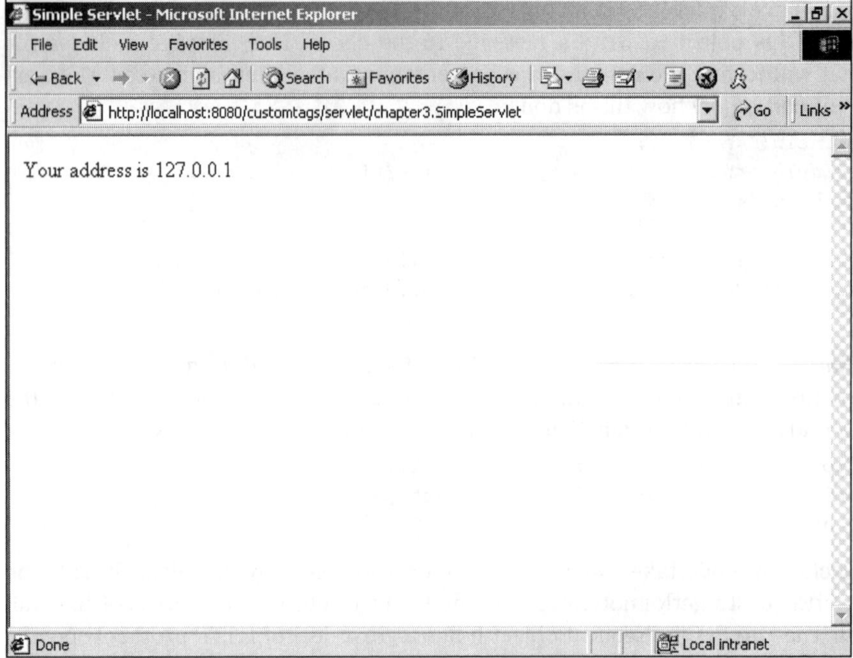

Figure 3.3 Output of the SimpleServlet.

NOTE **In the URL to access the SimpleServlet, the string *_/servlet_* immediately precedes the reference to the actual servlet name. This text tells the container that you are referencing a servlet.**

ServletContext

A *ServletContext* is an object defined in the javax.servlet package. It defines a set of methods used by server-side components of a Web application to communicate with the servlet container.

The ServletContext is used most frequently as a storage area for objects that need to be available to all the server-side components in a Web application. Think of the ServletContext as a shared memory segment for Web applications. When an object is placed in the ServletContext, it exists for the life of a Web application, unless it is explicitly removed or replaced. Four methods defined by the ServletContext are leveraged to provide this shared memory functionality; these methods are defined in Table 3.1.

Table 3.1 Shared Memory Methods of the ServletContext

METHOD	DESRIPTION
setAttribute()	Binds an object to a given name and stores the object in the current ServletContext. If the name specified is already in use, this method will remove the old object binding and bind the name to the new object.
getAttribute()	Returns the object referenced by the given name, or retuns null if there is no attribute bound to the given key.
removeAttribute()	Removes the attribute with the given name from the ServletContext.
getAttributeNames()	Returns an enumeration of strings containing the object names stored in the current ServletContext.

Relationship Between a Web Application and the ServletContext

The ServletContext acts as the container for a given Web application. For every Web application, there can be only one instance of a ServletContext. This relationship is required by the Servlet Specification, and is enforced by all servlet containers.

To see how this relationship affects Web components, let's use a servlet and a JSP. The first Web component is a servlet that stores an object in the ServletContext, with the purpose of making this object available to all server-side components in this Web application. The source code for this servlet can be found in Listing 3.2.

```
package chapter3;

import javax.servlet.*;
import javax.servlet.http.*;
import java.io.*;
import java.util.*;

public class ContextServlet extends HttpServlet {

  private static final String CONTENT_TYPE = "text/html";

  public void doGet(HttpServletRequest request,
    HttpServletResponse response)
    throws ServletException, IOException {
```

Listing 3.2 ContextServlet.java. *(continues)*

```
      doPost(request, response);
    }

    public void doPost(HttpServletRequest request,
      HttpServletResponse response)
      throws ServletException, IOException {

      // Get a reference to the ServletContext
      ServletContext context = getServletContext();

      // Get the userName attribute from the ServletContext
      String userName = (String)context.getAttribute("USERNAME");

      // If there was no attribute USERNAME, then create
      // one and add it to the ServletContext
      if ( userName == null ) {

        userName = new String("Bob Roberts");
        context.setAttribute("USERNAME", userName);
      }

      response.setContentType(CONTENT_TYPE);
      PrintWriter out = response.getWriter();
      out.println("<html>");
      out.println("<head><title>Context Servlet</title></head>");
      out.println("<body>");

      // Output the current value of the attribute USERNAME
      out.println("<p>The current User is : " + userName +
        ".</p>");
      out.println("</body></html>");
    }

  }
```

Listing 3.2 ContextServlet.java. *(continued)*

ContextServlet performs the following steps:

1. It gets a reference to the ServletContext, using the getServletContext() method:

```
ServletContext context = getServletContext();
```

2. It gets a reference to the object bound to the name USERNAME from the ServletContext, using the getAttribute() method:

```
String userName =
  (String)context.getAttribute("USERNAME");
```

3. It checks to see whether the reference returned was valid. If getAttribute() returned *null*, then no object was bound to the name USERNAME. If the attribute was not found, it is created and added to the ServletContext, bound to the name USERNAME, using the setAttribute() method:

```
// If there was no attribute USERNAME, then create
// one and add it to the ServletContext
if ( userName == null ) {

  userName = new String("Bob Roberts");
  context.setAttribute("USERNAME", userName);
}
```

4. The value of this reference is printed to the output stream, using the PrintWriter.println() method:

```
// Output the current value of the attribute USERNAME
out.println("<p>The current User is : " +
  userName + ".</p>");
```

After you have looked over this servlet, compile it and move the class file into the <TOMCAT_HOME>/webapps/customtags/WEB-INF/classes/chapter3 directory. This servlet is now deployed to the Web application customtags.

The JSP you will use is much like the servlet. The only differences are that the code to access the ServletContext is in a JSP scriptlet (discussed in Chapter 4), and if the JSP cannot find a reference to the USERNAME attribute, it does not add a new one. Otherwise it performs essentially the same actions, but in a JSP. The source for the JSP can be found in Listing 3.3.

```
<HTML>
<HEAD>
<TITLE>
Context
</TITLE>
</HEAD>
<BODY>
<%
  // Try to get the USERNAME attribute from the ServletContext
  String userName = (String)application.getAttribute("USERNAME");

  // If there was no attribute USERNAME, then create
  // one and add it to the ServletContext
  if ( userName == null ) {

    // Don't try to add it just, say that you can't find it
    out.println("<b>Attribute USERNAME not found");
  }
```

Listing 3.3 Context.jsp. *(continues)*

```
    else {

        out.println("<b>The current User is : " + userName +
            "</b>");
    }
%>
</BODY>
</HTML>
```

Listing 3.3 Context.jsp. *(continued)*

NOTE **Context.jsp uses two JSP implicit objects: the application object, which references the ServletContext; and the out object, which references an output stream to the client. These objects are discussed in Chapter 4.**

Copy Context.jsp to the <TOMCAT_HOME>webapps/customtags/directory directory, restart Tomcat, and open your browser to the following URL:

```
http://localhost:8080/customtags/Context.jsp
```

You should see a page similar to Figure 3.4.

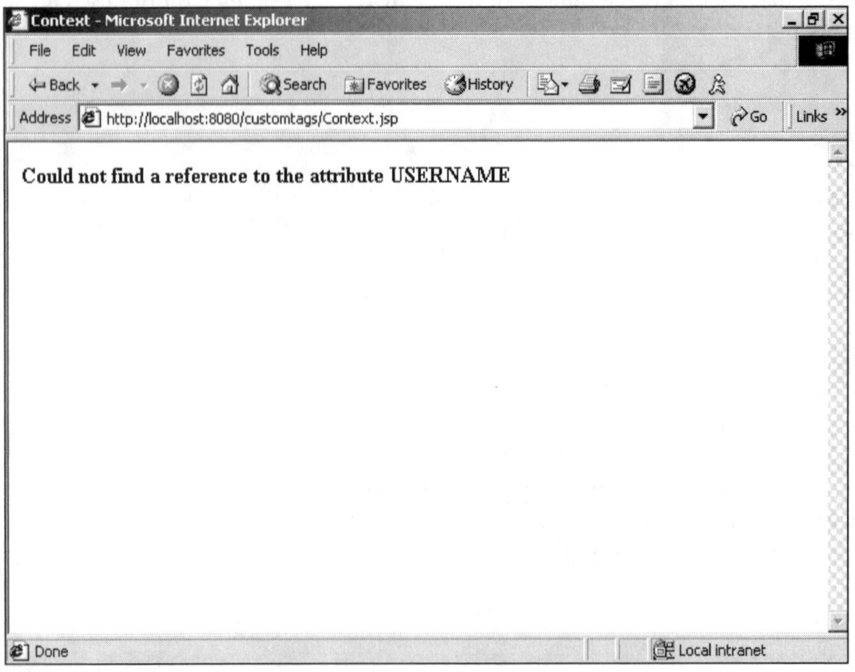

Figure 3.4 Output of the Context.jsp prior to the execution of the servlet ContextServlet.

Notice that the Context.jsp cannot find a reference to the attribute USERNAME. It will not be able to find this reference until the reference is placed there by the ContextServlet. To do this, open your browser to the following URL:

```
http://localhost:8080/customtags/servlet/chapter3.ContextServlet
```

You should see output similar to Figure 3.5.

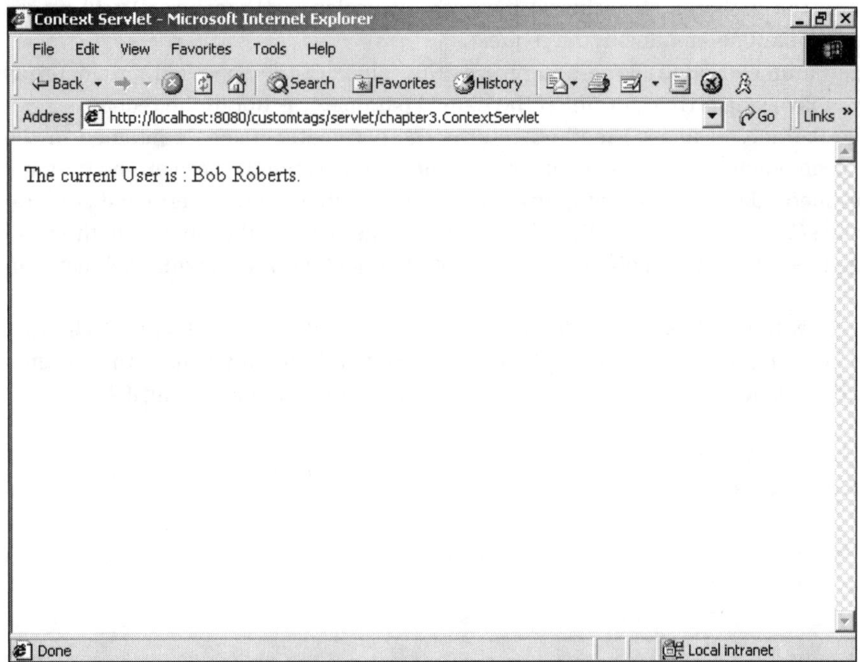

Figure 3.5 Output of the ContextServlet.

After running this servlet, the customtags Web application has an object bound to the name USERNAME stored in its ServletContext. To see how this affects another Web component in the customtags Web application, open the previous URL that references the Context.jsp, and look at the change in output. The JSP can now find the USERNAME, and it prints this value to the response.

NOTE **To remove an object from the ServletContext, restart the JSP/servlet container, or use the ServletContext.removeAttribute() method.**

Using Servlets to Retrieve HTTP Data

This final section on servlets examines how servlets can be used to retrieve information from the client. Three methods retrieve request parameters: the ServletRequest's getParameterNames(), getParameter(), and getParameterValues() methods. The method signatures are as follows.

```
public String ServletRequest.getParameter(String name);
public String[] ServletRequest.getParameterValues(String name);
public Enumeration ServletRequest.getParameterNames();
```

The getParameter() method returns a string containing the single value of the named parameter, or null if the parameter is not in the request. Use this method only if you are sure the request contains a single value for the parameter. If the parameter has multiple values, use the getParameterValues() method; otherwise, getParameter() will return only the first parameter value in the request.

The getParameterValues() method returns the values of the specified parameter as an array of java.lang.Strings, or null if the named parameter is not in the request.

The getParameterNames() method returns the parameter names contained in the request as an enumeration of strings, or an empty enumeration if there are no parameters. This method is used as a supporting method to both getParameter() and getParameterValues(). The enumerated list of parameter names returned from this method can be iterated over by calling getParameter() or getParameterValues() with each name in the list.

To see how to use these methods to retrieve <form> data, let's look at a servlet that services POST requests: It retrieves the parameters sent to it, and returns the parameters and their values back to the client. The servlet can be found in Listing 3.4.

```
package chapter3;

import javax.servlet.*;
import javax.servlet.http.*;
import java.io.*;
import java.util.*;

public class ParameterServlet extends HttpServlet {

  // Process the HTTP GET request
  public void doGet(HttpServletRequest request,
    HttpServletResponse response)
    throws ServletException, IOException {

    doPost(request, response);
  }

  // Process the HTTP POST request
  public void doPost(HttpServletRequest request,
    HttpServletResponse response)
    throws ServletException, IOException {

    response.setContentType("text/html");
    PrintWriter out = response.getWriter();
```

Listing 3.4 ParameterServlet.java. *(continues)*

```
    out.println("<html>");
    out.println("<head>");
    out.println("<title>Parameter Servlet</title>");
    out.println("</head>");
    out.println("<body>");

    // Get an enumeration of the parameter names
    Enumeration parameters = request.getParameterNames();

    String param = null;

    // Iterate over the paramter names,
    // getting the parameters values
    while ( parameters.hasMoreElements() ) {

      param = (String)parameters.nextElement();
      out.println(param + " : " +
        request.getParameter(param) +
        "<BR>");
    }

    out.println("</body></html>");
    out.close();
  }
}
```

Listing 3.4 ParameterServlet.java. *(continued)*

The servlet's first notable action is to get all the parameter names passed in on the request. It does this using the getParameterNames() method. Once it has this list, it performs a while loop to retrieve and print all the parameter values associated with the matching parameter names, using the getParameter() method. You can invoke the ParamaterServlet by encoding a URL string with parameters and values, or simply by using the HTML form found in Listing 3.5.

```
<HTML>
<HEAD>
<TITLE>
Parameter Servlet Form
</TITLE>
</HEAD>
<BODY>
```

Listing 3.5 Form.html. *(continues)*

```
<form
 action="servlet/chapter3.ParameterServlet"
 method=POST>
  <table width="400" border="0" cellspacing="0">
    <tr>
      <td>Name: </td>
      <td>
        <input type="text"
               name="name"
               size="20"
               maxlength="20">
      </td>
      <td>SSN:</td>
      <td>
        <input type="text" name="ssn" size="11" maxlength="11">
      </td>
    </tr>
    <tr>
      <td>Age:</td>
      <td>
        <input type="text" name="age" size="3" maxlength="3">
      </td>
      <td>email:</td>
      <td>
        <input type="text"
               name="email"
               size="30"
               maxlength="30">
      </td>
    </tr>
    <tr>
      <td> </td>
      <td>  </td>
      <td>  </td>
      <td>
        <input type="submit" name="Submit" value="Submit">
        <input type="reset" name="Reset" value="Reset"">
      </td>
    </tr>
  </table>
</FORM>

</BODY>
</HTML>
```

Listing 3.5 Form.html. *(continued)*

This HTML document contains a simple HTML form that can be used to pass data to the ParameterServlet. To see this example in action, compile the servlet and move the class file to the <TOMCAT_HOME>webapps/customtags/WEB-INF/classes/chapter3 directory and the HTML file to the <TOMCAT_HOME>webapps/customtags/ directory. Open your browser to the following URL:

```
http://localhost:8080/customtags/Form.html
```

You should see a page similar to Figure 3.6.

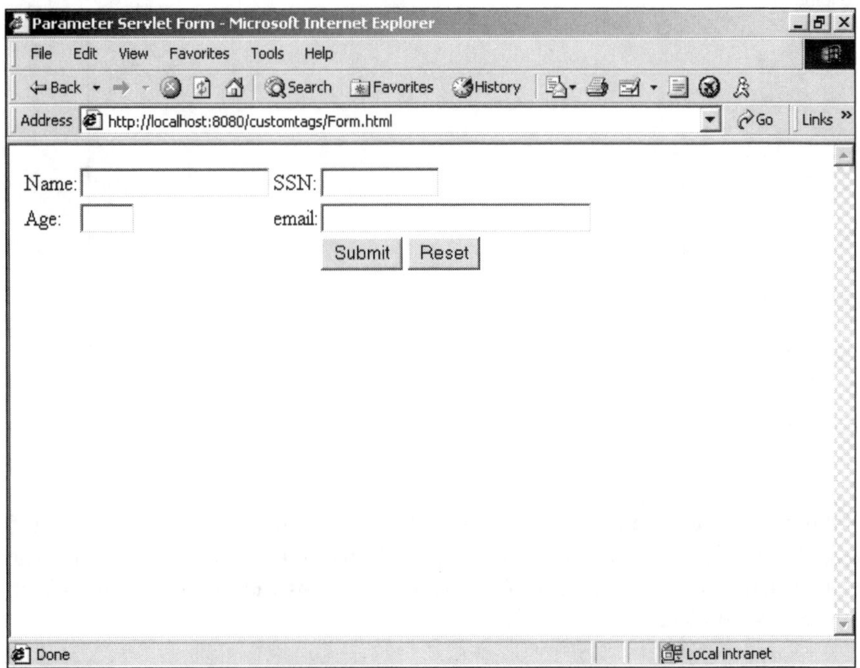

Figure 3.6 Output from Form.html.

Populate the form, and click the Submit button. The response will of course depend on your entries; it should look similar to Figure 3.7.

This example shows how easy it is to retrieve request parameters in a servlet. Although the ParameterServlet works well for most requests, it does contain an error. We chose to use getParameter() to retrieve the parameter values because we could count on receiving only one value per request parameter. If you can't rely upon this fact, then you should use the getParameterValues() method discussed previously.

Summary

This chapter introduced the Java servlet SDK. It began by describing the Java servlet architecture and then discussed the life cycle of a servlet and the methods that make up this life cycle. You then applied your knowledge by creating simple servlet. The chapter

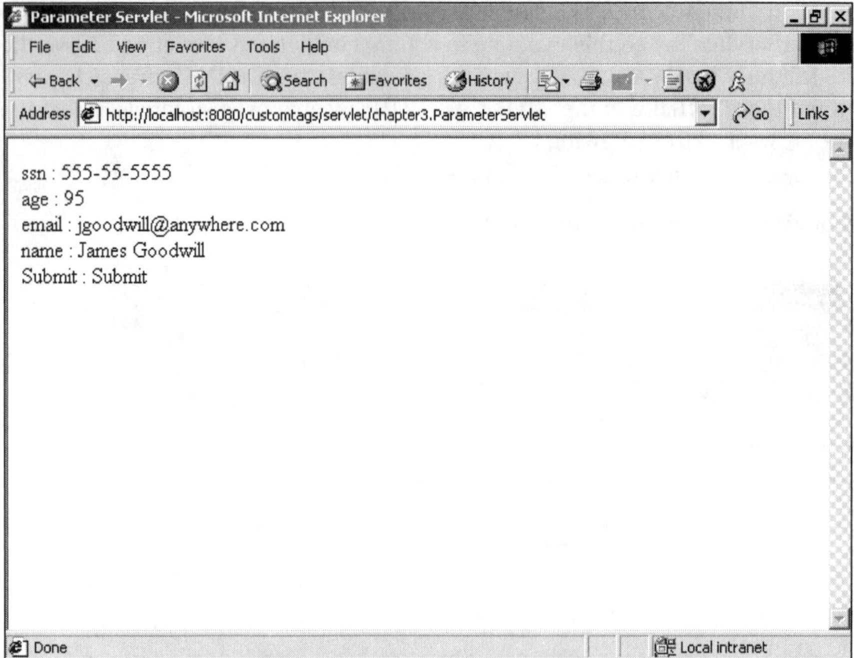

Figure 3.7 Response of the ParameterServlet.

also explained the relationship between a ServletContext and its Web application, and concluded with a discussion of how to retrieve HTTP parameters and values using the servlet SDK. The next chapter will describe JavaServer Pages and the components from which they are assembled.

CHAPTER

4

JSP Overview and Architecture

This chapter will:

- Define JavaServer Pages
- Describe the components of a JavaServer Page

JavaServer Pages, or JSPs, are a simple but powerful technology used most often to generate dynamic HTML on the server side. JSPs are a direct extension of Java servlets designed to let the developer embed Java logic directly into a requested document. A JSP document must end with the extension .jsp. The following hello.jsp code snippet contains a simple example of a JSP file (its output is shown in Figure 4.1):

```
<HTML>
<BODY>

<% out.println("HELLO JSP READER"); %>

</BODY>
</HTML>
```

This document looks like any other HTML document, with some added tags containing Java code. The source code is stored in a file called hello.jsp, and copied to the document directory of the Web application to which this JSP will be deployed. When a request is made for this document, the server recognizes the .jsp extension and realizes that special handling is required. The JSP is then passed to the JSP engine—which is just another servlet mapped to the extension .jsp—for processing.

The first time the file is requested, it is translated into a servlet and then compiled into an object that is loaded into resident memory. The generated servlet then services

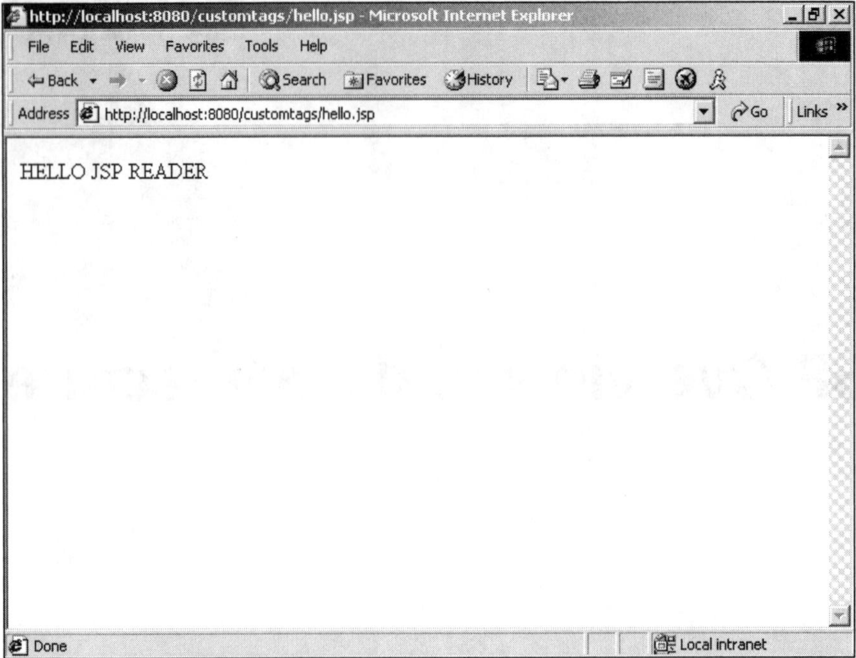

Figure 4.1 Output of hello.jsp.

the request, and the output is sent back to the requesting client. On all subsequent requests, the server will check to see whether the original .jsp source file has changed. If it has not changed, then the server invokes the previously compiled servlet object. If the source has changed, the JSP engine will reparse the JSP source. Figure 4.2 shows these steps graphically.

NOTE **It's essential to remember that JSPs are just servlets created from a combination of HTML and Java source. Therefore, they have the resources and functionality of a servlet.**

Components of a JavaServer Page

This section discusses the components of a JSP, including directives, JSP scripting, implicit objects, and JSP standard actions.

JSP Directives

JSP directives are JSP elements that provide global information about a JSP page. An example would be a directive that includes a list of Java classes to be imported into a JSP. The syntax of a JSP directive follows:

```
<%@ directive {attribute="value"} %>
```

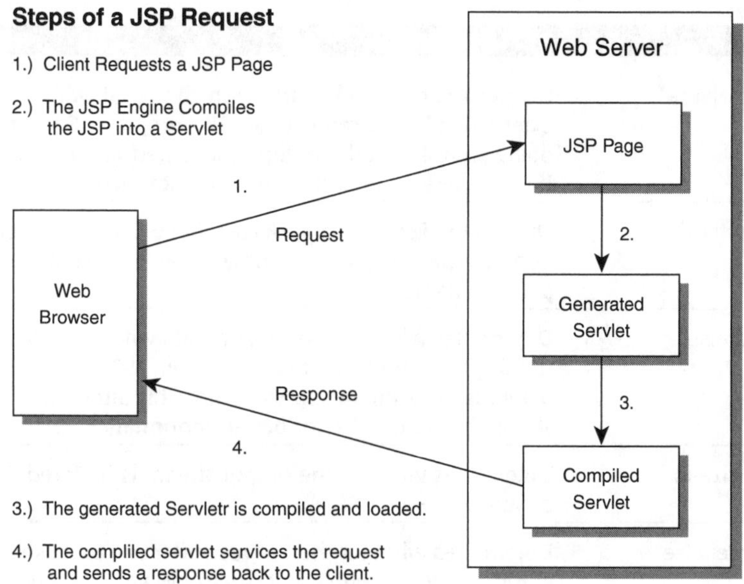
Steps of a JSP Request
1.) Client Requests a JSP Page
2.) The JSP Engine Compiles the JSP into a Servlet
Web Server
JSP Page
1.
Request
2.
Web Browser
Generated Servlet
Response
3.
4.
Compiled Servlet
3.) The generated Servletr is compiled and loaded.
4.) The compliled servlet services the request and sends a response back to the client.

Figure 4.2 Steps of a JSP request.

Three possible directives are currently defined by the JSP specification v1.2: page, include, and taglib. These directives are defined in the following sections.

page Directive

The *page directive* defines information that will globally affect the JavaServer Page containing the directive. The syntax of a JSP page directive follows:

```
<%@ page {attribute="value"} %>
```

Table 4.1 defines the attributes for the page directive.

NOTE **Because all mandatory attributes are defaulted, you are not required to specify any page directives.**

Table 4.1 Attributes for the page Directive

ATTRIBUTE	DEFINITION
language="scriptingLanguage"	Tells the server which language will be used to compile the JSP file. Java is currently the only available JSP language, but there will hopefully be other language support in the near future.

Table 4.1 Attributes for the page Directive (continued)

ATTRIBUTE	DEFINITION
extends="className"	Defines the parent class from which the JSP will extend. While you can extend JSP from other Servlets, doing so will limit the optimizations performed by the JSP/servlet engine and is therefore not recommened.
import="importList"	Defines the list of Java packages that will be imported into this JSP. It will be a comma-separated list of package names.
session="true|false"	Determines whether the session data will be available to this page. The default is true. If your JSP is not planning on using the session, then this attribute should be set to false for better performance.
buffer="none|size in kb"	Determines whether the output stream is buffered. The default value is 8KB.
autoFlush="true|false"	Determines whether the output buffer will be flushed automatically, or whether it will throw an exception when the buffer is full. The default is true.
isThreadSafe="true|false"	Tells the JSP engine that this page can service multiple requests at one time. By default, this value is true. If this attribute is set to false, the SingleThreadModel is used.
info="text"	Represents information about the JSP page that can be accessed by invoking the page's Servlet.getServletInfo() method.
errorPage="error_url"	Represents the relative URL to a JSP that will handle JSP exceptions.
isErrorPage="true|false"	States whether the JSP is an errorPage. The default is false.
contentType="ctinfo"	Represents the MIME type and character set of the response sent to the client.

The following code snippet includes a page directive that imports the java.util package:

```
<%@ page import="java.util.*" %>
```

include Directive

The *include directive* is used to insert text and/or code at JSP translation time. The syntax of the include directive is shown in the following code snippet:

```
<%@ include file="relativeURLspec" %>
```

The file attribute can reference a normal text HTML file or a JSP file, which will be evaluated at translation time. This resource referenced by the file attribute must be local to the Web application that contains the include directive. Here's an example include directive:

```
<%@ include file="header.jsp" %>
```

NOTE **Because the include directive is evaluated at translation time, this included text will be evaluated only once. Thus, if the included resource changes, these changes will not be reflected until the JSP/servlet container is restarted or the modification date of the JSP that includes that file is changed.**

taglib Directive

For our purposes, the most important directive of the JSP specification is used to include a tag library in a JSP. The taglib directive states that the including page uses a custom tag library, uniquely identified by a URI and associated with a prefix that will distinguish each set of custom tags. The syntax of the taglib directive is as follows:

```
<%@ taglib uri="tagLibraryURI" prefix="tagPrefix" %>
```

The taglib attributes are described in Table 4.2.

Table 4.2 Attributes for the taglib Directive

ATTRIBUTE	DEFINITION
uri	A URI that uniquely names a custom tag library
prefix	The prefix string used to distinguish a custom tag instance

The following code snippet includes an example of how the taglib directive is used:

```
<%@ taglib
  uri="http://jakarta.apache.org/taglibs/random-1.0"
  prefix="rand" %>
```

JSP Scripting

Scripting is a JSP mechanism for directly embedding Java code fragments into an HTML page. Three scripting language components are involved in JSP scripting. Each of these components has its appropriate location in the generated servlet. This section examines these components.

Declarations

JSP *declarations* are used to define Java variables and methods in a JSP. A JSP declaration must be a complete declarative statement.

JSP declarations are initialized when the JSP page is first loaded. After the declarations have been initialized, they are available to other declarations, expressions, and scriptlets within the same JSP. The syntax for a JSP declaration is as follows:

```
<%! declaration %>
```

A sample variable declaration using this syntax is shown here:

```
<%! String name = new String("BOB"); %>
```

A sample method declaration using the same syntax is as follows:

```
<%! public String getName() { return name; } %>
```

To get a better understanding of declarations, let's take the previous String declaration and embed it into a JSP document. The sample document would look similar to the following code snippet:

```
<HTML>
<BODY>

<%! String name = new String("BOB"); %>

</BODY>
</HTML>
```

When this document is initially loaded, the JSP code is converted to servlet code, and the name declaration is placed in the declaration section of the generated servlet. It is now available to all other JSP components in the JSP.

NOTE It should be noted that all JSP declarations are defined at the class level, in the servlet generated from the JSP, and will therefore be evaluated prior to all JSP expression and scriptlet code.

Expressions

JSP *expressions* are JSP components whose text, upon evaluation by the container, is replaced with the resulting value of the container evaluation. JSP expressions are evaluated at request-time, and the result is inserted at the expression's referenced position in the .jsp file. If the resulting expression cannot be converted to a String, then a translation-time error will occur. If the conversion to a String cannot be detected during translation, a ClassCastException will be thrown at request-time.

NOTE JSP Expressions should not to be confused with the JSP Tag Library (JSPTL) Expression Language, which is intended to for use with custom tags only. We will discuss the JSPTL in Chapter 24.

The syntax of a JSP expression is as follows:

```
<%= expression %>
```

A code snippet containing a JSP expression is shown here:

```
Hello <B><%= getName() %></B>
```

A sample JSP document containing a JSP expression is listed in the following code snippet:

```
<HTML>
<BODY>
```

```
<%! public String getName() { return "Bob"; } %>

Hello <B><%= getName() %></B>

</BODY>
</HTML>
```

Scriptlets

Scriptlets are the JSP components that bring all the JSP elements together. They can contain almost any coding statements that are valid for the language referenced in the language directive. They are executed at request-time, and they can make use of all the JSP components. The syntax for a scriptlet is as follows:

```
<% scriptlet source %>
```

When JSP scriptlet code is converted into servlet code, it is placed into the generated servlet's service() method. The following code snippet contains a simple JSP that uses a scripting element to print the text *Hello Bob* to the requesting client:

```
<HTML>
<BODY>

<% out.println("Hello Bob"); %>

</BODY>
</HTML>
```

You should note that although JSP scriplet code can be very powerful, composing all your JSP logic using scriptlet code can make your application difficult to manage. This problem led to the creation of custom tag libraries, which is the focus of this book.

JSP Error Handling

Like all development methods, JSPs need a robust mechanism for handling errors. The JSP architecture provides an error-handling solution through the use of JSPs that are written exclusively to handle JSP errors.

The errors that occur most frequently are runtime errors that can arise either in the body of the JSP page or in some other object that is called from the body of the JSP page. Request-time errors that result in an exception being thrown can be caught and handled in the body of the calling JSP, which signals the end of the error. Exceptions that are not handled in the calling JSP result in the forwarding of the client request, including the uncaught exception, to an error page specified by the offending JSP.

NOTE An errorpage can also be named in the web.xml file of a web application, using the <error-page> element. This would require a discussion of the <error-page> and all of its subelements, which is beyond the scope of this text.

Creating a JSP Error Page

Creating a JSP error page is a simple process: Create a basic JSP and then tell the JSP engine that the page is an error page. You do so by setting the JSP's page directive attribute, isErrorPage, to true. Listing 4.1 contains a sample error page.

```
<html>

<%@ page isErrorPage="true" %>

Error: <%= exception.getMessage() %> has been reported.

</body>
</html>
```

Listing 4.1 Creating a JSP error page: errorpage.jsp.

The first JSP-related line in this page tells the JSP compiler that this JSP is an error page. This code snippet is

```
<%@ page isErrorPage="true" %>
```

The second JSP-related section uses the implicit exception object that is part of all JSP error pages to output the error message contained in the unhandled exception that was thrown in the offending JSP.

Using a JSP Error Page

To see how an error page works, let's create a simple JSP that throws an uncaught exception. The JSP found in Listing 4.2 uses the error page created in the previous section.

```
<%@ page errorPage="errorpage.jsp" %>

<%

  if ( true ) {

    // Just throw an exception
    throw new Exception("An uncaught Exception");
  }

%>
```

Listing 4.2 Using a JSP error page: testerror.jsp.

Notice in this listing that the first line of code sets errorPage equal to errorpage.jsp, which is the name of the error page. To make a JSP aware of an error page, you simply need to add the errorPage attribute to the page directive and set its value equal to the location of your JSP error page. The rest of the example simply throws an exception that will not be caught. To see this example in action, copy both JSPs to the <TOMCAT_HOME>/webapps/customtags/ directory, and open the testerror.jsp page in your browser. You will see a page similar to Figure 4.3.

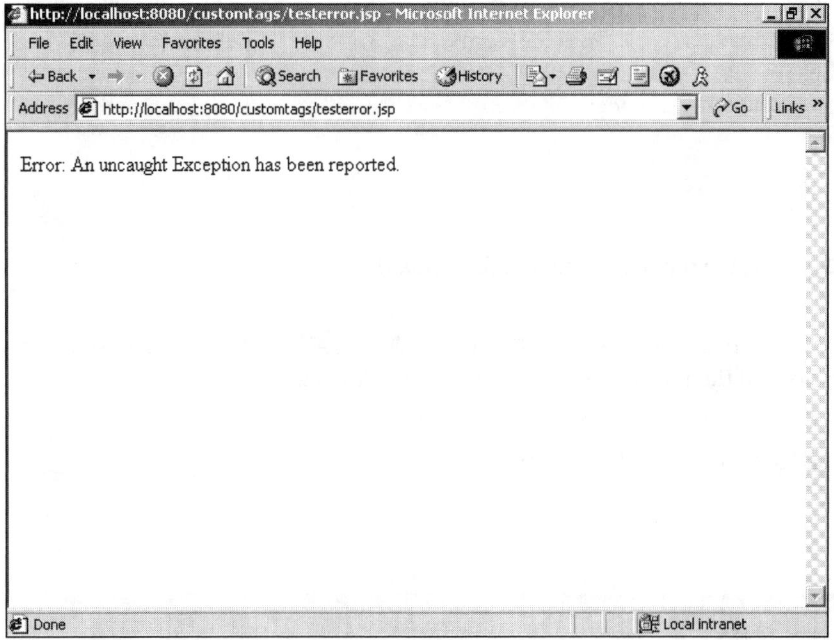

Figure 4.3 Output of the testerror.jsp example.

Implicit Objects

As a JSP author, you have implicit access to certain objects that are available for use in all JSP documents. These objects are parsed by the JSP engine and inserted into the generated servlet as if you defined them yourself.

out

The implicit *out* object represents a JspWriter (derived from a java.io.Writer) that provides a stream back to the requesting client. The most common method of this object is out.println(), which prints text that will be displayed in the client's browser. Listing 4.3 provides an example using the implicit out object.

```
<%@ page errorPage="errorpage.jsp" %>
```

Listing 4.3 Using the out object: out.jsp. *(continues)*

```
<html>
  <head>
    <title>Use Out</title>
  </head>
  <body>
    <%
      // Print a simple message using the implicit out object.
      out.println("<center><b>Hello Wiley" +
        " Reader!</b></center>");
    %>
  </body>
</html>
```

Listing 4.3 Using the out object: out.jsp. *(continued)*

To execute this example, copy this file to the <TOMCAT_HOME>/webapps/customtags/ directory and then open your browser to the following URL:

```
http://localhost:8080/customtags/out.jsp
```

You should see a page similar to Figure 4.4.

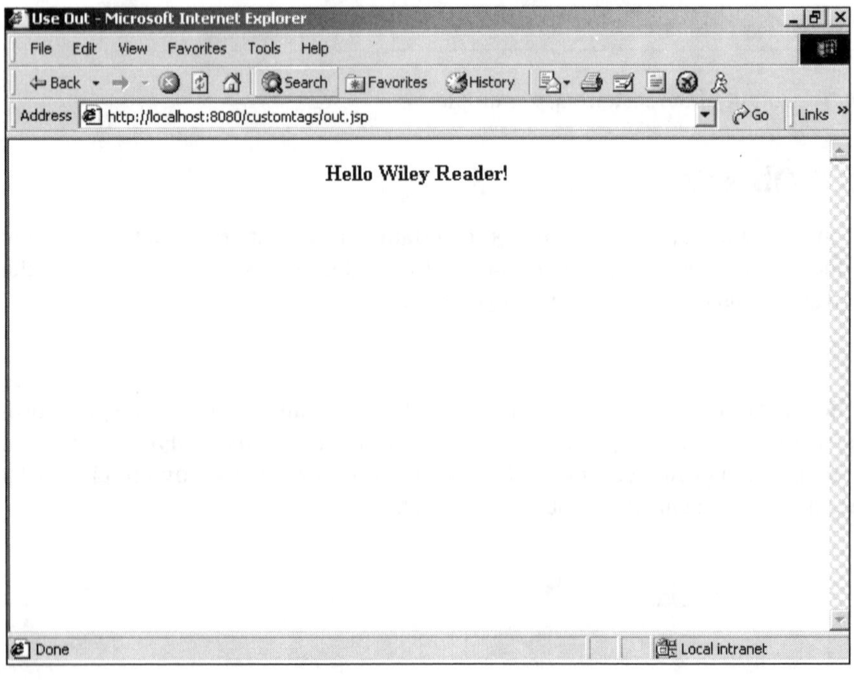

Figure 4.4 Output of out.jsp.

request

The implicit request object represents the javax.servlet.http.HttpServletRequest interface, as discussed in Chapter 3. The request object is associated with every HTTP request.

One of the more common uses for the request object is to access request parameters. You can do this by calling the request object's getParameter() method with the parameter name you are seeking. It will return a string with the value matching the named parameter. An example using the implicit request object can be found in Listing 4.4.

```
<%@ page errorPage="errorpage.jsp" %>

<html>
  <head>
    <title>UseRequest</title>
  </head>
  <body>
    <%
      out.println("<b>Welcome: " +
        request.getParameter("user") + "</b>");
    %>
  </body>
</html>
```

Listing 4.4 Using the request object: request.jsp.

This JSP calls the request.getParameter() method, passing in the parameter user. This method looks for the key user in the parameter list, and returns the value if it is found. Enter the following URL into your browser to see the results from this page:

```
http://localhost:8080/customtags/request.jsp?user=Robert
```

After loading this URL, you should see a page similar to Figure 4.5.

response

The implicit response object represents the javax.servlet.http.HttpServletResponse object. The response object is used to pass data back to the requesting client. This implicit object provides all the functionality of the HttpServletRequest, just as if you were executing in a servlet. One of the more common uses for the response object is writing HTML output back to the client browser; however, the JSP API already provides access to a stream back to the client using the implicit out object, as described earlier.

pageContext

The pageContext object provides access to the namespaces associated with a JSP page. It also provides accessors to several other JSP implicit objects. You will use the pageContext most often inside tag handlers developed in later chapters. A common use for the pageContext is setting and retrieving objects using the setAttribute() and getAttribute() methods.

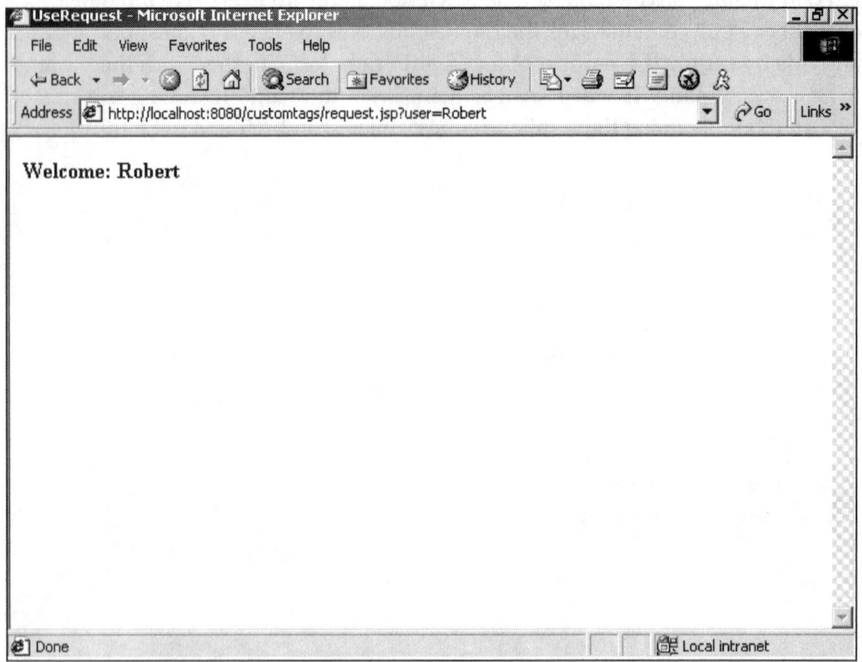

Figure 4.5 Output of request.jsp.

session

The implicit session object represents the javax.servlet.http.HttpSession object. It's used to store objects between client requests, thus providing an almost state-full HTTP interactivity.

An example of using the session object is shown in Listing 4.5.

```
<%@ page errorPage="errorpage.jsp" %>

<html>
  <head>
    <title>Session Example</title>
  </head>
  <body>
    <%
```

Listing 4.5 Using the session object: session.jsp. *(continues)*

```
        // get a reference to the current count from the session
        Integer count = (Integer)session.getAttribute("COUNT");

        if ( count == null ) {

          // If the count was not found create one
          count = new Integer(1);
          // and add it to the HttpSession
          session.setAttribute("COUNT", count);
        }
        else {

          // Otherwise increment the value
          count = new Integer(count.intValue() + 1);
          session.setAttribute("COUNT", count);
        }
        out.println("<b>You have accessed this page: "
          + count + " times.</b>");
      %>
    </body>
  </html>
```

Listing 4.5 Using the session object: session.jsp. *(continued)*

To use this example, copy the JSP to the <TOMCAT_HOME>webapps/customtags/ directory, and open your browser to the following URL:

```
http://localhost:8080/customtags/session.jsp
```

If everything went OK, you should see a page similar to Figure 4.6.

Click the Reload button a few times to see the count increment.

application

The application object represents the javax.servlet.ServletContext, as discussed in Chapter 3. The application object is most often used to access objects stored in the ServletContext to be shared between Web components in a global scope. It is a great place to share object between JSPs and servlets. An example using the application object can be found in Chapter 2 (in the section “The ServletContext”).

config

The implicit config object holds a reference to the ServletConfig, which contains configuration information about the JSP/servlet engine containing the Web application where this JSP resides.

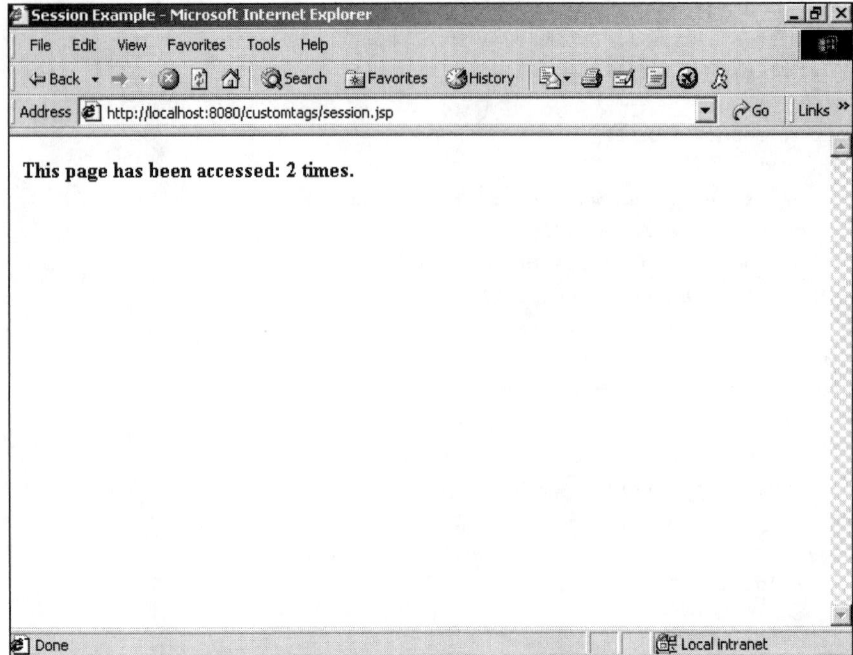

Figure 4.6 Output of session.jsp.

page

The page object contains a reference to the current instance of the JSP being accessed. The page object is used just like a *this* object, to reference the current instance of the generated servlet representing this JSP.

exception

The implicit *exception* object provides access to an uncaught exception thrown by a JSP. It is available only in JSPs that have a page with the attribute isErrorPage set to true.

Standard Actions

JSP standard actions are predefined custom tags that can be used to encapsulate common actions easily. There are two types of JSP standard actions: the first type is related to JavaBean functionality, and the second type consists of all other standard actions. Each group will be defined and used in the following sections.

JavaBean Standard Actions

Three predefined standard actions relate to using JavaBeans in a JSP: <useBean>, <setProperty>, and <getProperty>. After these tags are defined, you will create a simple example that uses them.

<jsp:useBean>

The <jsp:useBean> JavaBean standard action creates or looks up an instance of a JavaBean with a given scope and ID. The <jsp:useBean> action is very flexible. When a <useBean> action is encountered, the action tries to find an existing object using the same id and scope. If it cannot find an existing instance, it will attempt to create the object and store it in the named scope associated with the given ID. The syntax of the <jsp:useBean> action is as follows:

```
<jsp:useBean id="name"
        scope="page|request|session|application"
        typeSpec>
        body
</jsp:useBean>

typeSpec ::=class="className" |
        class="className" type="typeName" |
        type="typeName" class="className" |
        beanName="beanName" type="typeName" |
        type="typeName" beanName="beanName" |
        type="typeName"
```

Table 4.3 contains the attributes of the <jsp:useBean> action. The scope attribute listed in Table 4.3 can have four possible values, as described in Table 4.4.

Table 4.3 Attributes for the <jsp:useBean> Standard Action

ATTRIBUTE	DEFINITION
id	The key associated with the instance of the object in the specified scope. This key is case-sensitive. The id attribute is the same key as used in the page.getAttribute(id) method.
scope	The life of the referenced object. The scope options are page, request, session, and application. They are defined in a later section.
class	The fully qualified class name that defines the implementation of the object. The class name is case-sensitive.
beanName	The name of the JavaBean.
type	The type of scripting variable defined. If this attribute is unspecified, then the value is the same as the value of the class attribute.

Table 4.4 Scope Values for the <jsp:useBean> Standard Action

VALUE	DEFINITION
page	Beans with page scope are accessible only within the page where they were created. References to an object with page scope will be released when the current JSP has completed it evaluation.

Table 4.4 Scope Values for the <jsp:useBean> Standard Action *(continued)*

VALUE	DEFINITION
request	Beans with request scope are accessible only within pages servicing the same request, in which the object was instantiated, including forwarded requests. All references to the object will be released after the request is complete.
session	Beans with session scope are accessible only within pages processing requests that are in the same session as the one in which the bean was created. All references to beans with session scope will be released after their associated session expires.
application	Beans with application scope are accessible within pages processing requests that are in the same Web application. All references to beans will be released when the JSP/servlet container is shut down.

<jsp:setProperty>

The <jsp:setProperty> standard action sets the value of a bean's property. Its name attribute represents an object that must already be defined and in scope. The syntax for the <jsp:setProperty> action is as follows:

```
<jsp:setProperty name="beanName" propexpr />
```

In the preceding syntax, the name attribute represents the name of the bean whose property you are setting, and propexpr can be represented by any of the following expressions:

```
property="*" |
property="propertyName" |
property="propertyName" param="parameterName" |
property="propertyName" value="propertyValue"
```

Table 4.5 contains the attributes and their descriptions for the <jsp:setProperty> action.

Table 4.5 Attributes for the <jsp:setProperty> Standard Action

ATTRIBUTE	DEFINITION
name	The name of the bean instance defined by a <jsp:useBean> action or some other action.
property	The bean property for which you want to set a value. If you set propertyName to an asterisk (*), then the action will iterate over the current ServletRequest parameters, matching parameter names and value types to property names and setter method types, and setting each matched property to the value of the matching parameter. If a parameter has an empty string for a value, the corresponding property is left unmodified.

Table 4.5 Attributes for the <jsp:setProperty> Standard Action *(continued)*

ATTRIBUTE	DEFINITION
param	The name of the request parameter whose value you want to set the named property to. A <jsp:setProperty> action cannot have both param and value attributes referenced in the same action.
value	The value assigned to the named bean's property.

<jsp:getProperty>

The last standard action that relates to integrating JavaBeans into JSPs is <jsp:getProperty>. It takes the value of the referenced bean's instance property, converts it to a java.lang.String, and places it on the output stream. The referenced bean instance must be defined and in scope before this action can be used. The syntax for the <jsp:getProperty> action is as follows:

```
<jsp:getProperty name="name" property="propertyName" />
```

Table 4.6 contains the attributes and their descriptions for the <jsp:getProperty> action.

Table 4.6 Attributes for the <jsp:getProperty> Standard Action

ATTRIBUTE	DEFINITION
name	The name of the bean instance from which the property is obtained, defined by a <jsp:useBean> action or some other action.
property	The bean property for which you want to get a value.

JavaBean Standard Action Example

To learn how to use the JavaBean standard actions, let's create an example. This example uses a simple JavaBean that acts as a counter. The Counter bean has a single int property, count, that holds the current number of times the bean's property has been accessed. It also contains the appropriate methods for getting and setting this property. Listing 4.6 contains the source code for the Counter bean.

```
package chapter4;

public class Counter {

  int count = 0;
```

Listing 4.6 Example of a Counter bean: Counter.java. *(continues)*

```
    public Counter() {

    }

    public int getCount() {

      count++;

      return count;
    }

    public void setCount(int count) {

      this.count = count;
    }
  }
```

Listing 4.6 Example of a Counter bean: Counter.java. *(continued)*

Let's look at how to integrate this sample JavaBean into a JSP, using the JavaBean standard actions. Listing 4.7 contains the JSP that leverages the Counter bean.

```
<!-- Set the scripting language to java -->
<%@ page language="java" %>

<HTML>
<HEAD>
<TITLE>Bean Example</TITLE>
</HEAD>

<BODY>

<!-- Instantiate the Counter bean with an id of "counter" -->
<jsp:useBean id="counter" scope="session"
  class="chapter4.Counter" />

<%

  // write the current value of the property count
  out.println("Count from scriptlet code : "
    + counter.getCount() + "<BR>");

%>
```

Listing 4.7 A JSP that uses the Counter bean: counter.jsp. *(continues)*

```
<!-- Get the the bean's count property, -->
<!-- using the jsp:getProperty action. -->
Count from jsp:getProperty :
  <jsp:getProperty name="counter" property="count" /><BR>

</BODY>
</HTML>
```

Listing 4.7 A JSP that uses the Counter bean: counter.jsp. *(continued)*

Counter.jsp has four JSP components. The first component tells the JSP container that the scripting language is Java:

```
<%@ page language="java" %>
```

The next step uses the standard action <jsp:useBean> to create an instance of the class Counter with a scope of session and ID of counter. Now you can reference this bean using the name *counter* throughout the rest of the JSP. The code snippet that creates the bean is as follows:

```
<jsp:useBean id="counter" scope="session"
  class="chapter4.Counter" />
```

The final two actions demonstrate how to get the current value of a bean's property. The first of these two actions uses a scriptlet to access the bean's property, using an explicit method call. It simply accesses the bean by its ID, counter, and calls the getCount() method. The scriptlet snippet is listed here:

```
<%

  // write the current value of the property count
  out.println("Count from scriptlet code : "
    + counter.getCount() + "<BR>");

%>
```

The second example uses the <jsp:getProperty> standard action, which requires the ID of the bean and the property to be accessed. The action takes the attribute, calls the appropriate accessor, and embeds the results directly into the resulting HTML document, as follows:

```
<!-- Get the bean's count property, -->
<!-- using the jsp:getProperty action. -->
Count from jsp:getProperty :
  <jsp:getProperty name="counter" property="count" /><BR>
```

When you execute the Counter.jsp, notice that the second reference to the count property results in a value that is one greater that the first reference. This is the case because both methods of accessing the count property result in a call to the getCount() method, which increments the value of count.

To see this JSP in action, compile the Counter class, move it to the <TOMCAT_HOME>/customtags/WEB-INF/classes/chapter4/ directory, and copy the Counter.jsp file to the <TOMCAT_HOME>/customtags/ directory. Then, open your browser to the following URL:

```
http://localhost:8080/customtags/Counter.jsp
```

Once the JSP is loaded, you should see an image similar to Figure 4.7.

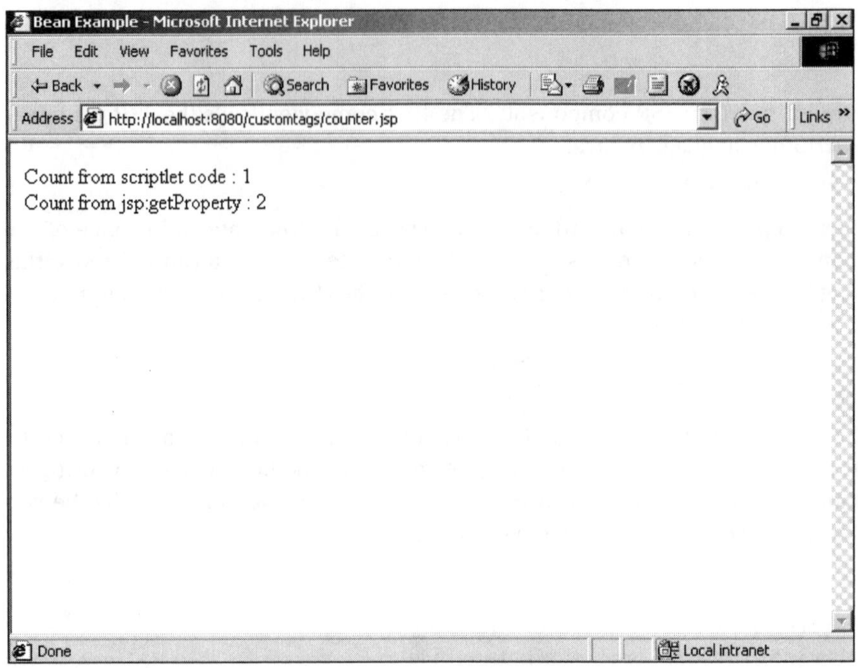

Figure 4.7 Results of counter.jsp.

Remaining Standard Actions

The remaining standard actions are used for generic tasks, from basic parameter action to an object plug-in action. These actions are described in the following sections.

<jsp:param>

The <jsp:param> action provides parameters and values to the JSP standard actions <jsp:include>, <jsp:forward>, and <jsp:plugin>. The syntax of the <jsp:param> action is as follows:

```
<jsp:param name="name" value="value"/>
```

Table 4.7 contains the attributes and their descriptions for the <jsp:param> action.

Table 4.7 Attributes for the <jsp:param> Action

ATTRIBUTE	DEFINITION
name	The name of the parameter being referenced
value	The value of the named parameter

<jsp:include>

The <jsp:include> standard action provides a method for including additional static and dynamic Web components in a JSP. The syntax for this action is as follows:

```
<jsp:include page="urlSpec" flush="true">
    <jsp:param ... />
</jsp:include>
```

Table 4.8 contains the attributes and their descriptions for the *<jsp:include>* action.

Table 4.8 Attributes for the <jsp:include> Action

ATTRIBUTE	DEFINITION
page	The relative URL of the resource to be included
flush	A mandatory Boolean value stating whether the buffer should be flushed

NOTE **It is important to note the difference between the *include directive* and the *include standard action*. The directive is evaluated only once, at translation time, whereas the standard action is evaluated with every request.**

The syntax description shows a request-time inclusion of a URL that is passed an optional list of param subelements used to argument the request. An example using the include standard action can be found in Listing 4.8.

```
<html>
  <head>
    <title>Include Example</title>
  </head>
  <body>
    <table width="100%" cellspacing="0">
      <tr>
        <td align="left">
          <jsp:include page="header.jsp" flush="true">
            <jsp:param name="user"
              value='<%= request.getParameter("user") %>' />
          </jsp:include>
```

Listing 4.8 Example of the include action: include.jsp. *(continues)*

```
            </td>
          </tr>
        </table>
    </body>
</html>
```

Listing 4.8 Example of the include action: include.jsp. *(continued)*

This file contains a single include action that includes the results of evaluating the JSP header.jsp, as shown in Listing 4.9.

```
<%
    out.println("<b>Welcome: </b>" +
      request.getParameter("user"));
%>
```

Listing 4.9 JSP evaluated in include.jsp: header.jsp.

This JSP simply looks for a parameter named user and outputs a string containing a welcome message. To deploy this example, copy these to JSPs to the <TOMCAT_HOME>/webapps/customtags/ directory. Open your browser to the following URL:

```
http://localhost:8080/customtags/include.jsp?user=Bob
```

The results should look similar to Figure 4.8.

Change the value of the user parameter to verify that the included JSP is evaluated at request time.

<jsp:forward>

The <jsp:forward> standard action enables the JSP engine to execute a runtime dispatch of the current request to another resource existing in the current Web application, including static resources, servlets, or JSPs. The appearance of <jsp:forward> effectively terminates the execution of the current JSP.

NOTE **A <jsp:forward> action can contain <jsp:param> subattributes. These subattributes act as parameters that will be forwarded to the targeted resource.**

The syntax of the <jsp:forward> action is as follows:

```
<jsp:forward page="relativeURL">
    <jsp:param .../>
</jsp:forward>
```

Table 4.9 contains the attribute and its description for the <jsp:forward> action.

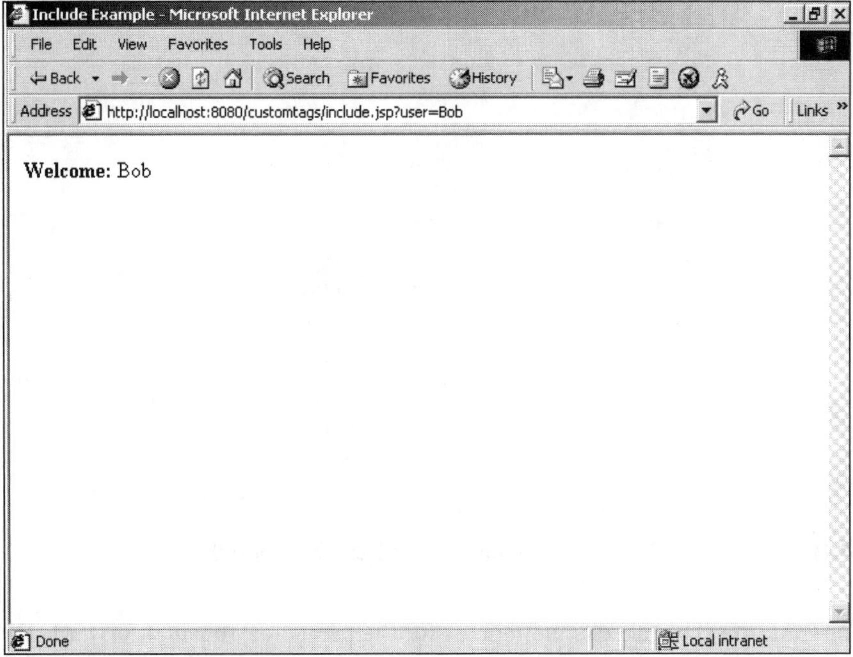

Figure 4.8 Results of include.jsp.

Table 4.9 Attribute for the <jsp:forward> Action

ATTRIBUTE	DEFINITION
page	The relative URL of the target of the forward

The example in Listing 4.10 contains a JSP that uses the <jsp:forward> action. This example checks a request parameter and forwards the request to one of two JSPs based on the value of the parameter.

```
<html>
  <head>
    <title>JSP Forward Example</title>
  </head>
  <body>
    <%

      if ( (request.getParameter("role")).equals("manager") ) {
```

Listing 4.10 Example of the forward action: forward.jsp. *(continues)*

```
        %>
          <jsp:forward page="management.jsp" />
        <%
      }
      else {
        %>
          <jsp:forward page="welcome.jsp">
          <jsp:param name="user"
            value='<%=request.getParameter("user") %>' />
          </jsp:forward>
        <%
      }
    %>
  </body>
</html>
```

Listing 4.10 Example of the forward action: forward.jsp. *(continued)*

The forward.jsp simply checks the request for the parameter role and forwards the request, along with a set of request parameters, to the appropriate JSP based on this value. Listings 4.11 and 4.12 contain the source of the targeted resources.

```
<html>
<!-- Set the scripting language to java -->
<%@ page language="java" %>

<HTML>
<HEAD>
<TITLE>Welcome Home</TITLE>
</HEAD>

<BODY>
<table>
  <tr>
    <td>
      Welcome User: <%= request.getParameter("user") %>
    </td>
  </tr>
</table>
```

Listing 4.11 welcome.jsp.

```
<html>
<!-- Set the scripting language to java -->
<%@ page language="java" %>

<HTML>
<HEAD>
<TITLE>Management Console</TITLE>
</HEAD>

<BODY>
<table>
  <tr>
    <td>
      Welcome Manager: <%= request.getParameter("user") %>
    </td>
  </tr>
</table>
```

Listing 4.12 management.jsp.

To test this example, copy all three JSPs to the <TOMCAT_HOME/webapps/customtags/ directory, and open your browser to the following URL:

```
http://localhost:8080/customtags/forward.jsp?role=user&user=Bob
```

You will see an image similar to Figure 4.9.

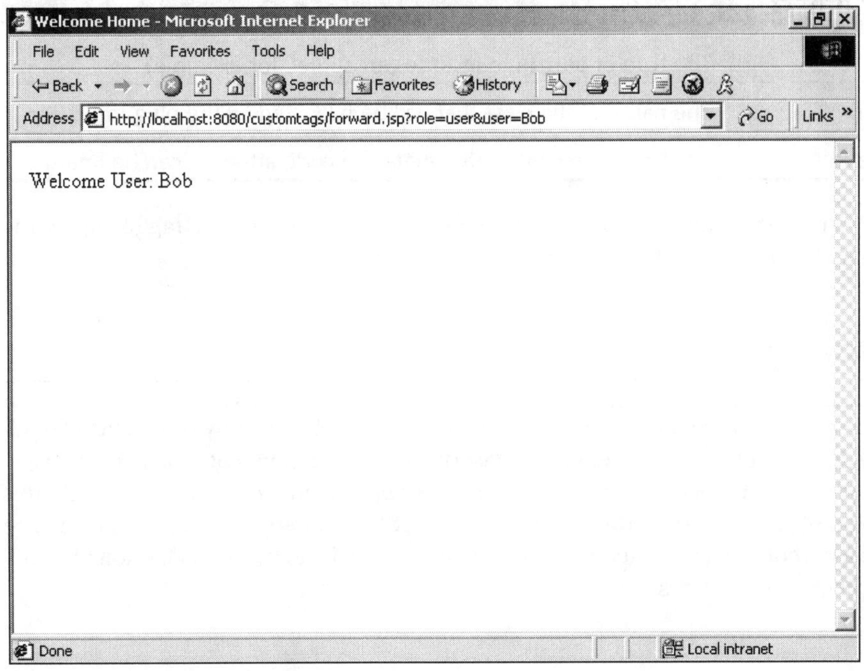

Figure 4.9 Output of forward.jsp.

You can also change the value of the role parameter to *manager*, to change the forwarded target.

<jsp:plugin>

The last standard action we will discuss is <jsp:plugin>. This action enables a JSP author to generate the required HTML, using the appropriate client-browser independent constructs, to result in the download and subsequent execution of the specified applet or JavaBeans component.

The <jsp:plugin> tag, once evaluated, will be replaced by either an <object> or <embed> tag, as appropriate for the requesting user agent. The attributes of the <jsp:plugin> action provide configuration data for the presentation of the embedded element. The syntax of the <jsp:plugin> action is as follows:

```
<jsp:plugin type="pluginType"
    code="classFile"
    codebase="relativeURLpath">

    <jsp:params>

    </jsp:params>
</jsp:plugin>
```

Table 4.10 contains the attributes and their descriptions for the <jsp:plugin> action.

Table 4.10 Attributes for the <jsp:plugin> Action

ATTRIBUTE	DEFINITION
type	The type of plug-in to include (an applet, for example)
code	The name of the class that will be executed by the plug-in
codebase	The base or relative path where the code attribute can be found

The <jsp:plugin> action also supports the use of the <jsp:params> tag to supply the plug-in with parameters, if necessary.

Summary

This chapter presented the JavaServer Pages technology. It began by providing a definition for JavaServer Pages. It went on to describe the components of a JavaServer Page, including directives, scripting elements, implicit objects, and standard actions. At this point, you should feel comfortable with the basic JSP technologies and how they can be used to assemble a Web application. The next chapter will begin our discussion of developing custom tag libraries.

CHAPTER

5

Simple Tags

In this chapter, we are going to begin our actual custom tag development discussions. We will start by developing a simple date tag without a body or attributes. We will then take our date tag and discuss how we can modify its behavior using tag attributes. We will conclude this chapter by describing how you can leverage the javax.servlet.jsp.tagext.TagSupport helper class to shortcut the Tag methods implemented in our date tag handler.

An object model depicting the javax.servlet.jsp.tagext objects covered in this chapter can be found in Figure 5.1.

Simple Tags

Simple tags are commonly used to perform straightforward tasks, such as printing the current date, getting or setting scripting variables, reading configuration values, or outputting some data back to a client. They perform much like any other custom tag, except that they do not intend to process their body, either because the tag has no body or it plans to simply pass its body through to the JSP container. This is the main characteristic separating a simple tag from its peers.

The Life Cycle of a Simple Custom Tag

Before we begin developing our own simple tag, we need to take a look at the life cycle of a simple tag. Figure 5.2 graphically depicts the flow of control that each method in the Tag interface goes through during a single evaluation. We will look at each of the methods in the tag's life cycle in the following sections.

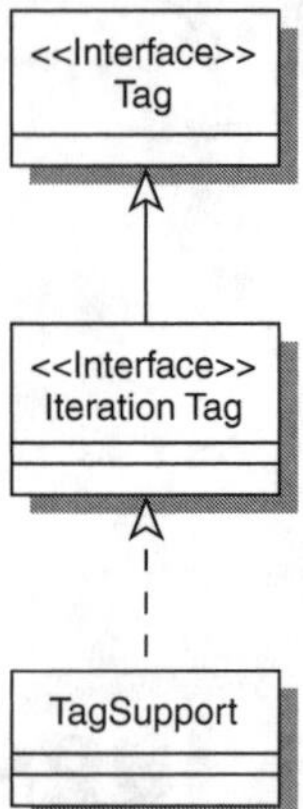

Figure 5.1 Simple tag objects.

As you examine Figure 5.2, you will note that the life of a simple tag can be broken down into the following steps. These steps should give you an understanding of the exact process a simple tag handler goes through during a single evaluation:

1. The JSP/servlet container receives a request for a JSP that contains a custom tag. The container matches the tag prefix of the encountered tag and retrieves the URI from the taglib directive in this JSP.
2. The JSP/servlet container looks in the TLD, referenced by the URI contained the JSP, for a tag name matching the tag name in the JSP.
3. If the container cannot find a matching tag in the TLD, a JspException is thrown and the response is sent back to the client.
4. If the matching tag name is found, the container tries to get a reference to the tag handler that matches the tag name. The tag handler can be in an instance pool.
5. If the tag handler is in an instance pool, the container retrieves the handler from the pool, and marks it "unavailable."
6. If the tag handler is not pooled, the container instantiates a new tag handler instance.
7. After the tag handler is retrieved or created, the container invokes the setPage-Context() method, with a reference to the javax.servlet.jsp.PageContext for the JSP containing this tag.
8. The container then calls the setParent() method, with a reference to the enclosing parent, or null if there is no parent.
9. The last initialization step performed by the container is to call the setters associated with each attribute included in the tag. We will cover tag attributes in a later section of this chapter.
10. At this point, the tag handler is completely initialized, and the doStartTag() method is invoked. The doStartTag() is the most common place to perform the business logic of a tag.

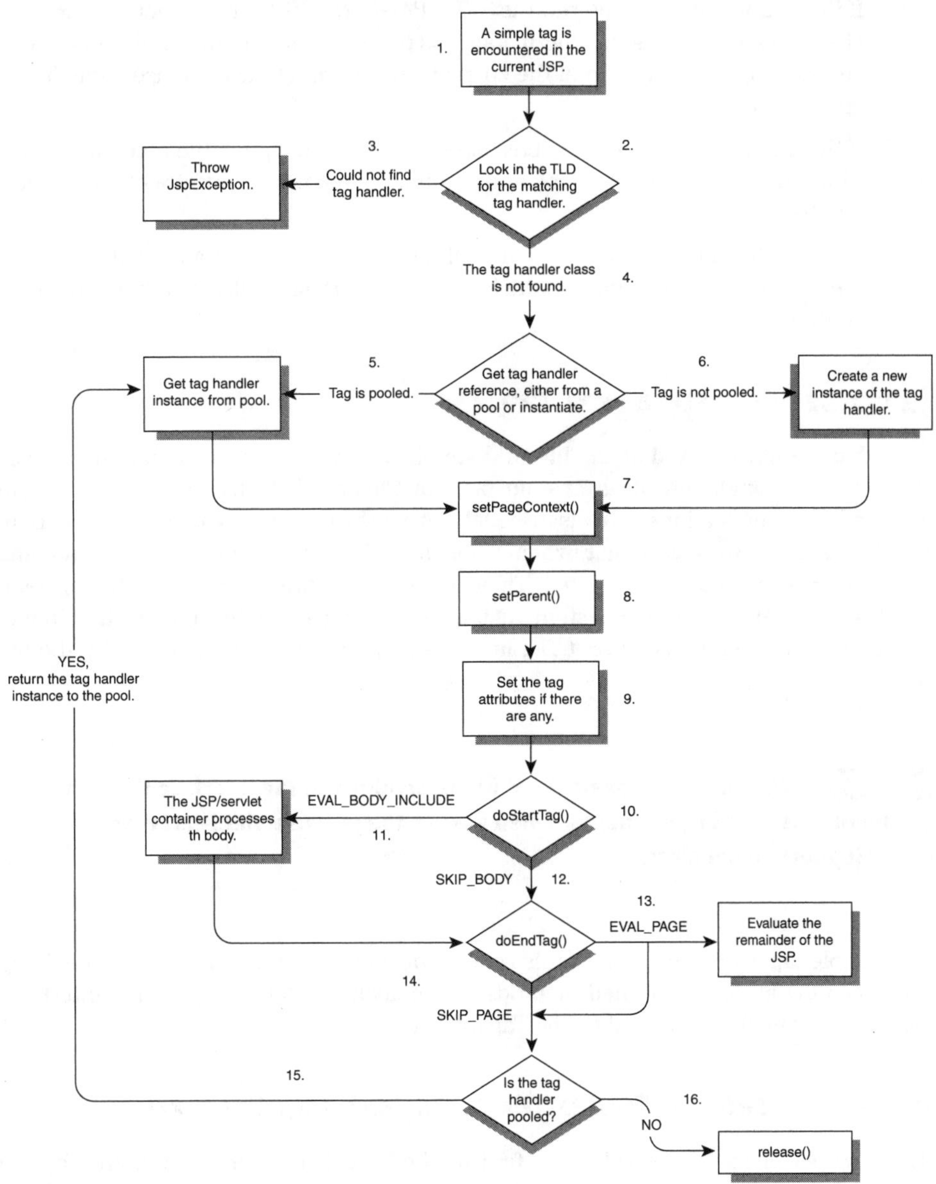

Figure 5.2 Flow of a simple tag.

11. If the doStartTag() method returns EVAL_BOY_INCLUDE, the container will evaluate the body of the tag before invoking the doEndTag().
12. If the doStartTag() method returns SKIP_BODY, the doEndTag() will be invoked immediately.
13. If the doEndTag() method returns EVAL_PAGE, the JSP/servlet container will check to see if the tag handler instance is pooled or not, going on to steps 15 or 16, and continue to evaluate the JSP.

14. If the doEndTag() method returns SKIP_PAGE, the JSP/servlet container will check to see if the tag handler instance is pooled or not, going on to steps 15 or 16, and stop its evaluation of the current JSP returning the response immediately to the client.
15. If the tag handler instance is determined to belong in a pool, the container will return the instance to the pool, and continue to the next request without invoking the release() method.
16. If the tag handler instance does not belong in a pool, the container will invoke the release() method and free the instance for garbage collection. It will then continue to the next request.

javax.servlet.jsp.tagext.Tag

Now that we have looked at the life of a simple tag, we need to examine the classes that act as a foundation of all custom tags. In Chapter 1, "Introducing JSP Custom Tags and Web Applications," we discussed the process that occurs when a tag is encountered in a JSP. We stated that when a tag in a JSP is encountered, its matching tag handler is located and executed. These tag handlers are where all of the tag logic resides. To develop your own custom tag handler, you must create an object that implements the javax.servlet.jsp.tagext.Tag interface, either explicitly or implicitly though inheritance.

NOTE **We will see an example of implementing the Tag interface through inheritance later in this chapter when we use the javax.servlet.jsp.tagext.TagSupport helper class.**

A simple tag is no exception to this rule. To develop a simple tag, we must begin by implementing all of the defined methods of the javax.servlet.jsp.tagext.Tag interface. There are six methods defined by the Tag interface.

public void setPageContext(PageContext pageContext)

The setPageContext() method is the first method invoked when encountered by the JSP/servlet container. It is used to set the current javax.servlet.jsp.PageContext object for the JSP containing the tag being evaluated.

A javax.servlet.jsp.PageContext is an abstract class that provides several convenience methods that can be used inside of a custom tag handler. These methods provide access to the javax.servlet.http.HttpServletRequest and javax.servlet.http.HttpServletResponse objects, the javax.servlet.ServletContext, and the javax.servlet.jsp.JspWriter that will be used to present data back to the requesting client. We will see this object used frequently throughout the remainder of this text.

public void setParent(Tag parent)

The setParent() method is used to set a Tag reference containing the closest enclosing tag of this tag handler. If there is no enclosing parent tag, then this value is *null*. This method is the second method invoked by the JSP/servlet container when a tag is encountered.

public Tag getParent()

The getParent() method is a convenience method that returns a reference to the closest enclosing tag of this tag handler. If there is no enclosing parent tag then null is returned.

public int doStartTag()

The doStartTag() method is the third Tag interface method invoked. It is invoked when the opening tag element is encountered, but not before the setPageContext() and setParent() methods are invoked. In a simple tag implementation, this method is often where you will perform most of your tag handler logic.

The doStartTag() method has two possible return values. The first return value, Tag.EVAL_BODY_INCLUDE, will result in the tag's body being evaluated by the JSP/servlet container. The result of the body evaluation is then included in the response sent back to the client.

The second available return value is Tag.SKIP_BODY. doStartTag() should return this value if it does not want its body to be evaluated. Returning Tag.SKIP_BODY will force the JSP/servlet container to skip the evaluation of the tag's body.

public int doEndTag()

The doEndTag() method is the fourth Tag interface method invoked. It is invoked after the doStartTag() method returns, when the closing tag element is encountered.

This method is often used to free resources allocated during tag processing. The resources that are freed using the doEndTag() method are those resources that must be unique to each instance of the tag encountered in a JSP. By using the doEndTag() to free resources, you make a tag instance that has been pooled available for reuse by the JSP/servlet engine.

The doEndTag() method has two possible return values. The first of these return values is Tag.EVAL_PAGE. If this value is returned, the JSP/servlet container will continue evaluating the JSP.

If doEndTag() returns SKIP_PAGE, the rest of the page is not evaluated, and the request is considered complete.

public void release()

The final Tag method that must be implemented is the release() method. This method is called when the tag is completely released by the JSP/servlet engine. After this method is called, a new Tag object must be created again before it can be used another time.

This method represents the death of a custom tag. It should be used to clean up any resources that were not accounted for in the doEndTag() method.

Current Date Tag

Now that we understand what a simple tag is and the methods involved when developing a simple tag, we are going to develop our own simple tag. Our tag will calculate the current date, and print it to the requesting client. The syntax of our simple tag is going to look something like the following snippet:

```
<chapter5:currentDate />
```

Current Date Tag Handler

To create the logic that will calculate the current date and print it to the requesting client, we need to create a tag handler that implements the six methods defined by the javax.servlet.jsp.Tag interface. The source for our date tag handler is shown in Listing 5.1.

```
package chapter5;

import javax.servlet.jsp.tagext.Tag;
import javax.servlet.jsp.JspWriter;
import javax.servlet.jsp.PageContext;
import javax.servlet.jsp.JspException;

import java.util.Date;
import java.io.*;
import java.text.SimpleDateFormat;

public class DateTag_v1 implements Tag {

  private Tag parent = null;
  protected PageContext pageContext = null;

  /**
   * Set the current page context.
   */
  public void setPageContext(PageContext pageContext) {

    System.err.println("---->inside setPageContext()<----");

    this.pageContext = pageContext;
  }
```

Listing 5.1 DateTag_v1.java *(continues)*

```
/**
 * Set the parent of this tag handler.
 */
public void setParent(Tag parent) {

  System.err.println("---->inside setParent()<----");

  this.parent = parent;
}

/**
 * Get the parent for this tag handler.
 */
public Tag getParent() {

  System.err.println("---->inside getParent()<----");

  return this.parent;
}

/**
 * The doStartTag method assumes that the properties
 * pageContext and parent have been set.
 * It also assumes that any properties exposed as
 * attributes have been set too.
 */
public int doStartTag()
  throws javax.servlet.jsp.JspException {

  System.err.println("---->inside doStartTag()<----");

  // Get the current date
  Date currentDate = new java.util.Date();

  // Provide a format to display the date
  String format =
    new String("yyyy.MM.dd G 'at' hh:mm:ss a zzz");

  try {

    // Format the current time.
    SimpleDateFormat formatter
      = new SimpleDateFormat(format);
```

Listing 5.1 DateTag_v1.java *(continues)*

```
        JspWriter out = pageContext.getOut();

        out.print(formatter.format(currentDate));
      }
      catch (Exception e) {

        throw new JspException("Exception thrown: " +
          e.getMessage());
      }
      return SKIP_BODY;
    }

    /**
     * If this method returns EVAL_PAGE, the rest of the page
     * continues to be evaluated.  If this method returns
     * SKIP_PAGE, the rest of the page is not evaluated
     * and the request is completed.
     */
    public int doEndTag()
      throws javax.servlet.jsp.JspException {

      System.err.println("---->inside doEndTag()<----");

      // return Tag.EVAL_PAGE
      return Tag.EVAL_PAGE;
    }

    /**
     * The release() mehtod is used to reset Tag Handler
     * data members. It is the final method called when a tag
     * is being processed.
     */
    public void release() {

      System.err.println("---->inside release()<----");
    }
  }
```

Listing 5.1 DateTag_v1.java *(continued)*

NOTE **You will notice that each of the methods in this tag handler has a simple System.err.println() statement. These statements are included only to provide trace statements showing the order in which each of the tag handler's methods are invoked.**

As you examine this class, you should note the first two methods: setPageContext() and setParent(). These two methods are used to prepare or initialize the tag handler for processing.

The setPageContext() method takes the current javax.servlet.PageContext object passed to it and places a reference to it in a local data member called pageContext. We will see this member being used later in the doStartTag() method.

The second of the initialization methods is the setParent() method. This method takes the javax.servlet.tagext.Tag object, representing the tag handler's parent, and places a reference to it in a local data member called parent. We will not use this object in this example, but we will make use of it in a later chapter.

The third method in this tag handler is the getParent() method. This method is simply an accessor for the parent tag.

doStartTag() Method

The final three methods in this handler represent the functional methods of the tag. The first of these methods is the doStartTag(). This method is invoked when the opening tag is encountered, immediately after the setPageContext() and setParent() methods are invoked. The following code snippet contains the source for the doStartTag() method:

```
public int doStartTag()
  throws javax.servlet.jsp.JspException {

  System.err.println("---->inside doStartTag()<----");

  try {

    // Get the current date
    Date currentDate = new java.util.Date();

    // Provide a format to display the date
    String format =
      new String("yyyy.MM.dd G 'at' hh:mm:ss a zzz");

    // Format the current time.
    SimpleDateFormat formatter
      = new SimpleDateFormat(format);

    JspWriter out = pageContext.getOut();

    out.print(formatter.format(currentDate));
  }
  catch (Exception e) {

    throw new JspException("IOException thrown: " +
      e.getMessage());
  }
  return SKIP_BODY;
}
```

The first part of this method creates a java.util.Date, java.lang.String, and java.text.SimpleDateFormat that will be used to format the current date according to the static format String.

NOTE **You should notice that the format used to print the current date is static. With the current implementation of this tag handler, there is no way to change the format without changing the source code for the tag handler. We will look at a solution for this problem in the following section.**

The next statement uses the previously stored PageContext to get a reference to the current javax.servlet.jsp.JspWriter. The JspWriter retrurned by the PageContext. getWriter() method is the same object represented by the JSP implicit out object, and therefore functions exactly the same.

Once we have a reference to the current JspWriter, we can write our response back to the client. The output from a simple tag will replace the JSP tag text. We will see this explicitly when we execute this handler.

The final executed line of this method uses the retrieved JspWriter to print the current date in the format contained in the format String.

After the doStartTag() method has finished its processing, it can return one of two values: EVAL_BODY_INCLUDE or SKIP_BODY. In this case, there is no reason for this tag to have a body; therefore, we return SKIP_BODY. This causes the JSP/servlet engine to skip a body if there is one, and invoke the doEndTag() method. If the doStartTag() did return EVAL_BODY_INCLUDE, the JSP/servlet engine would have evaluated the body of the tag, and the results would have been included with the output of the DateTag_v1.

doEndTag() Method

The second of the function methods is the doEndTag() method. This method is invoked when the closing tag is encountered. In the case of the <chapter5:currentDate />, the end of the tag is represented by the '/' character. The following code snippet contains the source for the doEndTag() method:

```
public int doEndTag()
  throws javax.servlet.jsp.JspException {

  System.err.println("---->inside doEndTag()<----");

  // return EVAL_PAGE
  return EVAL_PAGE;
}
```

As you can see, there is really nothing special happening in this method. We simply return the value EVAL_PAGE, which tells the JSP/servlet engine that we want the remainder of the JSP to be evaluated. If we encountered a condition that made us want to stop processing the current JSP, we could have returned SKIP_PAGE. This value would cause the JSP/servlet engine to stop processing the current JSP and immediately return the response to the client.

NOTE **A common reason to skip the remainder of the page is when a tag determines that the current user does not have permissions to view the results.**

The release() Method

The final of the functional methods is the release() method. This method is invoked when the JSP/servlet engine is finished using the tag, either pooled or not. In our implementation, the release method does nothing. This is because we have no resources that we need to release. If the tag handler had allocated resources that we not released in the doEndTag() method, this is where we would do it.

Current Date TLD

To publish the Current Date tag, we must create the TLD that tells the JSP/servlet engine how our custom tag is to be used. This is a very simple process, but without it the container would not have any knowledge of our tag. The TLD for our tag is shown in Listing 5.2.

```
<?xml version="1.0" encoding="ISO-8859-1" ?>
<!DOCTYPE taglib PUBLIC
"-//Sun Microsystems, Inc.//DTD JSP Tag Library 1.1//EN"
"http://java.sun.com/j2ee/dtds/web-jsptaglibrary_1_1.dtd">

<taglib>
  <tlibversion>1.0</tlibversion>
  <jspversion>1.2</jspversion>
  <shortname>chapter5</shortname>

  <tag>
    <name>currentDate</name>
    <tagclass>chapter5.DateTag_v1</tagclass>
    <bodycontent>empty</bodycontent>
  </tag>

</taglib>
```

Listing 5.2 chapter5.tld

All TLDs are made up of three sections. The three sections describe the XML document definition, the tag library as a whole, and the collection of tags that belong to this library.

The first section of our TLD will most often simply be a cut-and-paste from one TLD to another. This section describes the XML version we are using, the ISO encoding type, and the document type for this file. The most important piece of this section is the document type definition. It contains the name and location of the DTD that describes the possible values that can be used in a TLD. If you want to see the actual DTD, you can point your browser to the URL found in this definition. The URL for this definition is as follows:

```
http://java.sun.com/j2ee/dtds/web-jsptaglibrary_1_1.dtd
```

The next section of the TLD describes characteristics that are global to the entire tag library. For this tag library, we describe only the required global elements. The first, <tlibversion>, tells the JSP/servlet engine that we are using version 1 of the tag library implementation. The next element, <jspversion>, tells the JSP/servlet engine that this tag library depends upon version 1.2 of the JSP specification. The final global element, <short-name>, contains a simple string that can be used by a JSP authoring tool to identify the tag library to the user of the tool. This value is often used as a recommended tag prefix.

The third section of this TLD is used to describe the tag handlers packaged in this tag library. This section is composed of *n* number of <tag> elements and their appropriate subelements, each describing an individual tag in the library. Each tag can be made up of up to eleven subelements. The possible tag subelements are described in Table 5.1.

NOTE **In this chapter we cover only a fraction of the possible <tag> subelements. As we progress through this text we will cover the remainder of these subelements.**

Table 5.1 Subelements of a <tag>

SUBELEMENT	DESCRIPTION
name	The name subelement is used to identify the actual tag text that will be used in the hosting JSP. (required)
tag-class	The tag-class subelement contains the fully qualified class name of the tag handler that will be invoked when the named tag is encountered. (required)
tei-class	The tei-class subelement contains the fully qualified class name of the tag extra info class (TEI) associated with this tag. We will be discussing the use of a TEI class in Chapter 7. (optional)
body-content	The body-content subelement is used to identify what kind of body this tag will allow. The possible values for this element are none, JSP, and tag dependent. Each of these options is described in the final paragraph of this section. The default value is JSP. (optional)
display-name	The display-name subelement is used to identify the tag in a tag library tool. (optional)
small-icon	The small-icon subelement names a small icon that can represent the tag graphically in a tag library tool. (optional)
large-icon	The large-icon subelement names a large icon that can represent the tag graphically in a tag library tool. (optional)
description	The description subelement provides human-readable information about the custom tag. (optional)
variable	The variable subelement provides information about the tag's scripting variables, if there are any. (optional)

Table 5.1 Subelements of a <tag> *(continued)*

SUB-ELEMENT	DESCRIPTION
attribute	The attribute subelement is used to define all attributes associated with this tag. (optional)
example	The example subelement provides a simple description of how the tag can be used. (optional)

For this first example, our library contains only a single <tag> element. This is because we currently have only one tag in the library.

NOTE **If you want to include multiple tags in this library, you could simply add additional <tag> elements following the first <tag> element.**

In the <tag> element that describes our Current Date tag, we have four subelements, of which the first two are required when describing a tag. The first element, <name>, names the JSP text to be used when embedding the tag into a JSP. In this instance, we use the value currentDate, which implies that to use this tag in a JSP you need to embed the string <currentDate />.

The next element used to describe the currentDate tag is the <tagclass> element. Like the <name> element, the <tagclass> element is required. This element defines the tag handler class that will be invoked when the tag <currentDate /> is encountered. As we stated earlier, this class must implement the javax.servlet.jsp.tagext.Tag interface explicitly or implicitly. The value we are using for this handler is chapter5.DateTag_v1.class. This value matches the name of our tag handler defined in Listing 5.1.

The last element used to describe this tag is the <bodycontent> element. This element is not required, but is very useful when describing the usage of a custom tag. The <bodycontent> element tells the JSP/servlet engine what kind of body this tag will allow. The possible values for this element are *none*, *JSP*, and *tag dependent*. If this value is not specified, it is defaulted to *JSP*, which tells the container that the body can contain any JSP allowed syntax. If this element's value equals *tag dependent*, then the contents of the tag body would be processed in reference to the tag only. For the purposes of this example, we do not want this tag to contain a body, therefore we have set this value to *none*.

Deploying and Using the Current Date Tag

Now that we have the current date's tag handler and TLD defined, we can move on to actually using the tag. To do this we must first compile the DateTag_v1.java file, and move the resulting class file into the <TOMCAT_HOME>/webapps/customtags/WEB-INF/classes/chapter5/ directory. To compile this tag handler, you must have the latest JSP/servlet SDK in your classpath. If you are using Tomcat 4, you should be able to find the appropriate classes in the <TOMCAT_HOME>/common/lib/servlet.jar archive file.

NOTE **We will be using the /customtags Web application created in Chapter 3, "Java Servlet Overview and Architecture," for all of the remaining examples in this text.**

After you have compiled and moved the class file into the appropriate directory, you need to tell the JSP/servlet engine that you are making a new tag library available to the customtags Web application. You do this first by deploying the TLD, which is really just copying the TLD to the <TOMCAT_HOME>/webapps/customtags/WEB-INF/ directory. And then you need to add a taglib entry to the web.xml file for the customtags Web application. The following snippet contains the <taglib> entry describing this tag library:

```
<taglib>
  <taglib-uri>
    /chapter5
  </taglib-uri>
  <taglib-location>
    /WEB-INF/chapter5.tld
  </taglib-location>
</taglib>
```

NOTE **Make sure that your <taglib> entries are added directly after any <servlet> definitions that may exist in your web.xml file.**

This entry defines the URI that will identify the tag library and the location of its TLD. That is all there is to it. The new tag library is deployed.

Now it is time to use our newly developed tag. To do this, we need a simple JSP that references the tag library and the <currentDate /> tag. Listing 5.3 contains a simple JSP that does just this.

```
<%@ taglib uri="/chapter5" prefix="chapter5" %>

<html>
<head>
  <title>Custom Tags Demo</title>
</head>

The current date is : <chapter5:currentDate />

</body>
</html>
```

Listing 5.3 chapter5.jsp

As you look over this JSP, you will see that there is very little to it. It begins with a taglib directive that names the URI of the tag library that this JSP will use, which must match the <taglib_uri> value in the web.xml file. This directive also tells the JSP/servlet container that all tags in this page that begin with the prefix chapter5 will reference a tag found in the library referenced by the URI '/chapter5'.

The next statement to notice is the following line:

```
The current date is : <chapter5:currentDate />
```

The tag included in this line begins with the prefix chapter5, which will tell the JSP/servlet container that it must look in the tag library referenced by the /chapter5 URI. The container then looks up the tag named currentDate, which has a tag class named chapter5.DateTag_v1, and invokes the tag handler. The result of this executing replaces the tag text with the current date. To see this process in action, copy this JSP to the <TOMCAT_HOME>/webapps/customtags/ directory, and open your browser to the following URL:

```
http://localhost:8080/customtags/chapter5.jsp
```

If everything went according to plan, you should see a page similar to Figure 5.3.

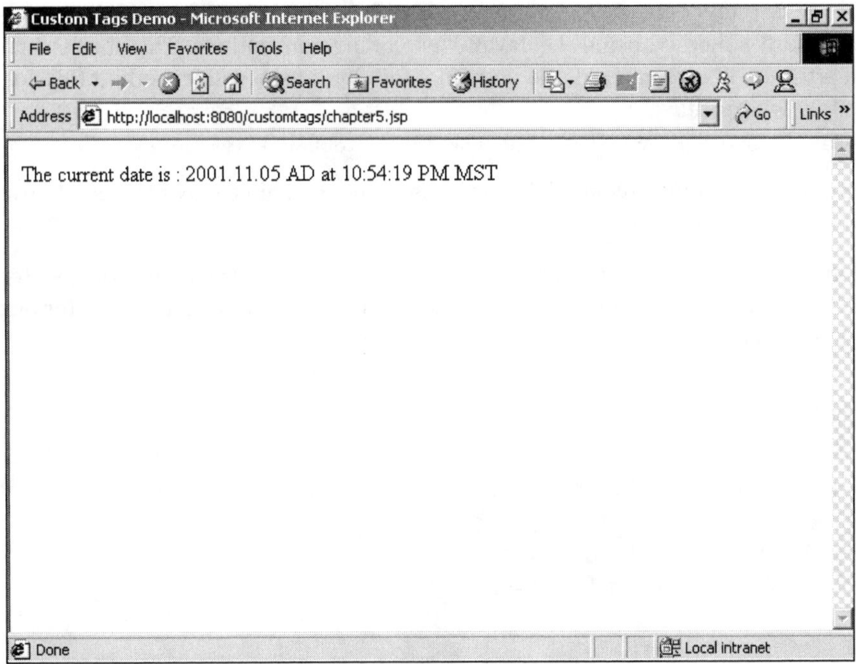

Figure 5.3 Output of the chapter 5.jsp.

After this JSP has finished its execution, select the View Source option for your particular browser. What you will see is that the tag text originally contained in the JSP has been replaced by the output of the <chapter5:currentDate /> tag handler.

You should also notice the text being printed to the Tomcat console. These text strings are being printed to the Tomcat standard error stream to show the order in which the tag handler's methods are being invoked. You will see that the output matches the data flow diagram contained in Figure 5.2.

Simple Tags with Attributes

In this section, we are going to change the <chapter5:currentDate /> to allow us to dynamically set the format of the date printed by this tag. This is accomplished using tag attributes. Tag attributes allow the user of a custom tag to change the behavior of the tag by simply changing the source of the JSP. An example of this is included in the following snippet:

```
<chapter5:currentDate format="yyyy.MM.dd" />
```

As you can see, the format of this tag is exactly the same as before, except that this tag includes an attribute named format that allows you to pass a string that will be used to format the current date.

Changing the Tag Handler to Accept an Attribute

When the JSP/servlet container encounters a tag with an attribute, it will call the appropriate tag handler method using the JavaBeans coding conventions. This means that when an attribute is encountered, the container will look for a setter method that follows the following syntax:

```
set + attribute name capitalizing the first letter + (value);
```

In our case, the method invoked following this syntax would be executed as follows:

```
setFormat("yyyy.MM.dd")
```

What this means to our original tag handler is that we must add an appropriate setter method to receive the passed in format attribute. Listing 5.4 contains the source for our modified tag handler.

```
package chapter5;

import javax.servlet.jsp.tagext.Tag;
import javax.servlet.jsp.JspWriter;
import javax.servlet.jsp.PageContext;
import javax.servlet.jsp.JspException;

import java.util.Date;
import java.io.*;
import java.text.SimpleDateFormat;

public class DateTag_v2 implements Tag {

  private Tag parent = null;
  protected PageContext pageContext = null;

  // Provide a default date format
  private String format =
    new String("yyyy.MM.dd G 'at' hh:mm:ss a zzz");

  public void setFormat(String format) {
```

Listing 5.4 DateTag_v2.java *(continues)*

```
    this.format = format;
  }

  public String getFormat() {

    return this.format;
  }

  /**
   * Set the current page context.
   */
  public void setPageContext(PageContext pageContext) {

    this.pageContext = pageContext;
  }

  /**
   * Set the parent of this tag handler.
   */
  public void setParent(Tag parent) {

    this.parent = parent;
  }

  /**
   * Get the parent for this tag handler.
   */
  public Tag getParent() {

    return this.parent;
  }

  public int doStartTag()
    throws javax.servlet.jsp.JspException {

    // Get the current date
    Date currentDate = new java.util.Date();

    try {

      // Format the current time using the
      // format passed using the format attribute.
      SimpleDateFormat formatter
```

Listing 5.4 DateTag_v2.java *(continues)*

```
            = new SimpleDateFormat(getFormat());

          JspWriter out = pageContext.getOut();

          out.print(formatter.format(currentDate));
        }
        catch (Exception e) {

          throw new JspException("IOException thrown: " +
            e.getMessage());
        }
        return SKIP_BODY;
      }

      public int doEndTag()
        throws javax.servlet.jsp.JspException {

        // reset the default format when the tags is released
        this.format =
     "yyyy.MM.dd G 'at'' hh:mm:ss a zzz";

        return EVAL_PAGE;
      }

      /**
       * The release() mehtod is used to reset Tag Handler
       * data members. It is the final method called when a tag
       * is being processed.
       */
      public void release() {

      }
    }
```

Listing 5.4 DateTag_v2.java *(continued)*

As you examine this tag handler, you will immediately notice several changes. The first of these changes is the name of the tag handler. We have changed the class name to DateTag_v2 purely to keep the progression of changes to this handler separate. This change will only be important when we modify the TLD to include our new attribute.

The next change that you should notice is the addition of the data member format. This data member will be set to whatever value is included in the format tag attribute. It is defaulted to the string "yyyy.MM.dd G 'at' hh:mm:ss a zzz" if no value is included in the format attribute.

The next change that you should notice is the two accessor methods that have been added to the handler. These methods, setFormat() and getFormat(), are used to modify the value of the format data member. The setFormat() method is the method that will be invoked by the container when a format attribute is encountered.

After you have examined the new accessor methods, we need to move on to the doStartTag() method. This is where we see how the addition of tag attributes can modify the behavior of a custom tag. In this instance, when we create the SimpleDateFormat that will be used to format the current date, we get the format contained in the format data member using the getFormat() method. The result is a date format that was configured dynamically using the format attribute.

The final change made to this tag handler is in the doEndTag() method. In this method we reset the format data member to the default value, allowing the tag to be reused in the case of pooled tag handlers.

Changing the TLD to Allow an Attribute

After the appropriate changes have been made to the tag handler, we must modify the TLD to reflect these changes. To add an attribute to a tag's definition, we must use the <attribute> subelement. This element is composed of up to five unique sub-elements that describe how the attribute will function. Each of these subelements is described in Table 5.2.

Table 5.2 Subelements of an <attribute>

SUBELEMENT	DESCRIPTION
name	The name subelement is used to define the name of the attribute that will be used in the JSP. (required)
required	The required subelement tells the JSP/servlet container that this attribute is required when using the tag. The default value is false. (optional)
rtexprvalue	The rtexprvalue subelement tells the JSP/servlet container that this attribute can be the result of a runtime expression. An example of this would be using a JSP assignment operator as follows: <%= request.getParameter("*parametername*") %>. The default value is false. (optional)
type	The type subelement is used to name the Java type of the attribute. If the type attribute is not included, it is assumed to be a java.lang.String. (optional)
description	The description subelement is used provide a human-readable description of the attribute. (optional)

Of the previously listed subelements, we are going to use three subelements to describe the currentDate tag's format attribute. The following code snippet contains the changes that need to be made to describe the format attribute:

```
<tag>
  <name>currentDate</name>
  <tagclass>chapter5.DateTag_v2</tagclass>
```

```
    <bodycontent>empty</bodycontent>
    <attribute>
      <name>format</name>
      <required>false</required>
      <rtexprvalue>true</rtexprvalue>
    </attribute>
  </tag>
```

There are two changes that have been made to this TLD. The first is the renaming of the value of the <tagclass> element from chapter5.DateTag_v2 to chapter5.DateTag_v2. We made this change so that the tag handler referenced by the <currentDate /> tag would point to the modified DateTag_v2 class defined in Listing 5.4, which contains the setters and getters for the new format attribute.

The second change includes the addition of the <attribute> subelement, which actually describes the new attribute. With the addition of the <attribute> subelement, there are three other subelements that have been included. The first of these subelements defines the name of the attribute as format.

The second subelement, which is set to false, tells the container that this tag is not required. If you look back at the source for the chapter5.DateTag_v2 tag handler, you will see that the attribute is defaulted to the String "yyyy.MM.dd G 'at' hh:mm:ss a zzz" when the format attribute is not used.

The last subelement used to describe this attribute is the <rtexprvalue> subelement. This element, which is set to true for this example, tells the container that this attribute can be the result of a runtime expression.

To see our new changes in action, we need to first compile the new tag handler, chapter5.DateTag_v2, and move it into the <TOMCAT_HOME>/webapps/customtags/WEB-INF/classes/chapter5/ directory. Next, we need to add the <attribute> subelement, listed previously, to the chapter5.tld file located in the <TOMCAT_HOME>/ webapps/customtags/WEB-INF / directory, and restart the Tomcat server.

Once the Tomcat server is up and running again, we need to change the syntax of the <chapter5:currentDate /> tag, contained in the chapter5.jsp file, to use our new attribute. Listing 5.5 contains our modified JSP.

```
<%@ taglib uri="/chapter5" prefix="chapter5" %>

<html>
<head>
  <title>Custom Tags Demo</title>
</head>

The current date is :
  <chapter5:currentDate format="yyyy.MM.dd" />

</body>
</html>
```

Listing 5.5 Modified chapter5.jsp

After examining the changes in Listing 5.5, you will notice that the only change is the addition of the format attribute. The new attribute is set to the string "yyyy.MM.dd", which will cause the current date to be printed using this format as defined by the java.text.SimpleDateFormat.

After these changes have been made to the chapter5.jsp file, save the file, and open your browser to the following URL:

```
http://localhost:8080/customtags/chapter5.jsp
```

If everything went according to plan, you should see a page similar to Figure 5.4, with a date in the format defined by the format attribute.

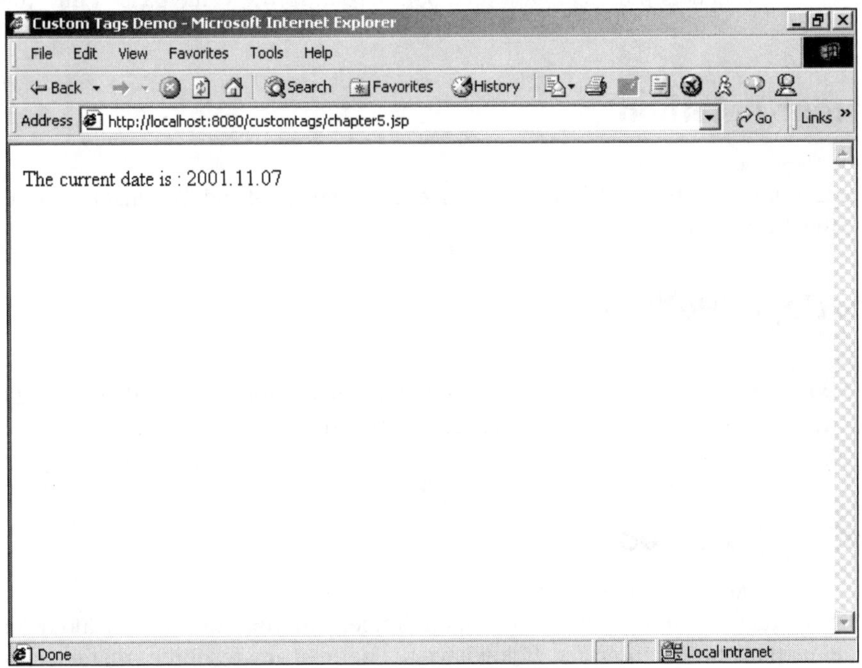

Figure 5.4 New output of the chapter 5.jsp.

Using the TagSupport Helper Class

The final section in this chapter covers a class that acts as a helper class for custom tags that do not process body content. It provides default implementations for all of the methods defined by the Tag interface and additional convenience methods that save the tag developer implementation time. This class is the javax.servlet.jsp.tagext.TagSupport class. It implements the javax.servlet.jsp.tagext.IterationTag interface, which extends the javax.servlet.jsp.tagext.Tag interface. Each of the methods defined by the javax.servlet.jsp.tagext.TagSupport is described in following sections.

setPageContext() Method

```
public void setPageContext(PageContext pageContext)
```

The setPageContext() method provides a default implementation for setting a tag's PageContext. This implementation sets the local data member, pageContext, to the value passed.

setParent() Method

```
public void setParent(Tag t)
```

The setParent() method provides a default implementation for setting a tag's parent. This implementation sets the local data member, parent, to the value passed into the method.

getParent() Method

```
public Tag getParent()
```

The getParent() method acts as a basic accessor returning the Tag instance that encloses this tag instance.

doStartTag() Method

```
public int doStartTag() throws JspException
```

The doStartTag() method acts as a default implementation for the doStartTag() method defined by the Tag interface. This implementation returns the value SKIP_BODY.

doEndTag() Method

```
public int doEndTag() throws JspException
```

The doEndTag() method acts as a default implementation for the doEndTag() method defined by the Tag interface. If you have not defined any resources that need to be released before the tag is used again, then this implementation will be sufficient for your tag. This implementation returns the value EVAL_PAGE.

release() Method

```
public void release()
```

The release() method acts a default implementation for the release() method defined by the Tag interface. If you have not defined any resources that need to be released before the tag is garbage collected, then this implementation will be sufficient for your tag.

findAncestorWithClass() Method

```
public static final Tag findAncestorWithClass(Tag from,
  java.lang.Class klass)
```

The findAncestorWithClass() method is used to find the instance of a given Tag that directly encloses the calling tag. This class is used for coordination among cooperating tags. If there is no parent tag, null is returned.

setId() Method

```
public void setId(java.lang.String id)
```

The setId() method is the basic accessor for setting the tag's id attribute.

getId() Method

```
public java.lang.String getId()
```

The getId() method returns the value of the id attribute of this tag, or null

setValue() Method

```
public void setValue(java.lang.String k, java.lang.Object o)
```

The setValue() method is a simple accessor that is used to set a key/value pair that will be stored in a tag's internal Hashtable for later retrieval. This method is often used to set a value in a parent tag. You will see an example of this methods usage in Chapter 9, "Cooperating Tags."

getValue() Method

```
public java.lang.Object getValue(java.lang.String k)
```

The getValue() method returns the value associated with named key/value pair previously set using the setValue() method.

getValues() Method

```
public java.util.Enumeration getValues()
```

The getValues() method returns an Enumeration containing all the keys set using the setValue() method. This Enumeration can then be iterated over and used, in conjunction with the getValue() method, to retrieve the matching values.

removeValue() Method

```
public void removeValue(java.lang.String k)
```

The removeValue() method removes a value associated with named key.

currentDate Tag Using TagSupport

After looking over the default implementations provided by the javax.servlet.jsp.tagext.TagSupport class, we see that it can really reduce the amount of code required to develop our <currentDate /> tag handler. To save this time, we simply need to extend our tag handler from the TagSupport class and remove the methods that are sufficiently implemented by TagSupport. These changes are shown in Listing 5.6.

```
package chapter5;

import java.io.*;
import java.text.SimpleDateFormat;
import java.util.Date;

import javax.servlet.jsp.*;
import javax.servlet.jsp.tagext.*;

// Extend the Helper Class TagSupport
public class DateTag_v3 extends TagSupport {

  // Provide a default date format
  private String format =
    new String("yyyy.MM.dd G 'at' hh:mm:ss a zzz");

  public void setFormat(String format) {

    this.format = format;
  }

  public String getFormat() {

    return this.format;
  }

  public int doStartTag() throws JspException {

    // Get the current date
    Date currentDate = new java.util.Date();

    try {

      // Format the current time.
      SimpleDateFormat formatter
        = new SimpleDateFormat(getFormat());

      JspWriter out = pageContext.getOut();

      out.print(formatter.format(currentDate));
    }
```

Listing 5.6 DateTag_v3.java *(continues)*

```
    catch (Exception e) {

      throw new JspException("IOException thrown: " +
        e.getMessage());
    }
    return SKIP_BODY;
  }

  public int doEndTag()
    throws javax.servlet.jsp.JspException {

    // reset the default format when the tags is released
    this.format =
      new String("yyyy.MM.dd G 'at'' hh:mm:ss a zzz");

    return EVAL_PAGE;
  }
}
```

Listing 5.6 DateTag_v3.java *(continued)*

As you can see in our updated tag handler, there is very little change. We first changed the name of the class by appending _v3 to the class and file name. We did this simply as a matter of convenience. It just helps us distinguish from class to class.

The second thing we changed is that now the tag handler extends the TagSupport class instead of implementing the Tag interface. This change made it possible to make our final change, which was to remove the tag handler methods that were sufficiently implemented by the TagSupport class. In particular, we were able to remove four methods, including the setPageContext(), setParent(), getParent(), and release() methods. The removal of these methods reduced the tag handler by approximately 40 percent.

To test these changes, first compile the new tag handler, move it into the <TOMCAT_HOME>/webapps/customtags/WEB-INF/classes/chapter5/ directory, and finally change the <tagclass> element, found in the chapter5.tld file, to reflect our new class name. This change is shown in the following code snippet:

```
<tag>
  <name>currentDate</name>
  <tagclass>chapter5.DateTag_v3</tagclass>
  <bodycontent>empty</bodycontent>
  <attribute>
    <name>format</name>
    <required>false</required>
    <rtexprvalue>true</rtexprvalue>
  </attribute>
</tag>
```

After you have made these changes, restart Tomcat, and open your browser to the following URL:

```
http://localhost:8080/customtags/chapter5.jsp
```

If everything went okay, then you should see a page similar to the one shown earlier in Figure 5.4.

Summary

In this chapter, we discussed simple custom tags. We described the classes and interfaces that are used when developing simple tags. We also explained how you can modify the behavior of a custom tag using attributes, and concluded the chapter with a discussion of how you can use the javax.servlet.jsp.tagext.TagSupport class as helper class. In the next chapter, we are going to discuss another tag implementation: tags with bodies.

CHAPTER

6

Tags with Bodies

In this chapter, we are going to describe custom tags that process their bodies. We will begin by describing what custom body tags are and how they can be used. We will then develop a custom tag that leverages the content of its body. After we have an understanding of how a custom body tag is developed, we will then create a tag that will use the javax.servlet.jsp.tagext.BodyTagSupport helper class to simplify the development of the tag handler.

At the end of this chapter, you should have a solid understanding of the components involved in creating a custom tag that processes its body. An object model depicting these components can be found in Figure 6.1.

NOTE **At this point, you can ignore the javax.servlet.jsp.tagext.IterationTag shown in Figure 6.1. We will implement the single method defined by this interface, doAfterBody(), but we will not leverage its iteration behavior until Chapter 8, "Iteration Tags."**

Tags with Bodies

Tags that process their bodies are different from simple custom tags in three major ways. First, their tag handlers must implement two methods defined by the javax.servlet.jsp.tagext.BodyTag interface and a single method defined by the javax.servlet.jsp.tagext.IterationTag. Second, they must set the <bodycontent> element in their TLD to either JSP or tagdependent. Lastly, tags that process their bodies, if they intend to write content back to the client, must use the JspWriter referenced by the javax.servlet.jsp.tagext.BodyContent passed to the tag handler during initialization. These differences are the topics that we are going to cover in this chapter.

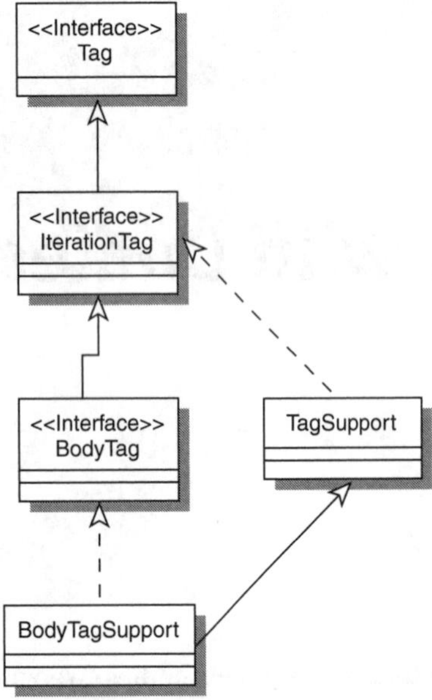

Figure 6.1 The body tag objects.

The BodyTag and IterationTag Interfaces

As we stated previously, the first major difference in a tag handler that processes its body is that it must implement the javax.servlet.jsp.tagext.BodyTag and javax.servlet.jsp.tagext.IterationTag interfaces, either directly or indirectly. In this section, we are going to describe the process of creating a custom tag that directly implements these two interfaces. We will begin this process by defining the methods of each interface.

NOTE **We will see an example of implementing these interfaces indirectly, later in this chapter, when we look at the javax.servlet.jsp.tagext.BodyTagSupport helper class.**

javax.servlet.jsp.tagext.BodyTag

The javax.servlet.jsp.tagext.BodyTag interface defines two methods that must be implemented when creating a custom tag handler that processes its body: setBodyContent() and doInitBody().

public void setBodyContent(BodyContent bodyContent)

The setBodyContent() method is used by the JSP/servlet engine to pass the tag's body content to the tag handler for this tag. It is invoked by the JSP/servlet engine after the doStartTag() method if the doStartTag() method returns EVAL_BODY_ BUFFERED. In your implementation of this method, you should store a reference to the passed in javax.servlet.jsp.tagext.BodyContent object in a local data member. An example implementation of this method is included in the following code snippet:

```
public void setBodyContent(BodyContent bodyContent) {

  this.bodyContent = bodyContent;
}
```

NOTE At this point, the body of the tag has not been evaluated by the JSP/servlet engine.

The single parameter passed to this method is a reference to a javax.servlet.jsp. tagext.BodyContent object, which contains the body of the current instance of the tag. This class is an abstract subclass of a javax.servlet.jsp.JspWriter.

The BodyContent object is most often used to read the contents of the tag body and write the result of processing this body back to the calling client. Although these are its two major functions, the BodyContent class defines additional methods that assist in the processing of a tag's body. All of the methods defined by the javax.servlet.jsp. tagext.BodyContent object are described in Table 6.1.

Table 6.1 Methods of the BodyContent Class

METHOD	DESCRIPTION
flush()	The flush() method has been defined as an illegal method. If it is executed, an IOException stating that it is "Illegal to flush within a custom tag" will be thrown.
clearBody()	The clearBody() method is another implementation of the JspWriter method clear(). The only difference is that clearBody() is guaranteed not to throw an exception.
getReader()	The getReader() method returns the value of the tag's body as a java.io.Reader.
getString()	The getString() method returns the value of the tag's body as a java.lang.String. This is the most common method of retrieving the body of a tag.
writeOut(Writer out)	The writeOut() method writes the contents of this BodyContent into the java.io.Writer object passed into this method.
getEnclosingWriter()	The getEnclosingWriter() method returns a unique instance of a JspWriter object that is used to write content back to the calling client.

public void doInitBody()

The doInitBody() method is invoked after the BodyContent has been set using the tag handler's setBodyContent() method and before the evaluation of the tag's body. This method is often used to perform any initialization that may be necessary prior the evaluation of the tag's body.

javax.servlet.jsp.tagext.IterationTag Interface

The javax.servlet.jsp.tagext.IterationTag interface extends the javax.servlet.jsp. tagext. Tag interface and defines an additional method, doAfterBody(), that is used to evaluate the body of a tag multiple times.

public int doAfterBody()

The doAfterBody() method is executed after the tag's body has been evaluated by the JSP/servlet engine. This method will not be invoked for simple tags or tags that return SKIP_BODY from the doStartTag() method. This method is where most of your business logic should be located.

NOTE **While doAfterBody() is defined by the IterationTag interface, for the purposes of this discussion, we will not use any of the iteration functionality defined by this interface. Because we are not interested in reevaluating the body of this tag, we will return SKIP_BODY for all examples in this chapter. We will examine tag iteration in much more detail in Chapter 8.**

Life Cycle of a Custom BodyTag

Now that we have taken a look at the methods defined by the javax.servlet.jsp. tagext.BodyTag and javax.servlet.jsp.tagext.IterationTag interfaces, we need to take a look at how these methods fit into the life cycle of a body tag.

As we stated in Chapter 4, when the JSP/servlet container compiles a JSP, it creates a servlet that contains the JSP and HTML code. If this JSP contains a tag, the servlet will create an instance of this tag and call the appropriate life cycle methods in their proper order. A simplified code example of this process is contained in the following snippet:

```
BodyTag tag = new BodyTag();
tag.setPageContext()
tag.setParent()
tag.doStartTag()
tag.setBodyContent()
tag.doInitBody()
tag.doAfterBody()
tag.doEndTag()
tag.release()
```

As you can see by this snippet, there is really no magic to this process. The servlet, which represents the compiled JSP, creates an instance of the tag handler, and executes the appropriate methods to evaluate the tag. We will look at each of these methods in the first example of this chapter. To see how these new methods fit into the tag life cycle, examine Figure 6.2, which presents the complete life cycle of a BodyTag.

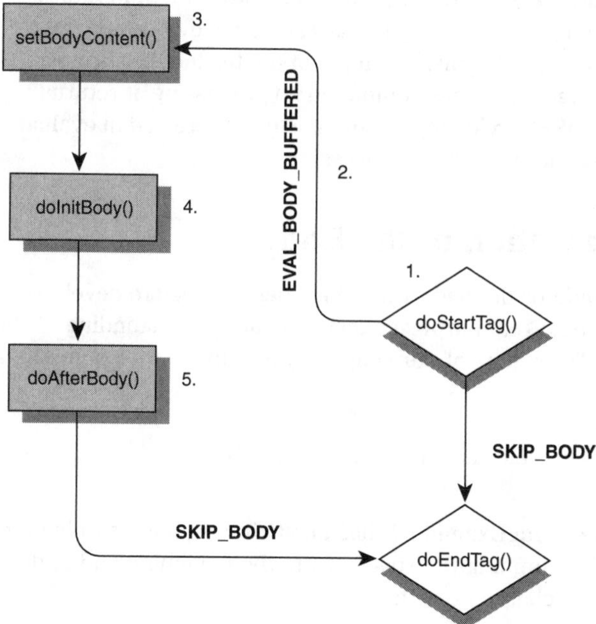

Figure 6.2 Flow of a BodyTag.

Figure 6.2 depicts the exact events that will occur during the evaluation of a body tag. These steps should give you an understanding of the process a body tag handler goes through during a single evaluation. Because a body tag handler follows the same life cycle as a simple tag, up until the invocation of the doStartTag() method, we will begin our discussions of this life cycle with the doStartTag() method.

1. At this point, the PageContext and Parent objects have been set, and the doStartTag() method is invoked. While the doStartTag() is the most common place to perform the business logic of a simple tag, it is not often used for this function when implementing a BodyTag. This is because at this point, you do not have access to the tag's body content. If the doStartTag() method returns SKIP_BODY, then the doEndTag() will be invoked immediately, the tag body will be ignored, and normal processing will continue. When creating a BodyTag, doStartTag() should return EVAL_BODY_BUFFERED.

2. If the doStartTag() method returns EVAL_BODY_BUFFERED, then the container knows that the tag handler wants to process its body, and it invokes the setBodyContent() method with a pre-evaluation version of the tag's body.

3. The setBodyContent() method most often does nothing more than store a reference to the passed in BodyContent object in a local data member. The setBodyContent() method has no return value.

4. After the setBodyContent() finishes its execution, the JSP/servlet engine executes the doInitBody(). This is the tag handler's opportunity to access the tag's body prior to its evaluation. The doInitBody() method has no return value.
6. The doAfterBody() method is executed after the doInitBody() method returns. At the point of its invocation, the tag's body has already been evaluated by the JSP/servlet engine. At this point, the business logic of the tag handler is most often executed. Once doAfterBody() has completed its processing, it returns SKIP_BODY. This tells the JSP/servlet engine that it is not interested in evaluating the body again and to continue normal processing.

An Example Implementation of the BodyTag

To really understand the new methods defined by the BodyTag, we need to develop our own body tag. Our tag will serve no real purpose except to gain understanding of the body tag development process. The syntax of our simple tag is going to look something like the following snippet:

```
<chapter6:bodyTagExample>
  This message should be written back to the client.
</chapter6:bodyTagExample>
```

This new tag will be named bodyTagExample. It has no attributes, and its only function will be to print out its body, trimming the spaces from the beginning and ending, and replacing the remaining space characters with a'-'.

BodyTagExample Handler

Now that we know what we want our tag to do, we need to create a tag handler that implements the javax.servlet.jsp.tagext.BodyTag interface. The source for our tag handler is shown in Listing 6.1. As you examine this source, focus on the bolded areas.

```
package chapter6;

import java.io.IOException;

import javax.servlet.jsp.JspWriter;
import javax.servlet.jsp.JspException;
import javax.servlet.jsp.tagext.BodyTag;
import javax.servlet.jsp.tagext.BodyContent;
import javax.servlet.jsp.tagext.Tag;
import javax.servlet.jsp.PageContext;

public class BodyTagExample implements BodyTag {

  private Tag parent = null;
```

Listing 6.1 BodyTagExample.java. *(continues)*

```
protected PageContext pageContext = null;
protected BodyContent bodyContent = null;

public void setPageContext(PageContext pageContext) {

  System.err.println("---->inside setPageContext()<----");

  this.pageContext = pageContext;
}

public void setParent(Tag parent) {

  System.err.println("---->inside setParent()<----");

  this.parent = parent;
}

public Tag getParent() {

  System.err.println("---->inside getParent()<----");

  return this.parent;
}
public int doStartTag()
  throws javax.servlet.jsp.JspException {

  System.err.println("--->inside doStartTag()<---");

  // return EVAL_BODY_BUFFERED instead of EVAL_BODY_INCLUDE
  // when implementing a BodyTag
  return EVAL_BODY_BUFFERED;
}

public void setBodyContent(BodyContent bodyContent) {

  this.bodyContent = bodyContent;
  System.err.println("---->inside setBodyContent()<----");
}

public void doInitBody()
  throws javax.servlet.jsp.JspException {

  System.err.println("---->inside doInitBody()<----");
}
```

Listing 6.1 BodyTagExample.java. *(continues)*

```
  public int doAfterBody()
    throws javax.servlet.jsp.JspException {

    System.err.println("---->inside doAfterBody()<----");
    String body = bodyContent.getString();

    // trim the spaces from the string
    body = body.trim();

    // replace the spaces with a '-'
    body = body.replace(' ', '-'');

    JspWriter writer = bodyContent.getEnclosingWriter();

    try {

      writer.write(body);
    }
    catch (IOException e) {

      throw new JspException(e.getMessage());
    }

    return SKIP_BODY;
  }

  public int doEndTag()
    throws javax.servlet.jsp.JspException {

    System.err.println("---->inside doEndTag()<----");

    bodyContent = null;

    // return EVAL_PAGE as an example
    return EVAL_PAGE;
  }

  public void release() {

    System.err.println("---->inside release()<----");
  }
}
```

Listing 6.1 BodyTagExample.java. *(continued)*

NOTE **You will notice that each of the methods in this tag handler has a simple System.err.println() statement. These statements are included only to provide trace statements showing the order in which each of the tag handler's methods are invoked.**

The first part of this tag handler that needs to be focused upon is the return value of the doStartTag() method. It returns the value EVAL_BODY_BUFFERED. This return value tells the JSP/servlet engine that this tag is interested in processing its body, and will cause the container to invoke the setBodyContent() method. The invocation of this method marks the beginning of a BodyTag's specific processing, which includes the setBodyContent(), doInitBody(), and doAfterBody() methods. Each of these methods, implemented by our body tag, is described in the following sections.

NOTE **The remaining methods contained in this tag handler function exactly as they did in the simple tag examples described in the previous chapter. These methods must be implemented, but are not pertinent to this discussion.**

setBodyContent() Method

The setBodyContent() method is the first javax.servlet.jsp.tagext.BodyTag method invoked by the JSP/servlet engine. Its purpose is very simple. It is simply meant to store the reference to the BodyContent object that is passed to it in a local data member. For this example, the reference is stored in the data member bodyContent.

```
public void setBodyContent(BodyContent bodyContent) {

  this.bodyContent = bodyContent;
  System.err.println("---->inside setBodyContent()<----");
}
```

doInitBody() Method

The doInitBody() method contained in this handler does absolutely nothing. This method is meant to give the tag handler a chance to read or modify the contents of the tag's body, prior to being evaluated by the JSP/servlet engine.

doAfterBody() Method

The final method that we need to look at is doAfterBody(). This method, which is actually defined by the javax.servlet.jsp.tagext.IterationTag interface, is invoked after the tag's body has been evaluated by the JSP/servlet container. This method is where we will most often perform our business logic. For this instance of the doAfterBody() method, we begin by getting a string reference to the tag's body by calling the BodyContent.getString() method. This bit of code is shown here:

```
String body = bodyContent.getString();
```

After we have a reference to the tag's body, we perform some simple modifications to this tag with no other purpose than to prove that we can. These modifications are shown in the following code snippet:

```
// trim the spaces from the string
body = body.trim();

// replace the spaces with a '-'
body = body.replace(' ', '-'');
```

As you can see, the modifications to the body are very simple. We first remove the extra space characters from both the beginning and ending of the body string. After we have trimmed the extra spaces, we replace all other space characters with a '-' character.

The next step performed by this handler is to print the modified body back to the client, as follows:

```
JspWriter writer = bodyContent.getEnclosingWriter();

try {

  writer.write(body);
}
catch (Exception e) {

  throw new JspException(e.getMessage());
}
```

The most important line of code in this snippet is the very first line. In this line, we use the BodyContent object's getEnclosingWriter() method to get a reference to a JspWriter that we can use to write data back to the client.

The difference between accessing a JspWriter using the BodyContent.getEnclosingWriter() and using the PageContext.getOut() method is that when the JSP engine begins processing the body of a BodyTag, it swaps the implicit out with a temporary JspWriter represented by the BodyContent. This reference acts as a buffer for the tag handler's output. Once the tag handler has completed its processing, then this buffer is written to the real JspWriter, represented by the implicit out object.

The PageContext.getOut() method is different in that it returns a direct reference to the JspWriter representing the implicit out object, therefore the tag handler's output will be written directly to the stream going back to the client.

For our purposes, after we have a reference to the JspWriter returned by this getEnclosingWriter() method, we use it just like any other JspWriter by calling it with the modified string containing the results of our tag handler's processing. This is done by simply calling the JspWriter.write() method with the results to be written back to the client.

Once the doAfterBody() method has written its results back to the client, it returns the value SKIP_BODY. This is done to prevent the tag body from being evaluated multiple times. At this point, the tag handler resumes normal processing, just like we described when using a simple tag.

NOTE **In Chapter 8, we will examine the doAfterBody()'s other return code, EVAL_BODY_AGAIN, and the effects it has on the processing of a BodyTag.**

BodyTagExample TLD

To publish the BodyTagExample, we must create the TLD that tells the JSP/servlet engine how our custom tag is to be used, and that it does contain a body. Creating a TLD for a body tag is just like creating a TLD for any other, with the exception of the contents of the <bodycontent> element. The possible values for this element are none, JSP, and tag dependent. If this value is not specified, it is defaulted to JSP, which tells the container that the body can contain any JSP-allowed syntax. If this element's value equals tagdependent, then the contents of the tag body would be processed in reference to the tag only. The <bodycontent> element cannot be set to the value none when describing a BodyTag, or a JspException will be thrown. The TLD for our tag is shown in Listing 6.2.

```
<?xml version="1.0" encoding="ISO-8859-1" ?>
<!DOCTYPE taglib PUBLIC
"-//Sun Microsystems, Inc.//DTD JSP Tag Library 1.1//EN"
"http://java.sun.com/j2ee/dtds/web-jsptaglibrary_1_1.dtd">

<taglib>
  <tlibversion>1.0</tlibversion>
  <jspversion>1.2</jspversion>
  <shortname>chapter6</shortname>

  <tag>
    <name>bodyTagExample</name>
    <tagclass>chapter6.BodyTagExample</tagclass>
    <bodycontent>JSP</bodycontent>
    <info>Just a Simple Tag with Body Example</info>
  </tag>

</taglib>
```

Listing 6.2 chapter6.tld.

Deploying and Using the ExampleBodyTag

Now that we have the current date's tag handler and TLD defined, let's actually deploy and use the new tag. To do this, we must first compile the BodyTagExample.java file, and move the resulting class file into the <TOMCAT_HOME>/webapps/customtags/WEB-INF/classes/chapter6/ directory.

Next, move the TLD to the <TOMCAT_HOME>/webapps/customtags/WEB-INF/ directory and then add a taglib entry to the web.xml file for the customtags Web application. The following snippet contains the <taglib> entry describing this tag library:

```
<taglib>
  <taglib-uri>/chapter6</taglib-uri>
  <taglib-location>/WEB-INF/chapter6.tld</taglib-location>
</taglib>
```

Now it is time to use the ExampleBodyTag. To do this, we need a simple JSP that references the tag library and the <exampleBodyTag /> tag. Listing 6.3 contains a simple JSP that does just this.

```
<%@ taglib uri="/chapter6" prefix="chapter6" %>

<html>
  <head>
    <title>Custom Tags Demo</title>
  </head>

  <body>

    <chapter6:bodyTagExample>
      This message should be written back to the client.
    </chapter6:bodyTagExample>

  </body>
</html>
```

Listing 6.3 chapter6.jsp.

There is very little to this JSP. It begins with a taglib directive that names the uri of the tag library that this JSP will use, which must match the <taglib-uri> value we added to the web.xml file. This directive also tells the JSP/servlet container that all tags in this page that begin with the prefix chapter6 will reference a tag found in the library referenced by the uri /chapter6.

The next section to notice is contained in the following snippet:

```
<chapter6:bodyTagExample>
  This message should be written back to the client.
</chapter6:bodyTagExample>
```

The tag included in this line begins with the prefix chapter6, which tells the JSP/servlet container that it must look in the tag library referenced by the /chapter6 uri. The container then looks up the tag named bodyTagExample, which references the tag handler class named chapter6.BodyTagExample, and invokes the retrieved object. The result of this execution replaces the tag text with the output of this tag. To see this process in action, copy this JSP to the <TOMCAT_HOME>/webapps/customtags/ directory, and open your browser to the following URL:

```
http://localhost:8080/customtags/chapter6.jsp
```

If everything went according to plan, you should see a page similar to Figure 6.3.

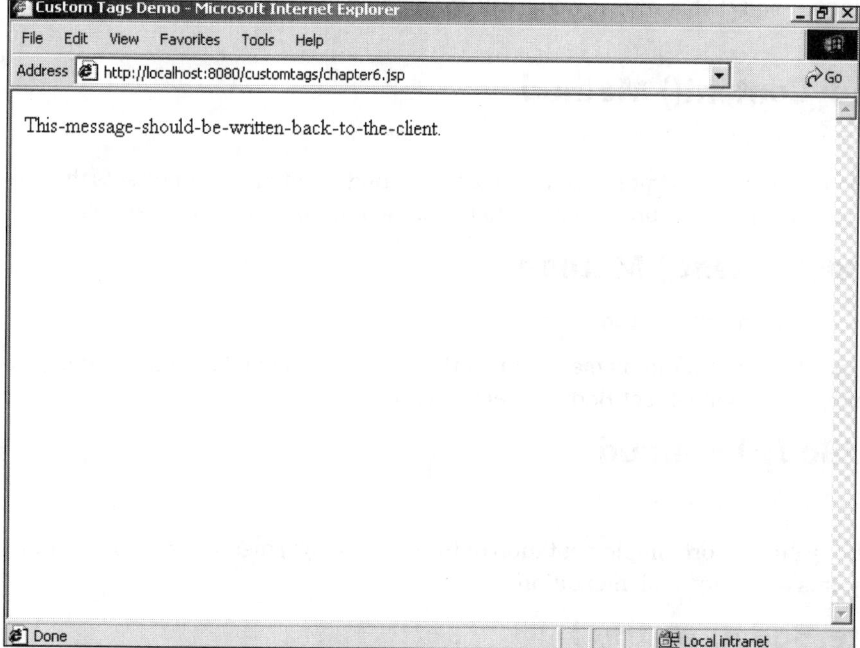

Figure 6.3 Output of the chapter6.jsp.

You should also notice the text being printed to the Tomcat console. These text strings are being printed to the Tomcat standard error stream to show the order in which the tag handler's methods are being invoked. You will see that the output matches the data flow diagram contained in Figure 6.2.

Using the BodyTagSupport Helper Class

The final section in this chapter covers javax.servlet.jsp.tagext.BodyTagSupport, a helper class for custom tags that process body content. It provides default implementations for all of the methods defined by the BodyTag interface, and default implementations of some of the Tag interface methods. The BodyTagSupport class implements the javax.servlet.jsp.tagext.IterationTag interface, and extends the javax.servlet.jsp.tagext.TagSupport helper class. Each of the methods defined by javax.servlet.jsp.tagext.BodyTagSupport are described in following sections.

doStartTag() Method

```
public int doStartTag() throws JspException
```

The doStartTag() method acts as a default implementation for the doStartTag() method defined by the Tag interface. This implementation returns the value EVAL_BODY_BUFFERED to tell the JSP/servlet engine that this tag is interested in processing its body. This return value will force the setBodyContent() method to be invoked next.

setBodyContent() Method

```
public void setBodyContet(BodyContent bodyContent)
```

The BodyTagSupport's implementation of the setBodyContent() method sets the protected local data member, bodyContent, to the passed-in BodyContent reference.

getBodyContent() Method

```
public BodyContent getBodyContet()
```

The BodyTagSupport's implementation of the getBodyContent() method is simply an accessor to the previously set BodyContent reference.

doInitBody() Method

```
public void doInitBody()
```

The BodyTagSupport's implementation of the doInitBody() method contains no functionality. It is an empty implementation.

doAfterBody() Method

```
public int doAfterBody()
```

The doAfterBody() method by default performs no function, except to return the value SKIP_BODY, which tells the JSP/servlet engine that the tag handler is not interested in evaluating the tag body again.

doEndTag() Method

```
public int doEndTag() throws JspException
```

The doEndTag() method implementation provided by the BodyTagSupport method simply calls its parent TagSupport.doEndTag() method, which does nothing more than return EVAL_PAGE. This return value tells the container that the remainder of the JSP should be evaluated.

release() Method

```
public void release()
```

This implementation of the release() method does nothing more than set the data member bodyContent to null, so that it is ready for processing a new tag occurrence.

getPreviousOut() Method

```
public JspWriter getPreviousOut()
```

The final BodyTag method implemented by the BodyTagSupport class, getPreviousOut(), acts as a simple accessor returning the JspWriter represented by the bodyContent data member.

Log Tag Using BodyTagSupport

After looking over the default implementations provided by the javax.servlet.jsp. tagext.BodyTagSupport class, we see that it really does reduce the amount of code required to develop a body tag handler. To see these savings in action, we are going to create a logging tag that leverages the functionality defined by the BodyTagSupport object.

The name of our tag is <chapter6:log />. It will not use any attributes, and its main function will be to take its evaluated body and write it to the ServletContext log. This log, when using the Tomcat 4 container, by default is represented by the file <TOMCAT_HOME>/logs/ localhost_log.<currentdate>.txt. The source for our <chapter6:log /> tag is shown in Listing 6.4.

```
package chapter6;

import javax.servlet.ServletContext;
import javax.servlet.jsp.JspException;
import javax.servlet.jsp.tagext.BodyTagSupport;

public class LogTag extends BodyTagSupport {

  public final int doAfterBody() throws JspException {

    // Get the evaluated body of the tag
    String message = bodyContent.getString();

    message = message.trim();

    // Get a reference to the ServletContext
    ServletContext context = pageContext.getServletContext();

    // Write the message to the ServletContext log
    context.log(message);

    return SKIP_BODY;
  }
}
```

Listing 6.4 LogTag.java.

As you can see, our tag handler contains a single method, doAfterBody. This is because our tag handler extends the BodyTagSupport class instead of implementing the BodyTag interface. All other methods defined by the BodyTag interface are adequately implemented by the BodyTagSupport class.

The doAfterBody() is explicitly implemented because it is where our business logic is going to exist. The first line of the tag handler's business logic, which is shown in the following code snippet, is used to get a String representation of the evaluated tag body.

```
String message = bodyContent.getString();
```

The next line trims the leading and trailing spaces from the tag's body. This is done to provide a more readable log message.

After the message text is ready to be logged, we get a reference to the javax.servlet. ServletContext object. This object contains a log method that will allow the tag handler to log its body to the ServletContext log file. Once we have this reference we can log the message. This code is accomplished using the following snippet:

```
// Get a reference to the ServletContext
ServletContext context = pageContext.getServletContext();

// Write the message to the ServletContext log
context.log(message);
```

Finally, the last action performed by this method is to return the value SKIP_BODY, which tells the container that we are finished with the tag's body and to continue normal processing.

To test these changes, first compile the new tag handler, move it into the <TOMCAT_HOME>/webapps/customtags/WEB-INF/classes/chapter6/ directory, and add the following code snippet to the previously described TLD:

```
  <tag>
    <name>log</name>
    <tagclass>chapter6.LogTag</tagclass>
    <bodycontent>JSP</bodycontent>
    <info>
      A Tag that Logs its body to the ServletContext Log
    </info>
  </tag>
The final step required to use the <chapter6:log /> tag is to create a
JSP that actually references the tag. This JSP can be found in Listing
6.5.
<%@ taglib uri="/chapter6" prefix="chapter6" %>

<html>
<head>
  <title>Custom Tags Demo</title>
</head>

  <body>

    <chapter6:log>
    This message should be logged to the ServletContext Log
    </chapter6:log>

  </body>
</html>
```

Listing 6.5 logExample.jsp.

After you have looked over this file, copy it to the <TOMCAT_HOME>/webapps/customtags directory, restart Tomcat, and open your browser to the following URL:

```
http://localhost:8080/customtags/logExample.jsp
```

There should be no output written to the calling client, but if everything went okay, then you should be able to open the latest ServletContext log file and see the body of the <chapter6:log /> tag written a the bottom of the file.

Summary

In this chapter, we discussed custom tags that processed their body contents. We described the classes and interfaces that are used when developing custom body tags. We also discussed how the javax.servlet.jsp.tagext.BodyTagSupport class can be used to shortcut the implementation required when developing a custom body tag. In the next chapter, we are going to discuss Tag Extra Info classes and how they can be utilized to validate tags and create scripting variables.

CHAPTER

7

Scripting Variables and Tag Validation

This chapter describes JSP scripting variables and translation-time attribute validation. It begins by describing the classes and methods used when creating JSP scripting variables and tag validators. You'll then create a custom tag that will expose a scripting variable containing the results of the tag's processing. The chapter concludes by extending your previously created tag to validate the attributes passed to it. At the end of this chapter, you should have a solid understanding of how scripting variables are created and how attribute validation is performed.

Supporting Classes

Before discussing scripting variables and validation, let's look at the supporting classes involved. You'll leverage three classes in this chapter: javax.servlet.jsp.tagext.VariableInfo, javax.servlet.jsp.tagext.TagData, and javax.servlet.jsp.tagext.TagExtraInfo.

VariableInfo Class

The VariableInfo class is used to describe a single instance of a scripting variable. A VariableInfo class must be created for each scripting variable being exposed to a JSP by a tag. The VariableInfo object defines a single constructor VariableInfo() and four methods: getClassName(), getDeclare(), getScope(), and getVarName().

VariableInfo() Method

VariableInfo() is the only defined constructor for the VariableInfo object; it takes four parameters. The signature of the VariableInfo() constructor is follows:

```
public VariableInfo(java.lang.String varName,
  java.lang.String className,
  boolean declare,
  int scope)
```

Table 7.1 describes the parameters passed to the VariableInfo() constructor and their purpose.

Table 7.1 Parameters of the VariableInfo() Constructor

PARAMETER	DESCRIPTION
varName	The name of the scripting variable. This value is used to access the scripting variable in a JSP.
className	The fully qualified class name of the type of object represented by the scripting variable. This parameter cannot name a Java primitive.
declare	A Boolean value that, if *true*, tells the JSP/servlet container a new instance of the scripting variable needs to be created. You will most often set this value to true. It has been introduced to allow compatibility with future languages.
scope	The accessibility of the scripting variable. It can be one of three possible values. The first value, *VariableInfo.NESTED*, tells the container that the scripting variable is visible only between the tag's beginning and ending elements. The second value, *VariableInfo.AT_BEGIN*, tells the container that the scripting variable is visible only after the tag's beginning element. The last value, *VariableInfo.AT_END*, tells the container that the scripting variable is visible only after the tag's ending element.

getClassName() Method

The getClassName() method acts as an accessor of the className data member, returning the fully qualified class name of the type of object represented by the scripting variable. The signature of the getClassName() method is as follows:

```
public java.lang.String getClassName()
```

getDeclare() Method

The getDeclare() method returns a boolean value that, if *true*, tells the JSP/servlet container that a new instance of the scripting variable needs to be created. The signature of the getDeclare() method is as follows:

```
public boolean getDeclare()
```

getScope() Method

The getScope() method returns an integer indicating the lexical scope of the scripting variable. The possible values returned by the getScope() method are listed in the scope parameter description of Table 7.1. The signature of the getScope() method is as follows:

```
public int getScope()
```

getVarName() Method

The getVarName() method returns the name of the scripting variable. This returned value is used to access the scripting variable in a JSP. The signature of the getVarName() method is as follows:

```
public java.lang.String getVarName()
```

TagData Class

The second of the supporting classes is javax.servlet.jsp.tagext.TagData. Its main function is to provide access to a tag's instance attributes and values (there is an example later in this chapter). It is passed to the TagExtraInfo.isValid() method (discussed later in this chapter) by the JSP/servlet container. It allows you to test the value of a tag's attributes. The TagData class has five methods: getAttribute(), getAttributeString(), getId(), setAttribute(), and getAttributes().

getAttribute() Method

The getAttribute() method returns the request-time value of the attribute represented by the java.lang.String parameter passed to it. We will use this method when validating a tag's attributes. The signature of the getAttribute() method is as follows:

```
public java.lang.Object getAttribute(java.lang.String name)
```

getAttributeString() Method

The getAttributeString() method returns the value of an attribute as a java.lang.String. This method functions exactly like the getAttribute() method, except that it always returns a string representation of the named attribute's value. The signature of the getAttributeString() method is as follows:

```
public java.lang.String
  getAttributeString(java.lang.String name)
```

getId() Method

The getId() method returns the value of the id attribute, or null if the id attribute is not set. The signature of the getId() method is as follows:

```
public java.lang.String getId()
```

setAttribute() Method

This method sets the value of an attribute/value pair. The signature of the setAttribute() method is as follows:

```
public void setAttribute(java.lang.String name,
  java.lang.Object value)
```

getAttributes() Method

The getAttributes() method returns an Enumeration of the attributes associated with the current TagData instance. The signature of the getAttributes() method is as follows:

```
public java.util.Enumeration
  getAttributes(java.lang.String name)
```

TagExtraInfo Class

The final supporting class is javax.servlet.jsp.tagext.TagExtraInfo. It is an abstract class that provides extra tag information about a custom tag. This class must be created when defining any scripting variables or if the tag wants to provide translation-time validation of the tag attributes passed to it. The TagExtraInfo class ties together all the supporting classes.

To define scripting variables or perform attribute validation, you must create a TagExtraInfo class that extends the abstract TagExtraInfo class. This class, although defined as abstract, provides default implementations for all its methods. Of these methods, we are interested in only two: getVariableInfo() and isValid().

getVariableInfo() Method

The getVariableInfo() method is used to create new scripting variables for use in a JSP, which is the first objective of this chapter. It returns an array of javax.servlet.jsp.tagext.VariableInfo objects (described earlier), describing the scripting variables defined by a tag. The default implementation of this method returns an array containing a single empty VariableInfo instance. The signature of the getVariableInfo() method is as follows:

```
public VariableInfo[] getVariableInfo(TagData data);
```

To create scripting variables, you must define an implementation of the getVariableInfo() method. This implementation must return an array of VariableInfo objects describing each scripting variable (this will be demonstrated in the scripting variable example later in this chapter).

isValid() Method

The isValid() method is used to perform translation-time validation of a tag's attributes, the second objective of this chapter. It takes a javax.servlet.jsp.tagext.TagData reference (described earlier) and returns a boolean value indicating the validity of the tag's attributes. The default implementation of the isValid() method, which always returns *true*, is as follows:

```
public boolean isValid(TagData data) {

  return true;
}
```

To test the attributes of a given tag, you must define an implementation of the isValid() method that examines the contents of the TagData object and returns either true or false, depending on the contents of the TagData reference.

Scripting Variables

A *scripting variable* is a Java object that is exposed to a JSP by a custom tag, making it accessible by simply including the scripting variable's name. This feature of the JSP architecture makes it possible for a tag to expose the results of its processing to other JSP elements. Once these scripting variables are created, they can then be accessed just like JSP implicit objects.

To create and expose scripting variables, you must complete three steps:

1. Create or have an existing tag handler that adds the object it wants to expose to the current PageContext.
2. Create a TagExtraInfo (TEI) object that describes the object you want to expose.
3. Modify the tag library descriptor (TLD) to name the TEI object used to describe the scripting variable.

The following sections describe each of these steps in detail, using a SQL tag example.

SQLTag Handler

As stated in the previous section, the first step in creating scripting variable is to have a tag that creates an object you would like to expose. This example uses the SQLTag tag handler for this step. It performs a SQL query, returns the results as a vector of hashtables, and adds the resulting vector to the PageContext. This tag handler is shown in Listing 7.1.

```
package chapter7;

import javax.servlet.jsp.tagext.BodyTagSupport;
import javax.servlet.jsp.JspException;
import javax.servlet.jsp.PageContext;

import java.util.Hashtable;
import java.util.Vector;
```

Listing 7.1 SQLTag.java. *(continues)*

```
import java.lang.StringBuffer;

import java.sql.ResultSet;
import java.sql.SQLException;
import java.sql.ResultSetMetaData;
import java.sql.Connection;
import java.sql.DriverManager;
import java.sql.Statement;

public class SQLTag extends BodyTagSupport {

  private String resultId = null;
  private String driver = null;
  private String url = null;
  private String username ="";
  private String password = "";

  public SQLTag() {

  }

  public void setResultId(String resultId) {

    this.resultId = resultId;
  }

  public String getResultId() {

    return resultId;
  }

  public void setDriver(String driver) {

    this.driver = driver;
  }

  public String getDriver() {

    return driver;
  }

  public void setUrl(String url) {

    this.url = url;
```

Listing 7.1 SQLTag.java. *(continues)*

```
}

public String getUrl() {

  return url;
}

public void setUsername(String username) {

  this.username = username;
}

public String getUsername() {

  return username;
}

public void setPassword(String password) {

  this.password = password;
}

public String getPassword() {

  return password;
}

// Returns a Vector containing the column names
// found in the passed in ResultSet
protected Vector getResultSetColumnNames(ResultSet rs)
  throws Exception {

  // Get a reference to the ResultSet's meta data
  ResultSetMetaData md = rs.getMetaData();

  // Get the number of columns returned in the Result Set
  int count = md.getColumnCount();
  // Create a Vector to hold the Column Names
  Vector columnNames = new Vector(count);

  // Get all of the Column Names
  for ( int x = 0; x < count; x++ ) {

    // The column name indexes begin at 1
```

Listing 7.1 SQLTag.java. *(continues)*

```
      columnNames.addElement(md.getColumnName(x + 1));
    }
    return columnNames;
  }

  protected Vector copyResultSet(ResultSet rs)
    throws Exception {

    // Create a Vector to hold the Hashtables representing
    // each row in the ResultSet
    Vector results = new Vector();
    // Retrieve a Vector of Column Names
    Vector columnNames = getResultSetColumnNames(rs);

    // Test the ResultSet
    if ( rs == null ) {

      throw new Exception("ResultSet is null");
    }

    // Iterate over the ResultSet
    while ( rs.next() ) {

      // Create a Hashtable for every row in the ResultSet
      Hashtable row = new Hashtable();

      // Add a key/value pair for each column name
      for ( int x = 0; x < columnNames.size(); x++ ) {

        String rsColumn = (String)columnNames.elementAt(x);
        String rsValue = rs.getString(rsColumn);

        if ( rsValue == null ) {

          rsValue = new String("");
        }
        row.put(rsColumn, rsValue);
      }
      // Add the new Hashtable to the Vector
      results.add(row);
    }
    // Return the result
    return results;
  }
```

Listing 7.1 SQLTag.java. *(continues)*

```
protected Vector selectData(String sqlString)
  throws Exception {

  Connection con = null;
  Vector results = null;
  ResultSet rs = null;

  try {

    // Load the JDBC Driver
    Class.forName(getDriver());

    // Create a JDBC Connection
    con = DriverManager.getConnection(getUrl(),
      getUsername(), getPassword());

    // Create a statement to execute the query
    Statement statement = con.createStatement();

    // Execute the query
    rs = statement.executeQuery(sqlString);

    // Copy the ResultSet to a Vector of Hashtables
    results = copyResultSet(rs);
  }
  catch (Exception e) {

    throw new Exception(e.getMessage());
  }
  finally {

    try {

      // Close the ResultSet
      if ( rs != null) {

        rs.close();
      }
      if ( con != null ) {

        // Close the connection no matter what
        con.close();
      }
```

Listing 7.1 SQLTag.java. *(continues)*

```
            }
            catch (SQLException sqle) {

              throw new Exception(sqle.getMessage());
            }
          }
          return results;
        }

        public int doAfterBody() throws JspException {

          // Get Query String from the body of the tag
          String sql = bodyContent.getString();

          try {

            // Trim the extra spaces from the query string
            sql = sql.trim();
            // Execute the query
            Vector rows = selectData(sql);
            // Add the Vector of results to the PageContext
            pageContext.setAttribute(getResultId(), rows);
          }
          catch (Exception e) {

            throw new JspException(e.getMessage());
          }
          return SKIP_BODY;
        }
      }
```

Listing 7.1 SQLTag.java. *(continued)*

This is a BodyTag that extends javax.servlet.jsp.tagext.BodyTagSupport. It contains basic accessors for setting the database connection attributes, an implementation of the doAfterBody() method, and three other business logic methods.

The first important feature of this tag is the methods it uses to set its data members. Five data members can be set when processing the database query. These data members, described in Table 7.2, map to a tag attribute in the actual JSP tag code.

Table 7.2 Data Members of the SQLTag

PARAMETER	DESCRIPTION
resultId	The name of the scripting variable that is used to access the query results

Table 7.2 Data Members of the SQLTag *(continued)*

PARAMETER	DESCRIPTION
driver	The fully qualified class name of the JDBC driver used to perform the database functions
url	The connection string used to connect to the JDBC data source
usename	The username used to connect to the database
password	The password used to connect to the database

The next important part of the SQLTag is the doStartTag() method. This is the only method from the BodyTagSupport implementation that this tag overrides. It is also the method that signals the beginning of this tag's unique processing. The following steps describe the actions performed by the SQLTag, beginning with doStartTag():

1. The doStartTag() method begins its processing by retrieving its body, and trimming the trailing and leading spaces contained in its body.
2. Once the doStartTag() method has a trimmed reference to the tag's body, it passes the body to the selectData() method.
3. The selectData() method, upon receiving the SQL string, uses the data members defined by the tag's attributes to connect to the database and execute the query.
4. Once the selectData() method receives the results of the SQL query, it passes the result set to the copyResultSet() method.
5. The copyResultSet() method retrieves the column names contained in the result set, using the getResultSetColumnNames() methods. It then builds a vector of hashtables, each representing a single row in the result set.
6. The copyResultSet() method returns the newly built vector to the selectData() method, which in turn returns the same vector to the doStartTag() method. At this point, the doStartTag() method contains a reference to the vector of hashtables with the results of the database query.
7. The doStartTag() method adds the vector, rows, to the PageContext, and binds it to the key referenced by the resultId data member.

The results of the query are accessible by using the pageContext.getAttribute() method, passing it the value named by the resultId attribute. This code looks something like the following:

```
<chapter7:sql driver="sun.jdbc.odbc.JdbcOdbcDriver"
          url="Jdbc:Odbc:contacts"
          resultId="results">
SELECT * FROM CONTACTS
</chapter7:sql>

<%
Vector res =
  (Vector)pageContext.getAttribute("results");
%>
```

The resultId value is the key used to retrieve the result set from the PageContext.

SQLTagTEI Class

Now that a tag handler is defined that adds its results to the PageContext, you need to make these results accessible by referencing a scripting variable. The result is the ability to access the SQLTag results using syntax similar to the following code snippet:

```
<chapter7:sql driver="sun.jdbc.odbc.JdbcOdbcDriver"
           url="Jdbc:Odbc:contacts"
           resultId="results">
SELECT * FROM CONTACTS
</chapter7:sql>

<table border="1" width="500">
  <tr>
    <th>Username</th><th>First Name</th><th>Last Name</th>
  </tr>
  <%

  for ( int x = 0; x < results.size(); x++) {

    out.println("<tr>");

    Hashtable table = (Hashtable)results.elementAt(x);

    out.println("<td>" + table.get("username") + "</td>");
    out.println("<td>" + table.get("firstname") + "</td>");
    out.println("<td>" + table.get("lastname") + "</td>");

    out.println("</tr>");
  }
  %>
</table>
```

To do this, you must first create a class that extends the javax.servlet.jsp. tagext. TagExtraInfo class and describes the resultId scripting variable using the getVariableInfo() method. This class is shown in Listing 7.2.

```
package chapter7;

import javax.servlet.jsp.tagext.TagExtraInfo;
import javax.servlet.jsp.tagext.TagData;
import javax.servlet.jsp.tagext.VariableInfo;

public class SQLTagTEI extends TagExtraInfo {

  public VariableInfo[] getVariableInfo(TagData data) {
```

Listing 7.2 SQLTagTEI.java. *(continues)*

```
        return new VariableInfo[]
        {
          new VariableInfo((String)data.getAttribute("resultId"),
                           "java.util.Vector",
                           true,
                           VariableInfo.AT_END)
        };
      }
    }
```

Listing 7.2 SQLTagTEI.java. *(continued)*

This class contains a single method, getVariableInfo(), that performs only one action: It creates a new VariableInfo object describing the scripting variable to expose. It creates the VariableInfo object using its default constructor with the appropriate parameters. The explicit parameter values for this instance are described in Table 7.3.

Table 7.3 Parameter Values of the VariableInfo() Constructor

PARAMETER VALUE	DESCRIPTION
(String)data.getAttribute("resultId")	Identifies the name of the scripting variable, which in this case is retrieved from the resultId attribute found the TagData object describing the associated tag.
java.util.Vector	Defines the type of object represented by the scripting variable as a vector.
true	Tells the JSP/servlet container that a new instance of the scripting variable needs to be created.
VariableInfo.AT_END	Tells the container that the scripting variable is visible only after the tag's ending element.

The combination of these parameters describes a scripting variable that has a name determined by the value of the tag's resultId attribute, that is of type java.util.Vector, that must be newly created with every occurrence of its associated tag, and that is visible only after the tag's ending element.

Adding the TEI Class to the TLD

When creating a scripting variable, the final step is to generate a TLD that describes the tag handler and its associated TEI class. This simple step requires only a single additional element to describe the tag: the <teiclass> element. Listing 7.3 contains the entire TLD used to describe this example's new tag, including its TEI class.

```
<?xml version="1.0" encoding="ISO-8859-1" ?>
<!DOCTYPE taglib PUBLIC
"-//Sun Microsystems, Inc.//DTD JSP Tag Library 1.1//EN"
"http://java.sun.com/j2ee/dtds/web-jsptaglibrary_1_1.dtd">

<taglib>
  <tlibversion>1.0</tlibversion>
  <jspversion>1.2</jspversion>
  <shortname>chapter7</shortname>

  <tag>
    <name>sql</name>
    <tagclass>chapter7.SQLTag</tagclass>
    <teiclass>chapter7.SQLTagTEI</teiclass>
    <bodycontent>JSP</bodycontent>
    <info>Example SQL Tag using a TEI Class</info>
      <attribute>
        <name>driver</name>
        <required>true</required>
        <rtexprvalue>true</rtexprvalue>
      </attribute>
      <attribute>
        <name>url</name>
        <required>true</required>
        <rtexprvalue>true</rtexprvalue>
      </attribute>
      <attribute>
        <name>username</name>
        <required>false</required>
        <rtexprvalue>true</rtexprvalue>
      </attribute>
      <attribute>
        <name>password</name>
        <required>false</required>
        <rtexprvalue>true</rtexprvalue>
      </attribute>
      <attribute>
        <name>resultId</name>
        <required>true</required>
        <rtexprvalue>true</rtexprvalue>
      </attribute>
  </tag>

</taglib>
```

Listing 7.3 taglib.tld.

Notice that this TLD contains only one tag element you have not seen: <teiclass>. This element simply tells the JSP/servlet container that this tag uses the TEI class chapter7.SQLTagTEI to define any extra information about this tag:

```
<teiclass>chapter7.SQLTagTEI</teiclass>
```

NOTE **The naming convention commonly used when naming a TagExtraInfo class is the tag handler name with TEI appended to it. The example TLD uses this exact nomenclature.**

Using the Defined Scripting Variable

To use the new scripting variable, complete the follow deployment steps:

1. Compile the SQLTag and SQLTagTEI classes, and move them to the <TOMCAT_HOME>/webapps/customtags/WEB-INF/classes/chapter7 directory.
2. Move the chapter7.tld file to the <TOMCAT_HOME>/webapps/customtags/WEB-INF directory.
3. Add the following <taglib> entry to the <TOMCAT_HOME>/webapps/customtags/WEB-INF/web.xml file:

```
<taglib>
  <taglib-uri>/chapter7</taglib-uri>
  <taglib-location>
    /WEB-INF /chapter7.tld
  </taglib-location>
</taglib>
```

4. Restart Tomcat.

Now that all of the tag's components are deployed, you can use the tag and its scripting variable in a JSP. Listing 7.4 shows the JSP that will use these elements.

```
<%@ taglib uri="/chapter7" prefix="chapter7" %>
<%@ page import="java.util.Hashtable, java.util.Iterator" %>
<%@ page import="java.util.Set" %>

<html>
<head>
  <title>Custom Tags Demo</title>
</head>

<body bgcolor="#FFFFFF">

<chapter7:sql driver="sun.jdbc.odbc.JdbcOdbcDriver"
          url="Jdbc:Odbc:contacts"
          resultId="results">
```

Listing 7.4 chapter7.jsp. *(continues)*

```
SELECT * FROM CONTACTS
</chapter7:sql>

<table border="1" width="500">
  <tr>
    <th>Username</th><th>First Name</th><th>Last Name</th>
  </tr>
  <%

  for ( int x = 0; x < results.size(); x++) {

    out.println("<tr>");

    Hashtable table = (Hashtable)results.elementAt(x);

    out.println("<td>" + table.get("username") + "</td>");
    out.println("<td>" + table.get("firstname") + "</td>");
    out.println("<td>" + table.get("lastname") + "</td>");

    out.println("</tr>");
  }
  %>
</table>

</body>
</html>
```

Listing 7.4 chapter7.jsp. *(continued)*

Notice a couple of items before making a request to this JSP. The first section is the <chapter7:sql> tag:

```
<chapter7:sql driver="sun.jdbc.odbc.JdbcOdbcDriver"
          url="Jdbc:Odbc:contacts"
          resultId="results">
SELECT * FROM CONTACTS
</chapter7:sql>
```

The JSP begins by setting three of the tag's five possible attributes. It first sets the driver attribute to the fully qualified class name of the JDBC:ODBC bridge driver. It then sets the URL of the tag to point to the ODBC datasource contacts used in Chapter 2, "Configuring and Testing the Web Application Environment." Last, it sets the resultId attribute to the value results. This value will be used to reference the scripting variable after this tag's execution is complete.

NOTE **The URL referenced by this instance of the <chapter7:sql> tag relies upon the previous configuration of the contacts datasource. If you did not configure this datasource in Chapter 2, you should do so prior to running this example.**

After the attributes are set to the appropriate values, the JSP sets the body of the <chapter7:sql> tag to a simple SQL query that retrieves all the values stored in all the rows in the contacts table. The result of this use of the <chapter7:sql> tag is a vector that contains a collection of hashtables representing each row returned in the result set.

The JSP prints the simple HTML needed to create an HTML table and then executes the following scriptlet section:

```
<%

  for ( int x = 0; x < results.size(); x++) {

    out.println("<tr>");

    Hashtable table = (Hashtable)results.elementAt(x);

    out.println("<td>" + table.get("username") + "</td>");
    out.println("<td>" + table.get("firstname") + "</td>");
    out.println("<td>" + table.get("lastname") + "</td>");

    out.println("</tr>");
  }
%>
```

This scriptlet code shows the result of exposing the scripting variable. Notice in this bit of code that the vector represented by the results scripting variable is referenced twice to display the results of the database query. This is the same vector that was added to the PageContext by the SQLTag and was exposed to the rest of the JSP by the SQLTagTEI class discussed earlier. You can now use this object in the same manner as an implicit JSP object.

To see this JSP perform, copy the chapter7.jsp file to the <TOMCAT_HOME> webapps/customtags/ directory and open your browser to the following URL:

```
http://localhost:8080/customtags/chapter7.jsp
```

The result should look similar to Figure 7.1.

Tag Validation

This section discusses a second use for the TagExtraInfo class: the translation-time validation of tag attributes and values using the TagExtraInfo.isValid() method. The isValid() utility method is invoked at translation time by the JSP/servlet engine with the intention of allowing the tag's attributes and attribute values to be validated prior to the evaluation of the tag. To perform this validation, the isValid() method is passed a TagData instance as its argument. This TagData object provides access to the tag's instance attributes and values, which allows the isValid() method to test for appropriate attribute data.

To use this mechanism, add to your TEI class an isValid() method that accesses the data contained in the TagData object. If the retrieved attribute values are valid, according to the business logic needed for your tag, then the isValid() should return true; otherwise, it should return false. If false is returned, then the JSP/servlet container will return an exception stating that the attributes are invalid.

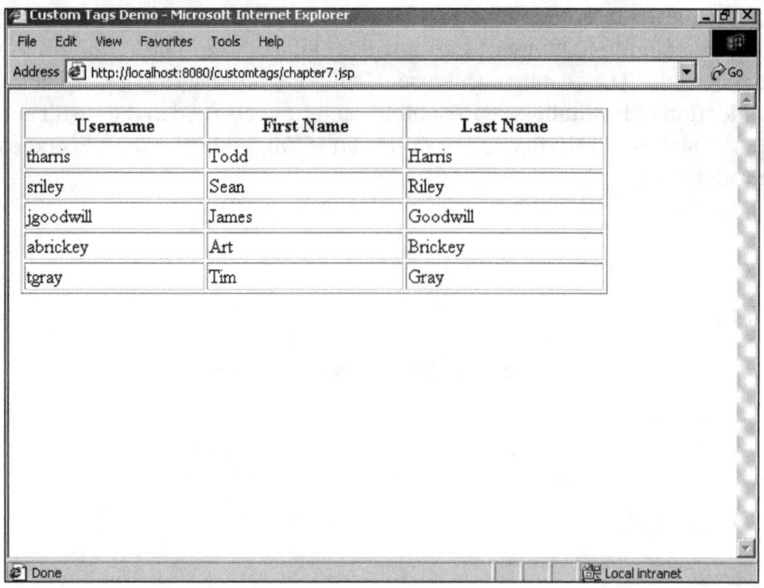

Username	First Name	Last Name
tharris	Todd	Harris
sriley	Sean	Riley
jgoodwill	James	Goodwill
abrickey	Art	Brickey
tgray	Tim	Gray

Figure 7.1 Output of chapter7.jsp.

To see how this works, add an isValid() method to the SQLTagTEI class. Listing 7.5 contains the modified TEI class.

```
package chapter7;

import javax.servlet.jsp.tagext.TagExtraInfo;
import javax.servlet.jsp.tagext.TagData;
import javax.servlet.jsp.tagext.VariableInfo;

public class SQLTagTEI extends TagExtraInfo {

  public boolean isValid(TagData data) {

    // if username != null then password cannot be null
    if ( data.getAttribute("username") != null &&
        data.getAttribute("password") == null ) {

      return false;
    }
    // if password != null then username cannot be null
    if ( data.getAttribute("password") != null &&
        data.getAttribute("username") == null ) {
```

Listing 7.5 Revised SQLTagTEI.java. *(continues)*

```
      return false;
    }
    return true;
  }

  public VariableInfo[] getVariableInfo(TagData data) {

    return new VariableInfo[]
    {
      new VariableInfo((String)data.getAttribute("resultId"),
                       "java.util.Vector",
                       true,
                       VariableInfo.AT_END)
    };
  }
}
```

Listing 7.5 Revised SQLTagTEI.java. *(continued)*

The isValid() method contains two if statements that test the username and password attribute values. These two statements make sure that if the username attribute has a value, the password attribute also has a value, and vice versa. If either test fails, then the isValid() method returns false, and an exception is reported to the user. If the isValid() method returns true, then normal processing continues.

NOTE **I have added this test to make this tag compatible with Microsoft Access, which does not currently support the use of usernames and passwords.**

You now have a TEI class that validates its attribute values at translation time. To see these changes in action, recompile the SQLTagTEI.java class, and move it to the <TOMCAT_HOME>/webapps/customtags/WEB-INF/classes/chapter7/ directory. Change the <chapter7:sql> tag attributes to include a password but no username in the chapter7.jsp listed previously, and open your browser to the following URL:

```
http://localhost:8080/customtags/chapter7.jsp
```

Summary

This chapter began by discussing the steps required when developing a tag that exposes a scripting variable. It then discussed the process of validating tag attributes a translation time. Chapter 8 will discuss iteration tags and how they can be employed when iterating over object collections.

CHAPTER 8

Iteration Tags

This chapter discusses iteration tags. It begins by describing what iteration tags are and how they can be used. You will then develop a custom tag that iterates over the results of the SQLTag developed in Chapter 7, "Scripting Variables and Tag Validation."

At the end of this chapter, you should feel comfortable with what iteration tags are and how they are developed. Figure 8.1 shows an object model of the components involved when developing an iteration tag.

IterationTag Interface

Iteration tags are one of the more useful components added with the JSP 1.2 specification. They were introduced to provide a simple interface for tags that need to evaluate their body for each item in a collection of objects. An example would be a SQL tag that evaluates its body once for each row in a JDBC result set.

javax.servlet.jsp.tagext.IterationTag Interface

To develop a custom iteration tag, you must implement the javax.servlet.jsp.tagext.IterationTag interface, either directly or though inheritance. IterationTag is a simple interface that extends the javax.servlet.jsp.tagext.Tag interface, adding a single method and data member.

The doAfterBody() method is the only method defined by the IterationTag interface:

```
public void doAfterBody()
```

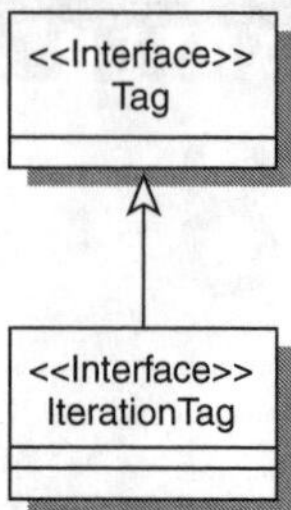

Figure 8.1 Iteration tag objects.

It is executed after the doStartTag() method and after the JSP/servlet engine has evaluated the tag's body one time. Most business logic should be located in this method.

The EVAL_BODY_AGAIN constant is used as a return value that, if returned by the doAfterBody() method, tells the JSP/servlet container to evaluate the tag's body again.

Life Cycle of an IterationTag

To see how the IterationTag interface works, let's examine its life cycle. As stated in Chapter 4, "JSP Overview and Architecture," when a JSP is first encountered, it is compiled into a servlet composed from JSP and HTML code. If the compiled JSP contains a tag, then the servlet will create an instance of this tag, and call the appropriate life cycle methods for the particular tag implementation. The following snippet contains a simplified code example showing the invocation order of an IterationTag:

```
IterationTag tag = new IterationTag();
tag.setPageContext()
tag.setParent()
if ( tag.doStartTag() == EVAL_BODY_INCLUDE ) {

while( tag.doAfterBody() == EVAL_BODY_AGAIN )
  { }
}
tag.doEndTag()
tag.release()
...
tag.setParent()
if(tag.doStartTag() == EVAL_BODY_INCLUDE) {
while(tag.doAfterBody() == EVAL_BODY_AGAIN);
}
tag.doEndTag()
...
```

As you can see, this pseudo-code represents a simplified view of the IterationTag's life cycle. Figure 8.2 shows the life cycle graphically.

The steps shown in Figure 8.2 represent the process an IterationTag handler goes through during a single evaluation. Because an IterationTag handler follows the same life cycle of a simple tag and body tag up to the invocation of the doStartTag() method, our discussion of this life cycle begins with the doStartTag() method:

1. At the point where we pick up the IterationTag's life cycle, the PageContext and Parent objects have been set, and the doStartTag() method is invoked. Once doStartTag() has finished executing, it can return one of two methods: SKIP_BODY or EVAL_BODY_INCLUDE.
2. If the doStartTag() method returns SKIP_BODY, then doEndTag() is invoked immediately, the tag's body is ignored, and normal tag processing continues.

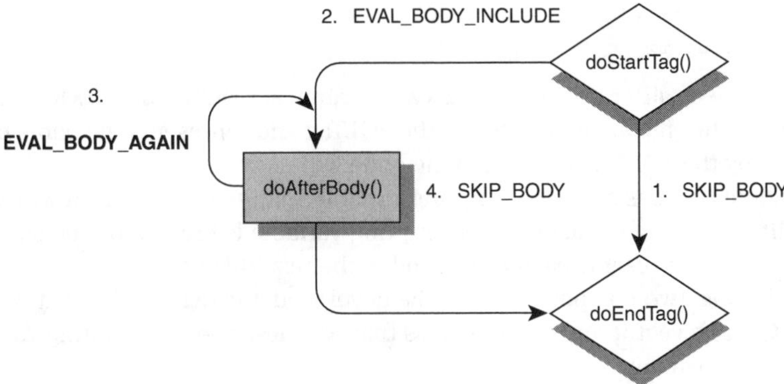

Figure 8.2 Flow of an IterationTag.

NOTE If the tag being evaluated is a BodyTag, then doStartTag() will return EVAL_BODY_BUFFERED instead of EVAL_BODY_INCLUDE, and the methods setBodyContent() and doInitBody() will be executed prior to the invocation of doAfterBody(). All other processing will be the same.

1. If the doStartTag() method returns EVAL_BODY_INCLUDE, then the container invokes the doAfterBody() method with an evaluated version of the tag's body.
2. When doAfterBody() is executed, the tag's body has already been evaluated by the JSP/servlet engine. The doAfterBody() method performs its processing, and returns either SKIP_BODY or EVAL_BODY_AGAIN.
3. If doAfterBody()returns EVAL_BODY_AGAIN, then the JSP/servlet container evaluates the body again, and invokes the doAfterBody() method another time.
4. If the doAfterBody() method returns SKIP_BODY, then the doEndTag() is invoked immediately, the tag's body is ignored, and normal tag processing continues.

Extending the SQLTag with an IterationTag

To see how IterationTags really work, let's create an IterationTag that evaluates its body for each row returned by the SQLTag from Chapter 7. The syntax of the new tag looks something like the following snippet.

```
<chapter8:sqlIterator resultId="results" rowId="rows">

  <%
out.println("<tr>");
out.println("<td>" + rows.get("username") + "</td>");
out.println("<td>" + rows.get("firstname") + "</td>");
out.println("<td>" + rows.get("lastname") + "</td>");
out.println("</tr>");
  %>

</chapter8:sqlIterator>
```

This new tag is named sqlIterator, and it has two attributes: resultId and rowId. The resultId attribute matches the attribute used in the SQLTag and represents the name of the vector exposed by the SQLTag over which the code will iterate.

The rowId attribute exposes a second scripting variable, accessible only from within the <chapter8:sqlIterator> tag elements. This scripting variable is created by the sqlIterator's tag handler, and represents each row found in the resultId vector.

To implement this tag, two components must be developed: the tag handler that will iterate over the SQLTag's vector and the TEI class that will describe the scripting variable created by the tag handler.

SQLIteratorTag Handler

The first component of IteratorTag is the tag handler containing the business logic of the tag. Listing 8.1 contains the source for the tag handler. As you examine this code, focus on the bolded areas.

NOTE **This tag does not implement the IterationTag interface directly, but instead extends the TagSupport class, which does directly implement the IterationTag interface. This approach keeps the SQLIteratorTag as simple as possible, and has no adverse affects on the execution of the tag.**

```
package chapter8;
import java.util.Hashtable;
import java.util.Vector;
import java.util.Enumeration;
import java.io.IOException;

import javax.servlet.jsp.tagext.TagSupport;
import javax.servlet.jsp.tagext.IterationTag;
import javax.servlet.jsp.JspException;
import javax.servlet.jsp.PageContext;
import javax.servlet.jsp.JspWriter;

public class SQLIteratorTag extends TagSupport {
```

Listing 8.1 SQLIteratorTag.java. *(continues)*

```
private String resultId = null;
private String rowId = null;
private Vector results = null;
private int currentrow = 0;
public SQLIteratorTag() {

  }

// Accessors used to set/get the id of
// the scripting variable exposed by the
// chapter7.SQLTag
public void setResultId(String resultId) {
this.resultId = resultId;
  }

public String getResultId() {
return resultId;
  }

// Accessors used to set/get the id of
// a scripting variable containing each
// Hashtable Row found in the resultId
public void setRowId(String rowId) {

this.rowId = rowId;
  }

public String getRowId() {
return rowId;
  }

public int doStartTag()
throws javax.servlet.jsp.JspException {
// Get a reference, from the PageContext, to the
// Vector of Hashtable named by the scripting variable
// resultId
results = (Vector)pageContext.getAttribute(getResultId());
// Make sure there are actually results to iterate over
if ( results != null && currentrow < results.size() ) {
// Get a reference to the current Hashtable
Hashtable table =
(Hashtable)results.elementAt(currentrow);
// Place the Hashtable in the PageContext bound
// to the key named by the rowId attribute
pageContext.setAttribute(rowId, table);
```

Listing 8.1 SQLIteratorTag.java. *(continues)*

```
// increment the Vector of Hashtable
currentrow++;
// We do want to evalaute our body
return EVAL_BODY_INCLUDE;
    }
// skip the body if the are no elements in the Vector
return SKIP_BODY;
  }

public int doAfterBody() throws JspException {
// Make sure there are actually results to iterate over
if ( results != null && currentrow < results.size() ) {
// Get a reference to the current Hashtable
Hashtable table =
(Hashtable)results.elementAt(currentrow);
// Place the Hashtable in the PageContext bound
// to the key named by the rowId attribute
pageContext.setAttribute(rowId, table);
// increment the Vector of Hashtable
currentrow++;
// Evaluate the body again
return EVAL_BODY_AGAIN;
    }
// skip the body if the are no more elements in the Vector
return SKIP_BODY;
  }

public int doEndTag() throws JspException {
// reset the tag's data members
results = null;
currentrow = 0;

return EVAL_PAGE;
  }
}
```

Listing 8.1 SQLIteratorTag.java. *(continued)*

This tag handler contains five methods. These methods are described in the following sections, in the order of their invocation.

setResultId() Method

The accessor setResultId() sets the id used to retrieve the results of the SQLTag. The value set using this method maps to the resultId attribute of the <chapter8:sqlIterator> tag, as follows:

```
<chapter8:sqlIterator resultId="results" rowId="rows" />
```

setRowId() Method

The accessor setRowId() sets the id used to create a scripting variable that will hold each hashtable contained in the vector referenced by the resultId from the previous attribute. The value set using this method maps to the rowId attribute of the <chapter8:sqlIterator> tag, as follows:

```
<chapter8:sqlIterator resultId="results" rowId="rows" />
```

doStartTag() Method

In the doStartTag() method, the tag begins its business logic. This method is invoked after the setPageContext(), setParent(), and attribute() methods have been invoked. The doStartTag() method begins by retrieving the vector identified by the resultId attribute:

```
results = (Vector)pageContext.getAttribute(getResultId());
```

After the vector is retrieved from the PageContext, it is checked to make sure that it is not empty. If it is empty, then doStartTag() returns SKIP_BODY, and doEndTag() is invoked.

If the vector is not empty, then the first element—a hashtable representing the row in a database—is retrieved and placed in the PageContext bound to the key passed in the rowId attribute:

```
// Get a reference to the current Hashtable
Hashtable table =
(Hashtable)results.elementAt(currentrow);
// Place the Hashtable in the PageContext bound
// to the key named by the rowId attribute
pageContext.setAttribute(rowId, table);
```

After the first element is added to the PageContext, the currentrow index is incremented so that it points to the next element in the vector, and EVAL_BODY_INCLUDE is returned:

```
// increment the Vector of Hashtable
currentrow++;

// We do want to evalaute our body
return EVAL_BODY_INCLUDE;
```

At this point, the first hashtable is stored in the PageContext and the tag's body is evaluated for the first time.

doAfterBody() Method

The doAfterBody() method is invoked once the doStartTag() has completed its processing and the tag's body has been evaluated once. The doAfterTag() method begins by making sure the results vector is not empty. If it is empty, then doStartTag() returns SKIP_BODY and doEndTag() is invoked.

If the vector is not empty, then the next element in the vector is retrieved. Processing continues just as it did in doStartTag(), except that doAfterBody() returns EVAL_BODY_AGAIN until all of the vector's elements have been retrieved. This return value causes the JSP/servlet engine to re-evaluate the tag's body.

Once all the vector's elements have been retrieved, the doAfterBody() method returns the value SKIP_PAGE, and the doEndTag() method is invoked.

doEndTag() Method

The doEndTag() method is invoked after doAfterBody() has completed its processing and has returned the value SKIP_BODY. The doEndTag() method, in this instance, serves only one function: to return all of the tag handler's data members to their original state.

SQLIteratorTagTEI Class

The second component that needs to be developed is the SQLIteratorTagTEI class. This class is a simple extension of the javax.servlet.jsp.tagext.TagExtraInfo class, and will be used to describe a scripting variable that represents each hashtable contained in the results vector.

As described in Chapter 7, to describe a scripting variable, you simply need to implement the getVariableInfo() method. This method returns a javax.servlet.jsp.tagext.VariableInfo object describing the scripting variable being exposed. Listing 8.2 contains the source for the TEI class.

```
package chapter8;
import javax.servlet.jsp.tagext.TagExtraInfo;
import javax.servlet.jsp.tagext.TagData;
import javax.servlet.jsp.tagext.VariableInfo;
public class SQLIteratorTagTEI extends TagExtraInfo {
public VariableInfo[] getVariableInfo(TagData data) {
return new VariableInfo[]
        {
new VariableInfo((String)data.getAttribute("rowId"),
"java.util.Hashtable",
true,
VariableInfo.NESTED)
        };
   }
}
```

Listing 8.2 SQLIteratorTagTEI.java.

There is little to the SQLIteratorTagTEI class. It implements the getVariableInfo() method and returns a single VariableInfo object. The VariableInfo object returned by this method, describes a scripting variable described by the parameters of the VariableInfo constructor. These parameters are described in Table 8.1.

Table 8.1 Parameter Values of the VariableInfo() Constructor

PARAMETER VALUE	DESCRIPTION
(String)data.getAttribute("rowId")	Identifies the name of the scripting variable, which in this case is retrieved from the rowId attribute found in the TagData object describing the current instance of the SQLIteratorTag.
"java.util.Hashtable"	Defines the type of object that is referenced by the scripting variable. For this instance, the scripting variable is a hashtable.
true	Tells the JSP/servlet container that a new instance of the scripting variable needs to be created.
VariableInfo.NESTED	Tells the container that the scripting variable is visible only between the <chapter8:sqlIterator> elements.

The combination of these parameters describes a scripting variable whose name is determined by the value of the tag's rowId attribute, that is a type of java.util.Hashtable, that must be newly created with every occurrence of its associated tag, and that is visible only between the <chapter8:sqlIterator>'s beginning and ending elements.

sqlIterator TLD

Now that the tag and its related classes have been defined, you need to create a TLD that describes them. Listing 8.3 contains the TLD used to describe the new tag.

```
<?xml version="1.0" encoding="ISO-8859-1" ?>
<!DOCTYPE taglib PUBLIC
"-//Sun Microsystems, Inc.//DTD JSP Tag Library 1.1//EN"
"http://java.sun.com/j2ee/dtds/web-jsptaglibrary_1_1.dtd">
<taglib>
<tlibversion>1.0</tlibversion>
<jspversion>1.2</jspversion>
<shortname>chapter8</shortname>

<tag>
<name>sqlIterator</name>
<tagclass>chapter8.SQLIteratorTag</tagclass>
<teiclass>chapter8.SQLIteratorTagTEI</teiclass>
<bodycontent>JSP</bodycontent>
<info>Example SQL Iterator Tag</info>
```

Listing 8.3 chapter8.tld. *(continues)*

```
<attribute>
<name>resultId</name>
<required>true</required>
<rtexprvalue>true</rtexprvalue>
</attribute>
<attribute>
<name>rowId</name>
<required>true</required>
<rtexprvalue>true</rtexprvalue>
</attribute>
</tag>
</taglib>
```

Listing 8.3 chapter8.tld. *(continued)*

Deploying and Using the sqlIterator Tag

To deploy the new tag, complete the following steps:

1. Compile the SQLIteratorTag.java and SQLIteratorTagTEI files, moving the resulting class files into the <TOMCAT_HOME>/webapps/customtags/WEB-INF/classes/chapter8/ directory.
2. Move the chapter8.tld file to the <TOMCAT_HOME>/webapps/customtags/WEB-INF/lib/ directory.
3. After the TLD is deployed, add the following snippet to the <TOMCAT_HOME>/webapps/customtags/WEB-INF/web.xml file:

```
<taglib>
<taglib-uri>/chapter8</taglib-uri>
<taglib-location>/WEB-INF/lib/chapter8.tld</taglib-location>
</taglib>
```

4. Restart Tomcat.

Now that the tag's components are deployed, you can use the tag to iterate over a collection of objects. This JSP is shown in Listing 8.4.

```
<%@ taglib uri="/chapter7" prefix="chapter7" %>
<%@ taglib uri="/chapter8" prefix="chapter8" %>
<%@ page import="java.util.HashMap, java.util.Iterator, java.util.Set"
%>
<html>
<head>
```

Listing 8.4 chapter8.jsp. *(continues)*

```
<title>Custom Tags Demo</title>
</head>
<chapter7:sql driver="sun.jdbc.odbc.JdbcOdbcDriver"
url="Jdbc:Odbc:contacts"
resultId="results">
SELECT * FROM CONTACTS
</chapter7:sql>

<table border="1" width="500">
<tr>
<th>Username</th><th>First Name</th><th>Last Name</th>
</tr>
<chapter8:sqlIterator resultId="results" rowId="rows">

 <%
out.println("<tr>");
out.println("<td>" + rows.get("username") + "</td>");
out.println("<td>" + rows.get("firstname") + "</td>");
out.println("<td>" + rows.get("lastname") + "</td>");
out.println("</tr>");
%>

</chapter8:sqlIterator>
</table>
</body>
</html>
```

Listing 8.4 chapter8.jsp. *(continued)*

The chapter8.jsp begins with the inclusion of taglib directives that name both the chapter7 and chapter8 tag libraries. The first action performed by this JSP is the evaluation of a <chapter7:sql> tag. This instance of the <chapter7:sql> tag executes the same query used in Chapter 7, storing the results in a vector referenced by the value of its resultId attribute.

After the <chapter7:sql> tag completes its processing, then the <chapter8:sqlIterator> begins its processing. It first defines two attributes: resultId and rowId. The first attribute, resultId, names the vector to be iterated over. Note that this attribute's value matches the resultId of the <chapter7:sql> tag. The rowId attribute names the scripting variable that references each hashtable contained in the resultId vector.

Now <chapter8:sqlIterator> knows what to iterate over and where to expose the results. It begins its iteration, repeating the evaluation of its body until there are no more elements in the vector.

The tag's body contains some scriptlet code that prints out the contents of each hashtable represented by the current row's scriptlet variable. The results of these repeated evaluations is a table that contains the results of the <chapter7:sql> tag.

To see this process in action, copy this JSP to the <TOMCAT_HOME>/webapps/customtags/ directory, and open your browser to the following URL:

```
http://localhost:8080/customtags/chapter8.jsp
```

You should see a page similar to Figure 7.1 in Chapter 7.

Summary

This chapter discussed custom tags that iterate over their bodies for every object found in a given collection. It described the classes and interfaces used when developing custom iteration tags. It also discussed the process involved when developing an iteration tag. The next chapter will discuss the built-in functionality provided by the Tag APIs that can be leveraged as a communication tool between custom tags.

CHAPTER

9

Cooperating Tags

This chapter looks at how to build custom tags that cooperate with each other. It first examines some of the different tag communication techniques and their associated shortcomings. The chapter then focuses on how these shortcomings can be overcome by leveraging tag communications techniques between parent and child tags.

At the end of this chapter, you should have a good understanding of the relationship that exists between a parent and child tag. You should also feel comfortable with how this relationship can be leveraged when communicating information between these tags.

Cooperation Techniques

Several techniques can be employed when trying to communicate between different custom tags: storing and retrieving objects using the HttpSession, HttpServletRequest, or ServletContext; using the PageContext to share data between tags; and creating scripting variables to be used by other custom tags. Although all these techniques work fine in most cases, they expose objects to other JSP objects that may or may not be trusted.

When an object is shared using one of the techniques just mentioned, the object can be retrieved and modified by any JSP component that has knowledge of the object. If other tags depend on the data contained in the shared object, and it has been changed by a foreign component, then the behavior of the tags with which you intended to communicate could change dramatically.

Creating custom tags that use a parent/child relationship to communicate with each other can conquer this problem. When a parent/child link exists, one tag—the child—is nested inside a second tag, which acts as the parent. The following code snippet shows an example:

```
<parentTag>
  <childTag>
  </childTag>
</parentTag>
```

Using a parent/child relationship allows the child tag to directly communicate with its parent tag. With this type of communication, the data being shared between tags is never exposed to other JSP components and, as a result, the shared data's integrity is guaranteed. This method of tag communication is the subject of this chapter.

TagSupport Convenience Methods

In Chapter 5, "Simple Tags," the javax.servlet.jsp.tagext.TagSupport class introduced several convenience methods. Of these methods, six were created with the purpose of communicating between parent and child tags. These methods can be separated into two groups, which are described in the following sections.

NOTE All of the tag classes that use this method of communication must extend the javax.servlet.jsp.tagext.TagSupport class, either directly or through inheritance.

Parent/Ancestor Accessor Methods

The first set of communication methods, defined by the TagSupport class, allows a child tag to retrieve an instance to a parent or ancestor tag. A child tag invokes these methods when it is interested in communicating with its parent/ancestor.

getParent() Method

The getParent() method acts as a basic accessor, allowing a child tag to retrieve an instance of its parent tag. The following code snippet shows an example of how getParent() is often used:

```
TagSupport parent = (TagSupport)getParent();
```

This example assumes that its parent is an extension of the TagSupport class.

findAncestorWithClass() Method

The findAncestorWithClass() method is used much like the getParent() method, except that it searches for a particular type of parent object. This method is used when the tag containing the data of interest is contained in an ancestor that may not be the direct parent of the child tag. If no ancestor tag of the named type exists, then null is returned. The following code snippet shows this kind of relationship:

```
<ancestorTag>
  <parentTag>
    <childTag>
```

```
    </childTag>
  </parentTag>
</ancestorTag>
```

If the <ancestorTag> was of type chapter9.SomeTagHandler, to retrieve an instance of the <ancestorTag>'s tag handler from the <childTag>'s tag handler, the findAncestorWithClass() method could be used in the following manner.

```
SomeTagHandler ancestor =
  (SomeTagHandler)findAncestorWithClass(this,
  class.forName("chapter9.SomeTagHandler"));
```

The findAncestorWithClass() method uses two parameters. The first parameter names the starting point to begin the search. Most often, this parameter will be set to *this*, which represents the calling class. The second parameter names the class type being searched for. This value will always be the type of ancestor the child tag is searching for.

Data Access Methods

The second group of convenience methods is used after a child tag has retrieved an instance its parent or ancestor. These methods are used to store and retrieve values from a child's parent or ancestor.

Each of these methods operates on an internal hashtable defined by the javax.servlet.jsp.tagext.TagSupport class. This hashtable is defined with the sole purpose of sharing data with a tag's children.

setValue() Method

The setValue() method is used to set a key/value pair that will be stored in a tag's internal hashtable for later retrieval. The parent tag can use this method to share a particular piece of data. The setValue() method can also be used by the child to push a piece of data back to its parent/ancestor. An example using the setValue() method is shown here:

```
TagSupport parent = (TagSupport)getParent();
parent.setValue(key, value);
```

getValue() Method

The getValue() method is used by a child tag to retrieve a value associated with a named key/value pair previously set using the setValue() method. An example using the getValue() method is shown here:

```
TagSupport parent = (TagSupport)getParent();
java.lang.Object object = parent.getValue(key);
```

getValues() Method

The getValues() method is most often used by a child tag to retrieve an Enumeration containing all the keys set using the setValue() method. This Enumeration can then be iterated over and used in conjunction with the getValue() method to retrieve the matching values. An example using the getValue() method is shown here:

```
TagSupport parent = (TagSupport)getParent();
java.util.Enumeration keys = parent.getValues();
```

removeValue() Method

```
public void removeValue(java.lang.String k)
```

The removeValue() method removes a value associated with a named key. An example using this method is shown here:

```
TagSupport parent = (TagSupport)getParent();
parent.removeValue(key);
```

SQLIteratorTag and its Children

To see how a parent/child relationship works, let's modify the SQLIteratorTag handler from Chapter 8, "Iteration Tags," to allow its children access to its data values. Once the appropriate changes have been made to the SQLIteratorTag, you will create the children that will communicate with the new SQLIteratorTag. The syntax of the new tag will look something like the following snippet:

```
<chapter9:sqlIterator resultId="results">

  <tr>

    <td><chapter9:getColumn column="username" /></td>
    <td><chapter9:getColumn column="firstname" /></td>
    <td><chapter9:getColumn column="lastname"" /></td>

  </tr>

</chapter9:sqlIterator>
```

SQLIteratorTag Parent

A parent tag that wants to allow its children access to its values must satisfy only a couple of requirements. The first of these changes requires the parent tag to extend the javax.sevlet.jsp.tagext.TagSupport class, either directly or through inheritance. The second requirement is that the parent tag must store the data that it intends to share in its internal hashtable.

Because the SQLIteratorTag already extends the TagSupport class, you only need to modify this class to satisfy the data storage requirement for sharing data. The changes to satisfy this requirement are shown in Listing 9.1. As you examine this source, focus on the bolded areas.

```
package chapter9;

import java.util.Hashtable;
import java.util.Vector;
import java.util.Enumeration;
```

Listing 9.1 SQLIteratorTag.java. *(continues)*

```
import javax.servlet.jsp.tagext.TagSupport;
import javax.servlet.jsp.tagext.IterationTag;
import javax.servlet.jsp.JspException;
import javax.servlet.jsp.PageContext;
import javax.servlet.jsp.JspWriter;

public class SQLIteratorTag extends TagSupport {

  private String resultId = null;

  private Vector results = null;

  private int currentrow = 0;

  public SQLIteratorTag() {

  }

  // Accessors used to set/get the id of
  // the scripting variable exposed by the
  // chapter7.SQLTag
  public void setResultId(String resultId) {

    this.resultId = resultId;
  }

  public String getResultId() {

    return resultId;
  }

  // The setRow method copies the current
  // Hashtable key/value pairs into the TagSupport.values
  // Hashtable
  private void setRow(Hashtable table) {

    // Get the keys from the current row
    Enumeration enum = table.keys();
    // Iterate over the current row retrieving the
    // column values
    while ( enum.hasMoreElements() ) {

   String key = (String)enum.nextElement();
```

Listing 9.1 SQLIteratorTag.java. *(continues)*

```
            // Add the retrieved key/value pair to the
            // TagSupport.values using the TagSupport.setValue()
            setValue(key, table.get(key));
        }
    }

    public int doStartTag()
    throws javax.servlet.jsp.JspException {

        // Get a reference, from the PageContext, to the
        // Vector of Hashtable named by the scripting
        // variable resultId
        results = (Vector)pageContext.getAttribute(getResultId());
        currentrow = 0;

        // Make sure there are actually results to iterate over
        if ( currentrow < results.size() ) {

            setRow((Hashtable)results.elementAt(currentrow));

            // increment the Vector of Hashtables
            currentrow++;

            // We do want to evalaute our body
            return EVAL_BODY_INCLUDE;
        }
        // skip the body if the are no elements in the Vector
        return SKIP_BODY;
    }

    public int doAfterBody() throws JspException {

        // Make sure there are actually results to iterate over
        if ( currentrow < results.size() ) {

            setRow((Hashtable)results.elementAt(currentrow));

            // increment the Vector of Hashtables
            currentrow++;

            // Evaluate the body again
            return EVAL_BODY_AGAIN;
        }
        // skip the body if the are no more elements in the Vector
```

Listing 9.1 SQLIteratorTag.java. *(continues)*

```
    return SKIP_BODY;
  }

  public int doEndTag() throws JspException {

    // reset the tag's data members
    results = null;
    currentrow = 0;

    return EVAL_PAGE;
  }
}
```

Listing 9.1 SQLIteratorTag.java. *(continued)*

To make the SQLIteratorTag satisfy the previously mentioned data storage requirement, three modifications have been made to the tag handler class. These changes are described in the following sections.

doStartTag() and doAfterBody() Methods

The first two changes have been made to both the doStartTag() and doAfterBody() methods. The first modification is the removal of the following two lines:

```
Hashtable table = (Hashtable)results.elementAt(currentrow);
pageContext.setAttribute(rowId, table);
```

The description of the SQLIteratorTag in Chapter 8 mentions that these two lines retrieve each hashtable representing a row in a database and place them in the PageContext object for use as a scripting variable.

The second modification to these methods is the addition of the following line of code:

```
setRow((Hashtable)results.elementAt(currentrow));
```

This line calls the setRow() method, passing it the current hashtable retrieved from each iteration over the results vector.

setRow() Method

The setRow() method is a local method defined to copy the contents of each hashtable retrieved from the results vector into the internal hashtable defined by the TagSupport class. It is a straightforward method that simply iterates over the hashtable from the results vector, copying each element to the TagSupport internal hashtable:

```
Enumeration enum = table.keys();

while ( enum.hasMoreElements() ) {

  String key = (String)enum.nextElement();
  setValue(key, table.get(key));
}
```

This method satisfies the data storage requirement.

Child Class

The child class that retrieves data from the SQLIteratorTag is a simple tag that extends the TagSupport class. This tag has a single attribute, column, which represents the name of the database column to retrieve. This tag must be nested inside the SQLIteratorTag. The source for the child tag's handler is shown in Listing 9.2.

```
package chapter9;

import javax.servlet.jsp.tagext.TagSupport;
import javax.servlet.jsp.JspWriter;
import javax.servlet.jsp.JspException;

public class GetColumnTag extends TagSupport {

  private String column = null;

  public GetColumnTag() {

  }

  // Basic accessors for setting and getting the column name
  public void setColumn(String column) {

    this.column  = column;
  }

  public String getColumn() {

    return column;
  }

  public int doStartTag()
    throws javax.servlet.jsp.JspException {

    // Get a reference to the page's JspWriter
    JspWriter writer = pageContext.getOut();

    try {

      // Get a reference to this tag's parent, which
      // in this case should be a chapter9.SQLIteratorTag
      TagSupport parent = (TagSupport)getParent();
      if ( parent == null ) {
```

Listing 9.2 GetColumnTag.java. *(continues)*

```
          // If the parent could not be retrieved,
          // throw an exception
          throw
            new JspException("This tag must be nested!");
        }
        // Get the value bound to the key referenced by
        // the column attribute
        String columnValue =
          (parent.getValue(getColumn())).toString();
        // Write the column to the output stream
        writer.write(columnValue);
      }
      catch (Exception e) {

        throw new JspException(e.getMessage());
      }
      return SKIP_BODY;
    }

      public int doEndTag() throws JspException {

      // reset the column name
      this.column = null;

      return EVAL_PAGE;
    }
  }
```

Listing 9.2 GetColumnTag.java. *(continued)*

There is nothing special about the GetColumnTag handler. It defines accessors for setting and getting the column name. It defines a doStartTag() method that contains its business logic and a doEndTag() method that resets its data members, allowing the tag instance to be reused.

doStartTag() Method

The bulk of the child tag's logic exists in the doStartTag() method. It begins by getting a reference to its parent tag handler—SQLIteratorTag, in this instance—and casting it to a TagSupport class:

```
TagSupport parent = (TagSupport)getParent();
```

Once the tag handler's parent is retrieved, doStartTag() calls its parent's getValue() method with the value of its column attribute:

```
String columnValue =
        (parent.getValue(getColumn())).toString();
```

This method retrieves from its parent's internal hashtable the value bound to the value referenced by the column attribute. The returned value represents a database column value placed in the hashtable by the SQLIteratorTag. Once the doStartTag() method has the column value, it writes the JspWriter:

```
writer.write(columnValue);
```

TLD

Now that the SQLIteratorTag has been modified, and GetColumTag handlers are defined, you need to create a tag library descriptor (TLD) that describes them both. Listing 9.3 contains the TLD used to describe the tags.

```
<?xml version="1.0" encoding="ISO-8859-1" ?>
<!DOCTYPE taglib PUBLIC
"-//Sun Microsystems, Inc.//DTD JSP Tag Library 1.1//EN"
"http://java.sun.com/j2ee/dtds/web-jsptaglibrary_1_1.dtd">

<taglib>
  <tlibversion>1.0</tlibversion>
  <jspversion>1.2</jspversion>
  <shortname>chapter9</shortname>

  <tag>
    <name>sqlIterator</name>
    <tagclass>chapter9.SQLIteratorTag</tagclass>
    <bodycontent>JSP</bodycontent>
    <info>Example SQL Iterator Tag</info>
      <attribute>
        <name>resultId</name>
        <required>true</required>
        <rtexprvalue>true</rtexprvalue>
      </attribute>
  </tag>
  <tag>
    <name>getColumn</name>
    <tagclass>chapter9.GetColumnTag</tagclass>
    <bodycontent>none</bodycontent>
    <info>Child of SQLIteratorTag using getValue()</info>
    <attribute>
      <name>column</name>
      <required>true</required>
      <rtexprvalue>true</rtexprvalue>
    </attribute>
  </tag>
</taglib>
```

Listing 9.3 chapter9.tld.

NOTE **The tag element describing the sqlIterator tag no longer has a subelement defining a TEI class. This class is no longer needed, because the code is not exposing a scriptlet variable.**

Deploying and Using the New Tags

To deploy this new library, complete the following steps:

1. Compile the chapter9.SQLIteratorTag.java and chapter9.GetColumnTag.java files, moving the resulting class files into the <TOMCAT_HOME>/webapps/customtags/WEB-INF/classes/chapter9/ directory.
2. Move the chapter9.tld file to the <TOMCAT_HOME>/webapps/customtags/WEB-INF/ directory.
3. After the TLD is deployed, add the following snippet to the <TOMCAT_HOME>/webapps/customtags/WEB-INF/web.xml file:

```
<taglib>
  <taglib-uri>/chapter9</taglib-uri>
  <taglib-location>/WEB-INF/ chapter9.tld</taglib-location>
</taglib>
```

4. Restart Tomcat.

At this point, the entire chapter9 tag library is deployed, and it is time to create a JSP that uses the new tag library. This JSP is shown in Listing 9.4.

```
<%@ taglib uri="/chapter7" prefix="chapter7" %>
<%@ taglib uri="/chapter9" prefix="chapter9" %>

<html>
<head>
  <title>Custom Tags Demo</title>
</head>

<chapter7:sql driver="sun.jdbc.odbc.JdbcOdbcDriver"
  url="Jdbc:Odbc:contacts"
  resultId="results">
SELECT * FROM CONTACTS
</chapter7:sql>

<table border="1" width="500">
  <tr>
    <th>Username</th><th>First Name</th><th>Last Name</th>
  </tr>
```

Listing 9.4 chapter9.jsp. *(continues)*

```
  <chapter9:sqlIterator resultId="results">

    <tr>

      <td><chapter9:getColumn column="username" /></td>
      <td><chapter9:getColumn column="firstname" /></td>
      <td><chapter9:getColumn column="lastname" /></td>

    </tr>

  </chapter9:sqlIterator>
</table>

</body>
</html>
```

Listing 9.4 chapter9.jsp. *(continued)*

The chapter9.jsp begins with the inclusion of taglib directives that name both the chapter7 and chapter9 tag libraries. The chapter7 library is used for its SQLTag, which performs the SQL query.

The first action performed by this JSP is the evaluation of a <chapter7:sql> tag. This instance of the <chapter7:sql> tag executes the same query used in Chapters 7 and 8, storing the results in a vector referenced by the value of its resultId attribute.

After the <chapter7:sql> tag completes its processing, the <chapter9:sqlIterator> begins its processing. The new implementation of this tag defines only one attribute, resultId, which is used to retrieve the vector of hashtables created by the SQLTag.

Once the <chapter9:sqlIterator> knows what it is going to iterate over, it begins its iteration, repeating the evaluation of its body until there are no more elements in the vector. During each evaluation of the <chapter9:sqlIterator> tag's body, each child <chapter9:getColumn> tag is evaluated, resulting in its replacement with the value retrieved from its parent.

To see the results of this JSP, copy it to the <TOMCAT_HOME>/webapps/customtags/ directory, and open your browser to the following URL:

```
http://localhost:8080/customtags/chapter9.jsp
```

The resulting page should be similar to Figure 7.1 in Chapter 7, "Scripting Variables and Tag Validation."

Summary

This chapter discussed custom tag communications. It described some of the different techniques used to communicate between tags and then focused on tag communications using a parent/child relationship. Chapter 10 begins to discuss the Jakarta custom tag libraries.

CHAPTER

10

Apache Jakarta Taglibs Project

This chapter begins the Apache's Jakarta Taglibs section of this text. It starts by defining the Taglibs project, including its purpose. It then moves on to discuss the steps required to download the taglibs archive and explores the contents of that archive.

What is the Apache Jakarta Taglibs Project?

The Apache Jakarta Taglibs project is an open source project dedicated to the development of a public JSP custom tag library. Its goal is to provide an open source storage area for JSP custom tag libraries.

The Taglibs project contains several individual JSP tag libraries, each packaged according to its purpose. Some of the libraries packaged in this project include the functionality to perform HttpServletRequest and HttpServletResponse processing, PageContext query and modifications, date and time formatting, logging, regular expression processing, and common JDBC queries and updates.

The homepage for the Jakarta Taglibs project contains the latest documentation and status of the project: http://jakarta.apache.org/taglibs/index.html.

Downloading and Examining the Apache Jakarta Tag Libraries Archive

To prepare for the remainder of this section, you need to download a copy of the latest taglib archive, and extract it to your local drive. The examples in this section use the binary distribution of the tag libraries found at http://jakarta.apache.org/taglibs/index.html.

Select the latest release, and download it to your local disk. Once the download is complete, extract the archive to a convenient directory, and open the top-level directory. The archive contents consist of several subdirectories. Each subdirectory contains a tag library JAR file, a tag library descriptor, a documentation WAR file, and an examples WAR file. Table 10.1 describes the use of these files.

Table 10.1 Files Found in the Jakarta Taglibs Binary Archive

FILE	DESCRIPTION
taglib JAR file	Contains the tag handlers associated with each tag library. This file should be copied into the lib directory of the Web application using the tag library.
tag library descriptor	Contains the descriptor for the tag handler of this library. This file should be copied into the /WEB-INF directory of the Web application using the tag library.
Documentation WAR file	Contains the documentation describing the tag library associated with this WAR file. To use the Web application contained in this WAR, copy the file to the <TOMCAT_HOME>/webapps/ directory, and restart Tomcat.
Examples WAR file	Contains examples of how to use the tags contained in this tag library. To use the Web application contained in this WAR, copy the file to the <TOMCAT_HOME>/webapps/ directory, and restart Tomcat.

Summary

This chapter introduced Apache's Jakarta Taglibs project. The remainder of the Jakarta tag libraries section of this text examine the greater part of the libraries contained in this project, but some libraries are not discussed in this book. These libraries have either been released after the writing of this section or have been integrated into the JSP standard tag libraries, which are discussed in the third section of this book.

CHAPTER

11

Request Tag Library

The Jakarta Request tag library provides a group of tags that encapsulate the logic to access the HTTP request information for a particular HTTP request. The request library is most commonly used when retrieving request parameters or attributes. It is also very useful when retrieving and modifying HTTP cookies.

This library is broken into seven logically related tag groupings: generic tags, session tags, attribute tags, cookie tags, header tags, parameter tags, and query string tags. This chapter describes these tags.

NOTE **The Request tag library requires a JSP/servlet container that supports JSP 1.1 and above.**

Configuration

To use the Request tag library in your Web application, you must complete the following steps, substituting for the value *webappname* the name of the Web application that will use the library:

1. Copy the request.tld tag library descriptor (TLD) packaged with this tag library to the <TOMCAT_HOME>/webapps/*webappname*/WEB-INF directory.
2. Copy the request.jar JAR file containing the Request tag library's tag handlers to the <TOMCAT_HOME>/webapps/*webappname*/WEB-INF/lib directory.

3. Add the following <taglib> subelement to the web.xml file of the Web application:

```
<taglib>
  <taglib-uri>
    http://jakarta.apache.org/taglibs/request-1.0
  </taglib-uri>
  <taglib-location>/WEB-INF/request.tld</taglib-location>
</taglib>
```

The following taglib directive must be added to each JSP that will leverage the Request tag library:

```
<%@ taglib
  uri="http://jakarta.apache.org/taglibs/request-1.0"
  prefix="req" %>
```

This directive identifies the URI defined in the previously listed <taglib> element and states that all Request tags should be prefixed with the string *req*.

Generic Tags

The generic request tags encapsulate basic HTTP request functionality. At the time of this writing, this set of request tags includes two unique tags that provide basic request logging and request parsing functionality: log and request.

<req:log />

The log tag is used to print the body content of a tag to the servlet context log. The syntax of the log tag is as follows:

```
<req:log>message to be logged</req:log>
```

There really isn't much to the log tag. It simply takes the content of its body and writes it to the servlet context log. This tag has a body type of JSP, and it contains no attributes.

<req:request />

The request tag retrieves information from the current request. It retrieves the properties of the current request and stores them in a properties object, referenced by the id attribute. The syntax of the request tag is as follows:

```
<req:request id="id of current request properties" />
```

This tag has no body. Its attribute is described in Table 11.1.

Table 11.1 Attribute of the request Tag

ATTRIBUTE	DESCRIPTION
id	Identifies the collection of request properties (required)

The properties returned by the request tag are stored in a properties object containing the request attributes. These properties can be accessed using the standard JSP action <jsp:getProperty> as follows:

```
<jsp:getProperty name="req" property="queryString"/>
```

This tag uses the id of the request tag as the parameter to the name attribute to identify the collection of properties, and the name of the property to retrieve as the parameter to the property attribute. Table 11.2 describes the properties returned by the request tag and the string used to access these properties.

Table 11.2 Properties Returned by the request Tag

PROPERTY	DESCRIPTION
authType	The value of the authentication method.
contextPath	The segment of the request URI that indicates the context path of the request. Examples would be BASIC, SSL, or Form authentication.
method	The HTTP request method of the current request.
pathInfo	The extra path information contained in the URL of the request.
pathTranslated	The extra path information after the servlet name but before the query string.
queryString	The entire query string of the request.
remoteUser	The authenticated login of the user making this request.
requestedSessionId	The session Id request by the calling client.
requestURI	The part of this request's URL from the protocol name up to the query string in the first line of the HTTP request.
requestURL	The URL up to the query string in the first line of the HTTP request.
servletPath	The part of this request's URL that calls the servlet.
characterEncoding	The character encoding type used in the body of this request.
contentLength	The length of the request made available by the input stream, or -1 if the length is not known. This value is in bytes.
contentType	The MIME type of the request body, or "" if the type is not known.
protocol	The name and version of the protocol the request uses in the form; for example, HTTP/1.1.
remoteAddr	The IP address of the requesting client.
remoteHost	The fully qualified host name of the calling client.
serverName	The host name of the server that is servicing the request.
serverPort	The port number on which this request was received.

Using the Generic Tags

This section provides an example of how the generic request tags can be leveraged. Listing 11.1 contains the source for this example.

```
<%@ taglib
  uri="http://jakarta.apache.org/taglibs/request-1.0"
  prefix="req" %>

<html>
  <head>
    <title>Generic Request Tag Library Example</title>
  </head>

  <body>
    <!-- Get the current request properties and place them -->
    <!-- in a scripting variable named reqprops -->
    <req:request id="reqprops" />

    <!-- Log all of the properties to the Context Log. -->
    <req:log>
      AuthType:
        <jsp:getProperty
         name="reqprops"
         property="authType"/>
      ContextPath:
        <jsp:getProperty
         name="reqprops"
         property="contextPath"/>
      Method:
        <jsp:getProperty
       name="reqprops"
       property="method"/>
      PathInfo:
        <jsp:getProperty
         name="reqprops"
         property="pathInfo"/>
      PathTranslated:
        <jsp:getProperty
         name="reqprops"
         property="pathTranslated"/>
      QueryString:
        <jsp:getProperty
       name="reqprops"
```

Listing 11.1 GenericRequestExample.jsp. *(continues)*

```
    property="queryString"/>
    RemoteUser:
      <jsp:getProperty
     name="reqprops"
     property="remoteUser"/>
    RequestedSessionId:
      <jsp:getProperty
     name="reqprops"
     property="requestedSessionId"/>
    RequestURI:
      <jsp:getProperty
     name="reqprops"
     property="requestURI"/>
    RequestURL:
      <jsp:getProperty
     name="reqprops"
     property="requestURL"/>
    ServletPath:
      <jsp:getProperty
     name="reqprops"
     property="servletPath"/>
    CharacterEncoding:
      <jsp:getProperty
     name="reqprops"
     property="characterEncoding"/>
    ContentLength:
      <jsp:getProperty
     name="reqprops"
     property="contentLength"/>
    ContentType:
      <jsp:getProperty
     name="reqprops"
     property="contentType"/>
    Protocol:
      <jsp:getProperty
     name="reqprops"
     property="protocol"/>
    RemoteAddr:
      <jsp:getProperty
     name="reqprops"
     property="remoteAddr"/>
    RemoteHost:
      <jsp:getProperty
     name="reqprops"
```

Listing 11.1 GenericRequestExample.jsp. *(continues)*

```
    property="remoteHost"/>
   Scheme:
     <jsp:getProperty
    name="reqprops"
    property="scheme"/>
   ServerName:
     <jsp:getProperty
    name="reqprops"
    property="serverName"/>
   ServerPort:
     <jsp:getProperty
    name="reqprops"
    property="serverPort"/>
</req:log>

<!-- Output all of the properties to the Client. -->
<h2>Request Properties</h2>
AuthType:
   <jsp:getProperty
     name="reqprops"
 property="authType"/><br>
ContextPath:
   <jsp:getProperty
     name="reqprops"
 property="contextPath"/><br>
Method:
   <jsp:getProperty
     name="reqprops"
 property="method"/><br>
PathInfo:
   <jsp:getProperty
     name="reqprops"
 property="pathInfo"/><br>
PathTranslated:
   <jsp:getProperty
     name="reqprops"
 property="pathTranslated"/><br>
QueryString:
   <jsp:getProperty
     name="reqprops"
 property="queryString"/><br>
RemoteUser:
   <jsp:getProperty
     name="reqprops"
```

Listing 11.1 GenericRequestExample.jsp. *(continues)*

```
     property="remoteUser"/><br>
    RequestedSessionId:
      <jsp:getProperty
        name="reqprops"
     property="requestedSessionId"/><br>
    RequestURI:
      <jsp:getProperty
        name="reqprops"
     property="requestURI"/><br>
    RequestURL:
      <jsp:getProperty
        name="reqprops"
     property="requestURL"/><br>
    ServletPath:
      <jsp:getProperty
        name="reqprops"
     property="servletPath"/><br>
    CharacterEncoding:
      <jsp:getProperty
        name="reqprops"
     property="characterEncoding"/><br>
    ContentLength:
      <jsp:getProperty
        name="reqprops"
     property="contentLength"/><br>
    ContentType:
      <jsp:getProperty
        name="reqprops"
     property="contentType"/><br>
    Protocol:
      <jsp:getProperty
        name="reqprops"
     property="protocol"/><br>
    RemoteAddr:
      <jsp:getProperty
        name="reqprops"
     property="remoteAddr"/><br>
    RemoteHost:
      <jsp:getProperty
        name="reqprops"
     property="remoteHost"/><br>
    Scheme:
      <jsp:getProperty
        name="reqprops"
```

Listing 11.1 GenericRequestExample.jsp. *(continues)*

```
      property="scheme"/><br>
    ServerName:
      <jsp:getProperty
        name="reqprops"
      property="serverName"/><br>
    ServerPort:
      <jsp:getProperty
        name="reqprops"
      property="serverPort"/><br>

  </body>
</html>
```

Listing 11.1 GenericRequestExample.jsp. *(continued)*

To install this example, copy this JSP to the <TOMCAT_HOME>/webapps/*webappname/* directory, and open your browser to the following URL:

```
http://localhost:8080/webappname/GenericRequestExample.jsp
```

If everything went according to plan, you should see a page similar to Figure 11.1.

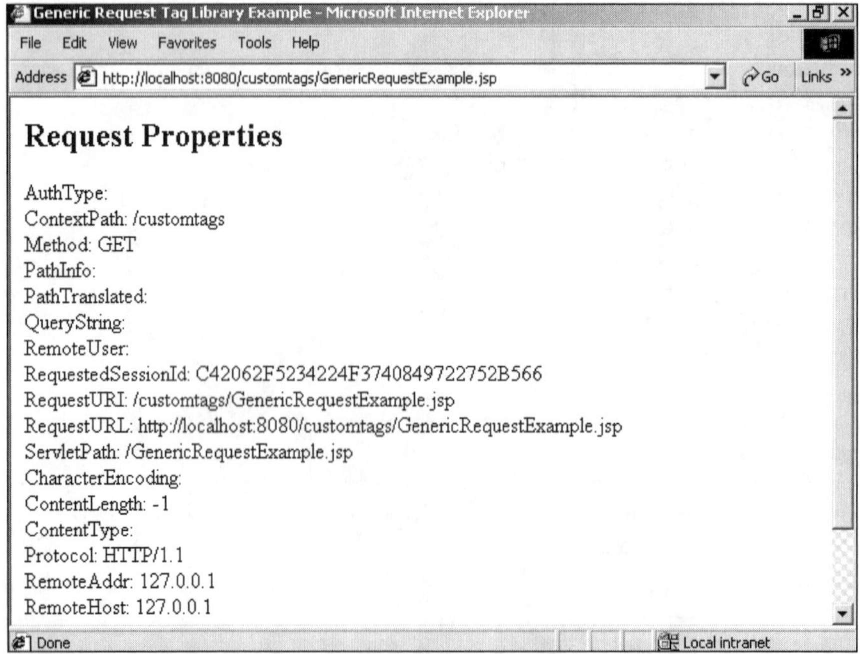

Figure 11.1 Output of the GenericRequestExample.jsp.

This example begins by using the <req:request> tag to create a scripting variable named reqprops, which contains all the properties in the current request. The JSP next logs the properties of this request using the <req:log> tag with an embedded <jsp:getProperty> standard action for each request property. (To view the output of this step, open the most recent localhost_log file, found in the <TOMCAT_HOME>/logs/ directory.) Finally, GenericRequestExample.jsp outputs all the request properties to the Web client.

Session Tags

The session tags in the request library retrieve information from the current HttpSession. At the time of this writing, this group includes five unique tags: isSecure, isSessionFromCookie, isSessionFromURL, isSessionValid, and isUserInRole.

<req:isSecure />

The isSecure tag tests the HttpSession to determine whether the HttpSession is secure. If the HttpSession object is secure, then the isSecure tag will evaluate its body. The syntax of the isSecure tag is as follows:

```
<req:isSecure>
     The requesting session is secure.
</req:isSecure>
```

This tag has a body type of JSP. The attribute of the isSecure tag is described in Table 11.3.

Table 11.3 Attribute of the isSecure Tag

ATTRIBUTE	DESCRIPTION
value	When set to false, causes the tag to evaluate its body if the session is not secure; the default value is true (optional)

NOTE **You should consult your web server to determine how the HttpSession can be secured.**

<req:isSessionFromCookie />

The isSessionFromCookie tag tests the HTTP session to determine whether it is being implemented using cookies. The syntax of the isSessionFromCookie tag is as follows:

```
<req:isSessionFromCookie>
     This session was implemented using a cookie.
</req:isSessionFromCookie>
```

The isSessionFromCookie tag will evaluate its body content if the session uses cookies in its implementation. This tag has a body type of JSP. The attribute of the isSessionFromCookie tag is described in Table 11.4.

Table 11.4 Attribute of the isSessionFromCookie Tag

ATTRIBUTE	DESCRIPTION
value	When set to false, causes the tag to evaluate its body if the session is implemented using cookies; the default value is true (optional)

<req:isSessionFromURL />

The isSessionFromURL tag tests the HTTP session to determine whether it is being implemented using URL rewriting. This tag will evaluate its body content if the session is implemented using URL rewriting. The syntax of the isSessionFromURL tag is as follows:

```
<req:isSessionFromURL >
     This session was implemented using a URL rewriting.
</req:isSessionFromURL >
```

This tag has a body type of JSP. The attribute of the isSessionFromURL tag is described in Table 11.5.

Table 11.5 Attribute of the isSessionFromURL Tag

ATTRIBUTE	DESCRIPTION
value	When set to false, causes the tag to evaluate its body if the session is implemented using URL rewriting; the default value is true (optional)

<req:isSessionValid />

The isSessionValid tag tests the HTTP session to determine whether it has expired or been explicitly invalidated. The syntax of the isSessionValid tag is as follows:

```
<req:isSessionValid >
     This session is still valid.
</req:isSessionValid >
```

The isSessionValid tag will evaluate its body content if the session is still valid. This tag has a body type of JSP. The attribute of the isSessionValid tag is described in Table 11.6.

Table 11.6 Attribute of the isSessionValid Tag

ATTRIBUTE	DESCRIPTION
value	When set to false, causes the tag to evaluate its body if the session in not valid; the default value is true (optional)

<req:isUserInRole />

The isUserInRole tag tests whether the current user has been authenticated with the named role. The syntax of the isUserInRole tag is as follows:

```
<req:isUserInRole role="manager">
  The current user is in the named role.
</req:isUserInRole>
```

The isUserInRole tag will evaluate its body content if the user has been authenticated with the role named in the role attribute.

This tag has a body type of JSP. The attributes of the isUserInRole tag are described in Table 11.7.

Table 11.7 Attributes of the isUserInRole Tag

ATTRIBUTE	DESCRIPTION
role	The role to test the user against (required)
value	When set to false, causes the tag to evaluate its body if the user is not in the named role; the default value is true (optional)

Using the Session Tags

This section presents an example of how the session request tags can be leveraged. Listing 11.2 contains the source for this example.

```
<%@ taglib
  uri="http://jakarta.apache.org/taglibs/request-1.0"
  prefix="req" %>

<html>
  <head>
    <title>Session Request Tag Library Example</title>
  </head>

  <body>

    <!-- Test to see if the session is using HTTPS. -->
    <req:isSecure>
      This request was made using the HTTPS protocol.<br>
    </req:isSecure>

    <!-- Test to see if the session is not using HTTPS. -->
    <req:isSecure value="false">
      This request was not made using the HTTPS protocol.<br>
```

Listing 11.2 SessionRequestExample.jsp. *(continues)*

```
    </req:isSecure>

    <!-- Test to see if the session was implemented -->
    <!-- using cookies. -->
    <req:isSessionFromCookie>
      This session was implemented using cookies.<br>
    </req:isSessionFromCookie>

    <!-- Test to see if the session was not implemented -->
    <!-- using cookies. -->
    <req:isSessionFromCookie value="false">
      This session was not implemented using cookies.<br>
    </req:isSessionFromCookie>

    <!-- Test to see if the session was implemented -->
    <!-- using URL rewriting. -->
    <req:isSessionFromUrl>
      This session was implemented using Url rewriting.<br>
    </req:isSessionFromUrl>

    <!-- Test to see if the session was not implemented -->
    <!-- using URL rewriting. -->
    <req:isSessionFromUrl value="false">
      This session was not implemented using Url rewriting.<br>
    </req:isSessionFromUrl>


  </body>
</html>
```

Listing 11.2 SessionRequestExample.jsp. *(continued)*

To test this example, copy the JSP to the <TOMCAT_HOME>/webapps/*webappname*/ directory, and open your browser to the following URL:

```
http://localhost:8080/webappname/SessionRequestExample.jsp
```

You should see a page similar to Figure 11.2.

This example begins by using two instances of the <req:isSecure> tag, which test the security of the request protocol. If the request protocol is HTTPS, then the body of the tag will be evaluated. The example uses one instance of the tag that evaluates its body if the request is secure, and a second instance that evaluates its body if the request is not secure.

The next tag, <req:isSessionFromCookie>, tests the session implementation method. The example uses two instances of this tag: The first evaluates its body if the session is implemented using cookies, and the second evaluates its body if the session is not implemented using cookies.

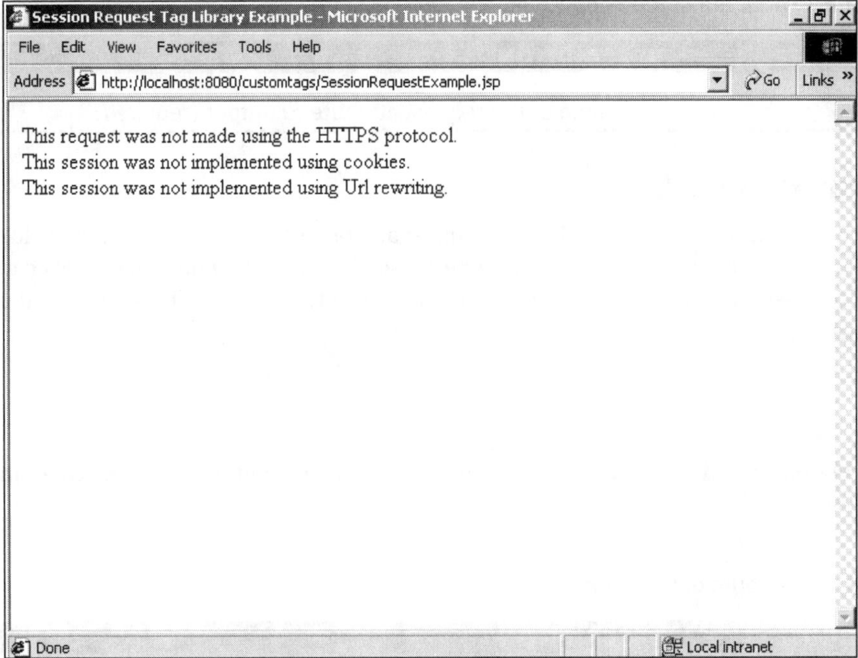

Figure 11.2 Output of the SessionRequestExample.jsp.

Finally, the <req:isSessionFromUrl> tag also tests the session implementation method. This tag evaluates its body if the session is implemented using URL rewriting. This example uses two instances of this tag: The first evaluates its body if the session is implemented using URL rewriting, and the second evaluates its body if the session is not implemented using URL rewriting.

Attribute Tags

The attribute tags in the Request tag library can be used to retrieve and modify information from the set of attributes bound to the current request. At the time of this writing, the attribute set of request tags includes six unique tags: attribute, attributes, equalsAttribute, existsAttribute, removeAttribute, and setAttribute.

<req:attribute />

The attribute tag outputs the value of a named request attribute. The syntax of the attribute tag is as follows:

```
<req:attribute name="request attribute name" />
```

This tag has no body. The attribute of the attribute tag is described in Table 11.8.

Table 11.8 Attribute of the attribute Tag

ATTRIBUTE	DESCRIPTION
name	The name of the request attribute to output (required)

<req:attributes />

The attributes tag loops through all of the request attributes, exposing each name/value pair as a scripting variable matching the value passed in the id attribute. The values can then be accessed using the JSP standard action <jsp:getProperty>. The syntax of the attributes tag is as follows:

```
<req:attributes id="scripting variable name" >
  Evaluated Body
<req:attributes/>
```

This tag has a body type of JSP. The attribute of the attributes tag is described in Table 11.9.

Table 11.9 Attribute of the attributes Tag

ATTRIBUTE	DESCRIPTION
id	The scripting variable that each name/value pair will be referenced as (required)

<req:equalsAttribute />

The equalsAttribute tag evaluates its body if the request attribute value equals the match attribute. The syntax of the equalsAttribute tag is as follows:

```
<req:equalsAttribute name="request attribute name"
  match="the value to compare the attribute to">
  Evaluated Body
<req:attributes/>
```

This tag has a body type of JSP. The attributes of the equalsAttribute tag are described in Table 11.10.

Table 11.10 Attributes of the equalsAttribute Tag

ATTRIBUTE	DESCRIPTION
name	The request attribute to compare (required)
value	When set to false, causes the tag to evaluate its body if there is no match; the default value is true (optional)
match	The string value to compare the attribute to (required)
ignoreCase	If false (the default), checks for equality, taking case into account; otherwise, the comparison ignores case

<req:existsAttribute />

The existsAttribute tag evaluates its body if the named request attribute exists in the request. The syntax of the existsAttribute tag is as follows:

```
<req:existsAttribute name="request attribute name">
  Evaluated Body
<req:existsAttribute />
```

This tag has a body type of JSP. The attributes of the existsAttribute tag are described in Table 11.11.

Table 11.11 Attributes of the existsAttribute Tag

ATTRIBUTE	DESCRIPTION
name	The request attribute to check for (required)
value	When set to false, causes the tag to evaluate its body if the named attribute does not exist in the request; the default value is true (optional)

<req:removeAttribute />

The removeAttribute tag removes the named attribute from the request. The syntax of the removeAttribute tag is as follows:

```
<req:removeAttribute name="request attribute name" />
```

This tag has no body. The attribute of the removeAttribute tag is described in Table 11.12.

Table 11.12 Attribute of the removeAttribute Tag

ATTRIBUTE	DESCRIPTION
name	The request attribute to remove from the request (required)

<req:setAttribute />

The setAttribute tag sets the value of the named request attribute to the content of the tag's body. The syntax of the setAttribute tag is as follows:

```
<req:setAttribute name="request attribute name" />
  The value of the new attribute
</req:setAttribute>
```

This tag has a body type of JSP. The attribute of the setAttribute tag is described in Table 11.13.

Table 11.13 Attribute of the setAttribute Tag

ATTRIBUTE	DESCRIPTION
name	The request attribute to be added to the request (required)

Using the Attribute Tags

This section presents an example of how the attribute tags in the request library can be leveraged. Listing 11.3 contains the source for this example.

```
<%@ taglib
  uri="http://jakarta.apache.org/taglibs/request-1.0"
  prefix="req" %>

<html>
  <head>
    <title>Attribute Request Tag Library Example</title>
  </head>

  <body>
  <!-- Use the setAttribute tag to set the username -->
  <!-- to the request. -->
  <req:setAttribute name="username">Bob</req:setAttribute>


  <!-- Check for the existence of username -->
  <req:existsAttribute name="username">
    <!-- If it exists, Test the value of username -->
    <req:equalsAttribute name="username" match="Bob">
      <!-- If the value of the request attribute equals -->
      <!-- Bob, then use the attribute tag to retrieve -->
      <!-- the username value. -->
      Welcome: <req:attribute name="username"/><br>
    </req:equalsAttribute>
  </req:existsAttribute>

  <h2> Display all of the request attributes.</h2>
  <req:attributes id="attrloop">
    Attribute Name: <jsp:getProperty name="attrloop"
      property="name"/>
    :
    Attribute Value: <jsp:getProperty name="attrloop"
      property="attribute"/>
    <br>
  </req:attributes>

  <!-- remove the username attribute -->
  <req:removeAttribute name="username" />
```

Listing 11.3 AttributeRequestExample.jsp. *(continues)*

```
<h2>Display all of the request attributes
after removing the username.</h2>
<req:attributes id="attrloop">
  Attribute Name: <jsp:getProperty name="attrloop"
    property="name"/>
  :
  Attribute Value: <jsp:getProperty name="attrloop"
    property="attribute"/>
  <br>
</req:attributes>

</body>
</html>
```

Listing 11.3 AttributeRequestExample.jsp. *(continued)*

To see this example in action, be sure the page tag library is installed, and copy this JSP to the <TOMCAT_HOME>/webapps/*webappname/* directory. Open your browser to the following URL:

http://localhost:8080/*webappname*/AttributeRequestExample.jsp

The resulting page should be similar to Figure 11.3.

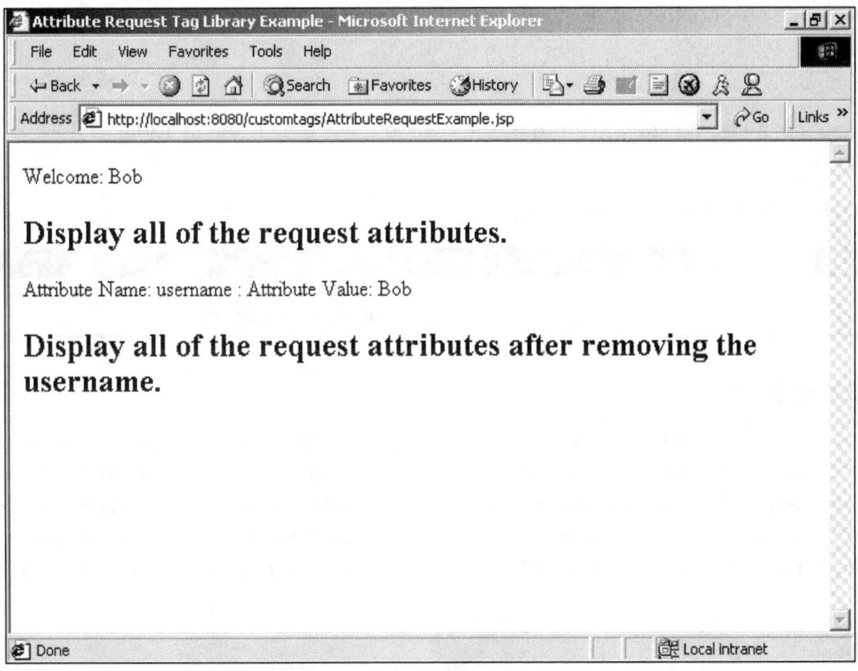

Figure 11.3 Output of the AttributeRequestExample.jsp.

This example begins by using the <req:setAttribute> tag to set a request level attribute that is bound to the key username, with a value of *Bob*. It then turns around and checks for the existence of the username attribute, using the <req:existsAttribute> tag. If the username exists, the JSP then checks the value of the attribute using <req:equalsAttribute>. If the username attribute has a value of *Bob*, which it does in this example, the JSP displays the text *Welcome: Bob*.

Next, AttributeRequestExample.jsp lists all the attributes currently in the HttpServletRequest. It does so using the <req:attributes> tag, which prints all the HttpServletRequest attributes. Unless you have added other attributes to the HttpServletRequest, you should see a single request attribute username.

After the JSP has listed the attributes of the HttpServletRequest, including the username attribute, it removes the username attribute using the <req:removeAttribute> tag. The JSP's final step is to redisplay the list of HttpServletRequest attributes. Note that this final list does not contain the username attribute.

Cookie Tags

The cookie tags in the Request tag library can be used to retrieve HTTP cookie information that has been bound to the current client. At the time of this writing, this set includes four unique tags: cookie, cookies, equalsCookie, and existsCookie.

<req:cookie />

The cookie tag outputs the value of a named HTTP cookie. The syntax of the cookie tag is as follows:

```
<req:cookie name="cookie name" />
```

This tag has no body. The attribute of the cookie tag is described in Table 11.14.

Table 11.14 Attribute of the cookie Tag

ATTRIBUTE	DESCRIPTION
name	The name of the cookie to output (required)

<req:cookies />

The cookies tag loops through all the HTTP request cookies, exposing a scripting variable containing the properties of each cookie in the request. If the name attribute is used, then the cookies tag exposes only the named cookie. The scripting variable is referenced using the value passed in the id attribute. The values can then be accessed using the JSP standard action <jsp:getProperty>. The syntax of the cookies tag is as follows:

```
<req:cookies id="scripting variable name" >
  <jsp:getProperty name="id attribute from cookies tag" />
<req:cookies/>
```

This tag has a body type of JSP. The attributes of the cookies tag are described in Table 11.15.

Table 11.15 Attributes of the cookies Tag

ATTRIBUTE	DESCRIPTION
id	The scripting variable that each name/value pair will be referenced as (required)
name	The cookie to retrieve from the request (optional)

The properties exposed by the cookies tag are described in Table 11.16.

Table 11.16 Properties Exposed by the cookies Tag

PROPERTYDESCRIPTION	
id	The scripting variable that each name/value pair will be referenced as (required)
comment	The comment associated with the retrieved cookie
domain	The domain name of the cookie
maxAge	An integer representing the length of time, in seconds, that a cookie will exist
name	The name of the cookie retrieved from the request
path	The server path of the retrieved cookie
value	The value of the retrieved cookie
version	The protocol used to implement the cookie

<req:equalsCookie />

The equalsCookie tag evaluates its body if the cookie value equals the match attribute. The syntax of the equalsCookie tag is as follows:

```
<req:equalsCookie name="cookie name"
  match="the value to compare the cookie to">
  Evaluated Body
<req:equalsCookie/>
```

This tag has a body type of JSP. The attributes of the equalsCookie tag are described in Table 11.17.

Table 11.17 Attributes of the equalsCookie Tag

ATTRIBUTE	DESCRIPTION
name	The cookie to compare (required)

Table 11.17 Attributes of the equalsCookie Tag *(continued)*

ATTRIBUTE	DESCRIPTION
value	When set to false, causes the tag to evaluate its body if there is no match; the default value is true (optional)
match	The string value to compare the cookie to (required)
ignoreCase	If false (the default), checks for equality, taking case into account; otherwise, the comparison ignores case (optional)

<req:existsCookie />

The existsCookie tag evaluates its body if the named cookie exists in the request. The syntax of the existsCookie tag is as follows:

```
<req:existsCookie name="cookie name">
  Evaluated Body
<req:existsCookie />
```

This tag has a body type of JSP. The attributes of the existsCookie tag are described in Table 11.18.

Table 11.18 Attributes of the existsCookie Tag

ATTRIBUTE	DESCRIPTION
name	The cookie to test for (required)
value	When set to false, causes the tag to evaluate its body if the named cookie does not exist in the request; the default value is true (optional)

Using the Cookie Tags

This section presents an example of how the cookie tags in the request library can be leveraged. Listing 11.4 contains the source for this example.

```
<%@ page import="javax.servlet.http.Cookie" %>

<%@ taglib
  uri="http://jakarta.apache.org/taglibs/request-1.0"
  prefix="req" %>

<html>
  <head>
    <title>Cookie Request Tag Library Example</title>
```

Listing 11.4 CookieRequestExample.jsp. *(continues)*

```
  </head>

  <body>

  <%
    Cookie cookie = new Cookie("username", "Bob");
    response.addCookie(cookie);
  %>

  <!-- Check for the existence of username -->
  <req:existsCookie name="username">
    <!-- If it exists, Test the value of username -->
    <req:equalsCookie name="username" match="Bob">
      <!-- If the value of the request level cookie equals -->
      <!-- Bob, then use the cookie tag to retrieve -->
      <!-- the username value. -->
      Welcome: <req:cookie name="username"/><br>
    </req:equalsCookie>
  </req:existsCookie>

  <h2> Display all of the request cookies.</h2>
  <req:cookies id="cookieloop">
    Cookie Name: <jsp:getProperty name="cookieloop"
      property="name"/>
      :
    Cookie Value: <jsp:getProperty name="cookieloop"
      property="value"/>
    <br>
  </req:cookies>

  </body>
</html>
```

Listing 11.4 CookieRequestExample.jsp. *(continued)*

To test this example, copy the JSP to the <TOMCAT_HOME>/webapps/*webapp-name*/ directory and open your browser to the following URL:

```
http://localhost:8080/webappname/CookieRequestExample.jsp
```

You should see a page similar to Figure 11.4.

This example begins by creating a new cookie and adding it to the HttpServletResponse using a scriptlet. The created cookie contains a key of username, with a value of *Bob*.

After the username cookie is created, the JSP uses <req:existsCookie> to test for the existence of the cookie. On the first request, the cookie does not exist; therefore, the body of <req:existsCookie> will not be evaluated.

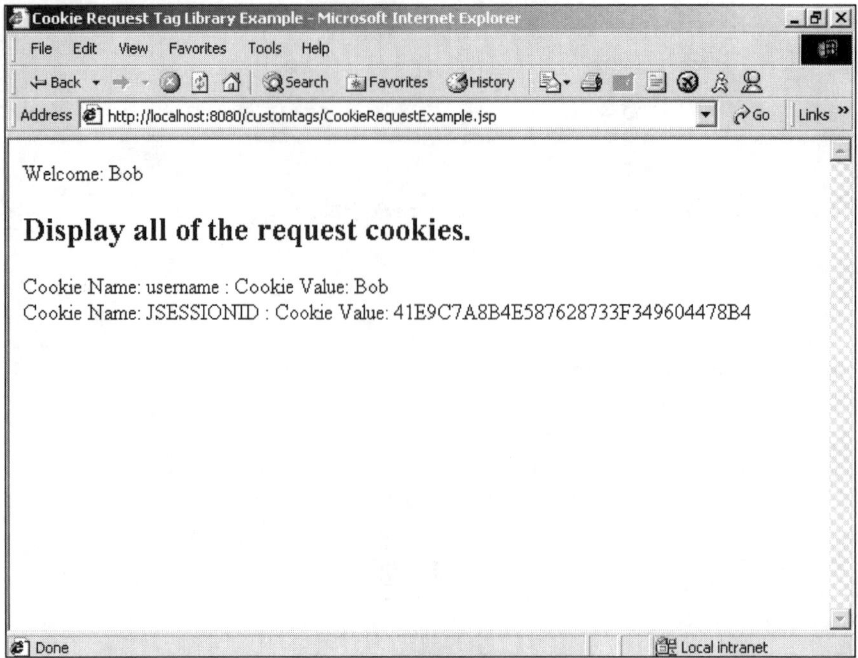

Figure 11.4 Output of the CookieRequestExample.jsp.

Next, the JSP uses the <req:cookies> tag to list all the cookies associated with this client. Note that at this time, the username cookie is not included in this list because the cookie is sent back to the client in the response. It will become visible with subsequent requests.

If you click Refresh, the JSP will perform much the same as the first request. The only difference will be that this time, the <req:existsCookie> tag will evaluate its body, because the request includes the username cookie.

The body of <req:existsCookie> contains an instance of the <req:equalsCookie> tag, which will test the value of the cookie for the string include in the match attribute. If the match attribute's value equals the value of the username cookie, then the <req:equalsCookie> tag will evaluate its body. In this case, the cookie value and the match value are equal, so the tag evaluates its body.

The body of the <req:equalsCookie> tag contains the string Welcome: plus a single instance of the <req:cookie> tag. This tag simply outputs the value of the username cookie. This evaluation results in the text *Welcome: Bob* being sent back to the client.

Finally, this JSP again prints the list of cookies in the client request. Note that this time the username cookie appears in the list.

Header Tags

The header tags in the Request tag library can be used to retrieve HTTP header information about the current request. At the time of this writing, this set includes five unique tags: header, headers, equalsHeader, existsHeader, and headerValues.

<req:header />

The header tag outputs the value of a named HTTP request header. The syntax of the header tag is as follows:

```
<req:header name="request header name" />
```

This tag has no body. The attribute of the header tag is described in Table 11.19.

Table 11.19 Attribute of the header Tag

ATTRIBUTE	DESCRIPTION
name	The name of the request header to output (required)

<req:headers />

The headers tag loops through all the HTTP request headers, exposing a scripting variable containing the properties of each header in the request. If the name attribute is used, then the headers tag exposes only the named header. The scripting variable is referenced using the value passed in the id attribute. The values can then be accessed using the JSP standard action <jsp:getProperty>. The syntax of the headers tag is as follows:

```
<req:headers id="scripting variable name" >
  <jsp:getProperty name="id attribute from headers tag"
    property="name of header property as described below" />
<req:headers/>
```

This tag has a body type of JSP. The attributes of the headers tag are described in Table 11.20. The properties exposed by the headers tag are described in Table 11.21.

Table 11.20 Attributes of the headers Tag

ATTRIBUTE	DESCRIPTION
id	The scripting variable that each name/value pair will be referenced as (required)
name	The header to retrieve from the request (optional)

Table 11.21 Properties Exposed by the headers Tag

PROPERTY	DESCRIPTION
name	The name of the header retrieved from the request
header	The value of the retrieved header
dateHeader	The header value for a date, measured in milliseconds since midnight January 1, 1970 GMT
intHeader	The request header value for an integer

<req:equalsHeader />

The equalsHeader tag evaluates its body if the header value equals the match attribute. The syntax of the equalsHeader tag is as follows:

```
<req:equalsHeader name="header name"
  match="the value to compare the header to">
  Evaluated Body
</req:equalsHeader>
```

This tag has a body type of JSP. The attributes of the equalsHeader tag are described in Table 11.22.

Table 11.22 Attributes of the equalsHeader Tag

ATTRIBUTE	DESCRIPTION
name	The header to compare (required)
value	When set to false, causes the tag to evaluate its body if there is no match; the default value is true (optional)
match	The string value to compare the header to (required)
ignoreCase	If false (the default), checks for equality, taking case into account; otherwise, the comparison ignores case (optional)

<req:existsHeader />

The existsHeader tag evaluates its body if the named header exists in the request. The syntax of the existsHeader tag is as follows:

```
<req:existsHeader name="header name">
  Evaluated Body
</req:existsHeader>
```

This tag has a body type of JSP. The attributes of the existsHeader tag are described in Table 11.23.

Table 11.23 Attributes of the existsHeader Tag

ATTRIBUTE	DESCRIPTION
name	The header to test for (required)
value	When set to false, causes the tag to evaluate its body if the named header does not exist in the request; the default value is true (optional)

<req:headerValues />

The headerValues tag loops through all the HTTP request headers that have multiple values, exposing a scripting variable containing the properties of the named header. The scripting variable is referenced using the value passed in the id attribute. The values can then be accessed using the JSP standard action <jsp:getProperty>. The syntax of the headerValues tag is as follows:

```
<req:headers id="id of headers scripting variable"
  name="name of header to retrieve">
  <req:headerValues id="scripting variable id">
    <jsp:getProperty name="id attribute from headerValues"
      property="header" />
  </req:headerValues>
</req:headers>
```

NOTE **This tag must be a child of the <headers> tag.**

This tag has a body type of JSP. The attribute of the headerValues tag is described in Table 11.24. The property exposed by the headerValues tag is described in Table 11.25.

Table 11.24 Attribute of the headerValues Tag

ATTRIBUTE	DESCRIPTION
id	The scripting variable that each name/value pair will be referenced as (required)

Table 11.25 Property Exposed by the headerValues Tag

PROPERTY	DESCRIPTION
header	The value of the multivalued header retrieved from the request

Using the Header Tags

This section provides an example of how the tags in the header requests library can be leveraged. Listing 11.5 contains the source for this example.

```
<%@ taglib
  uri="http://jakarta.apache.org/taglibs/request-1.0"
  prefix="req" %>

<html>
  <head>
    <title>Header Request Tag Library Example</title>
  </head>

  <body>
```

Listing 11.5 HeadersRequestExample.jsp. *(continues)*

```
    <!-- List all the headers in the current request -->
    <h2>Request Headers</h2>
    <req:headers id="hdrs1">
       <jsp:getProperty name="hdrs1" property="name"/>
       =
       <jsp:getProperty name="hdrs1" property="header"/><br>
    </req:headers>

    <!-- See if accept-language Header exists -->
    <h2>The Accepted Language</h2>
    <req:existsHeader name="accept-language">
      <req:header name="accept-language"/>
    </req:existsHeader>

    <!-- Check for multiple encoding values -->
    <h2>Encoding Headers</h2>
    <req:headers id="hdrs2"
      name="accept-encoding">
      <req:headerValues id="hvalues">
        <jsp:getProperty name="hvalues"
          property="header" /><br>
      </req:headerValues>
    </req:headers>

  </body>
</html
```

Listing 11.5 HeadersRequestExample.jsp. *(continued)*

To see this example in action, copy the JSP to the <TOMCAT_HOME>/webapps/*webappname/* directory, and open your browser to the following URL:

```
http://localhost:8080/webappname/HeadersRequestExample.jsp
```

The resulting page should be similar to Figure 11.5.

This example begins by outputting all the HTTP headers associated with this request. It does so using the <req:headers> tag, which creates a scripting variable that references the name and value of the current header in the list. These names and values are then printed to the client using the <jsp:getProperty> standard action.

Next, this JSP tests for the existence of the accept-language header. If this header is in the request (which it is, in this case), then the body of the <req:existsHeader> tag is evaluated. The body of this tag prints the value of the accept-language header using the <req:header> tag.

Finally, HeadersRequestExample.jsp prints out the values of the accept-encoding header. It does so using the <req:headerValues> tag, which prints all the values of a named request header. This example includes only one accept-encoding header, gzip, deflate.

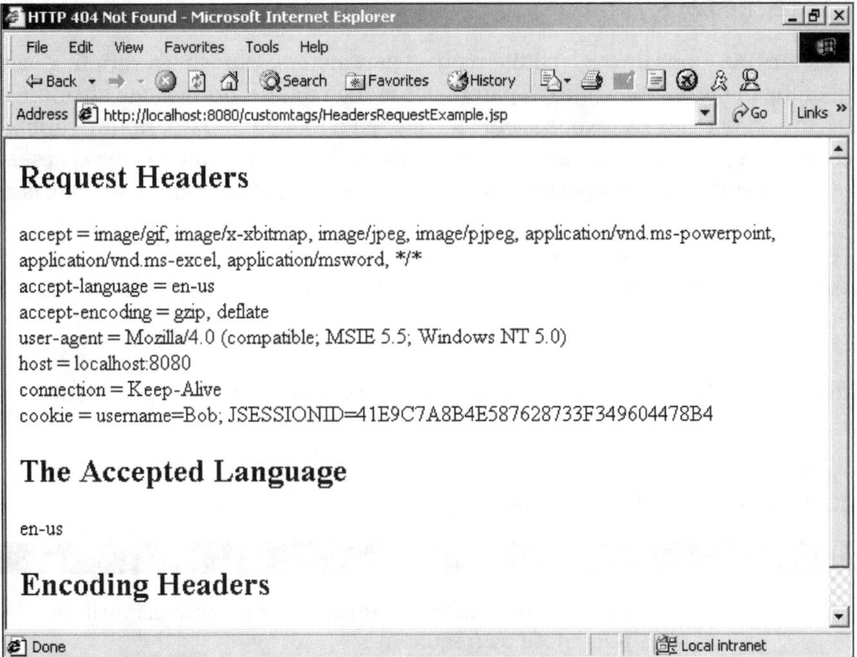

Figure 11.5 Output of the HeadersRequestExample.jsp.

Parameter Tags

The parameter tags in the Request tag library can be used to retrieve information about the current set of parameters bound to the current request. At the time of this writing, this set includes five unique tags: parameter, parameters, equalsParameter, existsParameter, and parameterValues.

<req:parameter />

The parameter tag outputs the value of a named HTTP request parameter. The syntax of the parameter tag is as follows:

```
<req:parameter name="request parameter name" />
```

This tag has no body. The attribute of the parameter tag is described in Table 11.26.

Table 11.26 Attribute of the parameter Tag

ATTRIBUTE	DESCRIPTION
name	The name of the request parameter to output (required)

<req:parameters />

The parameters tag loops through all the request parameters, exposing a scripting variable containing the properties of each parameter in the request. If the name attribute is used, then the parameters tag exposes only the named parameter. The scripting variable is referenced using the value passed in the id attribute. The values can then be accessed using the JSP standard action <jsp:getProperty>. The syntax of the parameters tag is as follows:

```
<req:parameters id="scripting variable name" >
  <jsp:getProperty name="id attribute from parameters tag"
property="name or value"/>
</req:parameters>
```

This tag has a body type of JSP. The attributes of the parameters tag are described in Table 11.27.

Table 11.27 Attributes of the parameters Tag

ATTRIBUTE	DESCRIPTION
id	The scripting variable that each name/value pair will be referenced as (required)
name	The parameter to retrieve from the request (optional)

The properties exposed by the parameters tag are described in Table 11.28.

Table 11.28 Properties Exposed by the parameters Tag

PROPERTY	DESCRIPTION
name	The name of the parameter retrieved from the request
value	The value of the retrieved parameter

<req:equalsParameter />

The equalsParameter tag evaluates its body if the parameter value equals the match attribute. The syntax of the equalsParameter tag is as follows:

```
<req:equalsParameter name="parameter name"
  match="the value to compare the parameter to">
  Evaluated Body
<req:equalsParameter/>
```

This tag has a body type of JSP. The attributes of the equalsParameter tag are described in Table 11.29.

Table 11.29 Attributes of the equalsParameter Tag

ATTRIBUTE	DESCRIPTION
name	The parameter to compare (required)
value	When set to false, causes the tag to evaluate its body if there is no match; the default value is true (optional)
match	The string value to compare the parameter to (required)
ignoreCase	If false (the default), checks for equality, taking case into account; otherwise, the comparison ignores case (optional)

<req:existsParameter />

The existsParameter tag evaluates its body if the named parameter exists in the request. The syntax of the existsParameter tag is as follows:

```
<req:existsParameter name="parameter name">
  Evaluated Body
<req:existsParameter />
```

This tag has a body type of JSP. The attributes of the existsParameter tag are described in Table 11.30.

Table 11.30 Attributes of the existsParameter Tag

ATTRIBUTE	DESCRIPTION
name	The parameter to test for (required)
value	When set to false, causes the tag to evaluate its body if the named parameter does not exist in the request; the default value is true (optional)

<req:parameterValues />

The parameterValues tag loops through an HTTP request parameter that has multiple values, exposing a scripting variable containing the properties of the named parameter. The scripting variable is referenced using the value passed in the id attribute. The values can then be accessed using the JSP standard action <jsp:getProperty>. The syntax of the parameterValues tag is as follows:

```
<req:parameters id="id of parameter scripting variable"
  name="name of parameter to retrieve">
  <req:parameterValues id="scripting variable id">
    <jsp:getProperty name="id attribute from parameterValues"
      property="value" />
  </req:parameterValues>
</req:parameters>
```

NOTE **This tag must be a child of the <parameters> tag.**

This tag has a body type of JSP. The attribute of the parameterValues tag is described in Table 11.31. The property exposed by the parameterValues tag is described in Table 11.32.

Table 11.31 Attribute of the parameterValues Tag

ATTRIBUTE	DESCRIPTION
id	The scripting variable that each name/value pair will be referenced as(required)

Table 11.32 Property Exposed by the parameterValues Tag

PROPERTY	DESCRIPTION
value	The value of the multivalued parameter retrieved from the request (optional)

Using the Parameter Tags

This section presents an example of how the parameter tags in the request library can be leveraged. Listing 11.6 contains the source for this example.

```
<%@ taglib
  uri="http://jakarta.apache.org/taglibs/request-1.0"
  prefix="req" %>

<html>
  <head>
    <title>Parameters Request Tag Library Example</title>
  </head>

  <body>

    <!-- List all the parameters in the current request -->
    <h2>Request Parameters</h2>
    <req:parameters id="params1">
       <jsp:getProperty name="params1" property="name"/>
       =
       <jsp:getProperty name="params1" property="value"/><br>
    </req:parameters>
```

Listing 11.6 ParametersRequestExample.jsp. *(continues)*

```
    <!-- See if username parameter exists -->
    <h2>Print the username parameter if it exists.</h2>
    <req:existsParameter name="username">
      <req:parameter name="username"/>
    </req:existsParameter>

    <!-- Print role parameter values -->
    <h2>Role Parameter Values</h2>
    <req:parameters id="params2"
      name="role">
      <req:parameterValues id="pvalues">
        <jsp:getProperty name="pvalues"
          property="value" /><br>
      </req:parameterValues>
    </req:parameters>

  </body>
</html>
```

Listing 11.6 ParametersRequestExample.jsp. *(continued)*

To see this example in action, copy the JSP to the <TOMCAT_HOME>/webapps/*webappname*/ directory, and open your browser to the following URL:

```
http://localhost:8080/webappname/ParametersRequestExample.jsp?username=Bob
&role=manager&role=user
```

You should see a page similar to Figure 11.6.

This example begins by retrieving all the single-value request parameters, using the <req:parameters> tag. The parameters printed using the URL given earlier are username and role. Note that only the first role parameter is printed, because the parameters tag retrieves only single-value parameters.

Next, ParametersRequestExample.jsp tests for the existence of the username parameter, using the <req:existsParameter> tag. With this occurrence of the <req:existsParameter> tag, the username parameter exists; therefore, the body of this tag will be evaluated. The body of the tag contains a single instance of the <jsp:getProperty> tag, which will print the value of the retrieved username parameter.

Finally, the JSP prints out the values of the role parameter. It does so using the <req:parameterValues> tag, which prints all the values of a named request parameter. This example includes two values for the role parameter: manager and user.

Query String Tags

The query string tags in the Request tag library can be used to retrieve the HTTP QUERY_STRING associated with the current request. At the time of this writing, this set includes three unique tags: queryString, queryStrings, and existsQueryString.

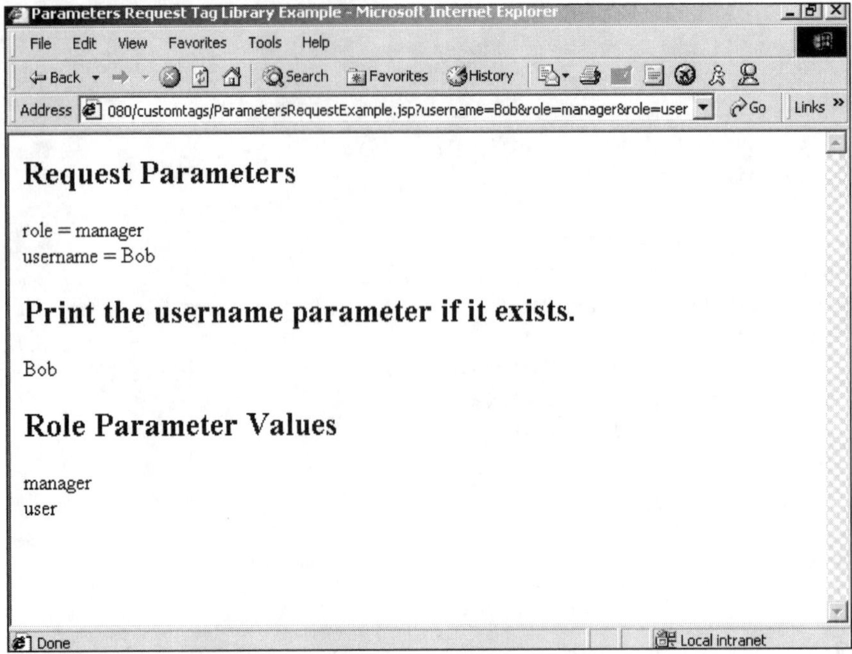

Figure 11.6 Output of the ParametersRequestExample.jsp.

<req:queryString />

The queryString tag outputs the value of a named HTTP QUERY_STRING parameter. The syntax of the queryString tag is as follows:

```
<req:queryString name="QUERY_STRING parameter name" />
```

This tag has no body. The attribute of the queryString tag is described in Table 11.33.

Table 11.33 Attribute of the queryString Tag

ATTRIBUTE	DESCRIPTION
name	The name of the QUERY_STRING parameter to output (required)

<req:queryStrings />

The queryStrings tag loops through all the QUERY_STRING parameters, exposing a scripting variable containing the properties of each QUERY_STRING parameter in the request. If the name attribute is used, then the queryStrings tag will expose only the named parameter. The scripting variable is referenced using the value passed in the id attribute. The values can then be accessed using the JSP standard action <jsp:getProperty>. The syntax of the queryStrings tag is as follows:

```
<req:queryStrings id="scripting variable name" >
  <jsp:getProperty name="id attribute from queryStrings tag" />
</req:queryStrings>
```

This tag has a body type of JSP. The attributes of the queryStrings tag are described in Table 11.34. The properties exposed by the queryStrings tag are described in Table 11.35.

Table 11.34 Attributes of the queryStrings Tag

ATTRIBUTE	DESCRIPTION
id	The scripting variable that each name/value pair will be referenced as (required)
name	The QUERY_STRING parameter to retrieve from the request (optional)

Table 11.35 Properties Exposed by the queryStrings Tag

PROPERTY	DESCRIPTION
name	The name of the QUERY_STRING parameter retrieved from the request
value	The value of the retrieved QUERY_STRING parameter
queryString	The entire QUERY_STRING parameter, including its name and value

<req:existsQueryString />

The existsQueryString tag evaluates its body, if the named QUERY_STRING parameter exists in the request. The syntax of the existsQueryString tag is as follows:

```
<req:existsQueryString name="QUERY_STRING parameter name">
  Evaluated Body
<req:existsQueryString />
```

This tag has a body type of JSP. The attributes of the existsQueryString tag are described in Table 11.36.

Table 11.36 Attributes of the existsQueryString Tag

ATTRIBUTE	DESCRIPTION
name	The QUERY_STRING parameter to test for (required)
value	When set to false, causes the tag to evaluate its body if the named QUERY_STRING parameter does not exist in the request; the default value is true (optional)

Using the Query String Tags

This section provides an example of how the tags in the query string library can be leveraged. Listing 11.7 contains the source for this example.

```
<%@ taglib
  uri="http://jakarta.apache.org/taglibs/request-1.0"
  prefix="req" %>

<html>
  <head>
    <title>QueryString Request Tag Library Example</title>
  </head>

  <body>

    <!-- List all the parameters in the current request -->
    <h2>QueryString Parameters</h2>
    <req:queryStrings id="strings">
        <h3>Parameter Name : Value</h3>
        <jsp:getProperty name="strings" property="name"/>
        :
        <jsp:getProperty name="strings" property="value"/><br>
        <h3>Query String Value</h3>
        <jsp:getProperty name="strings"
          property="queryString"/><br>
    </req:queryStrings>

    <!-- See if username queryString parameter exists -->
    <h2>Print the username parameter if it exists.</h2>
    <req:existsQueryString name="username">
      <req:queryString name="username"/>
    </req:existsQueryString>

  </body>
</html>
```

Listing 11.7 QueryStringRequestExample.jsp.

To see this example in action, copy the JSP to the <TOMCAT_HOME>/webapps/*webappname/* directory, and open your browser to the following URL:

```
http://localhost:8080/webappname/QueryStringRequestExample.jsp?username=
Bob&role=manager&role=user
```

You should see a page similar to Figure 11.7.

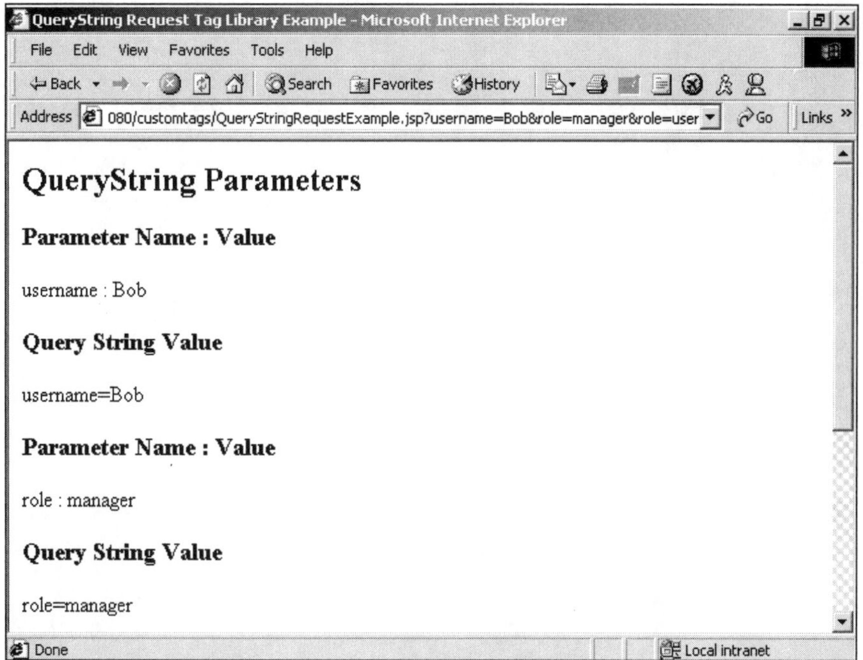

Figure 11.7 Output of the QueryStringRequestExample.jsp.

This example begins by retrieving all the QUERY_STRING parameters, using the <req:queryStrings> tag. The properties printed for each parameter include the parameter name, the parameter value, and the query string equivalent of the name/value pair.

The JSP then tests for the existence of the username QUERY_STRING parameter, using the <req:existsQueryString> tag. Because the username parameter is part of the query string, the body of this tag will be evaluated; as a result, the value of the retrieved username parameter is printed.

CHAPTER

12

Response Tag Library

This chapter examines the Jakarta Response tag library. This tag library contains tags that can be used to modify the HttpResponse object for a given request. The goal of this tag library is to allow a JSP developer to replace any HttpResponse object scriptlet code contained in a JSP with tags from this library. The Response library is broken into three logically related tag groupings: generic response tags, cookie tags, and header tags.

NOTE **This tag library requires a JSP/servlet container that supports JSP 1.1 and above.**

Configuration

To use the Response tag library in a Web application, complete the following steps, substituting for *webappname* the name of the Web application that will be using the library:

1. Copy the response.tld tag library descriptor (TLD) packaged with this tag library to the <TOMCAT_HOME>/webapps/*webappname*/WEB-INF directory.
2. Copy the response.jar JAR file containing the Response tag library's tag handlers to the <TOMCAT_HOME>/webapps/*webappname*/WEB-INF/lib directory.
3. Add the following <taglib> subelement to the web.xml file of the Web application:

```
<taglib>
  <taglib-uri>
```

```
    http://jakarta.apache.org/taglibs/response-1.0
  </taglib-uri>
  <taglib-location>
    /WEB-INF/response.tld
  </taglib-location>
</taglib>
```

The following taglib directive must be added to each JSP that will leverage the Response tag library:

```
<%@ taglib
  uri="http://jakarta.apache.org/taglibs/response-1.0"
  prefix="res" %>
```

This directive identifies the URI defined in the previously listed <taglib> element and states that all Response tags should be prefixed with the string *res*.

Generic Response Tags

The first grouping of response tags allow you to perform simple HTTP response modifications and queries. At the time of this writing, the generic set of response tags includes nine unique tags. These tags are discussed in the following sections.

<res:encodeRedirectUrl />

The encodeRedirectUrl tag encodes a URL with the JSESSIONID of the current user. The resulting URL is then used by the sendRedirect tag. The syntax of the encodeRedirectUrl tag is as follows:

```
<res:sendRedirect>
  <res:encodeRedirectUrl>
    the url to encode
  </res:encodeRedirectUrl >
</res:sendRedirect>
```

The encodeRedirectUrl tag has a body type of JSP and contains no attributes.

<res:encodeUrl />

The encodeUrl tag encodes a URL with the JSESSIONID, if necessary, of the current user. This tag differs from encodeRedirectUrl in that it uses the HttpServletResponse.encodeUrl() method, as opposed to the HttpServletResponse.encodeRedirectUrl() method, which is used by encodeRedirectUrl. The syntax of the encodeUrl tag is as follows:

```
<res:encodeUrl>
    the url to encode
</res:encodeUrl >
```

The encodeUrl tag has a body type of JSP and contains no attributes.

<res:flushBuffer />

The flushBuffer tag flushes any content in the current response buffer to the client. The syntax of the flushBuffer tag is as follows:

```
<res:flushBuffer />
```

The flushBuffer tag has no body and contains no attributes.

<res:isCommitted />

The isCommitted tag is a generic tag that will evaluate its body if the response has already been committed to the requesting client. This means that the content has already been written back to the client. The syntax of the isCommitted tag is as follows:

```
<res:isCommitted>
  The Body to evaluate if the response has been committed
</res:isCommitted>
```

The isCommitted tag has a body type of JSP. The attribute of the isCommitted tag is described in Table 12.1.

Table 12.1 Attribute of the isCommitted Tag

ATTRIBUTE	DESCRIPTION
value	If set to false, evaluates its body if the response has not been committed back to the client; the default value is true (optional)

<res:sendError />

The sendError tag sends an HTTP error back to the calling client. The body of this tag is used to send back a human-readable error. The syntax of the sendError tag is as follows:

```
<res:sendError error="HTTP error code">
  The human readable message reporting the error.
</res:sendError>
```

The sendError tag has a body type of JSP. The attributes of the sendError tag are described in Table 12.2.

Table 12.2 Attributes of the sendError Tag

ATTRIBUTE	DESCRIPTION
error	The HTTP error code that will be sent back to the client. The list of possible values can be found at http://jakarta.apache.org/taglibs/doc/response-doc/response-1.0-B1/index.html#codes. (required)
reset	If set to true, resets the response buffers, headers, and status codes by calling the HttpServletResponse.reset() method. (optional)

<res:sendRedirect />

The sendRedirect tag redirects the current user to a URL contained in the body of the tag, using the HttpServletResponse.sendRedirect() method. The syntax of the sendRedirect tag is as follows:

```
<res:sendRedirect>
  <res:encodeRedirectUrl>
    the url to encode
  </res:encodeRedirectUrl >
</res:sendRedirect>
```

The sendRedirect tag has a body type of JSP and no attributes.

<res:setContentType />

The setContentType tag sets the content type of the response sent to the requesting client. An example type would be text/html. The syntax of the setContentType tag is as follows:

```
<res:setContentType>
  the content type of the response such as text/html
</res:setContentType>
```

The setContentType tag has a body type of JSP and no attributes.

<res:setStatus />

The setStatus tag sends an HTTP status code back to the calling client. The syntax of the setStatus tag is as follows:

```
<res:setStatus status="HTTP status code" />
```

The setStatus tag has no body. Its attribute is described in Table 12.3.

Table 12.3 Attribute of the setStatus Tag

ATTRIBUTE	DESCRIPTION
status	The HTTP status code that will be sent back to the client. The list of possible values can be found at http://jakarta.apache.org/taglibs/doc/response-doc/response-1.0-B1/index.html#codes. (required)

<res:skipPage />

The skipPage tag skips the rest of the page when it is encountered. The syntax of the skipPage tag is as follows:

```
<res:skipPage />
```

The skipPage tag has no body or attributes.

Using the Generic Response Tags

This section presents a simple example of how the generic response tags can be used. Listing 12.1 contains the source for this example.

```
<%@ taglib
  uri="http://jakarta.apache.org/taglibs/response-1.0"
  prefix="res" %>

<%@ taglib
  uri="http://jakarta.apache.org/taglibs/request-1.0"
  prefix="req" %>

<html>
  <head>
    <title>Generic Response Taglib Example</title>
  </head>

  <body>

    <h1>Jakarta RESPONSE Taglib Example</h1>

    <%-- set the content type to text/html --%>
    <res:setContentType>text/html</res:setContentType>

    <%-- check for the Parameter skip --%>
    <%-- if it exits, then skip the remainder of the page --%>
    <req:existsParameter name="skip">
      <res:skipPage />
    </req:existsParameter>

    <%-- check for the Parameter target --%>
    <%-- if it exists encode the passed in URL --%>
    <%-- and perform a sendRedirect --%>
    <req:existsParameter name="target">
      <res:sendRedirect>
        <res:encodeRedirectUrl>
          <req:parameter name="target" />
        </res:encodeRedirectUrl>
      </res:sendRedirect>
    </req:existsParameter>

    <%-- test to see if the response has --%>
```

Listing 12.1 GenericRespExample.jsp. *(continues)*

```
    <%-- already been committed --%>
    <res:isCommitted>
      The response has already been committed.
    </res:isCommitted>
    <hr>

    <%-- flush the response output buffer: --%>
    <res:flushBuffer/>

    <%-- test to see if the response has --%>
    <%-- already been committed --%>
    <res:isCommitted>
      The response has already been committed.
    </res:isCommitted>
    <hr>

  </body>
</html>
```

Listing 12.1 GenericRespExample.jsp. *(continued)*

NOTE All the examples in this chapter leverage parts of the Request Tag library. Therefore, a second taglib directive appears in each of the JSPs.

To install this example, simply copy this JSP to the <TOMCAT_HOME>/webapps/*webappname/* directory, and open your browser to the following URL:

```
http://localhost:8080/webappname/GenericRespExample.jsp
```

The resulting page should be similar to Figure 12.1.

The GenericRespExample.jsp begins by setting the content type of the returned response to text/html, using the setContentType tag. The result of this tag evaluation tells the requesting browser that all returned content will be in the form of text/html.

Next, this JSP tests for the existence of the request parameter skip. If this parameter exists, then the remainder of the page will not be evaluated. The skipPage tag forces the skip. To see the skip page in action, add the following skip parameter and value to the previously listed query string:

```
?skip=True
```

NOTE The value of the skip parameter is not important. The skip parameter simply needs to exist to force the evaluation of the skipPage tag.

After the skipPage tag is either executed or ignored, the JSP performs a sendRedirect using an encoded URL that is passed as a request parameter target. If this request parameter does not exist, then sendRedirect is not evaluated. To see sendRedirect in action, add the following string to the originally listed URL, making sure CookieRespExample.jsp is in the same directory, and refresh your browser:

```
?target=CookieRespExample.jsp
```

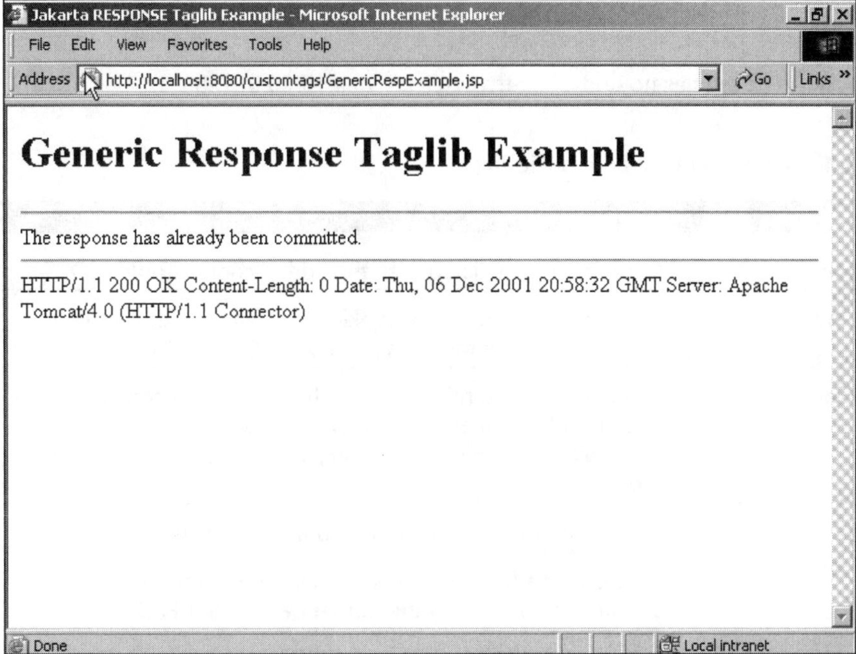

Figure 12.1 Output of the GenericRespExample.jsp.

The result should be the evaluated CookieRespExample.jsp, which is described in a later section of this chapter.

The GenericRespExample.jsp now checks the response to see if it has been committed to the client. In this case it has not; therefore, the body of the tag is not evaluated. This action is completed using the isCommitted tag.

Finally, the JSP flushes the output buffer using the flushBuffer tag and then checks the response again to see if it was committed. This time, the isCommitted tag does evaluate its body because the execution of the flushBuffer tag forces the response to be committed to the client.

Cookie Response Tags

The second group of response tags performs simple HTTP cookie modifications. At the time of this writing, there are eight cookie-related response tags, which are discussed in the following sections.

<res:addCookie />

The addCookie tag adds an HTTP cookie to the HttpServletResponse. The syntax of the addCookie tag is as follows:

```
<res:addCookie
  name="name of the cookie"
  value="the value of the cookie" />
```

The addCookie tag has no body. Its attributes are described in Table 12.4.

Table 12.4 Attributes of the addCookie Tag

ATTRIBUTE	DESCRIPTION
comment	A comment associated with the added cookie. (optional)
domain	The domain name of the cookie. The format of this attribute should satisfy the format defined in RFC 2109. (optional)
maxAge	An integer representing the length of time, in seconds, that the added cookie will exist. The default value is -1. Any negative value will cause the cookie to expire when the browser closes. (optional)
name	The name of the cookie added to the response. (required)
path	The server path of the added cookie. The format of this attribute should satisfy the format defined in RFC 2109. (optional)
value	The value of the added cookie. (optional)
version	The protocol used to implement the added cookie. The default version is 0. (optional)
secure	A Boolean attribute that tells the browser that this cookie should be sent using a secure protocol. The default value is false. (optional)

<res:comment />

The comment tag is used to replace the addCookie comment attribute. The syntax of the comment tag is as follows:

```
<res:addCookie
  name="name of the cookie"
  value="the value of the cookie">
  <res:comment>the comment of the cookie</res:comment>
</res:addCookie>
```

NOTE **The comment tag must be nested within an addCookie tag.**

The comment tag has a body type of JSP and no attributes.

<res:domain />

The domain tag is used to replace the addCookie domain attribute. The syntax of the domain tag is as follows:

```
<res:addCookie
  name="name of the cookie"
  value="the value of the cookie">
  <res:domain>the domain of the cookie</res:domain>
</res:addCookie>
```

NOTE **The domain tag must be nested within an addCookie tag.**

The domain tag has a body type of JSP and no attributes.

<res:maxAge />

The maxAge tag is used to replace the addCookie maxAge attribute. The syntax of the maxAge tag is as follows:

```
<res:addCookie
  name="name of the cookie"
  value="the value of the cookie">
  <res:maxAge>the maximum age of the cookie</res:maxAge>
</res:addCookie>
```

NOTE **The maxAge tag must be nested within an addCookie tag.**

The maxAge tag has a body type of JSP and no attributes.

<res:path />

The path tag is used to replace the addCookie path attribute. The syntax of the path tag is as follows:

```
<res:addCookie
  name="name of the cookie"
  value="the value of the cookie">
  <res:path>the path of the cookie</res:path>
</res:addCookie>
```

NOTE **The path tag must be nested within an addCookie tag.**

The path tag has a body type of JSP and no attributes.

<res:secure />

The secure tag is used to replace the addCookie secure attribute. The syntax of the secure tag is as follows:

```
<res:addCookie
  name="name of the cookie"
  value="the value of the cookie">
  <res:secure>true or false</res:secure>
</res:addCookie>
```

NOTE **The secure tag must be nested within an addCookie tag.**

The secure tag has a body type of JSP and no attributes.

<res:value />

The value tag is used to replace the addCookie value attribute. The syntax of the value tag is as follows:

```
<res:addCookie
  name="name of the cookie">
  <res:value>the value of the cookie</res:value>
</res:addCookie>
```

NOTE **The value tag must be nested within an addCookie tag.**

The value tag has a body type of JSP and no attributes.

<res:version />

The version tag is used to replace the addCookie version attribute. The syntax of the version tag is as follows:

```
<res:addCookie
  name="name of the cookie"
  value="the value of the cookie">
  <res:version>
    the version of the cookie
    implementation
  </res:version>
</res:addCookie>
```

NOTE **The version tag must be nested within an addCookie tag.**

The version tag has a body type of JSP and no attributes.

Using the Cookie Response Tags

This section presents an example of how the cookie response tags can be utilized in a JSP. Listing 12.2 contains the source for this example.

```
<%@ taglib
          uri="http://jakarta.apache.org/taglibs/response-1.0"
          prefix="res" %>

<%@ taglib
          uri="http://jakarta.apache.org/taglibs/request-1.0"
```

Listing 12.2 CookieRespExample.jsp. *(continues)*

```
  prefix="req" %>

<html>
  <head>
    <title>Cookie Response Taglib Example</title>
  </head>

  <body>

    <h1>Cookie Response Taglib Example</h1>

    <%-- add a new cookie to the response --%>
    <res:addCookie
      name="UserId"
      value="bob" />

    <h2>The added cookie's properties.</h2>
    <req:cookies id="cookieloop" name="UserId">
      Cookie Name: <jsp:getProperty
                     name="cookieloop"
                     property="name"/>
      <br>
      Cookie Value: <jsp:getProperty
                      name="cookieloop"
                      property="value"/>
      <br>
      Cookie Max Age: <jsp:getProperty
                        name="cookieloop"
                        property="maxAge"/>
    </req:cookies>
  </body>
</html>
```

Listing 12.2 CookieRespExample.jsp. *(continued)*

To install this example, copy this JSP to the <TOMCAT_HOME>/webapps/*webapp-name*/ directory, and open your browser to the following URL:

```
http://localhost:8080/webappname/CookieRespExample.jsp
```

The cookie will not be available in the first request processed by the container because the cookie is added to the response. To see the newly added cookie, click the browser's refresh button. The resulting page should be similar to Figure 12.2.

This example begins by adding a cookie with the name UserId and the value *Bob* to the response sent back to the client. It does so using the addCookie tag. This cookie will be available to all subsequent requests.

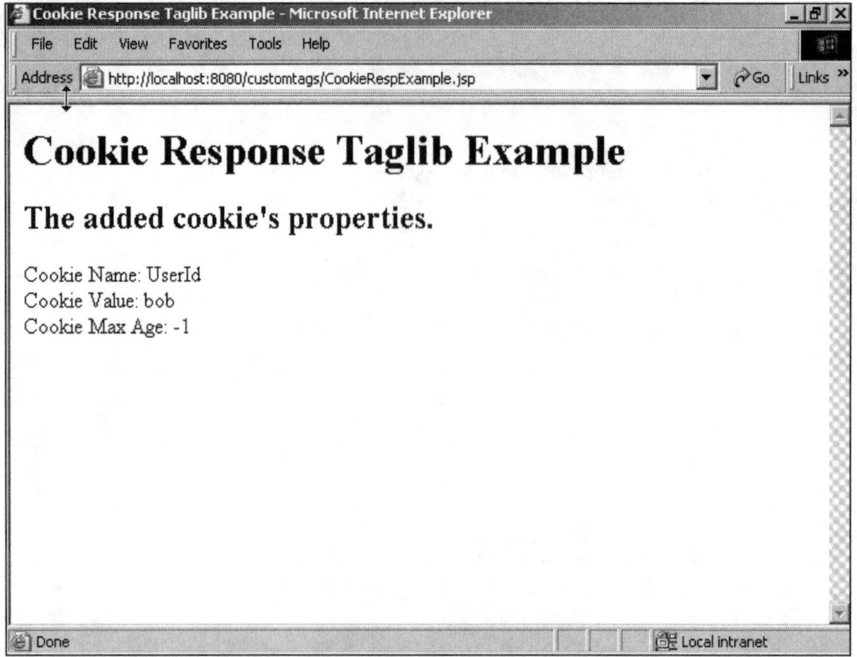

Figure 12.2 Output of the CookieRespExample.jsp.

After the cookie has been added to the response, the JSP uses the cookies tag, discussed in Chapter 11, to retrieve information about the new cookie. It does so using the <jsp:getProperty> standard action. There is nothing special about the remaining cookie tags; they simply set cookie properties dynamically.

Response Header Tags

The final group of response tags perform simple HTTP header modifications and queries. At the time of this writing, there are seven header-related response tags, which are discussed in the following sections.

NOTE **The list of possible HTTP headers is described in RFC 2616, which can be found at ftp://ftp.isi.edu/in-notes/rfc2616.txt.**

<res:addHeader />

The addHeader tag adds an HTTP header to the response object that will be sent back to the calling client. The value of the header is set using the result of the evaluated tag body. The syntax of the addHeader tag is as follows:

```
<res:addHeader name="HTTP header name">
  The value to add to the header
</res:addHeader>
```

NOTE **The addHeader tag allows you to add multiple values to a single header.**

The addHeader tag has a body type of JSP. Its attribute is described in Table 12.5.

Table 12.5 Attribute of the addHeader Tag

ATTRIBUTE	DESCRIPTION
name	The HTTP header to add (required)

<res:addDateHeader />

The addDateHeader tag adds an HTTP header containing a date value to the response object that will be sent back to the calling client. The date value of the header is set using the result of the evaluated tag body. The value must be in the form of milliseconds since Jan 1, 1970 GMT. The syntax of the addDateHeader tag is as follows:

```
<res:addDateHeader name="HTTP header name">
  The date value to add to the header
</res:addDateHeader>
```

NOTE **The addDateHeader tag allows you to add multiple values to a single header.**

The addDateHeader tag has a body type of JSP. Its attribute is described in Table 12.6.

Table 12.6 Attribute of the addDateHeader Tag

ATTRIBUTE	DESCRIPTION
name	The HTTP header to add (required)

<res:addIntHeader />

The addIntHeader tag adds an HTTP header containing an integer value to the response object that will be sent back to the calling client. The integer value of the header is set using the result of the evaluated tag body. The syntax of the addIntHeader tag is as follows:

```
<res:addIntHeader name="HTTP header name">
  The integer value to add to the header
</res:addIntHeader>
```

NOTE **The addIntHeader tag allows you to add multiple values to a single header.**

The addIntHeader tag has a body type of JSP. Its attribute is described in Table 12.7.

Table 12.7 Attribute of the addIntHeader Tag

ATTRIBUTE	DESCRIPTION
name	The HTTP header to add (required)

<res:containsHeader />

The containsHeader tag evaluates its body if the named header exists in the response. The syntax of the containsHeader tag is as follows:

```
<res:containsHeader name="HTTP header name">
  the evaluated body
</res:containsHeader>
```

The containsHeader tag has a body type of JSP. Its attributes are described in Table 12.8.

Table 12.8 Attributes of the containsHeader Tag

ATTRIBUTE	DESCRIPTION
name	The HTTP header to test for (required)
value	If set to false, causes the tag body to be evaluated if the header does not exist in the request; the default value is true (optional)

<res:setHeader />

The setHeader tag sets an HTTP header value. The value of the header is set using the result of the evaluated tag body. If the header already exists, then the previous value is replaced. The syntax of the setHeader tag is as follows:

```
<res:setHeader name="HTTP header name">
  The value to set the header to
</res:setHeader>
```

The setHeader tag has a body type of JSP. Its attribute is described in Table 12.9.

Table 12.9 Attribute of the setHeader Tag

ATTRIBUTE	DESCRIPTION
name	The HTTP header to set (required)

<res:setDateHeader />

The setDateHeader tag sets an HTTP header to a date value. The date value of the header is set using the result of the evaluated tag body. The value must be in the form of milliseconds since Jan 1, 1970 GMT. If the header already exists, then the previous value is replaced. The syntax of the setDateHeader tag is as follows:

```
<res:setDateHeader name="HTTP header name">
  The date value to set the header to
</res:setDateHeader>
```

The setDateHeader tag has a body type of JSP. Its attribute is described in Table 12.10.

Table 12.10 Attribute of the setDateHeader Tag

ATTRIBUTE	DESCRIPTION
name	The HTTP header to set (required)

<res:setIntHeader />

The setIntHeader tag sets an HTTP header to an integer value. The integer value of the header is set using the result of the evaluated tag body. If the header already exists, then the previous value is replaced. The syntax of the setIntHeader tag is as follows:

```
<res:setIntHeader name="HTTP header name">
  The integer value to set the header to
</res:setIntHeader>
```

The setIntHeader tag has a body type of JSP. Its attribute is described in Table 12.11.

Table 12.11 Attribute of the setIntHeader Tag

ATTRIBUTE	DESCRIPTION
name	The HTTP header to set (required)

Using the Header Response Tags

This section presents an example of how the header request tags can be used to change the response headers sent to the client. Listing 12.3 contains the source for this example.

```
<%@ taglib
  uri="http://jakarta.apache.org/taglibs/response-1.0"
  prefix="res" %>

<%@ taglib
  uri="http://jakarta.apache.org/taglibs/request-1.0"
  prefix="req" %>

<html>
  <head>
    <title>Header Response Taglib Example</title>
```

Listing 12.3 HeaderRespExample.jsp. *(continues)*

```
  </head>

  <body>

    <h1>Header Response Taglib Example</h1>

    <%-- Set the Cache-Control Header --%>
    <res:setHeader name="Cache-Control">
      no-cache
    </res:setHeader>

    <%-- Add a user defined header --%>
    <%-- if it does not already exist --%>
    <res:containsHeader name="User-Defined" value="false">
      The User-Defined header does not exist. Adding it.
      <res:setIntHeader name="User-Defined">
        25
      </res:setIntHeader>
    </res:containsHeader>
    <hr>

    <res:containsHeader name="User-Defined">
      The User-Defined header does exist. Modifying it.
      <res:setIntHeader name="User-Defined">
        10
      </res:setIntHeader>
    </res:containsHeader>
    <hr>

  </body>
</html>
```

Listing 12.3 HeaderRespExample.jsp. *(continued)*

To install this example, copy this JSP to the <TOMCAT_HOME>/webapps/*webappname*/ directory, and open your browser to the following URL:

```
http://localhost:8080/webappname/HeaderRespExample.jsp
```

The resulting page should be similar to Figure 12.3.

This final Response tag example begins by telling the client browser not to cache this page. This code forces the browser to request a new copy of the HeaderRespExam ple. jsp every time that the JSP is requested. The Cache-Control HTTP header controls the cache. The JSP performs this action using the setHeader tag, passing it the name of Cache-Control and the value *no-cache.*

After the client has been told not to cache this page, the JSP checks for a header named User-Defined. This is not a predefined header; the code uses this name to

provide an example of setting a user-defined header. In this example, the containsHeader tag cannot find the User-Defined header, which will cause the tag body to be evaluated. In the body of the containsHeader tag, the JSP adds the User-Defined header using setIntHeader, which sets the header value to the integer 25.

Finally, the HeaderRespExample.jsp again checks for the User-Defined header, which is found this time, and sets it to the integer 10. This action overwrites the current value of 25 with the new value 10.

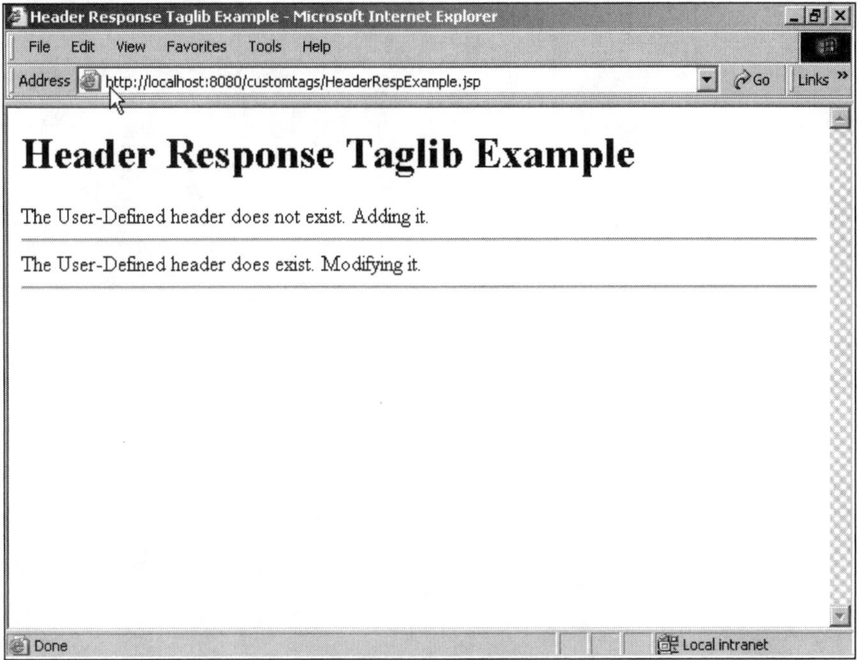

Figure 12.3 Output of the HeaderRespExample.jsp.

CHAPTER

13

Page Tag Library

The Jakarta Page tag library provides a group of tags that encapsulate the logic to access and modify the objects stored in the PageContext of the current JSP. This library focuses mainly on allowing the JSP author the ability to add attributes, remove attributes, and test for the existence of attributes in the PageContext. If you wanted the objects you were using to exist only for the life of the current JSP, then you would use this tag library as opposed to the Application, Request, or Session libraries. The Page library is named for the implicit JSP page object, which is used to reference the PageContext.

NOTE This tag library requires a JSP/servlet container that supports JSP 1.1 and above.

Configuration

To use the Page tag library in a Web application, complete the following steps. Substitute for *webappname* the name of the Web application that will be using this library:

1. Copy the page.tld tag library descriptor (TLD) packaged with this tag library to the <TOMCAT_HOME>/webapps/*webappname*/WEB-INF/lib directory.
2. Copy the page.jar JAR file containing the Page tag library's tag handlers to the <TOMCAT_HOME>/webapps/*webappname*/WEB-INF/lib directory.
3. Add the following <taglib> subelement to the web.xml file of the Web application:

```
<taglib>
  <taglib-uri>
    http://jakarta.apache.org/taglibs/page-1.0
  </taglib-uri>
  <taglib-location>
    /WEB-INF/page.tld
  </taglib-location>
</taglib>
```

The following taglib directive must be added to each JSP that will leverage the Page tag library:

```
<%@ taglib
  uri="http://jakarta.apache.org/taglibs/page-1.0"
  prefix="page" %>
```

This directive identifies the URI defined in the previously listed <taglib> element and states that all Page tags should be prefixed with the string *page*.

Page Tags

The Page tags provide the functionality to retrieve and modify the data stored in the current JSP's PageContext. The objects that are stored in the PageContext exist for the life of the requested JSP. They have page scope.

<page:attribute />

The attribute tag retrieves the value of the named attribute in the PageContext. The syntax of the attribute tag is as follows:

```
<page:attribute name="PageContext attribute name" />
```

This tag has no body. The attribute of the attribute tag is described in Table 13.1.

Table 13.1 Attribute of the attribute Tag

ATTRIBUTE	DESCRIPTION
name	Name of the PageContext attribute to retrieve (required)

<page:attributes />

The attributes tag loops through all the PageContext attributes, exposing each attribute as a name/value pair that can be referenced by a scripting variable matching the value passed in the id attribute. The values of the attribute can then be accessed using the JSP standard action <jsp:getProperty>. The syntax of the attributes tag is as follows:

```
<page:attributes id="scripting variable name" >
  <jsp:getProperty
    name="id attribute from attributes tag"
    property="name" />
```

```
<jsp:getProperty
  name="id attribute from attributes tag"
  property="attribute" />
</page:attributes>
```

This tag has a body type of JSP. The attribute of the attributes tag is described in Table 13.2.

Table 13.2 Attribute of the attributes Tag

ATTRIBUTE	DESCRIPTION
id	The scripting variable by which each name/value pair will be referenced (required)

<page:equalsAttribute />

The equalsAttribute tag evaluates its body if the named PageContext attribute has a value equal to the value of the match attribute. The syntax of the equalsAttribute tag is as follows:

```
<page:equalsAttribute name="PageContext attribute name"
  match="the value to compare the attribute to"
  value="true|false" ignoreCase="true|false">
  Evaluated Body
</page:attributes>
```

The <page:equalsAttribute />'s body will be evaluated by the JSP/servlet engine. The attributes of the equalsAttribute tag are described in Table 13.3.

Table 13.3 Attributes of the equalsAttribute Tag

ATTRIBUTE	DESCRIPTION
name	The PageContext attribute to compare (required)
value	When set to false, causes the tag to evaluate its body if there is no match; the default value is true (optional)
match	The string value to compare the named attribute to (required)
ignoreCase	If false (the default), will check for equality, taking case into account (optional)

<page:existsAttribute />

The existsAttribute tag evaluates its body if the named attribute exists in the PageContext. The syntax of the existsAttribute tag is as follows:

```
<page:existsAttribute name="PageContext attribute name">
  Evaluated Body
</page:existsAttribute>
```

This tag has a body type of JSP. The attributes of the existsAttribute tag are described in Table 13.4.

Table 13.4 Attributes of the existsAttribute Tag

ATTRIBUTE	DESCRIPTION
name	The PageContext attribute being tested for equality (required)
value	When set to false, causes the tag to evaluate its body if the named attribute does not exist in the PageContext; the default value is true (optional)

<page:removeAttribute />

The removeAttribute tag removes the named attribute from the PageContext. The syntax of the removeAttribute tag is as follows:

```
<page:removeAttribute name="PageContext attribute name" />
```

This tag has no body. The attribute of the removeAttribute tag is described in Table 13.5.

Table 13.5 Attribute of the removeAttribute Tag

ATTRIBUTE	DESCRIPTION
name	The attribute to remove from the PageContext (required)

<page:setAttribute />

The setAttribute tag sets the value of the named PageContext attribute to the content of the tag's body. The syntax of the setAttribute tag is as follows:

```
<page:setAttribute name="PageContext attribute name" />
  The value of the new attribute
</page:setAttribute>
```

This tag has a body type of JSP. The attribute of the setAttribute tag is described in Table 13.6.

Table 13.6 Attribute of the setAttribute Tag

ATTRIBUTE	DESCRIPTION
name	The attribute to be added to the PageContext (required)

Using the Page Tags

This section provides an example of how the tags in the Page library can be leveraged. Listing 13.1 contains the source for this example, and Figure 13.1 shows the results.

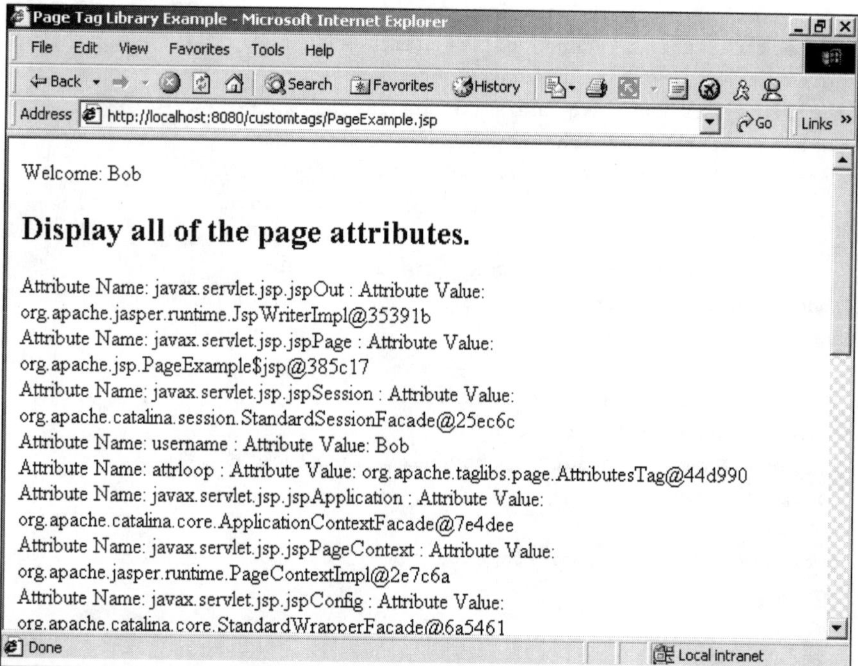

Figure 13.1 Output of PageExample.jsp.

```
<%@ taglib
  uri="http://jakarta.apache.org/taglibs/page-1.0"
  prefix="page" %>

<html>
  <head>
    <title>Page Tag Library Example</title>
  </head>

  <body>
  <!-- Use the setAttribute tag to add the username -->
  <!-- to the page. -->
  <page:setAttribute name="username">Bob</page:setAttribute>
```

Listing 13.1 PageExample.jsp. *(continues)*

```
    <!-- Check for the existence of username -->
    <page:existsAttribute name="username">
      <!-- If it exists, Test the value of username -->
      <page:equalsAttribute name="username" match="Bob">
        <!-- If the value of the page level attribute equals -->
        <!-- Bob, then use the attribute tag to retrieve -->
        <!-- the username value. -->
        Welcome: <page:attribute name="username"/><br>
      </page:equalsAttribute>
    </page:existsAttribute>

    <h2> Display all of the page attributes.</h2>
    <page:attributes id="attrloop">
      Attribute Name: <jsp:getProperty name="attrloop"
        property="name"/>
      :
      Attribute Value: <jsp:getProperty name="attrloop"
        property="attribute"/>
      <br>
    </page:attributes>

    <!-- remove the username attribute -->
    <page:removeAttribute name="username" />

    <h2>Display all of the page attributes
    after removing the username.</h2>
    <page:attributes id="attrloop">
      Attribute Name: <jsp:getProperty name="attrloop"
        property="name"/>
      :
      Attribute Value: <jsp:getProperty name="attrloop"
        property="attribute"/>
      <br>
    </page:attributes>

    </body>
  </html>
```

Listing 13.1 PageExample.jsp. *(continued)*

To see this example in action, be sure the Page tag library is installed, copy the JSP to the <TOMCAT_HOME>/webapps/*webappname/* directory, and open your browser to the following URL:

```
http://localhost:8080/webappname/PageExample.jsp
```

This example begins by using the <page:setAttribute> tag to set a page level attribute bound to the key username with a value of *Bob*. It then turns around and checks for the existence of the username attribute using the <page:existsAttribute> tag. If the username exists, the JSP then checks the value of the attribute using <page:equalsAttribute>. If the username attribute has a value of *Bob*, which it does in this example, the JSP displays the text Welcome: Bob.

Next, PageExample.jsp uses the <page:attributes> tag to list all the attributes currently in the PageContext. This tag prints all the PageContext attributes, including attributes that are placed in the context by the container. You should search this list of attributes, looking for an attribute with the username.

After the JSP has listed the attributes of the PageContext, including the username attribute, it removes the username attribute using the <page:removeAttribute> tag.

Finally, PageExample.jsp redisplays the list of PageContext attributes. Note that this final list does not contain the username attribute.

CHAPTER

14

Session Tag Library

The Jakarta Session tag library provides a group of tags that encapsulate the logic to access and modify the objects stored in the HttpSession. The Session library is named for the implicit JSP session object, which is used to reference the HttpSession. It is most commonly used when storing and retrieving information about a unique user's experience. A frequent piece of information that is stored in the HttpSession is a shopping cart.

The Session library is broken into two logically related tag groupings: generic session tags and attribute-related session tags. This chapter discusses these tags.

NOTE **This tag library requires a JSP/servlet container that supports JSP 1.1 and above.**

Configuration

To use the Session tag library in your Web application, you must complete the following steps, substituting for *webappname* the name of the Web application that will be using this library:

1. Copy the session.tld TLD packaged with this tag library to the <TOMCAT_HOME>/webapps/*webappname*/WEB-INF directory.
2. Copy the session.jar JAR file containing the Session tag library's tag handlers to the <TOMCAT_HOME>/webapps/*webappname*/WEB-INF/lib directory.

3. Add the following <taglib> subelement to the web.xml file of the Web application:

```
<taglib>
  <taglib-uri>
    http://jakarta.apache.org/taglibs/session-1.0
  </taglib-uri>
  <taglib-location>
    /WEB-INF/session.tld
  </taglib-location>
</taglib>
```

The following taglib directive must be added to each JSP that will leverage the Session tag library:

```
<%@ taglib
  uri="http://jakarta.apache.org/taglibs/session-1.0"
  prefix="sess" %>
```

This directive identifies the URI defined in the previously listed <taglib> element, and states that all Session tags should be prefixed with the string *sess*.

Generic Session Tags

The generic Session tags provide the generic HttpSession functionality. This group includes four tags: session, isNew, invalidate, and maxInactiveInterval.

<sess:session />

The session tag retrieves HttpSession-specific information, including the session creation time, id, last access time, and maximum inactive time interval. This information is exposed in name/value pairs that can be referenced by a scripting variable matching the value passed in the id attribute. The values of these pairs can then be accessed using the JSP standard action <jsp:getProperty>. The syntax of the session tag is as follows:

```
<sess:session id="scripting variable name" />

<jsp:getProperty
  name="id attribute from session tag"
  property="session property" />
```

This tag has no body. The attribute of the session tag is described in Table 14.1. The session tag returns the properties described in Table 14.2.

Table 14.1 Attribute of the session Tag

ATTRIBUTE	DESCRIPTION
id	The scripting variable by which each name/value pair will be referenced (required)

Table 14.2 Session Properties Returned by the session Tag

ATTRIBUTE	DESCRIPTION
creationTime	The creation time of this session, measured in milliseconds since midnight January 1, 1970 GMT
sessionId	The unique identifier identifying this session
lastAccessedTime	The last time the client sent a request linked to this session, represented as the number of milliseconds since midnight January 1, 1970 GMT
maxInactiveInterval	The maximum time interval, in seconds, that the servlet container will keep this session open without client interaction

The following example code snippet retrieves the last time the session was accessed:

```
<sess:session id="sessid" />
  This session was accessed :
  <jsp:getProperty
    name="sessid"
    property="lastAccessTime" />
```

<sess:isNew />

The isNew tag evaluates its body if the HttpSession is newly created. The syntax of the isNew tag is as follows:

```
<sess:isNew>
  Evaluated Body
</sess:isNew>
```

This tag has a body type of JSP. The attribute of the isNew tag is described in Table 14.3.

Table 14.3 Attribute of the isNew Tag

ATTRIBUTE	DESCRIPTION
value	When set to false, causes the tag to evaluate its body if the HttpSession object was not created with this request; the default value is true (optional)

<sess:invalidate/>

The invalidate tag invalidates the current HttpSession. The syntax of the invalidate tag is as follows:

```
<sess:invalidate />
```

This tag has no body or attributes.

<sess:maxInactiveInterval/>

The maxInactiveInterval tag sets the maximum time interval, in seconds, that the servlet container will keep this session open without client interaction. The syntax of the maxInactiveInterval tag is as follows:

```
<sess:maxInactiveInterval>

  The number of seconds to set the inactive interval.

</sess:maxInactiveInterval>
```

This tag has a body type of JSP. The maxInactiveInterval tag has no attributes.

Using the Generic Session Tags

This section presents an example of how the generic Session tags can be leveraged. Listing 14.1 contains the source for this example.

```
<%@ taglib
  uri="http://jakarta.apache.org/taglibs/session-1.0"
  prefix="sess" %>

<html>
  <head>
    <title>Generic Session Tag Library Example</title>
  </head>

  <body>

    <!-- List the current HTTP Session's Properties. -->
    <sess:session id="sessionId" />

    This session was created : <jsp:getProperty
      name="sessionId"
      property="creationTime" /><br>
    The session id is : <jsp:getProperty
      name="sessionId"
      property="sessionId" /><br>
    This session was last accessed : <jsp:getProperty
      name="sessionId"
      property="lastAccessedTime" /><br>
    The maximum inactive interval is : <jsp:getProperty
      name="sessionId"
      property="maxInactiveInterval" /><br>

    <sess:isNew>
```

Listing 14.1 GenericSessionExample.jsp. *(continues)*

```
    This HTTP session was just created.<br>
  </sess:isNew>

  <!-- Change the maxInactiveInterval to 60 minutes. -->
  <sess:maxInactiveInterval>
    3600
  </sess:maxInactiveInterval>

  <hr>

  <!-- List the current HTTP Session's Properties. -->
  This session was created : <jsp:getProperty
    name="sessionId"
    property="creationTime" /><br>
  The session id is : <jsp:getProperty
    name="sessionId"
    property="sessionId" /><br>
  This session was last accessed : <jsp:getProperty
    name="sessionId"
    property="lastAccessedTime" /><br>
  The maximum inactive interval is : <jsp:getProperty
    name="sessionId"
    property="maxInactiveInterval" /><br>

  <!-- Invalidate the session -->
  <sess:invalidate />

 </body>
</html>
```

Listing 14.1 GenericSessionExample.jsp. *(continued)*

To test this example, copy the JSP to the <TOMCAT_HOME>/webapps/*webapp-name*/ directory, and open your browser to the following URL:

```
http://localhost:8080/webappname/GenericSessionExample.jsp
```

You should see a page similar to Figure 14.1.

This example begins by retrieving the values of the current client session, using the <sess:session> tag. This tag takes the returned values and assigns them to a scripting variable named sessionId. After this scripting variable is created, the JSP prints the current values of the session using the standard <jsp:getProperty> action.

Next, the <sess:isNew> tag tests the current session to determine if it was just created. Every time this page is loaded, the <sess:isNew> tag should evaluate to true because of the last tag in the JSP (<sess:invalidate>, discussed in a moment).

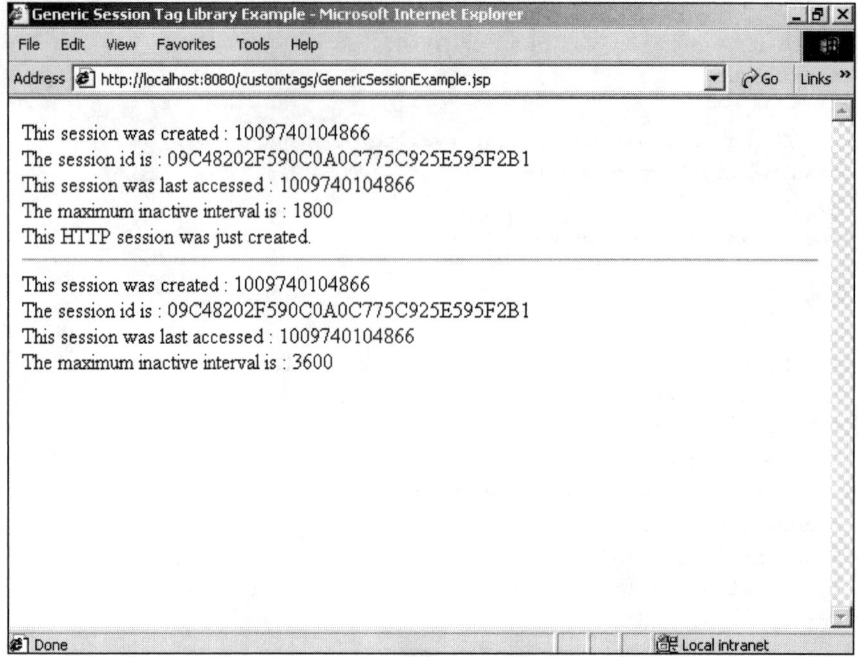
Generic Session Tag Library Example - Microsoft Internet Explorer
File Edit View Favorites Tools Help
Address http://localhost:8080/customtags/GenericSessionExample.jsp
Go
Links
This session was created : 1009740104866
The session id is : 09C48202F590C0A0C775C925E595F2B1
This session was last accessed : 1009740104866
The maximum inactive interval is : 1800
This HTTP session was just created.
This session was created : 1009740104866
The session id is : 09C48202F590C0A0C775C925E595F2B1
This session was last accessed : 1009740104866
The maximum inactive interval is : 3600
Done
Local intranet

Figure 14.1 Output of the GenericSessionExample.jsp.

NOTE **To make sure you get a new session, with the first request of this JSP, close all of your current browser instances.**

The third generic session tag used in this JSP, <sess:maxInactiveInterval>, sets the length of time an inactive session will exist before it is invalidated. This example sets the value to 3600, which equals 60 minutes.

After the maxInactiveInterval has been changed, the JSP prints the updated values of the session. It does so again using the standard <jsp:getProperty> action.

Finally, GenericSessionExample.jsp invalidates the HTTP session using the <sess: invalidate> tag. As stated earlier, this tag causes the <sess:isNew> tag to evaluate to true with every request for this JSP, because <sess:invalidate> forces a new session to be created upon a subsequent request. To see the <sess:isNew> return false, remove this line from the JSP two additional times.

Session Attribute Tags

The Session attribute tags provide the functionality to retrieve and modify the data stored in the current HttpSession. The objects stored in the HttpSession exist for the life of the HttpSession. There are six Session attribute tags: attribute, attributes, equalsAttribute, existsAttribute, removeAttribute, and setAttribute.

<sess:attribute />

The attribute tag retrieves the value of the named attribute in the HttpSession. The syntax of the attribute tag is as follows:

```
<sess:attribute name="HttpSession attribute name" />
```

This tag has no body. The attribute of the attribute tag is described in Table 14.4.

Table 14.4 Attribute of the attribute Tag

ATTRIBUTE	DESCRIPTION
name	The name of the HttpSession attribute to retrieve (required)

<sess:attributes />

The attributes tag loops through all the HttpSession attributes, exposing each attribute as a name/value pair that can be referenced by a scripting variable matching the value passed in the id attribute. The values of the attribute can then be accessed using the JSP standard action <jsp:getProperty>. The syntax of the attributes tag is as follows:

```
<sess:attributes id="scripting variable name" >
  <jsp:getProperty
    name="id attribute from attributes tag"
    property="HttpSession attribute name" />
</sess:attributes>
```

This tag has a body type of JSP. The attribute of the attributes tag is described in Table 14.5.

Table 14.5 Attribute of the attributes Tag

ATTRIBUTE	DESCRIPTION
id	The scripting variable by which each name/value pair will be referenced (required)

<sess:equalsAttribute />

The equalsAttribute tag evaluates its body if the named HttpSession attribute has a value equal to the value of the match attribute. The syntax of the equalsAttribute tag is as follows:

```
<sess:equalsAttribute name="HttpSession attribute name"
  match="the value to compare the attribute to">
  Evaluated Body
</sess:equalsAttribute>
```

This tag has a body type of JSP. The attributes of the equalsAttribute tag are described in Table 14.6.

Table 14.6 Attributes of the equalsAttribute Tag

ATTRIBUTE	DESCRIPTION
name	The HttpSession attribute to compare (required)
value	When set to false, causes the tag to evaluate its body if there is no match; the default value is true (optional)
match	The string value to compare the named attribute to (required)
ignoreCase	If false (the default), checks for equality, taking case into account (optional)

<sess:existsAttribute />

The existsAttribute tag evaluates its body if the named attribute exists in the HttpSession. The syntax of the existsAttribute tag is as follows:

```
<sess:existsAttribute name="HttpSession attribute name">
  Evaluated Body
<sess:existsAttribute />
```

This tag has a body type of JSP. The attributes of the existsAttribute tag are described in Table 14.7.

Table 14.7 Attributes of the existsAttribute Tag

ATTRIBUTE	DESCRIPTION
name	The HttpSession attribute being test for equality (required)
value	When set to false, causes the tag to evaluate its body if the named attribute does not exist in the HttpSession; the default value is true (optional)

<sess:removeAttribute />

The removeAttribute tag removes the named attribute from the HttpSession. The syntax of the removeAttribute tag is as follows:

```
<sess:removeAttribute name="HttpSession attribute name" />
```

This tag has no body. The attribute of the removeAttribute tag is described in Table 14.8.

Table 14.8 Attribute of the removeAttribute Tag

ATTRIBUTE	DESCRIPTION
name	The attribute to remove from the HttpSession (required)

<sess:setAttribute />

The setAttribute tag sets the value of the named HttpSession attribute to the content of the tag's body. The syntax of the setAttribute tag is as follows:

```
<sess:setAttribute name="HttpSession attribute name" />
  The value of the new attribute
</sess:setAttribute>
```

This tag has a body type of JSP. The attribute of the setAttribute tag is described in Table 14.9.

Table 14.9 Attribute of the setAttribute Tag

ATTRIBUTE	DESCRIPTION
name	The attribute to be added to the HttpSession (required)

Using the Session Attribute Tags

This section provides an example of how the attribute tags in the Session library can be leveraged. Listing 14.2 contains the source for this example.

```
<%@ taglib
  uri="http://jakarta.apache.org/taglibs/request-1.0"
  prefix="sess" %>

<html>
  <head>
    <title>Attribute Session Tag Library Example</title>
  </head>

  <body>
  <!-- Use the setAttribute tag to set the add the role -->
  <!-- to the session. -->
  <sess:setAttribute name="role">manager</sess:setAttribute>

  <!-- Check for the existence of role -->
  <sess:existsAttribute name="role">
    <!-- If it exists, Test the value of role -->
    <sess:equalsAttribute name="role" match="manager">
      <!-- If the value of the session attribute equals -->
      <!-- manager, then use the session tag to retrieve -->
      <!-- the role value. -->
```

Listing 14.2 AttributeSessionExample.jsp. *(continues)*

```
      Role: <sess:attribute name="role"/><br>
    </sess:equalsAttribute>
  </sess:existsAttribute>

  <h2> Display all of the session attributes.</h2>
  <sess:attributes id="attrloop">
    Attribute Name: <jsp:getProperty name="attrloop"
      property="name"/><br>
  </sess:attributes>

  <!-- remove the role attribute -->
  <sess:removeAttribute name="role" />

  <h2>Display all of the session attributes
  after removing the role.</h2>
  <sess:attributes id="attrloop">
    Attribute Name: <jsp:getProperty name="attrloop"
      property="name"/><br>
  </sess:attributes>

  </body>
</html
```

Listing 14.2 AttributeSessionExample.jsp. *(continued)*

To see this example in action, copy the JSP to the <TOMCAT_HOME>/webapps/*webappname*/ directory, and open your browser to the following URL:

`http://localhost:8080/webappname/AttributeSessionExample.jsp`

You should see a page similar to Figure 14.2.

This example begins by using the <sess:setAttribute> tag to set a session-level attribute that is bound to the key role, with a value of *manager*. It then turns around and checks for the existence of the role attribute, using the <sess:existsAttribute> tag. If the role attribute does exist, the JSP then checks the value of the attribute using <sess:equalsAttribute>. If the role attribute has a value of *manager*, which it does in this example, the JSP will display the text *Role: manager*.

Next, AttributeSessionExample.jsp lists all the attributes currently in the HttpSession object. It does so using the <sess:attributes> tag, which prints all the HttpSession attributes. Unless you have added other attributes to the HttpSession, you should see a single request attribute role.

Finally, the JSP removes the role attribute using the <sess:removeAttribute> tag and redisplays the modified contents of the HttpSession. Note that this final list does not contain the role attribute.

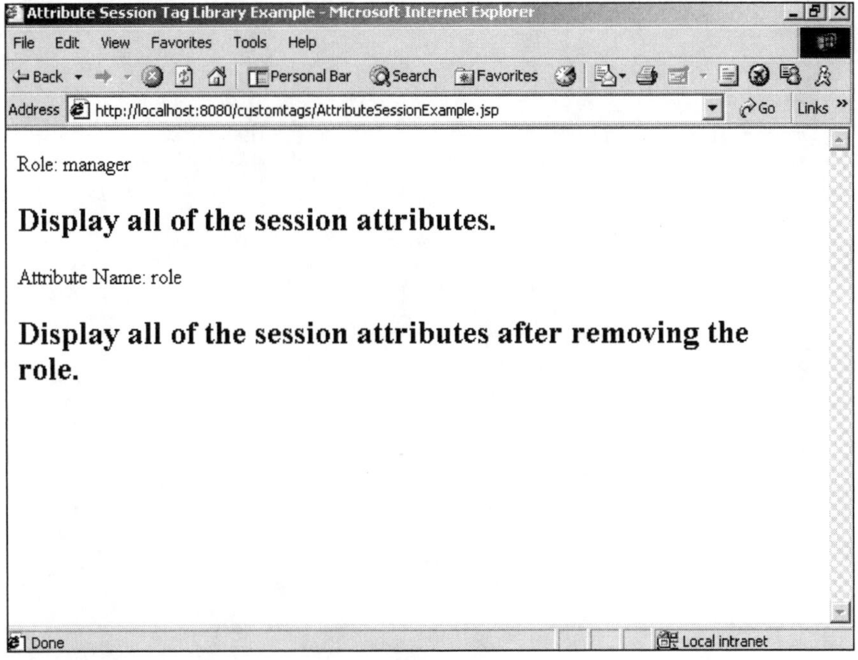

Figure 14.2 Output of the AttributeSessionExample.jsp.

Display all of the session attributes:

Display all of the session attributes after removing [illegible]

Figure 14.2 Output of the Attributes session example.

CHAPTER

15

Application Tag Library

The Jakarta Application tag library provides a group of tags that encapsulate the logic to access objects stored in the ServletContext of the current Web application. The application is named for the implicit JSP application object, which is used to reference the ServletContext. It is most commonly used to store and retrieve information that is relevant to the entire Web application. A common object that would be stored in the application is a Properties object containing configuration settings for the entire application.

This library is broken into two logically related tag groupings: attribute tags and initialization parameter tags. This chapter describes these tags.

NOTE **This tag library requires a JSP/servlet container that supports JSP 1.1 and above.**

Configuration

To use the Application tag library in your Web application, you must complete the following steps, substituting for *webappname* the name of the Web application that will be using this library:

1. Copy the application.tld TLD packaged with this tag library to the <TOMCAT_HOME>/webapps/*webappname*/WEB-INF/lib directory.
2. Copy the application.jar JAR file containing the Application tag library's tag handlers to the <TOMCAT_HOME>/webapps/*webappname*/WEB-INF/lib directory.

3. Add the following <taglib> subelement to the web.xml file of the Web application:

```
<taglib>
  <taglib-uri>
    http://jakarta.apache.org/taglibs/application-1.0
  </taglib-uri>
  <taglib-location>
    /WEB-INF/application.tld
  </taglib-location>
</taglib>
```

The following taglib directive must be added to each JSP that will leverage the Application tag library:

```
<%@ taglib
  uri="http://jakarta.apache.org/taglibs/application-1.0"
  prefix="app" %>
```

This directive identifies the URI defined in the previously listed <taglib> element and states that all Application tags should be prefixed with the string *app*.

Attribute Tags

The Application attribute tags provide the functionality to retrieve and modify the data stored in the current Web application's ServletContext. The objects that are stored in the ServletContext exist for the life of the Web application. This set includes six tags: attribute, attributes, equalsAttribute, existsAttribute, removeAttribute, and setAttribute.

<app:attribute />

The attribute tag retrieves the value of the named attribute in the ServletContext. The syntax of the attribute tag is as follows:

```
<app:attribute name="ServletContext attribute name" />
```

This tag has no body. The attribute of the attribute tag is described in Table 15.1.

Table 15.1 Attribute of the attribute Tag

ATTRIBUTE	DESCRIPTION
name	The name of the ServletContext attribute to output (required)

<app:attributes />

The attributes tag loops through all the ServletContext attributes, exposing each attribute as a name/value pair that can be referenced by a scripting variable matching the value passed in the id attribute. The values of the attribute can then be accessed using the JSP standard action <jsp:getProperty>. The syntax of the attributes tag is as follows:

```
<app:attributes id="scripting variable name" >
  <jsp:getProperty
    name="scripting variable name"
    property="name|value" />
</app:attributes>
```

This tag has a body type of JSP. The attribute of the attributes tag is described in Table 15.2.

Table 15.2 Attribute of the attributes Tag

ATTRIBUTE	DESCRIPTION
id	The scripting variable by which each name/value pair will be referenced (required)

<app:equalsAttribute />

The equalsAttribute tag evaluates its body if the named ServletContext attribute has a value equal to the value of the match attribute. The syntax of the equalsAttribute tag is as follows:

```
<app:equalsAttribute name="ServletContext attribute name"
  match="the value to compare the attribute to">
  Evaluated Body
</app: equalsAttribute>
```

This tag has a body type of JSP. The attributes of the equalsAttribute tag are described in Table 15.3.

Table 15.3 Attributes of the equalsAttribute Tag

ATTRIBUTE	DESCRIPTION
name	The ServletContext attribute to compare (required)
value	When set to false, causes the tag to evaluate its body if there is no match; the default value is true (optional)
match	The string value to compare the named attribute to (required)
ignoreCase	If false, checks for equality, taking case into account; the default value is false (optional)

<app:existsAttribute />

The existsAttribute tag evaluates its body if the named attribute exists in the Servlet-Context. The syntax of the existsAttribute tag is as follows:

```
<app:existsAttribute name="ServletContext attribute name">

  Evaluated Body
</app:existsAttribute>
```

This tag has a body type of JSP. The attributes of the existsAttribute tag are described in Table 15.4.

Table 15.4 Attributes of the existsAttribute Tag

ATTRIBUTE	DESCRIPTION
name	The ServletContext attribute being test for equality (required)
value	When set to false, causes the tag to evaluate its body if the named attribute does not exist in the ServletContext; the default value is true (optional)

<app:removeAttribute />

The removeAttribute tag removes the named attribute from the ServletContext. The syntax of the removeAttribute tag is as follows:

```
<app:removeAttribute name="ServletContext attribute name" />
```

This tag has no body. The attribute of the removeAttribute tag is described in Table 15.5.

Table 15.5 Attribute of the removeAttribute Tag

ATTRIBUTE	DESCRIPTION
name	The attribute to remove from the ServletContext (required)

<app:setAttribute />

The setAttribute tag sets the value of the named ServletContext attribute to the content of the tag's body. The syntax of the setAttribute tag is as follows:

```
<app:setAttribute name="ServletContext attribute name" />
  The value of the new attribute
</app:setAttribute>
```

This tag has a body type of JSP. The attribute of the setAttribute tag is described in Table 15.6.

Table 15.6 Attribute of the setAttribute Tag

ATTRIBUTE	DESCRIPTION
name	The attribute to be added to the ServletContext (required)

Using the Application Tags

This section presents an example of how the Application attribute tags can be leveraged. Listing 15.1 contains the source for this example.

```
<%@ taglib
  uri="http://jakarta.apache.org/taglibs/application-1.0"
  prefix="app" %>

<html>
  <head>
    <title>Attribute Application Tag Library Example</title>
  </head>

  <body>
  <!-- Use the setAttribute tag to add --->
  <!-- a JDBC url -->
  <!-- to the ServletContext. -->
  <app:setAttribute
    name="url">Jdbc:Odbc:contacts</app:setAttribute>

  <!-- Check for the existence of url -->
  <app:existsAttribute name="url">
    <!-- If it exists, Test the value of url -->
    <app:equalsAttribute name="url" match="Jdbc:Odbc:contacts">
      <!-- If the value of the application attribute equals -->
      <!-- Jdbc:Odbc:contacts, then use the attribute tag -->
      <!-- to retrieve the url value. -->
      URL: <app:attribute name="url"/><br>
    </app:equalsAttribute>
  </app:existsAttribute>

  <hr>

  <h2>Display all of the application attributes.</h2>
  <app:attributes id="attrloop">
    <b><jsp:getProperty name="attrloop" property="name"/>:</b>
    <jsp:getProperty name="attrloop" property="value"/><br>
  </app:attributes>

  <!-- remove the role attribute -->
  <app:removeAttribute name="url" />

  <h2>Display all of the application attributes
  after removing the url.</h2>
  <app:attributes id="attrloop">
    <b><jsp:getProperty name="attrloop" property="name"/>:</b>
    <jsp:getProperty name="attrloop" property="value"/><br>
  </app:attributes>

  </body>
</html>
```

Listing 15.1 AttributeApplicationExample.jsp.

To test this example, copy the JSP to the <TOMCAT_HOME>/webapps/*webapp-name/* directory, and open your browser to the following URL:

```
http://localhost:8080/webappname/AttributeApplicationExample.jsp
```

You should see a page similar to Figure 15.1.

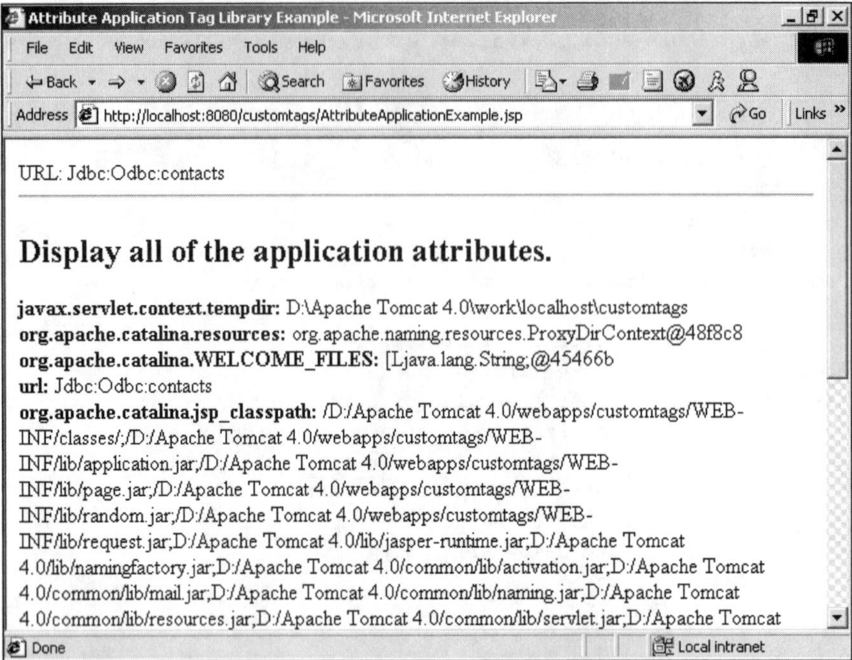

Figure 15.1 Output of the AttributeApplicationExample.jsp.

This example begins by using the <app:setAttribute> tag to set a ServletContext-level attribute bound to the key url, with a value of *Jdbc:Odbc:contacts*. It then checks for the existence of the url attribute, using the <app:existsAttribute> tag. If the url attribute does exist, the JSP then checks the value of the attribute using the <app:equalsAttribute>. If the url attribute has a matching value, which it does in this example, the JSP displays the text *URL:Jdbc:Odbc:contacts.*

Next, AttributeApplicationExample.jsp lists all the attributes currently in the ServletContext object. It does so using the <app:attributes> tag, which prints all the ServletContext attributes, including the added url attribute.

Finally, the JSP removes the url attribute, using the <app:removeAttribute> tag, and then redisplays the modified contents of the ServletContext. Note that this final list does not contain the url attribute.

Initialization Parameter Tags

The Application initialization parameter tags provide the functionality to retrieve the current set of initialization parameters existing in the Web application's ServletContext.

This set consists of four tags: initParameter, initParameters, equalsInitParameter, and existsInitParameter.

<app:initParameter />

The initParameter tag retrieves the value of a named initialization parameter from the ServletContext. The syntax of the initParameter tag is described as follows:

```
<app:initParameter name="init parameter name" />
```

This tag has no body. The attribute of the initParameter tag is described in Table 15.7.

Table 15.7 Attribute of the initParameter Tag

ATTRIBUTE	DESCRIPTION
name	The name of the initialization parameter to retrieve (required)

<app:initParameters />

The initParameters tag loops through all the initialization parameters from the Servlet-Context, exposing each name/value pair as a scripting variable matching the value passed in the id attribute. The values can then be accessed using the JSP standard action <jsp:getProperty>. The syntax of the initParameters tag is as follows:

```
<app:initParameters id="scripting variable name" >
  <jsp:getProperty
    name="scripting variable name"
    property="name|value" />
</app:initParameters>
```

This tag has a body type of JSP. The attribute of the initParameters tag is described in Table 15.8.

Table 15.8 Attribute of the initParameters Tag

ATTRIBUTE	DESCRIPTION
id	The scripting variable by which each name/value pair will be referenced (required)

<app:equalsInitParameter />

The equalsInitParameter tag evaluates its body if the init parameter value equals the match attribute. The syntax of the equalsInitParameter tag is as follows:

```
<app:equalsInitParameter
  name="init parameter name"
  match="the value to compare the init parameter to">
  Evaluated Body
</app:equalsInitParameter>
```

This tag has a body type of JSP. The attributes of the equalsInitParameter tag are described in Table 15.9.

Table 15.9 Attributes of the equalsInitParameter Tag

ATTRIBUTE	DESCRIPTION
name	The init parameter to compare (required)
value	When set to false, causes the tag to evaluate its body if there is no match; the default value is true (optional)
match	The string value to compare the init parameter to (required)
ignoreCase	If false (the default), checks for equality, taking case into account; otherwise the comparison will ignore case (optional)

<app:existsInitParameter />

The existsInitParameter tag evaluates its body if the named init parameter exists in the ServletContext. The syntax of the existsInitParameter tag is as follows:

```
<app:existsInitParameter
  name="init parameter name">
  Evaluated Body
</app:existsInitParameter>
```

This tag has a body type of JSP. The attributes of the existsInitParameter tag are described in Table 15.10.

Table 15.10 Attributes of the existsInitParameter Tag

ATTRIBUTE	DESCRIPTION
name	The ServletContext init parameter being test for equality (required)
value	When set to false, causes the tag to evaluate its body if the named init parameter does not exist in the ServletContext; the default value is true (optional)

Using the Initialization Parameter Tags

This section provides an example of how the init parameter application tags can be leveraged. This example is similar to the previous application, but implements init parameters. Listing 15.2 contains the source.

```
<%@ taglib
  uri="http://jakarta.apache.org/taglibs/application-1.0"
```

Listing 15.2 InitParamApplicationExample.jsp. *(continues)*

```
    prefix="app" %>

  <html>
    <head>
      <title>Init Param Application Tag Library Example</title>
    </head>

    <body>

    <!-- Check for the existence of url -->
    <app:existsInitParameter name="url">
      <!-- If it exists, Test the value of url -->
      <app:equalsInitParameter name="url"
        match="Jdbc:Odbc:contacts">
        <!-- If the value of the init parameter equals -->
        <!-- Jdbc:Odbc:contacts, then use the parameter tag -->
        <!-- to retrieve the url value. -->
        URL: <app:initParameter name="url"/><br>
      </app:equalsInitParameter>
    </app:existsInitParameter>

    <hr>

    <h2>Display all of the init parameters.</h2>
    <app:initParameters id="attrloop">
      <b><jsp:getProperty name="attrloop" property="name"/>:</b>
      <jsp:getProperty name="attrloop" property="value"/><br>
    </app:initParameters>

    </body>
  </html>
```

Listing 15.2 InitParamApplicationExample.jsp. *(continued)*

For this example, add a <context-param> entry to the web.xml file for the application. This entry will add a ServletContext init parameter to the deployed Web application, with a name of url and a value of *Jdbc:Odbc:contacts*:

```
<context-param>
  <param-name>url</param-name>
  <param-value>Jdbc:Odbc:contacts</param-value>
</context-param>
```

NOTE **Before this init parameter will take effect, Tomcat must be restarted.**

To test this example, copy the JSP to the <TOMCAT_HOME>/webapps/*webappname*/ directory, and open your browser to the following URL:

```
http://localhost:8080/webappname/InitParamApplicationExample.jsp
```

The result should be similar to Figure 15.2.

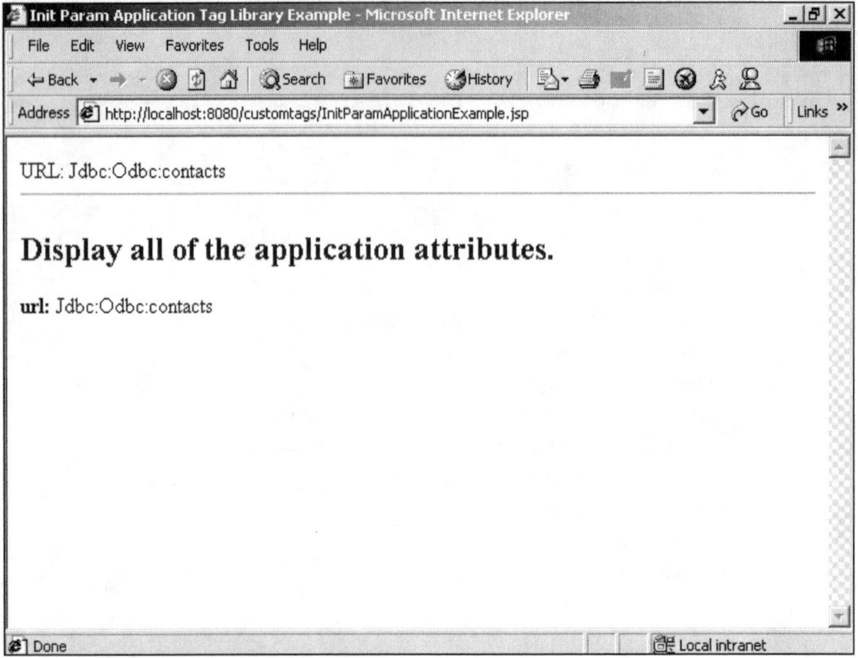

Figure 15.2 Output of the InitParamApplicationExample.jsp.

This example begins by testing for the existence of the url init parameter, using the <app:existsInitParameter> tag. If the url attribute does exist, the JSP then checks the value of the init parameter using <app:equalsInitParameter>. If the url attribute has a matching value, which it does in this example, the JSP displays the text *URL:Jdbc: Odbc:contacts*.

Next, the JSP displays all the ServletContext init parameters. Note that this list contains the url attribute.

As you can see, this example is just as functional as the previous application example. It is also a more practical solution because it requires only a change in the Web application deployment descriptor, as opposed to a JSP source code change.

CHAPTER

16

Datetime Tag Library

The Jakarta Datetime tag library provides a group of tags that encapsulate the logic to perform date and time functions, including outputting and formatting the results. The Datetime library is broken into two logically related tag groupings: generic date/time tags and localization related date/time tags. This chapter describes these tags.

NOTE This tag library requires a JSP/servlet container that supports JSP 1.1 and above.

Configuration

To use the Datetime tag library in a Web application, you must complete the following steps, substituting for *webappname* the name of the Web application that will be using this library:

1. Copy the datetime.tld TLD packaged with this tag library to the <TOMCAT_HOME>/webapps/*webappname*/WEB-INF directory.
2. Copy the datetime.jar JAR file containing the Datetime tag library's tag handlers to the <TOMCAT_HOME>/webapps/*webappname*/WEB-INF/lib directory.
3. Add the following <taglib> subelement to the web.xml file of the Web application:

```
<taglib>
  <taglib-uri>
    http://jakarta.apache.org/taglibs/datetime-1.0
```

```
    </taglib-uri>
    <taglib-location>
      /WEB-INF/datetime.tld
    </taglib-location>
  </taglib>
```

The following taglib directive must be added to each JSP that will leverage the Datetime tag library:

```
<%@ taglib
  uri="http://jakarta.apache.org/taglibs/datetime-1.0"
  prefix="dt" %>
```

This directive identifies the URI defined in the previously listed <taglib> element and states that all Datetime tags should be prefixed with the string *dt*.

Generic Datetime Tags

The generic datetime tags provide the necessary functionality required to output generic date and time information. There are four generic datetime tags: currentTime, format, parse, and timeZone.

<dt:currentTime />

The currentTime tag retrieves the current time in milliseconds since January 1, 1970 GMT. The syntax of the currentTime tag is as follows:

```
<dt:currentTime />
```

This tag has no body and no attributes.

<dt:format />

The format tag formats a date in milliseconds since January 1, 1970 GMT for output as a date string. The date that will be formatted is the evaluated body of the format tag. A common value used for the body is the <dt:currentTime /> tag, described previously. The syntax of the format tag is as follows:

```
<dt:format>
  A date in milliseconds since January 1, 1970 GMT
</dt:format>
```

This tag has a body type of JSP. The attributes of the format tag are described in Table 16.1.

Table 16.1 Attributes of the format Tag

ATTRIBUTE	DESCRIPTION
pattern	The string to use when formatting the date. The java.text.SimpleDateFormat class defines the possible date formats. (optional)

Table 16.1 Attributes of the format Tag *(continued)*

ATTRIBUTE	DESCRIPTION
patternId	An id representing a scripting variable that holds a reference to a java.text.SimpleDateFormat to be used to format the date in the body. The pattern and patternId attributes are mutually exclusive. (optional)
timeZone	A timeZone script id variable, created by the timeZone tag described later in this chapter, that will be used to adjust the time format. The timeZone date formatting is adjusted for the time zone. (optional)
date	Used to set the date to format by passing in a Date object using a runtime expression value. If this attribute is set, then the body will not be evaluated. (optional)
default	Used to set the default text to output if there is no valid date input. Passed either as a Date object or in the tag body. (optional)
locale	If set to true, forces the format tag to use the locale value associated with the client browser. (optional)

<dt:parse/>

The parse tag parses a date string, and outputs the time in milliseconds since January 1, 1970 GMT. The syntax of the parse tag is as follows:

```
<dt:parse pattern="yyyy MM dd">2000 11 5</dt:parse>
```

This tag has a body type of JSP. The attributes of the parse tag are described in Table 16.2.

Table 16.2 Attributes of the parse Tag

ATTRIBUTE	DESCRIPTION
pattern	The string to use when formatting the date. The java.text.SimpleDateFormat class defines the possible date formats. (optional)
patternId	An id representing a scripting variable that holds a reference to a java.text.SimpleDateFormat to be used to format the date in the body. (optional)
timeZone	A timeZone script id variable, created by the timeZone tag described later in this chapter, that will be used to adjust the time format. The timeZone date formatting is adjusted for the time zone. (optional)
locale	If set to true, forces the parse tag to use the locale value associated with the client browser. (optional)

<dt:timeZone/>

The timeZone tag sets a time zone script variable of type java.util.TimeZone for use with the parse and format tags. The syntax of the timeZone tag is as follows:

```
<dt:timeZone id="id of timeZone scripting variable">
  A Time Zone as defined by java.util.TimeZone
</dt:timeZone>
```

This tag has a body type of JSP. The attribute of the timeZone tag is described in Table 16.3.

Table 16.3 Attribute of the timeZone Tag

ATTRIBUTE	DESCRIPTION
id	The variable id of the time zone for use with the parse and format tags (required)

Using the Generic Datetime Tags

This section presents an example of how the generic datetime tags can be leveraged. Listing 16.1 contains the source for this example.

```
<%@ taglib
  uri="http://jakarta.apache.org/taglibs/datetime-1.0"
  prefix="dt" %>

<html>
<head>
   <title>Date Datetime Taglib Example</title>
</head>

  Setting the time zone for this session:
  <dt:timeZone id="tz">America/Denver</dt:timeZone><br>

  The local current time is:
  <dt:format timeZone="tz"
    pattern="yyyy.MM.dd G 'at' hh:mm:ss a zzz">
      <dt:currentTime/>
  </dt:format><br>

  The number of milliseconds since January 1, 1970 :
  <dt:parse pattern="yyyy.MM.dd G 'at' hh:mm:ss a zzz">
    <dt:format timeZone="tz"
```

Listing 16.1 DateDatetimeExample.jsp. *(continues)*

```
        pattern="yyyy.MM.dd G 'at' hh:mm:ss a zzz">
          <dt:currentTime/>
        </dt:format>
      </dt:parse>

      </body>
    </html>
```

Listing 16.1 DateDatetimeExample.jsp. *(continued)*

To test this example, copy the JSP to the <TOMCAT_HOME>/webapps/*webapp-name/* directory, and open your browser to the following URL:

`http://localhost:8080/`*`webappname`*`/DateDatetimeExample.jsp`

You should see a page similar to Figure 16.1.

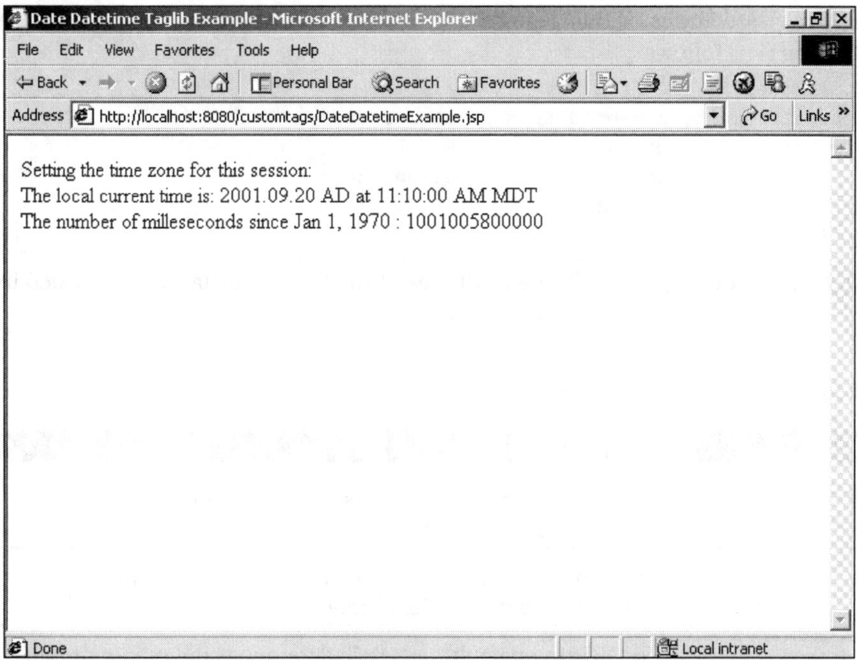

Figure 16.1 Output of the DateDatetimeExample.jsp.

This example begins by using the <dt:timeZone> tag to set the current time zone, which is represented using the *tz* scripting variable. After this scripting variable is created, the JSP prints the current time using a <dt:currentTime> tag. The output of the <dt:currentTime> tag is formatted according to the pattern attribute of its parent <dt:pattern> tag. Note that the <dt:format> tag takes the previously set time zone into account.

Finally, the JSP calculates and prints the number of milliseconds that have passed, based upon the current time, since January 1, 1970. It does so using the <dt:parse> tag, with a pattern equal to the pattern used to generate the current time embedded in the body of this tag.

Localized Datetime Tags

The localized datetime tags provide the necessary functionality required to output date information, taking the locale of the client into consideration. There are five localized datetime tags: timeZones, months, weekdays, amPms, and eras.

<dt:timeZones />

The timeZones tag loops through all the available time zones, defined by the java.util.TimeZone class, creating a scripting variable identified by the id attribute that contains the zoneId and displayName of each time zone. The created scripting variable can then be accessed by using the <jsp:getProperty /> standard action. The syntax of the timeZones tag is as follows:

```
<dt:timeZones id="id of scripting variable">
  <jsp:getProperty name="id from timeZones tag"
    property="zoneId" />
  <jsp:getProperty name="id from timeZones tag"
    property="displayName" />
</dt:timeZones>
```

This tag has a body type of JSP. The attributes of the timeZones tag are described in Table 16.4.

Table 16.4 Attributes of the timeZones Tag

ATTRIBUTE	DESCRIPTION
id	The variable id of the time zone for use with the parse and format tags (required)
locale	If set to true, forces the format tag to use the locale value associated with the client browser (optional)
style	SHORT (the default) or LONG; determines the output of the displayName property (optional)

<dt:months />

The months tag loops through the months of the year, as defined by the java.text.SimpleDateFormat class, creating a scripting variable identified by the id attribute that contains the monthOfYear, month, and shortMonth for each defined month. The created scripting variable can then be accessed by using the <jsp:getProperty/> standard action. The syntax of the months tag is as follows:

```
<dt:months id="id of scripting variable">
  <jsp:getProperty name="id from months tag"
    property="monthOfYear" />
  <jsp:getProperty name="id from months tag"
    property="month" />
  <jsp:getProperty name="id from months tag"
    property="shortMonth" />
</dt:months>
```

This tag has a body type of JSP. The attributes of the months tag are described in Table 16.5.

Table 16.5 Attributes of the months Tag

ATTRIBUTE	DESCRIPTION
id	The variable id containing the month properties (required)
locale	If set to true, forces the months tag to use the locale value associated with the client browser (optional)
style	SHORT (the default) or LONG; determines the output of the displayName property (optional)

Table 16.6 shows the properties contained in the object referenced by the scripting variable defined by the id attribute of the months tag.

Table 16.6 Properties Returned by the months Tag

PROPERTY	DESCRIPTION
monthOfYear	The number representing the month of the year
month	The full name of the month
shortMonth	The short name of the month

<dt:weekdays />

The weekdays tag loops through the days of the week, as defined by the java.text.SimpleDateFormat class, creating a scripting variable identified by the id attribute that contains the days of the week in three different formats. The created scripting variable can then be accessed by using the <jsp:getProperty /> standard action. The syntax of the weekdays tag is as follows:

```
<dt:weekdays id="id of scripting variable">
  <jsp:getProperty name="id from weekdays tag"
    property="dayOfWeek" />
  <jsp:getProperty name="id from weekdays tag"
```

```
    property="weekday" />
  <jsp:getProperty name="id from weekdays tag"
    property="shortWeekday" />
</dt:weekdays >
```

This tag has a body type of JSP. The attributes of the weekdays tag are described in Table 16.7.

Table 16.7 Attributes of the weekdays Tag

ATTRIBUTE	DESCRIPTION
id	The variable id containing the weekday properties (required)
locale	If set to true, forces the weekdays tag to use the locale value associated with the client browser (optional)

Table 16.8 shows the properties contained in the object referenced by the scripting variable defined by the id attribute of the weekdays tag.

Table 16.8 Properties Returned by the weekdays Tag

PROPERTY	DESCRIPTION
dayOfWeek	The number representing the day of the week
weekday	The full name of the day of the week
shortWeekday	The short name of the day of the week

<dt:amPms />

The amPms tag is used to loop through the AM and PM names, as defined by the java.text.SimpleDateFormat class, creating a scripting variable identified by the id attribute that contains the two values. The created scripting variable can then be accessed by using the <jsp:getProperty /> standard action. The syntax of the amPms tag is as follows:

```
<dt:amPms id="id of scripting variable">
  <jsp:getProperty name="id from weekdays tag"
    property="name" />
</dt:amPms>
```

This tag has a body type of JSP. The attributes of the amPms tag are described in Table 16.9.

Table 16.9 Attributes of the amPms Tag

ATTRIBUTE	DESCRIPTION
id	The variable id containing the amPms properties (required)
locale	If set to true, forces the amPms tag to use the locale value associated with the client browser (optional)

Table 16.10 shows the property contained in the object referenced by the scripting variable defined by the id attribute of the amPms tag.

Table 16.10 Property Returned by the amPms Tag

PROPERTY	DESCRIPTION
name	The AM or PM name returned by the amPms tag

<dt:eras />

The eras tag loops through the eras, as defined by the java.text.SimpleDateFormat class, creating a scripting variable identified by the id attribute that contains the defined eras. The created scripting variable can then be accessed by using the <jsp:getProperty/> standard action. The syntax of the eras tag is as follows:

```
<dt:eras id="id of scripting variable">
  <jsp:getProperty name="id from eras tag"
    property="name" />
</dt:eras>
```

This tag has a body type of JSP. The attributes of the eras tag are described in Table 16.11.

Table 16.11 Attributes of the eras Tag

ATTRIBUTE	DESCRIPTION
id	The variable id containing the eras properties (required)
locale	If set to true, forces the eras tag to use the locale value associated with the client browser (optional)

Table 16.12 shows the property contained in the object referenced by the scripting variable defined by the id attribute of the eras tag.

Table 16.12 Property Returned by the eras Tag

PROPERTY	DESCRIPTION
name	The B.C. or A.D. value returned by the amPms tag

Using the Localized Datetime Tags

This section provides an example of how the localized datetime tags can be leveraged. Listing 16.2 contains the source for this example.

```
<%@ taglib
  uri="http://jakarta.apache.org/taglibs/datetime-1.0"
```

Listing 16.2 LocalizedDatetimeExample.jsp. *(continues)*

```
  prefix="dt" %>

<html>
<head>
  <title>Localized Datetime Taglib Example</title>
</head>

  <form action="LocalizedDatetimeExample.jsp">

  <!-- Create a select list of time zones -->
  <select name="timezones">
    <dt:timeZones id="tz">
      <option
        value="<jsp:getProperty name="tz" property="zoneId"/>">
        <jsp:getProperty name="tz" property="displayName"/>
      </option>
    </dt:timeZones>
  </select>

  <!-- Create a select list of months -->
  <select name="months">
    <dt:months id="mon" locale="true">
      <option
        value="<jsp:getProperty name="mon"
          property="monthOfYear"/>">
        <jsp:getProperty name="mon" property="month"/>
      </option>
    </dt:months>
  </select>

  <!-- Create a select list of days -->
  <select name="days">
    <dt:weekdays id="day" locale="true">
      <option
        value="<jsp:getProperty name="day"
          property="shortWeekday"/>">
        <jsp:getProperty name="day" property="weekday"/>
      </option>
    </dt:weekdays>
  </select>

  <!-- Create a select list of AMPM -->
  <select name="ampms">
    <dt:amPms id="ampm" locale="true">
```

Listing 16.2 LocalizedDatetimeExample.jsp. *(continues)*

```
        <option
          value="<jsp:getProperty name="ampm" property="name"/>">
          <jsp:getProperty name="ampm" property="name"/>
        </option>
      </dt:amPms>
    </select>

    <!-- Create a select list of eras -->
    <select name="eras">
      <dt:eras id="eras" locale="true">
        <option
          value="<jsp:getProperty name="eras" property="name"/>">
          <jsp:getProperty name="eras" property="name"/>
        </option>
      </dt:eras>
    </select>

    <input type="Submit" name="Submit" value="Submit">

    </form>

    </body>
  </html>
```

Listing 16.2 LocalizedDatetimeExample.jsp. *(continued)*

To test this example, copy the JSP to the <TOMCAT_HOME>/webapps/*webapp-name*/ directory, and open your browser to the following URL:

`http://localhost:8080/`*`webappname`*`/LocalizedDatetimeExample.jsp`

The resulting page should be similar to Figure 16.2.

The LocalizedDatetimeExample.jsp provides a simple example of how the localized datetime tags can be used within an HTML form. It does this using a combination of each of the localized datetime tags with the <jsp:getProperty> standard action to retrieve the values returned by these tags. These values are then used to create HTML select lists.

When this JSP loads, it displays a select list for each tag. You can select items from these lists, and click the Submit button. The target of the submitted form is the same JSP. This approach makes it possible to demonstrate how the tag values can be submitted in a request. Note that the values selected can be seen in the address box after you click Submit.

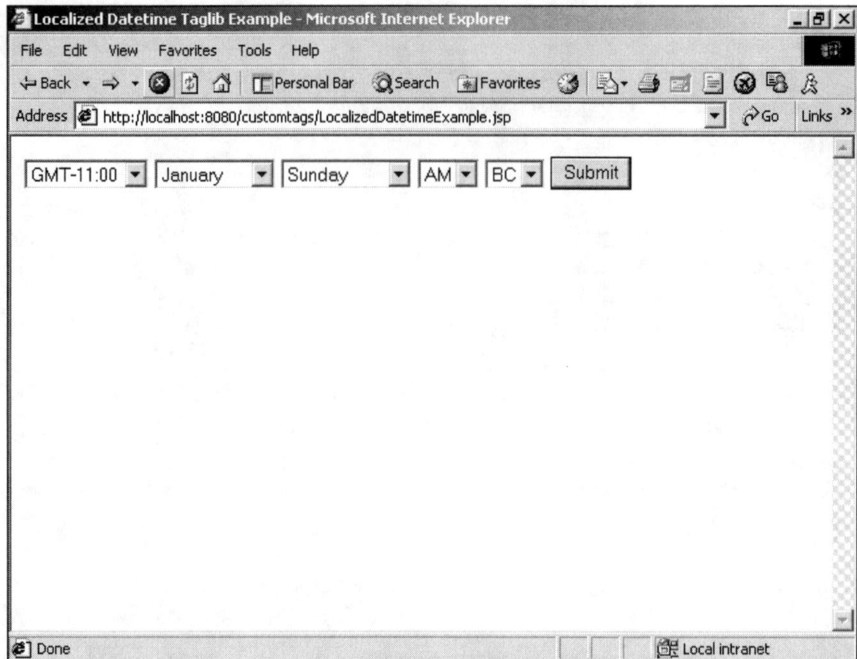

Figure 16.2 Output of the LocalizedDatetimeExample.jsp.

CHAPTER

17

DBTags Tag Library

The Jakarta DBTags Tag Library provides a group of tags that encapsulate the logic required to perform basic JDBC functionality inside a JSP. The JDBC tags provided by this library include the functionality to open and connect to JDBC DataSources, perform SQL queries, updates, inserts, and deletes. They also include the functionality to perform JDBC prepared statements.

NOTE **A fully functional Web application that uses the DBTags can be found in Chapter 2, "Configuring and Testing the Web Application Environment."**

The DBTags library is broken into three logically related tag groupings: Connection tags, Statement and PreparedStatement tags, and ResultSet tags. Each of these tags is described in the following sections.

NOTE **This tag library requires a JSP/servlet container that supports JSP 1.2 and above.**

Configuration

To use the DBTags tag library in your Web application, you must complete the following steps, substituting the value of the *webappname* with the name of the Web application that will be using this library:

1. Copy the TLD packaged with this tag library, dbtags.tld, to the <TOMCAT_HOME>/webapps/*webappname*/WEB-INF directory.
2. Copy the JAR file containing the Page tag library's tag handlers, dbtags.jar, to the <TOMCAT_HOME>/webapps/*webappname*/WEB-INF/lib directory.
3. Add the following <taglib> subelement to the web.xml file of the Web application:

```
<taglib>
  <taglib-uri>
    http://jakarta.apache.org/taglibs/dbtags
  </taglib-uri>
  <taglib-location>
    /WEB-INF/dbtags.tld
  </taglib-location>
</taglib>
```

The following taglib directive must be added to each JSP that will leverage the Session tag library:

```
<%@ taglib
  uri="http://jakarta.apache.org/taglibs/dbtags"
  prefix="sql" %>
```

This directive identifies the URI defined in the previously listed <taglib> element and states that all DBTags tags should be prefixed with the string *sql*.

Connection Tags

The Connection tags encapsulate the necessary logic required when creating or retrieving JDBC database connections. There are currently seven tags in the Connection tags.

<sql:connection />

The <sql:connection> tag creates or retrieves a JDBC connection. This connection can be established by creating a new connection, retrieving a DataSource from the page context, or retrieving a DataSource using a JNDI lookup. The syntax for each of these methods of using the connection tag follows:

Method 1. Opening a new database connection:

```
<sql:connection
  id="id of used to access the connection">
  <sql:url>url pointing to database</sql:url>
  <sql:driver>driver name used to access database</sql:driver>
  <sql:userId>id of connecting user</sql:driver>
  <sql:password>password of connecting user</sql:password>
</sql:connection>
```

Method 2. Retrieving a DataSource from the PageContext:

```
<sql:connection
  id="id of used to access the connection"
```

```
  dataSource="the name of the DataSource in the PageContext">
  <sql:userId>id of connecting user</sql:driver>
  <sql:password>password of connecting user</sql:password>
</sql:connection>
```

Method 3. Retrieving a DataSource from a JNDI server:

```
<sql:connection
  id="id of used to access the connection">
  <sql:jndiName>
    the name used to lookup a JNDI DataSource
  </sql:jndiName>
</sql:connection>
```

NOTE This example uses DBTags that we have not discussed. At this moment, you can ignore these tags. We will be examining each of them later in the chapter.

This tag has a body type of JSP. The attributes of the <sql:connection> tag are described in Table 17.1.

Table 17.1 <sql:connection> Tag Attributes

ATTRIBUTE	DESCRIPTION
id	The id attribute names the scripting variable that will be used to reference the newly created or retrieved connection properties. (required)
dataSource	The dataSource attribute names the DataSource, which exists in the PageContext, to retrieve. (optional)
jndiName	The jndiName attribute contains the name used to look up the JNDI DataSource. (optional)

The connection tag returns all of the properties described in Table 17.2.

Table 17.2 Connection Properties Returned by the connection Tag

ATTRIBUTE	DESCRIPTION
catalog	The catalog property contains the catalog of the database referenced by the connection tag.
closed	The closed property contains a Boolean value signifying whether the database connection is open (false) or closed (true).
readOnly	The readOnly property contains a Boolean value signifying whether the database connection can be used to update the database.

<sql:url />

The <sql:url> tag is used to set the url of the <sql:connection> tag. The syntax of the url tag is as follows:

```
<sql:connection
  id="id of used to access the connection">
  <sql:url>url pointing to database</sql:url>
  <sql:driver>driver name used to access database</sql:driver>
  <sql:userId>id of connecting user</sql:driver>
  <sql:password>password of connecting user</sql:password>
</sql:connection>
```

NOTE **The <sql:url> tag must be nested inside the <sql:connection> tag.**

This tag has a body type of JSP. The attribute of the url tag is described in Table 17.3.

Table 17.3 url Tag Attribute

ATTRIBUTE	DESCRIPTION
initParameter	The initParameter attribute names a ServletContext initialization parameter that can be used as the value of the url. (optional)

<sql:jndiName />

The <sql:jndiName> tag is used to set the name used to look up a JNDI DataSource used by the <sql:connection> tag. The syntax of the jndiName tag is as follows:

```
<sql:connection
  id="id of used to access the connection">
  <sql:jndiName>
    the name used to lookup a JNDI DataSource
  </sql:jndiName>
</sql:connection>
```

NOTE **The <sql:jndiName /> tag must be nested inside the <sql:connection> tag.**

This tag has a body type of JSP. The attribute of the jndiName tag is described in Table 17.4.

Table 17.4 jndiName Tag Attribute

ATTRIBUTE	DESCRIPTION
initParameter	The initParameter attribute names a ServletContext initialization parameter that can be used as the value of the JNDI DataSource name. (optional)

<sql:driver />

The <sql:driver> tag is used to set the name of the JDBC driver that will be used by the <sql:connection> tag when opening a database connection. The syntax of the driver tag is as follows:

```
<sql:connection
  id="id of used to access the connection">
  <sql:url>url pointing to database</sql:url>
  <sql:driver>driver name used to access database</sql:driver>
  <sql:userId>id of connecting user</sql:driver>
  <sql:password>password of connecting user</sql:password>
</sql:connection>
```

NOTE **The <sql:driver /> tag must be nested inside the <sql:connection> tag.**

This tag has a body type of JSP. The attribute of the driver tag is described in Table 17.5.

Table 17.5 driver Tag Attribute

ATTRIBUTE	DESCRIPTION
initParameter	The initParameter attribute names a ServletContext initialization parameter that can be used as the value of the driver. (optional)

<sql:userId />

The <sql:userId> tag is used to set the user id of the user, which will be used by the <sql:connection> tag, when opening a database connection. The syntax of the userId tag is as follows:

```
<sql:connection
  id="id of used to access the connection">
  <sql:url>url pointing to database</sql:url>
  <sql:driver>driver name used to access database</sql:driver>
  <sql:userId>id of connecting user</sql:driver>
  <sql:password>password of connecting user</sql:password>
</sql:connection>
```

NOTE **The <sql:userId/ > tag must be nested inside the <sql:connection> tag.**

This tag has a body type of JSP. The attribute of the userId tag is described in Table 17.6.

Table 17.6 userId Tag Attribute

ATTRIBUTE	DESCRIPTION
initParameter	The initParameter attribute names a ServletContext initialization parameter that can be used as the value of the user id. (optional)

<sql:password />

The <sql:password> tag is used to set the password of the user, which will be used by the <sql:connection> tag when opening a database connection. The syntax of the password tag is as follows:

```
<sql:connection
  id="id of used to access the connection">
  <sql:url>url pointing to database</sql:url>
  <sql:driver>driver name used to access database</sql:driver>
  <sql:userId>id of connecting user</sql:driver>
  <sql:password>password of connecting user</sql:password>
</sql:connection>
```

NOTE **The <sql:password /> tag must be nested inside the <sql:connection> tag.**

This tag has a body type of JSP. The attribute of the password tag is described in Table 17.7.

Table 17.7 password Tag Attribute

ATTRIBUTE	DESCRIPTION
initParameter	The initParameter attribute names a ServletContext initialization parameter that can be used as the value of the password. (optional)

<sql:closeConnection />

The <sql:closeConnection> tag is used to set the database connection referenced by the conn attribute. The syntax of the closeConnection tag is as follows:

```
<sql:closeConnection
  conn="name of connection stored in PageContext" />
```

This tag has a body type of JSP. The attribute of the closeConnection tag is described in Table 17.8.

Table 17.8 closeConnection Tag Attribute

ATTRIBUTE	DESCRIPTION
conn	The conn attribute names the connection stored in PageContext that you wish to close. (required)

Statement and PreparedStatement Tags

The Statement and PreparedStatement tags encapsulate the necessary functionality required to perform SQL commands, using both JDBC Statements and PreparedStatements. There are five tags associated with this group of DBTags.

<sql:statement />

The <sql:statement> tag creates and executes a database statement (note that the <sql:execute /> tag is required when executing a statement). The syntax for the statement tag follows:

```
<sql:statement
  id="id of used to identify the statement"
  conn="id created using the connection tag">
  <sql:query>
    SQL Statement to execute
  </sql:query>
  <sql:execute />
</sql:statement>
```

NOTE This example uses DBTags that we have not discussed. At this moment, you can ignore these tags. We will be examining each of them later in the chapter.

This tag has a body type of JSP. The attributes of the statement tag are described in Table 17.9.

Table 17.9 statement Tag Attributes

ATTRIBUTE	DESCRIPTION
id	The id attribute names the scripting variable that will be used to reference the newly created JDBC statement. (required)
conn	The conn attribute names the JDBC connection id that was used in the <sql:connection> tag. (required)

The statement tag can set or get all of the properties described in Table 17.10 using the JSP standard actions <jsp:setProperty> and <jsp:getProperty>, respectively.

Table 17.10 Properties Returned by the statement Tag

PROPERTY	DESCRIPTION
fetchSize	The fetchSize property is used to set or get the number of rows that should be or have been returned from the database.
maxRows	The maxRows property is used to set or get the maximum number of rows that should or can be returned from the database.
queryTimeout	The queryTimeout property is used to set or get the maximum length of time that a query will remain active before timing out.

<sql:query />

The <sql:query> tag is used to pass a SQL query to a <sql:statement> or <sql:prepared-Statement> tag. The syntax for the query tag follows:

```
<sql:statement
  id="id of used to identify the statement"
  conn="id created using the connection tag">
  <sql:query>
    SQL Statement to execute
  </sql:query>
  <sql:execute />
</sql:statement>
```

NOTE **This tag must be nested inside a <sql:statement> or <sql:preparedStatement> tag.**

This tag has a body type of JSP. The tag has no attributes.

<sql:execute />

The <sql:execute> tag is used to actually perform the database action described by the <sql:statement> or <sql:preparedStatement> tags. The <sql:execute> tag can have a nested set of <sql:setColumn> tags, if it is nested in a <sql:preparedStatement> tag. The syntax for the *execute* tag follows:

```
<sql:statement
  id="id of used to identify the statement"
  conn="id created using the connection tag">
  <sql:query>
    SQL Statement to execute
  </sql:query>
  <sql:execute />
</sql:statement>
```

NOTE **This tag must be nested inside a <sql:statement> or <sql:preparedStatement> tag.**

This tag has a body type of JSP. This tag has no attributes.

<sql:preparedStatement />

The <sql:preparedStatement> tag creates and executes a JDBC PreparedStatement (note that the <sql:execute /> tag is required when executing a statement). The syntax for the preparedStatement tag follows:

```
<sql:preparedStatement
  id="id of used to identify the PreparedStatement"
  conn="id created using the connection tag">
  <sql:query>
```

```
    <%-- SQL Prepared Statement to create and execute --%>
    select * from user where userid = ?
  </sql:query>
  <sql:execute>
    <sql:setColumn position="1">userid</sql:setColumn>
  </sql:execute>
</sql:preparedStatement>
```

This tag has a body type of JSP. The attributes of the preparedStatement tag are described in Table 17.11.

Table 17.11 preparedStatement Tag Attributes

ATTRIBUTE	DESCRIPTION
id	The id attribute names the scripting variable that will be used to reference the newly created JDBC PreparedStatement. (required)
conn	The conn attribute names the JDBC connection id that was used in the <sql:connection> tag. (required)

The preparedStatement tag can set or get all of the properties described in Table 17.12, using the JSP standard actions <jsp:setProperty> and <jsp:getProperty>, respectively.

Table 17.12 Properties of the preparedStatement Tag

PROPERTY	DESCRIPTION
fetchSize	The fetchSize property is used to set or get the number of rows that should be or have been returned from the database.
maxRows	The maxRows property is used to set or get the maximum number of rows that should or can be returned from the database.
queryTimeout	The queryTimeout property is used to set or get the maximum length of time that a query will remain active before timing out.

<sql:setColumn />

The <sql:setColumn> tag is used to set the value of a <sql:query> parameter that is nested in a <sql:preparedStatement>. The body of this tag will contain the value to set the column equal. The syntax for the setColumn tag follows:

```
<sql:preparedStatement
  id="id of used to identify the PreparedStatement"
  conn="id created using the connection tag">
```

```
    <sql:query>
      <%-- SQL Prepared Statement to create and execute --%>
      select * from user where userid = ?
    </sql:query>
    <sql:execute>
      <sql:setColumn position="1">userid</sql:setColumn>
    </sql:execute>
  </sql:preparedStatement>
```

NOTE **The <sql:setColumn /> tag must be nested inside a <sql:execute> tag that is nested inside a <sql:preparedStatement> tag.**

This tag has a body type of JSP. The attribute of the setColumn tag is described in Table 17.13.

Table 17.13 setColumn Tag Attributes

ATTRIBUTE	DESCRIPTION
position	The position attribute names the column position of the SQL parameter associated with a PreparedStatement. (required)

ResultSet Tags

The ResultSet tags encapsulate the necessary functionality required to perform basic operations on a JDBC ResultSet. There are eleven tags associated with this group of DBTags.

<sql:resultSet />

The <sql:resultSet> tag executes a query, generated by a parent <sql:statement> or <sql:preparedStatement> tag, and iterates over the results evaluating its body once per row in the returned ResultSet. The syntax for the resultSet tag follows:

```
<sql:statement
  id="id of used to identify the statement"
  conn="id created using the connection tag">
  <sql:query>
    SQL Statement to execute
  </sql:query>
  <table>
  <sql:resultSet id="id of used to identify the ResultSet">
    <tr>
      <td><sql:getColumn position="column position" /></td>
      <td><sql:getColumn position="column position" /></td>
      <td><sql:getColumn position="column position" /></td>
      <td><sql:getColumn position="column position" /></td>
    </tr>
```

```
    </sql:resultSet>
    </table>
  </sql:statement>
```

This tag has a body type of JSP. The attributes of the *resultSet* tag are described in Table 17.14.

Table 17.14 resultSet Tag Attributes

ATTRIBUTE	DESCRIPTION
id	The id attribute names the scripting variable that will be used to reference the newly created JDBC ResultSet. (required)
loop	The loop attribute, if set to true, will force the <sql:resultSet> tag to evaluate its body for every row in the ResultSet. (optional)
name	The name attribute names a scripting variable that contains a reference to a ResultSet object that was created without using a parent <sql:statement> or <sql:preparedStatement> tag. (optional)
scope	The scope attribute is used to access the ResultSet named using the name attribute, if the name attribute is used. If the name attribute has been used and the scope tag is left empty, then the <sql:resultSet> tag will search all scopes. (optional)

The resultSet tag can set or get the property described in Table 17.15, using the JSP standard actions <jsp:setProperty> and <jsp:getProperty>, respectively.

Table 17.15 Properties Returned by the resultSet Tag

ATTRIBUTE	DESCRIPTION
fetchSize	The fetchSize property is used to set or get the number of rows that should be or have been returned from the database.

<sql:wasNull />

The <sql:wasNull> tag will evaluate its body if the last <sql:getColumn> tag retrieved a null value from the database. The <sql:wasNull> tag must be nested inside a <sql:resultSet> tag and must be immediately preceded by a <sql:getColumn> tag. The syntax for the wasNull tag follows:

```
<sql:statement
  id="id of used to identify the statement"
  conn="id created using the connection tag">
  <sql:query>
    SQL Statement to execute
```

```
    </sql:query>
    <table>
    <sql:resultSet id="id of used to identify the ResultSet">
      <tr>
        <td><sql:getColumn position="column position" /></td>
        <td><sql:getColumn position="column position" /></td>
        <td><sql:getColumn position="column position" /></td>
        <td>
          <sql:getColumn position="column position" />
          <sql:wasNull>
            The evaluated body, if the column was null
          </sql:wasNull>
        </td>
      </tr>
    </sql:resultSet>
    </table>
  </sql:statement>
```

This tag has a body type of JSP. This tag has no attributes.

<sql:wasNotNull />

The <sql:wasNotNull> tag is the exact opposite of the <sql:wasNull> tag. It will evaluate its body if the last <sql:getColumn> tag did not retrieve a null value from the database. The <sql:wasNotNull> tag must be nested inside a <sql:resultSet> tag, and must be immediately preceded by a <sql:getColumn> tag. The syntax for wasNotNull tag follows:

```
  <sql:statement
    id="id of used to identify the statement"
    conn="id created using the connection tag">
    <sql:query>
      SQL Statement to execute
    </sql:query>
    <table>
    <sql:resultSet id="id of used to identify the ResultSet">
      <tr>
        <td><sql:getColumn position="column position" /></td>
        <td><sql:getColumn position="column position" /></td>
        <td><sql:getColumn position="column position" /></td>
        <td>
          <sql:getColumn position="column position" />
          <sql:wasNotNull>
            The evaluated body, if the column was not null
          </sql:wasNotNull>
        </td>
      </tr>
    </sql:resultSet>
    </table>
  </sql:statement>
```

This tag has a body type of JSP. This tag has no attributes.

<sql:getColumn />

The <sql:getColumn> tag retrieves the value, as a String, of a column in the parent ResultSet. The syntax for statement tag follows:

```
<sql:statement
  id="id of used to identify the statement"
  conn="id created using the connection tag">
  <sql:query>
    SQL Statement to execute
  </sql:query>
  <table>
  <sql:resultSet id="id of used to identify the ResultSet">
    <tr>
      <td><sql:getColumn position="column position" /></td>
      <td><sql:getColumn position="column position" /></td>
      <td><sql:getColumn position="column position" /></td>
      <td><sql:getColumn position="column position" /></td>
    </tr>
  </sql:resultSet>
  </table>
</sql:statement>
```

This tag has no body. The attributes of the statement tag are described in Table 17.16.

Table 17.16 getColumn Tag Attributes

ATTRIBUTE	DESCRIPTION
position	The position attribute names the column position to retrieve. (optional)
colName	The colName attribute names the column name to retrieve, as opposed to the column position. (optional)
to	The to attribute names an attribute to store the retrieved column value, as opposed to simply outputting the column value. (optional)
scope	The scope attribute specifies the scope of the attribute named in the to attribute, if the to attribute was set. (optional)

<sql:getNumber />

The <sql:getNumber> tag is comparable to the <sql:getColumn> tag, with the main exception being the ability to apply locale and format constraints on the output of retrieved numbers. The syntax for the getNumber tag follows:

```
<sql:statement
  id="id of used to identify the statement"
  conn="id created using the connection tag">
  <sql:query>
```

```
    SQL Statement to execute
  </sql:query>
  <table>
  <sql:resultSet id="id of used to identify the ResultSet">
    <tr>
      <td>
        <sql:getNumber
          position="column position"
          locale="en_US"
          format="CURRENCY" />
      </td>
    </tr>
  </sql:resultSet>
  </table>
</sql:statement>
```

This tag has no body. The attributes of the getNumber tag are described in Table 17.17.

Table 17.17 getNumber Tag Attributes

ATTRIBUTE	DESCRIPTION
position	The position attribute names the column position to retrieve. (optional)
colName	The colName attribute names the column name to retrieve, as opposed to the column position. (optional)
to	The to attribute names an attribute to store the retrieved column value, as opposed to simply outputting the column value. (optional)
scope	The scope attribute specifies the scope of the attribute named in the to attribute, if the to attribute was set. (optional)
locale	The locale attribute names the combined ISO Language Code and ISO Country code to associate the printed value. You can find documentation on both of these in the Java API description for the java.util.Locale object. (optional)
format	The format attribute names the style to use when printing the retrieved value. The available options include all formats defined by the class java.text.DecimalFormat or the tag-defined formats CURRENCY, PERCENT, or NUMBER. (optional)

<sql:getTime />

The <sql:getTime> tag is comparable to the <sql:getColumn> tag, with the main exception being the ability to apply locale and format constraints on the output of a retrieved java.sql.Time object. The syntax for getTime tag follows:

```
<sql:statement
```

```
  id="id of used to identify the statement"
  conn="id created using the connection tag">
  <sql:query>
    SQL Statement to execute
  </sql:query>
  <table>
  <sql:resultSet id="id of used to identify the ResultSet">
    <tr>
      <td>
        <sql:getTime
          position="column position"
          locale="en_US"
          format="SHORT" />
      </td>
    </tr>
  </sql:resultSet>
  </table>
</sql:statement>
```

This tag has no body. The attributes of the getTime tag are described in Table 17.18.

Table 17.18 getTime Tag Attributes

ATTRIBUTE	DESCRIPTION
position	The position attribute names the column position to retrieve. (optional)
colName	The colName attribute names the column name to retrieve, as opposed to the column position. (optional)
to	The to attribute names an attribute to store the retrieved column value, as opposed to simply outputting the column value. (optional)
scope	The scope attribute specifies the scope of the attribute named in the to attribute, if the to attribute was set. (optional)
locale	The locale attribute names the combined ISO Language Code and ISO Country code to associate the printed value. You can find documentation on both of these in the Java API description for the java.util.Locale object. (optional)
format	The format attribute names the style to use when printing the retrieved value. The available options include all formats defined by the class java.text.SimpleDateFormat or the tag-defined formats FULL, LONG, MEDIUM, or SHORT. (optional)

<sql:getTimestamp />

The <sql:getTimestamp> tag is comparable to the <sql:getTime> tag, with the main exception being the ability to apply locale and format constraints on the output of a retrieved java.sql.Timestamp object as opposed to a java.sql.Time object. The syntax for the getTimestamp tag follows:

```
<sql:statement
  id="id of used to identify the statement"
  conn="id created using the connection tag">
  <sql:query>
    SQL Statement to execute
  </sql:query>
  <table>
  <sql:resultSet id="id of used to identify the ResultSet">
    <tr>
      <td>
        <sql:getTimestamp
          position="column position"
          format="FULL" />
      </td>
    </tr>
  </sql:resultSet>
  </table>
</sql:statement>
```

This tag has no body. The attributes of the getTimestamp tag are described in Table 17.19.

Table 17.19 getTimestamp Tag Attributes

ATTRIBUTE	DESCRIPTION
position	The position attribute names the column position to retrieve. (optional)
colName	The colName attribute names the column name to retrieve, as opposed to the column position. (optional)
to	The to attribute names an attribute to store the retrieved column value, as opposed to simply outputting the column value. (optional)
scope	The scope attribute specifies the scope of the attribute named in the to attribute, if the to attribute was set. (optional)
locale	The locale attribute names the combined ISO Language Code and ISO Country code to associate the printed value. You can find documentation on both of these in the Java API description for the java.util.Locale object. (optional)
format	The format attribute names the style to use when printing the retrieved value. The available options include all formats defined by the class java.text.SimpleDateFormat or the tag-defined formats FULL, LONG, MEDIUM, or SHORT. (optional)

<sql:getDate />

The <sql:getDate> tag is comparable to the <sql:getTime> and <sql:getTimestamp> tags, with the main exception being the ability to apply locale and format constraints on the output of a retrieved java.sql.Date object as opposed to a java.sql.Time and java.sql.Timestamp objects. The syntax for the getDate tag follows:

```
<sql:statement
  id="id of used to identify the statement"
  conn="id created using the connection tag">
  <sql:query>
    SQL Statement to execute
  </sql:query>
  <table>
  <sql:resultSet id="id of used to identify the ResultSet">
    <tr>
      <td>
        <sql:getDate
          position="column position"
          format="FULL" />
      </td>
    </tr>
  </sql:resultSet>
  </table>
</sql:statement>
```

This tag has no body. The attributes of the getDate tag are described in Table 17.20.

Table 17.20 getDate Tag Attributes

ATTRIBUTE	DESCRIPTION
position	The position attribute names the column position to retrieve. (optional)
colName	The colName attribute names the column name to retrieve, as opposed to the column position. (optional)
to	The to attribute names an attribute to store the retrieved column value, as opposed to simply outputting the column value. (optional)
scope	The scope attribute specifies the scope of the attribute named in the to attribute, if the to attribute was set. (optional)
locale	The locale attribute names the combined ISO Language Code and ISO Country code to associate the printed value. You can find documentation on both of these in the Java API description for the java.util.Locale object. (optional)
format	The format attribute names the style to use when printing the retrieved value. The available options include all formats defined by the class java.text.SimpleDateFormat or the tag-defined formats FULL, LONG, MEDIUM, or SHORT. (optional)

<sql:wasEmpty />

The <sql:wasEmpty> tag will evaluate its body if the parent ResultSet was empty. The <sql:wasEmpty> tag must be nested inside a <sql:statement> or <sql:preparedStatement> tag and be preceded by a <sql:resultSet> tag. The syntax for the wasEmpty tag follows:

```
<sql:statement
  id="id of used to identify the statement"
  conn="id created using the connection tag">
  <sql:query>
    SQL Statement to execute
  </sql:query>
  <table>
  <sql:resultSet id="id of used to identify the ResultSet">
    <tr>
      <td><sql:getColumn position="column position" /></td>
      <td><sql:getColumn position="column position" /></td>
      <td><sql:getColumn position="column position" /></td>
      <td><sql:getColumn position="column position" /></td>
    </tr>
  </sql:resultSet>
  </table>
  <sql:wasEmpty>
    The evaluated body, if the ResultSet was empty
  </sql:wasEmpty>
</sql:statement>
```

This tag has a body type of JSP. This tag has no attributes.

<sql:wasNotEmpty />

The <sql:wasNotEmpty> tag will evaluate its body if the parent ResultSet was not empty. The <sql:wasNotEmpty> tag must be nested inside a <sql:statement> or <sql:preparedStatement> tag and be preceded by a <sql:resultSet> tag. The syntax for the wasNotEmpty tag follows:

```
<sql:statement
  id="id of used to identify the statement"
  conn="id created using the connection tag">
  <sql:query>
    SQL Statement to execute
  </sql:query>
  <table>
  <sql:resultSet id="id of used to identify the ResultSet">
    <tr>
      <td><sql:getColumn position="column position" /></td>
      <td><sql:getColumn position="column position" /></td>
      <td><sql:getColumn position="column position" /></td>
      <td><sql:getColumn position="column position" /></td>
    </tr>
  </sql:resultSet>
```

```
    </table>
    <sql:wasNotEmpty>
      The evaluated body, if the ResultSet was not empty
    </sql:wasNotEmpty>
  </sql:statement>
```

This tag has a body type of JSP. This tag has no attributes.

<sql:rowCount />

The <sql:rowCount> tag prints the number of rows returned in a ResultSet. The <sql:rowCount> tag must be nested inside a <sql:statement> or <sql:preparedStatement> tag and be preceded by a <sql:resultSet> tag. The syntax for rowCount tag follows:

```
<sql:statement
  id="id of used to identify the statement"
  conn="id created using the connection tag">
  <sql:query>
    SQL Statement to execute
  </sql:query>
  <table>
  <sql:resultSet id="id of used to identify the ResultSet">
    <tr>
      <td><sql:getColumn position="column position" /></td>
    </tr>
  </sql:resultSet>
  </table>
  Total Rows = <sql:rowCount />
</sql:statement>
```

This tag has neither body nor attributes.

CHAPTER

18

Scrape Tag Library

The Jakarta Scrape tag library enables you to retrieve anchored blocks of text from a named resource. The Scrape tag library relies upon the Jakarta ORO Perl Regular Expression package to perform the parsing of retrieved text. This Scrape library can be very useful when trying to build a portal-like interface composed of many disparate resources. A common use would be to retrieve a stock quote from yahoo.com.

NOTE **This tag library requires a JSP/servlet container that supports JSP 1.1 and above.**

Configuration

To use the Scrape tag library in a Web application, you must complete the following steps, substituting for *webappname* the name of the Web application that will be using this library:

1. Copy the scrape.tld TLD packaged with this tag library to the <TOMCAT_HOME>/webapps/*webappname*/WEB-INF/ directory.
2. Copy the scrape.jar JAR file containing the Scrape tag library's tag handlers to the <TOMCAT_HOME>/webapps/*webappname*/WEB-INF/lib directory.
3. Add the following <taglib> subelement to the web.xml file of the Web application:

```
<taglib>
  <taglib-uri>
```

```
    http://jakarta.apache.org/taglibs/scrape
  </taglib-uri>
  <taglib-location>
    /WEB-INF/scrape.tld
  </taglib-location>
</taglib>
```

4. If the Jakarta-Taglib archive did not include the Jakarta ORO Perl Regular Expression package, download and extract Version 2.0 or later from http://jakarta.apache.org/oro/.
5. Copy the jakarta-oro-2.0.x.jar file to the <TOMCAT_HOME>/webapps/*webapp-name*/WEB-INF/lib directory.

NOTE **The Jakarta ORO Perl Regular Expression package contains a set of text-processing classes that include Perl5 and AWK-like compatible regular expressions processing functionality. You can find more information about the ORO project at http://jakarta.apache.org/oro/.**

The following taglib directive must be added to each JSP that will leverage the Scrape tag library:

```
<%@ taglib
  uri="http://jakarta.apache.org/taglibs/scrape"
  prefix="scrp" %>
```

This directive identifies the URI defined in the previously listed <taglib> element and states that all Scrape tags should be prefixed with the string *scrp*.

Scrape Tags

Four custom tags are packaged in the Scrape tag library: result, scrape, page, and url.

<scrp:result />

The result tag retrieves and prints the results of a previously executed scrape tag. The syntax of the result tag is as follows:

```
<scrp:page url="the url to be scraped">
  <scrp:scrape
    id="id that will be used to reference this scrape"
    begin="beginning text anchor"
    end="ending text anchor" />
</scrp:page>

<scrp:result scrape="id from a previous scrape tag"/>
```

This tag has no body and a single attribute, scrape, used to define a previously executed scrape tag.

<scrp:scrape />

The <scrp:scrape> tag names the starting and ending anchors, with additional optional attributes that mark the text block that will be removed from a page or URL. The anchors act as delimiters, where the inner text is the text that is being returned. The syntax of the <scrp:scrape> tag is as follows:

```
<scrp:page url="the url to be scraped">
  <scrp:scrape
    id="id that will be used to reference this scrape"
    begin="beginning text anchor"
    end="ending text anchor" />
</scrp:page>

<scrp:result scrape="id from a previous scrape tag"/>
```

NOTE **The <scrp:scrape> tag must be nested inside a <scrp:page> tag.**

This tag has no body. The attributes of the <scrp:scrape> tag are described in Table 18.1.

Table 18.1 Attributes of the scrape Tag

ATTRIBUTE	DESCRIPTION
id	The id of the scraped results that will be used in the <scrp:results> tag to output the retrieved text block (required)
begin	The beginning of the text block to retrieve (required)
end	The ending of the text block to retrieve (required)
strip	If set to true, removes all markup language, including HTML, XML, and so on, from the retrieved text; the default value is false (optional)
anchors	If set to true, removes the anchors named using the begin and end attributes; the default value is false (optional)

<scrp:page />

The <scrp:page> tag names the URL of the document to be scraped. This tag also initiates the actual scraping of resource when its doEndTag() method is invoked. The syntax of the <scrp:page> tag is as follows:

```
<scrp:page url="the url to be scraped">
  <scrp:scrape
    id="id that will be used to reference this scrape"
    begin="beginning text anchor"
    end="ending text anchor" />
</scrp:page>

<scrp:result scrape="id from a previous scrape tag"/>
```

This tag has a body type of JSP. The attributes of the <scrp:page> tag are described in Table 18.2.

NOTE **If the URL of the resource needs to be created dynamically, then you should use the <scrp:url> tag. Combining these tags will require the omission of the url attribute.**

Table 18.2 Attributes of the page Tag

ATTRIBUTE	DESCRIPTION
url	The fully qualified URL of the resource to scrape. (required)
time	The length of time, in minutes, before the targeted resource will be scraped again. The minimum scrape interval, which is also the default, is 10 minutes. (optional)

<scrp:url />

The url tag names the fully qualified URL of the document to be scraped. This tag should be used in combination with the page tag when creating a URL dynamically. The syntax of the url tag is as follows:

```
<scrp:page>
    <scrp:url>
      fully qualified URL to the resource being scraped
    </scrp:url>
    <scrp:scrape
    id="id that will be used to reference this scrape"
    begin="beginning text anchor"
    end="ending text anchor" />
</scrp:page>

<scrp:result scrape="id from a previous scrape tag"/>
```

NOTE **The url tag must be nested inside a page tag.**

This tag has a body type of JSP and no attributes.

Using the Scrape Tags

This section provides an example of how the Scrape tags can be used to retrieve text blocks from a named resource. Listing 18.1 contains the source for this example.

```
<%@ taglib
  uri="http://jakarta.apache.org/taglibs/scrape"
  prefix="scrp" %>
```

Listing 18.1 ScrapeExample.jsp *(continues)*

```
<html>
  <head>
   <title>Scrape Taglib Example</title>
  </head>

  <body>

  <scrp:page>
    <scrp:url>
      http://www.weather.com/weather/local/<%=
request.getParameter("zip") %>
    </scrp:url>
    <scrp:scrape
      id="currentTemp"
      begin="<!-- insert current temp -->"
      end="</B>" />
  </scrp:page>

  The current temperature at zip code
   <%= request.getParameter("zip") %>
   : <scrp:result scrape="currentTemp"/> &deg;F

  </body>
</html>
```

Listing 18.1 ScrapeExample.jsp *(continued)*

This example takes a ZIP code, which is passed in on the requesting URL, to make a call to the Weather Channel. The text that is returned will contain the current temperature for the referenced ZIP code. To test this example, copy the JSP to the <TOMCAT_HOME>/webapps/*webappname*/ directory, and open your browser to the following URL:

```
http://localhost:8080/webappname/ScrapeExample.jsp?zip=80112
```

You should see a page similar to Figure 18.1.

NOTE **This example uses the ZIP code for Englewood, Colorado. You can just as easily substitute any U.S. ZIP code.**

The ScrapeExample.jsp's main functionality exists inside a single page tag, which acts as the parent to a url and a scrape tag. The url tag creates the URL that references the resource to be scraped. This example references the Weather Channel home page and appends the value of the zip parameter.

Next, the scrape tag names the starting and ending anchors of the text block to scrape. It also names the id used to identify the scraped results. Finally, the JSP outputs the block of text that was scraped, using the result tag.

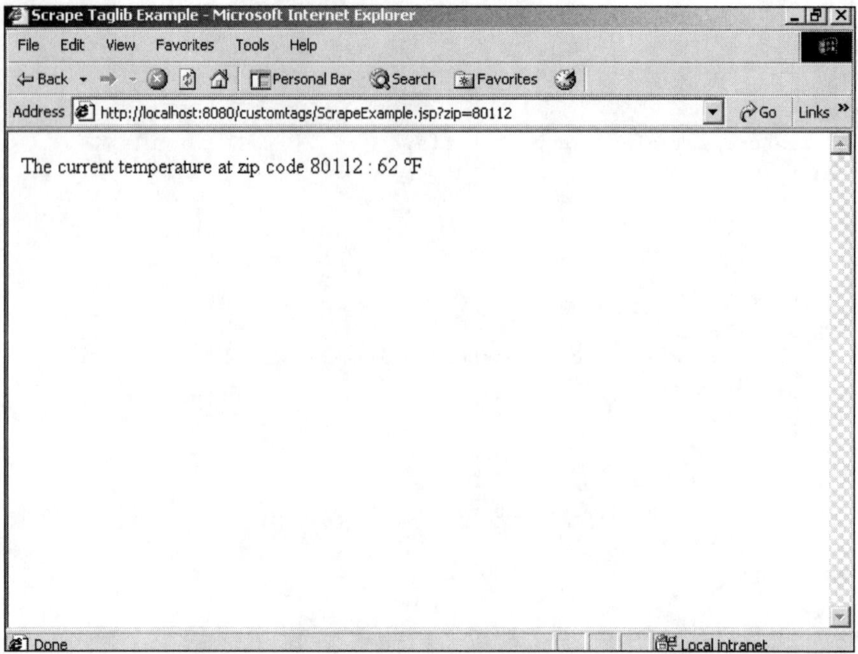

Figure 18.1 Output of the ScrapeExample.jsp.

CHAPTER

19

Logging Tag Library

The Jakarta Logging tag library enables you to insert Apache log4j functionality directly into your JSP documents. The Apache log4j project is an open source package that enables you to embed multiple target logging statements in your Java applications. The Logging tag libraries enable you to embed log4j statements in your JSPs.

NOTE **This tag library requires a JSP/servlet container that supports JSP 1.1 and above.**

Configuration

To use the Logging tag library in a Web application, you must complete the following steps, substituting for *webappname* the name of the Web application that will be using this library:

1. Download the log4j archive from the http://jakarta.apache.org Web site.
2. Extract the JAR file log4j.jar, and copy it to the <TOMCAT_HOME>/webapps/*webappname*/WEB-INF/lib directory.
3. Create a log4j properties file named log4j.properties, and copy it to the <TOMCAT_HOME>/webapps/*webappname*/WEB-INF/classes directory. The following code snippet shows our example properties file:

```
log4j.rootCategory= FATAL, console
log4j.category.chapter19= WARN, file
```

```
# console is set to be a ConsoleAppender which outputs to System.out.
log4j.appender.console=org.apache.log4j.ConsoleAppender

# console is set to be a ConsoleAppender which outputs to System.out.
log4j.appender.file=org.apache.log4j.RollingFileAppender
log4j.appender.file.File=<TOMCAT_HOME>/webapps/webappname/WEB-
INF/log.txt

# console uses PatternLayout.
log4j.appender.console.layout=org.apache.log4j.PatternLayout
log4j.appender.file.layout=org.apache.log4j.PatternLayout

# The conversion pattern uses format specifiers. You
# might want to change the pattern and watch the output
# layout change.
log4j.appender.console.layout.ConversionPattern=%3x - %m%
```

4. Copy the log.tld TLD packaged with this tag library to the <TOMCAT_HOME>/webapps/*webappname*/WEB-INF directory.
5. Copy the log.jar JAR file containing the Logging tag library's tag handlers to the <TOMCAT_HOME>/webapps/*webappname*/WEB-INF/lib directory.
6. Add the following <taglib> subelement to the web.xml file of the Web application:

```
<taglib>
  <taglib-uri>
    http://jakarta.apache.org/taglibs/log-1.0
  </taglib-uri>
  <taglib-location>
    /WEB-INF/log.tld
  </taglib-location>
</taglib>
```

The following taglib directive must be added to each JSP that will leverage the Logging tag library:

```
<%@ taglib
  uri="http://jakarta.apache.org/taglibs/log-1.0"
  prefix="log" %>
```

This directive identifies the URI defined in the previously listed <taglib> element and states that all Logging tags should be prefixed with the string *log*.

Logging Tags

The Logging tag library encapsulates the necessary functionality to embed Apache Jakarta log4j functionality into your JSPs. To understand the Logging tags, you must know the following facts about log4j:

- Log4j uses a properties object that is dynamically created or created using a log4j.properties file.

- When logging a message using log4j, you must choose a defined category to log your message to. This category is assigned a priority level, which determines which messages will be displayed; and an appender, which determines the target the messages will be logged to.
- Log4j defines five priority levels, listed as follows in priority order: debug, info, warn, error, and fatal. A combination of the priority level assigned to a message and the priority level assigned to a category, which is assigned in the properties object, determines if a message will be logged. If a message has a priority greater than or equal to the priority assigned to the category in the properties object, then the message will be logged. Otherwise, the message will be ignored.

NOTE **A complete discussion of log4j is beyond the scope of this text. To learn more about the functionality included in the log4j project, please see the documentation found on the Jakarta Web site: http://jakarta.apache.org.**

<log:debug />

The debug tag writes a debug-level message to the category defined in the log4j properties object, if the priority level of the defined category is set to debug. The syntax of the debug tag is as follows:

```
<log:debug>
  Message to log.
</log:debug>
```

This tag has a body type of JSP. The attributes of the debug tag are described in Table 19.1.

Table 19.1 Attributes of the debug Tag

ATTRIBUTE	DESCRIPTION
category	The defined category that will be used to log this message; if not specified, then the default log4j category is used (optional)
message	The message to log to the defined category; if not specified, then the tag body is logged to the category (optional)

<log:info />

The info tag writes an info-level message to the category defined in the log4j properties object, if the defined category has a priority of *info* or less. The syntax of the info tag is as follows:

```
<log:info>
  Message to log.
</log:info>
```

This tag has a body type of JSP. The attributes of the info tag are described in Table 19.2.

Table 19.2 Attributes of the info Tag

ATTRIBUTE	DESCRIPTION
category	The defined category that will be used to log this message; if not specified, then the default log4j category is used (optional)
message	The message to log to the defined category; if not specified, then the tag body is logged to the category (optional)

<log:warn />

The warn tag writes a warn-level message to the category defined in the log4j properties object, if the defined category has a priority of warn or less. The syntax of the warn tag is as follows:

```
<log:warn>
  Message to log.
</log:warn>
```

This tag has a body type of JSP. The attributes of the warn tag are described in Table 19.3.

Table 19.3 Attributes of the warn Tag

ATTRIBUTE	DESCRIPTION
category	The defined category that will be used to log this message; if not specified, then the default log4j category is used (optional)
message	The message to log to the defined category; if not specified, then the tag body is logged to the category (optional)

<log:error />

The error tag writes an error-level message to the category defined in the log4j properties object, if the defined category has a priority of error or less. The syntax of the error tag is as follows:

```
<log:error>
  Message to log.
</log:error>
```

This tag has a body type of JSP. The attributes of the error tag are described in Table 19.4.

Table 19.4 Attributes of the error Tag

ATTRIBUTE	DESCRIPTION
category	The defined category that will be used to log this message; if not specified, then the default *log4j* category is used (optional)
message	The message to log to the defined category; if not specified, then the tag body is logged to the category (optional)

<log:fatal />

The fatal tag writes a fatal-level message to the category defined in the log4j properties object, if the defined category has a priority of fatal or less. The syntax of the fatal tag is as follows:

```
<log:fatal>
  Message to log.
</log:fatal>
```

This tag has a body type of JSP. The attributes of the fatal tag are described in Table 19.5.

Table 19.5 Attributes of the fatal Tag

ATTRIBUTE	DESCRIPTION
category	The defined category that will be used to log this message; if not specified, then the default log4j category is used (optional)
message	The message to log to the defined category; if not specified, then the tag body is logged to the category (optional)

<log:dump />

The dump tag writes all the attributes in the named scope to the JspWriter associated with the requesting client. The syntax of the dump tag is as follows:

```
<log:dump scope="page|request|application|session" />
```

This tag has no body. The attribute of the dump tag is described in Table 19.6.

Table 19.6 Attribute of the dump Tag

ATTRIBUTE	DESCRIPTION
scope	The implicit JSP object whose attributes are displayed (required)

NOTE **The dump tag does not use the log4j project. It simply writes its output back to the calling client.**

Using the Logging Tags

This section provides an example of how the tags in the Logging tag library can be leveraged. Listing 19.1 contains the source for this example.

```
<%@ taglib
  uri="http://jakarta.apache.org/taglibs/log-1.0"
  prefix="log" %>

<html>
  <head>
    <title>Log4J Tag Library Example</title>
  </head>

  <body>

    <log:debug>
      This is a debug message using body content.
    </log:debug>
    <log:debug message="This is a debug message." />
    <log:debug category="chapter19">
      This is a debug message using category chapter19.
    </log:debug>

    <log:info>
      This is an info message using body content.
    </log:info>
    <log:info message="This is an info message." />
    <log:info category="chapter19">
      This is an info message using category chapter19.
    </log:info>

    <log:warn>
      This is a warn message using body content.
    </log:warn>
    <log:warn message="This is a warn message." />
    <log:warn category="chapter19">
      This is a warn message using category chapter19.
    </log:warn>
```

Listing 19.1 Log4JExample.jsp. *(continues)*

```
    <log:error>
      This is an error message using body content.
    </log:error>
    <log:error message="This is an error message." />
    <log:error category="chapter19">
      This is an error message using category chapter19.
    </log:error>

    <log:fatal>
      This is a fatal message using body content.
    </log:fatal>
    <log:fatal message="This is a fatal message." />
    <log:fatal category="chapter19">
      This is a fatal message using category chapter19.
    </log:fatal>

  </body>
</html>
```

Listing 19.1 Log4JExample.jsp. *(continued)*

Before examining the output from this JSP, let's look at the categories defined by the previously listed log4j.properties file. This file defines two categories: rootCategory and chapter19.

The rootCategory category has a log priority of fatal and uses an appender named console. These values signify that only fatal messages will be logged, and they will be logged to the console of the Tomcat application.

The chapter19 category has a log priority of warn and uses an appender named file; therefore, only messages with a priority of warn or higher will be logged to the file appender. Looking further into the properties file, you will find a file appender definition. This definition creates an appender that logs messages to a file named log.txt that exists in the <TOMCAT_HOME>/webapps/webappname/WEB-INF/ directory.

NOTE **Log4j will not evaluate the <TOMCAT_HOME> entry in the log4j.properties file. You must make this entry a fully qualified directory path.**

To see this example in action, make sure the Logging tag library is installed, and copy the JSP to the <TOMCAT_HOME>/webapps/*webappname*/ directory. Open your browser to the following URL:

```
http://localhost:8080/webappname/Log4JExample.jsp
```

You should see a blank Web page because all the output from this JSP is sent to the two appenders defined in the previously listed log4j.properties files.

This example contains five sections of log statements, grouped by the prioritiesdebug, info, warn, error, and fatal. Each grouping contains the same statement attributes and bodies. Which statements are logged depends on the combination of their named category and the implicit priority level of the tag used. The first two debug statements, because they does not explicitly name a category, will try to log a message to the appender defined by the root category. As discussed earlier, the root category logs only messages with a fatal priority; therefore the only log tag that will actually produce output using the root appender is <log:fatal>. All other tags will be ignored.

The last log tag of each grouping explicitly names the category it will use: chapter19. The category chapter19 has a priority of warn, which implies that all log statements with a priority of warn or higher will be logged to the appender defined by the category chapter19, including <log:warn>, <log:error>, and <log:fatal>.

To see the complete results of this JSP, monitor the Tomcat console window and the log file named in the file appender of the log4j.properties file. The contents of the console window are shown in the following code snippet:

```
This is a warn message using category chapter19.
This is an error message using category chapter19.
This is a fatal message using body content.
This is a fatal message.
This is a fatal message using category chapter19.
```

The contents of the log.txt file should look similar to the following code snippet:

```
This is a warn message using category chapter19.
This is an error message using category chapter19.
This is a fatal message using category chapter19.
```

NOTE The chapter19 log messages are included in the console window because all categories implicitly inherit the appenders from the root category. To examine the hierarchies of log4j, look at the documentation found on the log4j home page http://jakarta.apache.org/log4j/docs/index.html.

CHAPTER

20

Mailer Tag Library

This chapter examines the Jakarta Mailer tag library. This tag library allows you to integrate JavaMail functionality directly into JSP documents.

NOTE **This tag library requires a JSP/servlet container that supports JSP 1.1 and above.**

Configuration

To use the Mailer tag library in a Web application, complete the following steps, substituting for *webappname* the name of the Web application that will be using this library:

1. Download the JavaMail 1.2 archive from the http://java.sun.com/products/javamail/ Web site.
2. Extract the JAR file mail.jar, and copy it to the <TOMCAT_HOME>/webapps/*webappname*/WEB-INF/lib directory.
3. Download the Java Activation 1.0.1 archive from the http://java.sun.com/products/javabeans/glasgow/jaf.html Web site.
4. Extract the JAR file activation.jar, and copy it to the <TOMCAT_HOME>/webapps/*webappname*/WEB-INF/lib directory.
5. Copy the mailer.tld TLD packaged with this tag library to the <TOMCAT_HOME>/webapps/*webappname*/WEB-INF directory.

6. Copy the mailer.jar JAR file containing the Mailer tag library's tag handlers to the <TOMCAT_HOME>/webapps/*webappname*/WEB-INF/lib directory.
7. Add the following <taglib> subelement to the web.xml file of the Web application:

```
<taglib>
  <taglib-uri>
    http://jakarta.apache.org/taglibs/mailer-1.0
  </taglib-uri>
  <taglib-location>
    /WEB-INF/mailer.tld
  </taglib-location>
</taglib>
```

The following taglib directive must be added to each JSP that will leverage the Mailer tag library:

```
<%@ taglib
  uri="http://jakarta.apache.org/taglibs/mailer-1.0"
  prefix="mt" %>
```

This directive identifies the URI defined in the previously listed <taglib> element and states that all Mailer tags should be prefixed with the string *mt*.

Mailer Tags

The Mailer custom tag library is used to send email, using the JavaMail API. The Mailer library allows for the sending of email using three distinct methods. The first method requires the explicit name of the SMTP host being used to send the mail. The second method requires the name of a JNDI resource for a JavaMail session. The final method requires the name of a JNDI resource for a JavaMail MimePartDataSource. This chapter's examples use the first method.

The Mail tag library consists of 11 tags: mail, message, header, setrecipient, addrecipient, replyto, from, attach, subject, send, and error.

<mt:mail />

The mail tag is used to create, but not send, an email message. The mail tag can be used to send email without the use of other tags, but most often, these values will be set using a tag within the body of this tag. The attributes set using the child tags in the body of the mail tag will take precedence over any value set as an attribute in this tag. The syntax of the mail tag is as follows:

```
<mt:mail
  server="some smtp server"
  to="the to address"
  from="the from address"
  subject="subject of the message">
  <mt:message>
    the body of the message
```

```
  </mt:message>
  <mt:send/>
</mt:mail>
```

NOTE This example uses the message and send tags. For now, ignore these tags. We will examine them both later in the chapter.

This tag has a body type of JSP. The attributes of the mail tag are described in Table 20.1.

Table 20.1 Attributes of the mail Tag

ATTRIBUTE	DESCRIPTION
server	The SMTP host to use when sending email. If this attribute is not specified, then the default server, localhost, will be used. (optional)
session	Allows a message to be created using a predefined JNDI-named Session object. (optional)
mimeMessage	Allows a message to be created using a predefined, JNDI-named MimePartDataSource. (optional)
to	The To address of the email message. To send email to multiple recipients, use a comma-separated list of recipients. (optional)
replyTo	The Reply To address of the email message. To add multiple recipients to the Reply To address, use a comma-separated list of recipients. (optional)
from	The From address of the email message. (optional)
cc	The carbon copy address of the email message. To send email to multiple recipients, use a comma-separated list of recipients. (optional)
bcc	The blind carbon copy address of the email message. To send email to multiple recipients, use a comma-separated list of recipients. (optional)
subject	The subject of the message. (optional)

<mt:message />

The message tag sets the body of a message. The resulting message will appear as it is written; any carriage returns and spaces in the JSP will be present in the delivered message. The syntax of the message tag is as follows:

```
<mt:mail to="the to address" from="the from address"
  subject="subject of the message">
  <mt:message>
```

```
    the body of the message
  </mt:message>
  <mt:send/>
</mt:mail>
```

NOTE **The message tag must be nested within the mail tag.**

This tag has a body type of JSP. The attribute of the message tag is described in Table 20.2.

Table 20.2 Attribute of the message Tag

ATTRIBUTE	DESCRIPTION
type	The content type of the message: text or html. If text is selected, the body of the message is plain text. If html is selected, then the body of the message can contain HTML tags. The default value for this attribute is text. (optional)

<mt:header />

The header tag is used to set extra headers in an email message. The syntax of the header tag is as follows:

```
<mt:mail to"the to address" from="the from address"
  subject="subject of the message">
  <mt:header name="header name" value="header value" />
  <mt:message>
    the body of the message
  </mt:message>
  <mt:send/>
</mt:mail>
```

NOTE **The header tag must be nested within the mail tag.**

This tag has a body type of JSP. The attributes of the header tag are described in Table 20.3.

Table 20.3 Attributes of the header Tag

ATTRIBUTE	DESCRIPTION
name	The name of the header to set in the message (required)
value	The value to set the header equal to; if not specified, the tag body will be used as the header value (optional)

<mt:setto />

The setto tag is used to set the to address of an email message. The syntax of the setto tag is as follows:

```
<mt:mail from="the from address"
  subject="subject of the message">
  <mt:setto
    >
    the to address
  <mt:message>
    the body of the message
  </mt:message>
  <mt:send/>
</mt:mail>
```

NOTE **The setto tag must be nested within the mail tag.**

This tag has a body type of JSP and no attributes.

<mt:addto />

The addto tag is used to add a recipient to the list of to addresses. The syntax of the addto tag is as follows:

```
<mt:mail from="the from address"
  subject="subject of the message">
  <mt:setto>
    the to address
  </mt:setto>
  <mt:addto>
    another to address
  </mt:addto>
</mt:mail>
```

NOTE **The addto tag must be nested within the mail tag.**

This tag has a body type of JSP and no attributes.

<mt:setcc />

The setcc tag is used to set a cc (carbon copy) recipient in the mail tag. The syntax of the setcc tag is as follows:

```
<mt:mail from="the from address"
  subject="subject of the message">
  <mt:setto>
    the to address
  </mt:setto>
  <mt:setcc>
    the cc address
  </mt:setcc>
</mt:mail>
```

NOTE **The setcc tag must be nested within the mail tag.**

This tag has a body type of JSP and no attributes.

<mt:addcc />

The addcc tag is used to add a cc recipient to the list of cc addresses. The syntax of the addcc tag is as follows:

```
<mt:mail from="the from address"
  subject="subject of the message">
  <mt:setto>
    the to address
  </mt:setto>
  <mt:setcc>
    the cc address
  </mt:setcc>
  <mt:addcc>
    another cc address
  </mt:addcc>
</mt:mail>
```

NOTE **The addcc tag must be nested within the mail tag.**

This tag has a body type of JSP and no attributes.

<mt:setbcc />

The setbcc tag is used to set a bcc (blind carbon copy) recipient in the mail tag. The syntax of the setbcc tag is as follows:

```
<mt:mail from="the from address"
  subject="subject of the message">
  <mt:setto>
    the to address
  </mt:setto>
  <mt:setbcc>
    the bcc address
  </mt:setbcc>
</mt:mail>
```

NOTE **The setbcc tag must be nested within the mail tag.**

This tag has a body type of JSP and no attributes.

<mt:addbcc />

The addbcc tag is used to add a recipient to the list of bcc addresses. The syntax of the addbcc tag is as follows:

```
<mt:mail from="the from address"
  subject="subject of the message">
  <mt:setto>
    the to address
  </mt:setto>
  <mt:addto>
    another to address
  </mt:addto>
  <mt:setbcc>
    the bcc address
  </mt:setbcc>
  <mt:addbcc>
    another bcc address
  </mt:addbcc>

</mt:mail>
```

NOTE **The addto tag must be nested within the mail tag.**

This tag has a body type of JSP and no attributes.

<mt:replyto />

The replyto tag sets one or more Reply To addresses in an email message. The syntax of the replyto tag is as follows:

```
<mt:mail from="the from address"
  subject="subject of the message">
  <mt:replyto>email address</mt:replyto>
  <mt:message>
    the body of the message
  </mt:message>
  <mt:send/>
</mt:mail>
```

NOTE **The replyto tag must be nested within the mail tag.**

This tag has a body type of JSP. No attributes are associated with the replyto tag.

<mt:from />

The from tag is used to set the From address of an email message. This value supercedes the to attribute used in the mail tag. The syntax of the from tag is as follows:

```
<mt:mail
  subject="subject of the message">
  <mt:from>the from address</mt:from>
  <mt:message>
    the body of the message
  </mt:message>
```

```
  <mt:send/>
</mt:mail>
```

NOTE **The from tag must be nested within the mail tag.**

This tag has a body type of JSP. No attributes are associated with the from tag.

<mt:attach />

The attach tag adds an attachment to an email message. Three methods can be used to add an attachment to an email: providing the name of the file by using the file attribute, providing the URL that references the resource to be added using the url attribute, or including the attachment in the body of the attach tag. The last method requires you to set the type attribute of the attach tag to the appropriate file type of the included attachment. The syntax of the attach tag, using each of these methods, is as follows:

Using the file attribute:

```
<mt:mail to="the to address"
  from="the from address"
  subject="subject of the message">
  <mt:attach file="relative path to file" />
  <mt:message>
    the body of the message
  </mt:message>
  <mt:send/>
</mt:mail>
```

Using the url attribute:

```
<mt:mail to="the to address"
  from="the from address"
  subject="subject of the message">
  <mt:attach url="fully qualified url path to file" />
  <mt:message>
    the body of the message
  </mt:message>
  <mt:send/>
</mt:mail>
```

Using the type attribute:

```
<mt:mail to="the to address"
  from="the from address"
  subject="subject of the message">
  <mt:attach type="file MIME type">
    Contents of file to include as an attachment
  </mt:attach>
  <mt:message>
    the body of the message
  </mt:message>
  <mt:send/>
</mt:mail>
```

NOTE **The attach tag must be nested within the mail tag.**

This tag has a body type of JSP. The attributes of the attach tag are described in Table 20.6.

Table 20.6 Attributes of the *attach* Tag

ATTRIBUTE	DESCRIPTION
file	The name of the file to be included as an attachment. It must be a path or filename relative to the root directory of the Web application. If the value of the file attribute contains an empty string (""), the file contents will be assumed to be included in the body of the tag. (optional)
url	The URL of the resource to be attached to the email, in the format of a fully qualified URL. If the value of the url attribute contains an empty string (""), the URL will be assumed to be included in the body of the tag. (optional)
type	The MIME type of the attachment. When using the type attribute, the body of the attach tag will be used as the attachment. (optional)

<mt:subject />

The subject tag sets the subject of an email message. This tag will supercede the subject attribute of the mail tag. The syntax of the subject tag is as follows:

```
<mt:mail to="the to address"
  from="the from address">
  <mt:subject>
    the subject of the message
  </mt:subject>
  <mt:message>
    the body of the message
  </mt:message>
  <mt:send/>
</mt:mail>
```

NOTE **The subject tag must be nested within the mail tag.**

This tag has a body type of JSP. No attributes are associated with the subject tag.

<mt:send />

The send tag is used to send the email message. If an error occurs while the email message is being created, then the body of the send tag will be written back to the browser. The syntax of the send tag is as follows:

```
<mt:mail to="the to address"
  from="the from address">
  <mt:subject>
```

```
    the subject of the message
  </mt:attach>
  <mt:message>
    the body of the message
  </mt:message>
  <mt:send>
    An Error Message!
  </mt:send>
</mt:mail>
```

NOTE **The send tag must be nested within the mail tag.**

This tag has a body type of JSP. No attributes are associated with the send tag.

<mt:error />

The error tag retrieves error messages that occurred when sending email. If an error occurred, this tag will retrieve the error message from its parent mail tag and create a scripting variable containing the error message. This scripting variable can then be accessed using the <jsp:getProperty> standard action. The syntax of the error tag is as follows:

```
<mt:mail to="the to address"
  from="the from address">
  <mt:subject>
    the subject of the message
  </mt:attach>
  <mt:message>
    the body of the message
  </mt:message>
  <mt:send>
    Error Messages:
    <mt:error id="errid">
      <jsp:getProperty name="errid" property="error" />
    </mt:error>
  </mt:send>
</mt:mail>
```

NOTE **The error tag must be nested within the send tag.**

This tag has a body type of JSP. The attribute of the error tag is described in Table 20.7.

Table 20.7 Attribute of the error Tag

ATTRIBUTE	DESCRIPTION
id	The name of the scripting variable that will be accessed by the <jsp:getProperty> standard action (required)

Using the Mailer Tags

This section provides an example of how the tags in the Mailer library can be leveraged. The example creates an HTML form that takes the necessary parameters to send an email. These parameter values are submitted to a sample JSP that creates an email message, attaches a file to it, and sends the mail. Listing 20.1 contains the source for the HTML portion of the example.

```
<html>
<head>
<title>
Mail Form
</title>
</head>
<body>

<form
  action="/webappname/MailExample.jsp"
  method=POST>
  <table width="300" border="0" cellspacing="0">
    <tr>
      <td>To:
        <input type="text" name="to" size="30" maxlength="30">
      </td>
      <td>From:
        <input type="text" name="from" size="30"
          maxlength="30">
      </td>
      <td>Subject:
        <input type="text" name="subject">
      </td>
    </tr>
    <tr valign="top">
      <td colspan="3">
        <textarea name="message" cols="65"
          rows="15"></textarea>
      </td>
    </tr>
    <tr>
      <td>  </td>
      <td>  </td>
      <td>
        <input type="submit" name="Submit" value="Submit">
        <input type="reset" name="Reset" value="Reset">
      </td>
    </tr>
```

Listing 20.1 MailForm.html. *(continues)*

```
  </table>
</form>

</body>
</html>
```

Listing 20.1 MailForm.html. *(continued)*

There is nothing special about this HTML document; it simply contains a form with the appropriate input to send a message. The only thing notable is the form action, which names the JSP found in Listing 20.2 as its target.

```
<%@ taglib
  uri="http://jakarta.apache.org/taglibs/mailer-1.0"
  prefix="mt" %>

<html>
  <head>
    <title>Mailer Tag Library Example</title>
  </head>

  <body>

    <mt:mail
      server="smtp.somesmtpserver.com">
      <mt:setto>
        <%= request.getParameter("to") %>
      </mt:setto>
      <mt:from>
        <%= request.getParameter("from") %>
      </mt:from>
      <mt:subject>
        <%= request.getParameter("subject") %>
      </mt:subject>
      <mt:message>
        <%= request.getParameter("message") %>
      </mt:message>
      <mt:attach file="images/someimagefile.gif" />
      <mt:send>
        An Error was received!
      </mt:send>
    </mt:mail>

  </body>
</html>
```

Listing 20.2 MailExample.jsp. *(continued)*

The first thing to note about this JSP is the mail tag, which acts as the parent to all other tags belonging to the Mailer library. The only attribute set in this tag is server, which points to the SMTP server that will handle sending this message. You will need to substitute the value of your mail server for the value indicated in this JSP.

Next, the JSP sets the recipient of this email. It does so using the setto tag, which has a body that will be evaluated to the to parameter from the MailForm.html's form. This process is followed by the from, subject, and message tags.

After setting all the basic mail parameters required when sending most messages, the JSP uses the attach tag to attach a image file to the email. It does so by setting the file attribute to the relative path of the image file. You will need to substitute the file you would like to attach for the value used in this example.

Finally, the JSP sends the email by referencing the send tag. Notice that this tag has a body, which will be sent to the client browser if an error occurs.

To see this example in action, make sure the Mailer tag library is installed. Copy the HTML and JSP files to the <TOMCAT_HOME>/webapps/*webappname*/ directory and open your browser to the following URL:

```
http://localhost:8080/webappname/MailForm.html
```

You should see an image similar to Figure 20.1.

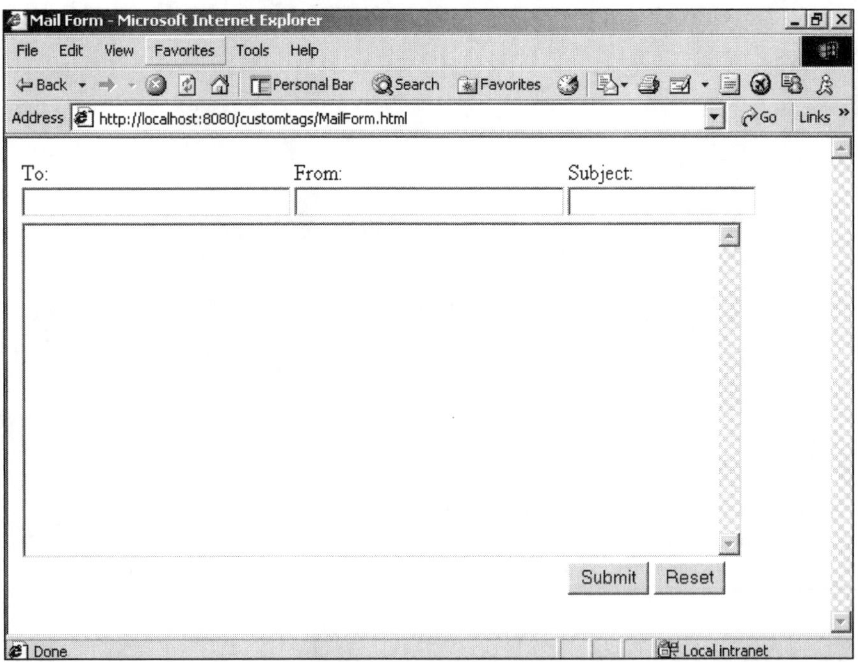

Figure 20.1 Output of the MailForm.html document.

Fill in the form fields with the appropriate data, including your email address, and click the Submit button. You should see a blank Web page because no output results from a successful execution.

To see the results of this JSP, open your email client, and check for the new message.

CHAPTER

21

Random Tag Library

The Jakarta Random tag library provides a group of tags that encapsulate the logic to generate random numbers and strings in your JSPs, as defined by the class java.security.SecureRandom. This library consists of two tags: <rand:number> and <rand:string>. This chapter discusses each of these tags.

NOTE **This tag library requires a JSP/servlet container that supports JSP 1.1 and above.**

Configuration

To use the Random tag library in a Web application, you must complete the following steps, substituting for *webappname* the name of the Web application that will be using this library:

1. Copy the random.tld TLD packaged with this tag library to the <TOMCAT_HOME>/webapps/*webappname*/WEB-INF directory.
2. Copy the random.jar JAR file containing the Random tag library's tag handlers to the <TOMCAT_HOME>/webapps/*webappname*/WEB-INF/lib directory.
3. Add the following <taglib> subelement to the web.xml file of the Web application:

```
<taglib>
  <taglib-uri>
```

```
    http://jakarta.apache.org/taglibs/ramdom
  </taglib-uri>
  <taglib-location>
    /WEB-INF/random.tld
  </taglib-location>
</taglib>
```

The following taglib directive must be added to each JSP that will leverage the Random tag library:

```
<%@ taglib
  uri="http://jakarta.apache.org/taglibs/ramdom"
  prefix="rand" %>
```

This directive identifies the URI defined in the previously listed <taglib> element and states that all Random tags should be prefixed with the string *rand*.

Random Tags

The Random tag library encapsulates the necessary functionality to create random strings and numbers. Two custom tags are packaged in the Random tag library: <rand:string> and <rand:number>.

<rand:string />

The string tag creates a scripting variable of type org.apache.taglibs.random.RandomStrg, referenced by the id attribute. This object will generate a new random string whenever its random property is accessed. This property can be accessed using the JSP standard action <jsp:getProperty>. The syntax of the string tag is as follows:

```
<rand:string id="scripting variable name" />

<jsp:getProperty
  name="id attribute from string tag"
  property="random" />
```

NOTE To access the random string using the <jsp:getProperty> standard action, you must set the property attribute to random, as shown in the previous code snippet.

This tag has no body. The attributes of the string tag are described in Table 21.1.

Table 21.1 Attributes of the string Tag

ATTRIBUTE	DESCRIPTION
id	The scripting variable to be used in the <jsp:getProperty> standard action. (required)

Table 21.1 Attributes of the string Tag *(continued)*

ATTRIBUTE	DESCRIPTION
length	The length of the random string; the default length is 8. (optional)
map	The name of a bean or script variable that is a Java HashMap object. The random string generated will be a new unique key for the HashMap. (optional)
charset	The set of characters to use when creating the random string. The default character set is "a-zA-Z0-9". To use the entire set of characters, pass the value all. (optional)
algorithm	The algorithm to use if a SecureRandom object will be used to generate the random string. (optional)
provider	The package to search for the previously included algorithm attribute, if the algorithm is to be used for a SecureRandom object. (optional)

<rand:number />

The number tag creates a scripting variable of type org.apache.taglibs.random.RandomNum, referenced by the id attribute. This object will generate a new random number whenever its random property is accessed. This property can be accessed using the JSP standard action <jsp:getProperty>. The syntax of the number tag is as follows:

```
<rand:number id="scripting variable name" />

<jsp:getProperty
  name="id attribute from number tag"
  property="random" />
```

NOTE To access the random number using the <jsp:getProperty> standard action, you must set the property attribute to random, as shown in the previous code snippet.

This tag has no body. The attributes of the number tag are described in Table 21.2.

Table 21.2 Attributes of the number Tag

ATTRIBUTE	DESCRIPTION
id	The scripting variable to be used in the <jsp:getProperty> standard action. (required)

Table 21.2 Attributes of the number Tag *(continued)*

ATTRIBUTE	DESCRIPTION
range	The lower and upper bounds of the generated random number. If the range attribute is set to 0-1, then a float value between 0 and 1 will be generated when the random property is accessed. All other values should return an integer. The default range is 0 to 100. The maximum size of the generated random number is limited only by the size of the primitive long. (optional)
algorithm	The algorithm to use if a SecureRandom object will be used to generate the random number. (optional)
provider	The package to search for the previously included algorithm attribute, if the algorithm is to be used for a SecureRandom object. (optional)

Using the Random Tags

This section provides an example of how the tags in the Random tag library can be leveraged. Listing 21.1 contains the source for this example.

```
<%@ taglib
  uri="http://jakarta.apache.org/taglibs/random-1.0"
  prefix="rand" %>

<html>
  <head>
    <title>Random Tag Library Example</title>
  </head>

  <body>

    <h2>Create a random number between 1 and 100</h2>
      <rand:number id="randomNumber" range="1-100"/><br/>

      <jsp:getProperty name="randomNumber"
        property="random"/>

    <h2>Create a random string using all possible
      characters and numbers.</h2>
      <rand:string id="randomString" charset="all"/>
```

Listing 21.1 RandomExample.jsp. *(continues)*

```
          <jsp:getProperty name="randomString"
             property="random"/>

      </body>
   </html>
```

Listing 21.1 RandomExample.jsp. *(continued)*

To see this example in action, make sure the Random tag library is installed, copy the JSP to the <TOMCAT_HOME>/webapps/*webappname*/ directory, and open your browser to the following URL:

`http://localhost:8080/webappname/RandomExample.jsp`

You should see a page similar to Figure 21.1.

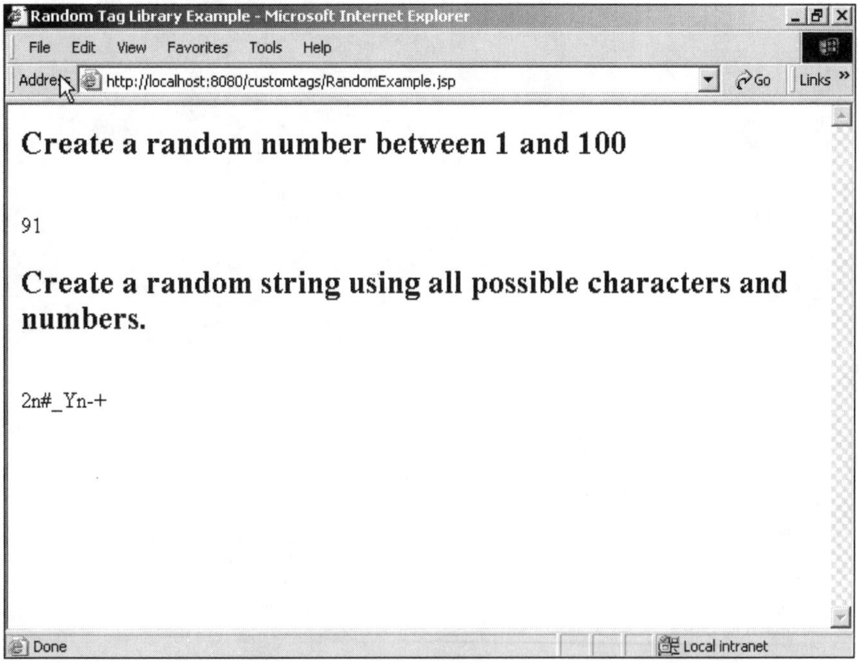

Figure 21.1 Output of the RandomExample.jsp.

This example performs two simple functions using the Random tag library. It first sets the properties of a random number generator using the number tag. The only property set by this tag is the range, which tells the generator to create a number between 1 and 100. After the generator has been created, the JSP standard action <jsp:getProperty> displays the results. When the <jsp:getProperty> action is invoked, it retrieves the random property; at that point, the random number is generated.

The second step performed by RandomExample.jsp is to set the properties of a random string generator using the string tag. This tag creates a random string generator that uses the entire range of characters and digits to create a random string. After the generator has been created, the JSP standard action <jsp:getProperty> displays the results. As with the number tag, invoking <jsp:getProperty> marks the actual creation of the random string.

CHAPTER 22

Regular Expression Tag Library

This chapter looks at the Jakarta Regular Expression (Regexp) tag library. Leveraging the Jakarta ORO Project, the Regexp tag library allows Perl5 and AWK-like compatible regular expressions' processing functionality to be inserted into a JSP.

NOTE **This tag library requires a JSP/servlet container that supports JSP 1.1 and above.**

Configuration

To use the Regexp tag library in a Web application, complete the following steps, substituting for *webappname* the name of the Web application that will be using this library:

1. Copy the regexp.tld TLD packaged with this tag library to the <TOMCAT_HOME>/webapps/*webappname*/WEB-INF directory.
2. Copy the regexp.jar JAR file containing the Regexp tag library's tag handlers to the <TOMCAT_HOME>/webapps/*webappname*/WEB-INF/lib directory.
3. Add the following <taglib> subelement to the web.xml file of the Web application:

```
<taglib>
  <taglib-uri>
    http://jakarta.apache.org/taglibs/regexp-1.0
  </taglib-uri>
  <taglib-location>
```

```
    /WEB-INF/regexp.tld
  </taglib-location>
</taglib>
```

4. Download and extract version 2.0 or later of the Jakarta ORO Perl Regular Expression package from http://jakarta.apache.org/oro/.
5. Copy the jakarta-oro-2.0.x.jar file to the <TOMCAT_HOME>/webapps/*webapp-name*/WEB-INF/lib directory.

NOTE The Jakarta ORO Perl Regular Expression package contains a set of text-processing classes that include Perl5 and AWK-like compatible regular expressions' processing functionality. You can find more information about the ORO project at http://jakarta.apache.org/oro/.

The following taglib directive must be added to each JSP that will leverage the Regexp tag library:

```
<%@ taglib
  uri="http://jakarta.apache.org/taglibs/regexp-1.0"
  prefix="rx" %>
```

This directive identifies the URI defined in the previously listed <taglib> element, and states that all Regexp tags should be prefixed with the string *rx*.

Regular Expression Tags

Six custom tags are packaged in the Regexp tag library: regexp, text, existsMatch, substitute, split, and match. These tags are described in the following sections.

<rx:regexp />

The regexp tag creates a scripting variable that contains a regular expression to be used in cooperation with the existsMatch, substitute, split, and match tags, which are discussed later in this chapter. The body of the tag contains the regular expression to create. The syntax of the regexp tag is as follows:

```
<rx:regexp id="scripting variable id">
  The regular expression to create
</rx:regexp>
```

This tag has a body type of JSP and a single attribute, id, used to define the id of the created scripting variable. The scripting variable defines a single property, regexp, containing the text of the regular expression. You can access this property using the <jsp:getProperty> standard action. The following code snippet includes an example of this action:

```
<jsp:getProperty
  name="id from regexp"
  property="regexp" />
```

<rx:text />

The text tag creates a scripting variable that contains a text string to be used in cooperation with the existsMatch, substitute, split, and match tags. The body of the tag contains the text string to create. The syntax of the text tag is as follows:

```
<rx:text id="scripting variable id">
  The text string to create
</rx:text>
```

This tag has a body type of JSP and a single attribute, id, used to define the id of the created scripting variable. The created scripting variable defines a single property, text, containing the text string. You can access this property using the <jsp:getProperty> standard action. The following code snippet includes an example of this action:

```
<jsp:getProperty
  name="id from text"
  property="text" />
```

<rx:existsMatch />

The existsMatch tag evaluates its body if the named regexp attribute finds a match in the named text attribute. The syntax of the existsMatch tag is as follows:

```
<rx:regexp id="scripting variable id">
  The regular expression to create
</rx:regexp>

<rx:text id="scripting variable id">
  The text string to create
</rx:text>

<rx:existsMatch
  regexp="the id from the regexp tag"
  text="the id from the text tag"
  value="true|false">
  The body to be evaluated if a match is found.
</rx:existsMatch>
```

This tag has a body type of JSP. The attributes of the existsMatch tag are described in Table 22.1.

Table 22.1 Attributes of the existsMatch Tag

ATTRIBUTE	DESCRIPTION
regexp	The id of the regexp scripting variable, created using the regexp tag, to use when looking for a match in the text attribute. (required)
text	The id of the text string scripting variable, created using the text tag, that will be searched for a match using the named regexp attribute. (required)

Table 22.1 Attributes of the existsMatch Tag *(continued)*

ATTRIBUTE	DESCRIPTION
value	If false, causes the existsMatch tag to evaluate its body if a match does not exist. The default value is true. (optional)

<rx:substitute />

The substitute tag performs a regular expression string substitution, and outputs the resulting string if the named regexp attribute finds a match in the named text attribute. The syntax of the substitute tag is as follows:

```
<rx:regexp id="scripting variable id">
  s/text to search for/text to use as replacement/g
</rx:regexp>

<rx:text id="scripting variable id">
  The text string to create
</rx:text>

<rx:substitute
  regexp="the id from the regexp tag"
  text="the id from the text tag" />
```

This tag has a body type of JSP. The attributes of the substitute tag are described in Table 22.2.

Table 22.2 Attributes of the substitute Tag

ATTRIBUTE	DESCRIPTION
regexp	The id of the regexp scripting variable, created using the regexp tag, to use when performing the regular expression substitution in the text attribute (required)
text	The id of the text string scripting variable, created using the text tag, that will be searched for a match using the named regexp attribute (required)

<rx:split />

The split tag performs a Perl-like split on the named text attribute, created using the text tag, and iterates through the split strings making each tokenized string available in a property named split. The syntax of the split tag is as follows:

```
<rx:text id="scripting variable id">
  The text string to create
</rx:text>

<rx:split text="the id from the text tag">
```

```
  <jsp:getProperty
    name="id from split"
    property="split" />
</rx:split>
```

NOTE **The split tag performs much like the Java utility class java.util.StringTokenizer.**

This tag has a body type of JSP. The attributes of the split tag are described in Table 22.3.

Table 22.3 Attributes of the split Tag

ATTRIBUTE	DESCRIPTION
id	The scripting variable to be used in the <jsp:getProperty> standard action. (required)
regexp	The id of the regexp scripting variable, created using the regexp tag, to use when performing the regular expression split on the text attribute. If the regexp attribute is not included, then the split will be performed on whitespace. (optional)
text	The id of the text string scripting variable, created using the text tag, that will be searched for a match using the named regexp attribute. (required)
limit	The maximum number of splits that will be performed on the named text attribute. (optional)

<rx:match />

The match tag is much like the existsMatch tag, except that it evaluates its body for every occurrence of the regexp match found in the named text attribute. With each of these occurrences, the match tag creates a scripting variable containing properties that can be referenced using the <jsp:getProperty> standard action. The syntax of the match tag is as follows:

```
<rx:regexp id="scripting variable id">
  The regular expression to create
</rx:regexp>

<rx:text id="scripting variable id">
  The text string to create
</rx:text>

<rx:match
  id="id used to expose match as scripting variable"
  regexp="the id from the regexp tag"
```

```
    text="the id from the text tag"
    value="true|false"">
    <jsp:getProperty
      name="id from match"
      property="match" />
  </rx:match>
```

This tag has a body type of JSP. The attributes of the match tag are described in Table 22.4.

Table 22.4 Attributes of the match Tag

ATTRIBUTE	DESCRIPTION
id	The scripting variable to be used in the <jsp:getProperty> standard action (required)
regexp	The id of the regexp scripting variable, created using the regexp tag, to use when performing the regular expression search on the text attribute (required)
text	The id of the text string scripting variable, created using the text tag, that will be searched for a match using the named regexp attribute (required)

This tag has a body type of JSP. The properties exposed by the match tag are described in Table 22.5.

Table 22.5 Properties Returned by the match Tag

PROPERTY	DESCRIPTION
match	The matching string found by the match tag
preMatch	The string immediately preceding the string contained in the match property
postMatch	The string immediately following the string contained in the match property

Using the Regular Expression Tags

This section presents an example of how each of the localized Regexp tags can be leveraged. Listing 22.1 contains the source for this example.

```
<%@ taglib
  uri="http://jakarta.apache.org/taglibs/regexp-1.0"
  prefix="rx" %>
```

Listing 22.1 RegexpExample.jsp. *(continues)*

```
<html>
  <head>
   <title>Regular Expression Taglib Example</title>
  </head>

  <body>

    <rx:regexp id="regexpId">m/Detroit/mi</rx:regexp>

    <rx:text id="textId">
      Bob left on a train headed for Detroit at 76 mph.
    </rx:text>

    <rx:existsMatch regexp="regexpId" text="textId">
       "Detroit" was found.
    </rx:existsMatch>

    <hr>

    <rx:regexp id="regexpId2">s/Detroit/Denver/gmi</rx:regexp>

    <rx:substitute regexp="regexpId2" text="textId"/>

    <hr>

    <rx:split id="split" text="textId">
      <jsp:getProperty name="split" property="split"/><br>
    </rx:split>

    <hr>

    <rx:match id="match" regexp="regexpId" text="textId">
      Match: <jsp:getProperty
               name="match"
               property="match"/><br>
      PreMatch: <jsp:getProperty
                  name="match"
                  property="preMatch"/><br>
      PostMatch: <jsp:getProperty
                   name="match"
                   property="postMatch"/><br>
    </rx:match>
  </body>
</html>
```

Listing 22.1 RegexpExample.jsp. *(continued)*

To test this example, copy the JSP to the <TOMCAT_HOME>/webapps/*webapp-name*/ directory, and open your browser to the following URL:

```
http://localhost:8080/webappname/RegexpExample.jsp
```

If everything went according to plan, you should see a page similar to Figure 22.1.

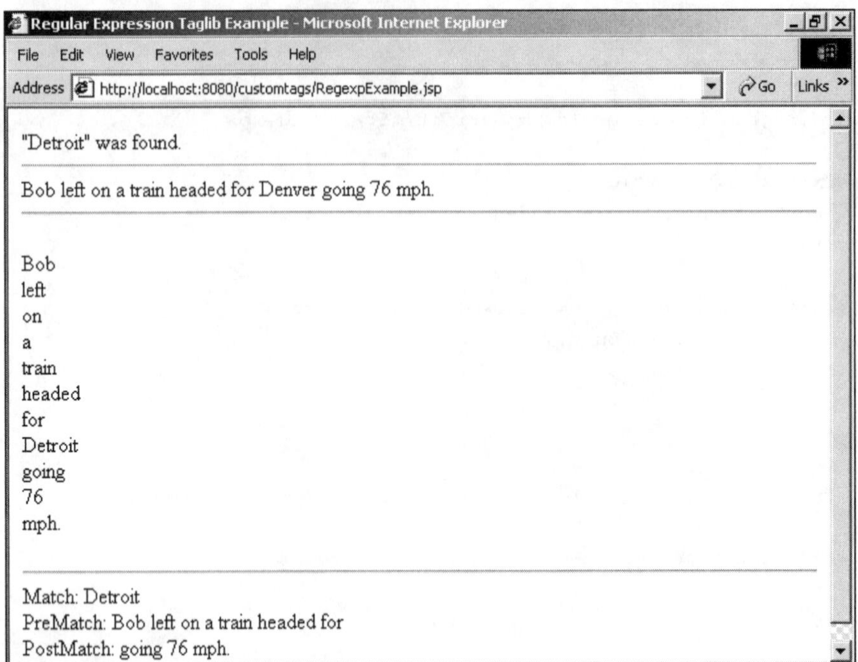

Figure 22.1 Output of the RegexpExample.jsp.

RegexpExample.jsp begins by creating a regular expression and a text string, using the regexp and text tag, respectively. Both of these components are used in the subsequent existsMatch tag, which performs a case-insensitive search for the text *Detroit*. In this case, it finds the match and evaluates its body, printing the following text: *"Detroit" was found.*

The JSP next creates another regular expression that is used in the substitute tag. The substitute tag replaces the string *Detroit* with the string *Denver*, and prints the result.

This JSP then uses the split tag to tokenize the original text string and print out each token using the <jsp:getProperty> tag. Note that the tokenized string still contains the text *Detroit* because the substitute tag does not change the original string created by the text tag.

The final action performed by the RegexpExample.jsp is to use the original regular expression and text string in the match tag. This tag evaluates its body for every occurrence of the string *Detroit*, printing the exposed properties match, preMatch, and postMatch. In this instance, there is only one occurrence of the string; therefore these properties are printed a single time.

CHAPTER

23

JSP Standard Tag Library Project (JSTL)

This chapter marks the beginning of our JSP Standard Tag Library (JSTL) discussions. We will start this chapter by defining the JSTL project, including its purpose. We will then conclude this chapter with a discussion of the steps required to download and configure the JSTL archive.

The goal of this chapter is to give you an understanding of the purpose behind the JSTL and to cover the steps required when installing the JSTL.

What Is the JSP Standard Tag Library Project?

The JSTL is a group of JSP custom tags and expression languages that were created by the JSR-052 expert group as part of the Java Community Process (JCP). The JSTL was created with the intention of encapsulating the core functionality common to most JSP Web applications and ultimately eliminating the need for scriptlet code in your JSPs.

The current release of the JSTL is Early-Access 3, and can be changed without notice; therefore, we focus on the core tag library that should remain relatively unchanged until the final release of the JSTL. We also discuss the SQL tags because of their importance to Web application development. The core library contains four groups of custom tags and the SQL tags packaged into a single library. An overview of each of these libraries is provided in the following sections. These tag groupings will be the focus of the remainder of this section.

NOTE **The homepage for the JSTL Project contains the latest documentation and project status. You can find this information at http://jakarta.apache.org/taglibs/doc/standard-doc/intro.html.**

Expression Language and Expression Language Tags

The current version of the JSTL has the capability to leverage an expression language as a method of communicating information from JSP custom tags to other the JSP elements. The goal of providing support for an expression language is to make it possible to easily access application data without having to use scriptlets or request-time expression values. The default expression language used in the current JSTL release is ECMAScript. We will discuss this expression language and three expression language tags in Chapter 24, "Expression Language and Tags."

Conditional Tags

The conditional tags provide simple tags that can be used to evaluate mutually exclusive conditions. The JSTL EA2 provides four tags that can be used when performing basic conditional evaluations: <if>, <choose>, <when>, and <otherwise>. We will describe each of these tags in Chapter 25, "Conditional Tags."

Iteration Tags

The iteration tags are used when iterating over standard Java collections or tokenizing string objects. At the time of this writing, there are two unique tags that perform basic iteration: <forEach> and <forTokens>. We will describe both of these tags in Chapter 26, "Iterator Tags."

Import Tags

The import tags were created with the intention of solving some of the shortcomings of the JSP standard action tag <jsp:include>. It does so with the inclusion of three unique tags: <import>, <urlEncode>, and <param>. We will describe each of these tags in Chapter 27, "Import Tags."

The SQL Tags

The SQL tags were created to provide the JSP developer with a set of custom tags that encapsulate the more common database functions. It does so with the creation of five unique tags: <driver>, <query>, <update>, <transaction>, and <param>. We will describe each of these tags in Chapter 28, "SQL Tags."

Downloading and Installing the JSP Standard Tag Library Archive

To prepare for the remainder of this section, you need to download a copy of the latest Standard Tag Library archive. For the examples in this section, we are going to use the binary distribution of the tag libraries, which can be found by pointing your browser to the following URL:

```
http://jakarta.apache.org/builds/jakarta-taglibs/releases/standard/
```

Select the latest archive, and download it to your local disk. When the download is complete, extract the archive to a convenient directory, and open the top-level directory. As you examine the archive contents, you will see a single subdirectory, which contains two JAR files, several tag library descriptors, a documentation WAR file, and an examples WAR file. Each of these files is described in Table 23.1.

Table 23.1 Files Found in the Standard Taglibs Binary Archive

FILE	DESCRIPTION
jstl.jar	The jstl.jar file contains the tag handlers associated with JSTL tag libraries. This file should be copied into the lib directory of the Web application using the tag library.
jstl-api.jar	The jstl-api.jar file contains the APIs that are used when developing your own tag libraries that conform to the JSTL architecture. We will not be discussing this file in this text because of its unpredictable status.
The TLDs	The TLDs contained in this archive are used to describe each tag library in the JSTL. For our discussion, we will only be using the c.tld. This file should be copied into either the /WEB-INF or /WEB-LIB/lib directory of the Web application using the tag library.
standard-doc.war	The documentation WAR file contains documentation describing the JSTL tag library. To use the Web application contained in this WAR, copy the file to the <TOMCAT_HOME>/webapps/ directory, and restart Tomcat.
standard-examples.war	The examples WAR file contains examples of how to use the tags contained in this tag library. To use the Web application contained in this WAR, copy the file to the <TOMCAT_HOME>/webapps/ directory, and restart Tomcat.

After you have the JSTL archive, perform the following steps to install and configure the tag library for use.

NOTE **When performing the following steps, make sure you substitute the value of the *webappname* with the name of the Web application that will be using this library. For our examples, we will continue to use the Web application /customtags.**

1. Copy the TLD packaged with this tag library, c.tld, to the <TOMCAT_HOME>/webapps/*webappname*/WEB-INF directory.

NOTE **The JSTL EA3 does provide a version of the Standard Tag Library that allows you to use runtime expressions for setting tag attributes, but this library does not support the expression language. Because of this limitation, we will only be deploying the c.tld, which supports the expression language attributes.**

2. Copy the JAR file containing the JSTL tag library's tag handlers, jstl.jar, to the <TOMCAT_HOME>/webapps/*webappname*/WEB-INF/lib directory.
3. Extract the standard-examples.war file and copy the files crimson.jar and js.jar to the <TOMCAT_HOME>/webapps/*webappname*/WEB-INF/lib directory.

NOTE **This may seem like a needless step, but at the time of this release of EA3, these JAR files are only packaged in the standard-examples.war file. This issue will probably not exist at the JSTL release.**

4. Add the following <taglib> subelement to the web.xml file of the Web application:

```
<taglib>
  <taglib-uri>http://java.sun.com/jstl/ea/core</taglib-uri>
  <taglib-location>/WEB-INF/c.tld</taglib-location>
</taglib>
```

NOTE **The installation of the SQL Tag Library is discussed in Chapter 28, "SQL Tags."**

At this point, the Standard Tag Library is deployed. To use the library, the following taglib directive must be added to each JSP that will leverage the JSTL:

```
<%@ taglib prefix="c" uri="http://java.sun.com/jstl/ea/core" %>
```

This directive identifies the URI defined in the previously listed <taglib> element and states that all JSTL core tags should be prefixed with the string *c*. You can change this prefix, but this is the recommended method of referencing the JSTL core tags.

Summary

In this chapter, we introduced Standard Tag Library Project. We referenced the location of the JSTL archive. We also described the installation process required when using the JSTL. The remainder of this text will be dedicated to examining the greater part of this library, with an explicit focus on the core tags and the ECMAScript expression language.

CHAPTER

24

Expression Language and Tags

In this chapter, we are going to discuss the default JSTL expression language (EL) and the supporting tags provided by the JSTL when using the EL. We will begin by providing a brief definition of expression languages. We will then move on to a discussion of the three tags that provide support for JSTL expression languages. After the supporting custom tags have been discussed, we then move on to describing the ECMAScript, which is the default expression language for EA2 of the JSTL. We will conclude this chapter with an example of how the EL and its supporting tags can be used.

NOTE **It should be noted that the current version of the JavaScript client-side scripting language is based on ECMAScript.**

The Expression Language

An EL defines a set of variables, operators, and expressions that when evaluated return a single value. The purpose of integrating an EL into the JSTL is to allow a JSP developer to replace the standard JSP expression syntax, which does include JSP scriptlet code with a more readable and hopefully more easily maintained EL.

Currently, the JSTL does not define a standard EL and probably will not do so anytime soon, but it does come configured with a default EL. This default EL is the ECMAScript scripting language.

To use any ECMAScript EL, you must take note of two characters that are used when creating an expression. The first character is the "$" character. This character signifies the beginning of an expression to be evaluated. An example of using the <c:expr> tag, which is described later in this chapter, is shown in the following code snippet:

```
<c:expr value="$user" />
```

The second character important to expression creation is the "." character. This character is used to access a property or function of a given variable. An example of using the <c:expr> tag is shown in the following code snippet:

```
<c:expr value="$user.name" />
```

NOTE **You can read the PDF found at http://www.mozilla.org/js/language/E262-3.pdf to learn more about the ECMAScript scripting language.**

Expression Language Tags

The current version of the JSTL provides three custom support tags that allow you to integrate EL functionality into your JSPs: the <c:expr> tag, the <c:declare> tag, and the <c:set> tag. The following three sections describe each of these support tags.

<c:expr />

The <c:expr> tag is probably the most common EL tag. It is used to evaluate an expression, outputting the result of the evaluation to the current JspWriter. It is the functional equivalent of a JSP expression, but is intended solely for integrating an EL into a JSP.

The <c:expr> tag also provides the functionality to set a default value, which will be written to the JspWriter if the tag cannot evaluate the expression passed to it. The default value can be set using either the default attribute or the body of the tag. The syntax of the <c:expr> tag is as follows:

```
<c:expr value="$expression to evaluate" />
```

This tag has a body type of JSP and supports two attributes, which are described in Table 24.1.

Table 24.1 <c:expr> Tag Attributes

ATTRIBUTE	DESCRIPTION
value	Contains the expression to be evaluated (required)
default	Used to set a default value, which will be written to the JspWriter if the tag cannot evaluate the expression passed to it (optional)

<c:set />

The <c:set> tag is used to create and set the value of an EL variable. The variable can be placed in any defined JSP scope page, request, session, or application. The value of the

EL variable can be set using the value attribute or the body of the <c:set> tag. The syntax of the <c:set> tag is as follows:

```
<c:set var="EL variable name">
  Value of the EL variable.
</c:set>
```

This tag has a body type of JSP and supports three attributes, which are described in Table 24.2.

Table 24.2 <c:set> Tag Attributes

ATTRIBUTE	DESCRIPTION
var	The var attribute names the EL scripting variable. (required)
value	The value attribute is used to set the EL variable's value. If this attribute is not used, the tag should set the value using the body of the tag. (optional)
scope	The scope attribute represents the location in which the EL variable will be stored. The possible values are page, request, session, and application. The default value is page. (optional)

<c:declare />

The <c:declare> tag is used to create a JSP scripting variable from an EL variable. This is useful in cases where you have a custom tag that does not currently support ELs. The visibility of the scripting variable begins with the <c:declare> closing tag. The syntax of the <c:declare> tag is as follows:

```
<c:set var="EL variable name" />
<c:declare
  id="scripting variable name mathcing EL variable name" />
```

NOTE **It is important to note that the id attribute of the <c:declare> tag must match the name of the EL variable that it intends to expose.**

This tag has no body, but does support two attributes, which are described in Table 24.3.

Table 24.3 <c:declare> Tag Attributes

ATTRIBUTE	DESCRIPTION
id	The id attribute names the scripting variable that is exported by the <c:declare> tag. (required)
type	The type attribute names the scripting variable's type. If this value is not included, the exposed scripting variable will be of type java.lang.Object. (optional)

ECMAScript Operators

There are four functional areas of the ECMAScript language that we need to take a look at before we can actually begin developing JSPs that use the default EL. These functional areas include comparison operators, arithmetic operators, logical operators, and a single string operator. Each of these areas is described in the following sections.

Comparison Operators

The comparison operators are used to compare operands, returning a true or false value based upon the results of an EL comparison. The expression operands can be numerical, string, logical, or object values. If the operands being compared are strings, they are compared based on standard lexicon graphical ordering, using Unicode values. All of the defined comparison operators are described in Table 24.4.

Table 24.4 Comparison Operators

OPERATOR	DESCRIPTION
==	The == operator evaluates to true if the operands are equal.
!=	The != operator evaluates to true if the operands are not equal.
===	The === operator evaluates to true if the operands are equal and of the same type.
!==	The !== operator evaluates to true if the operands are not equal and of the same type.
>	The > operator evaluates to true if the left operand is greater than the right operand.
>=	The >= operator evaluates to true if the left operand is greater than or equal to the right operand.
<	The < operator evaluates to true if the left operand is less than the right operand.
<=	The <= operator evaluates to true if the left operand is less than or equal to the right operand.

An example comparison, testing the variables *a* and *b* for equality, is shown in the following code snippet:

```
<c:expr value="$a == b"/>
```

Arithmetic Operators

The arithmetic operators are used to perform simple mathematical operations on EL operands, returning a single numerical value. All of the defined arithmetic operators are described in Table 24.5.

Table 24.5 Arithmetic Operators

OPERATOR	DESCRIPTION
+	The + operator adds the values of the two operands together, returning the integer result of the addition.
-	The - operator subtracts the values of the two operands, returning the integer result of the subtraction.
*	The * operator multiplies the values of the two operands, returning the integer result of the multiplication.
/	The / operator performs simple division of the two operands contained in the expression, returning a float result.
%	The % operator acts just like the Java modulas operator, returning the integer remainder of the divided operands.
++	The ++ operator acts just like the Java ++ (increment) operator, returning the original integer incremented by one. The ++ operator can be used in both prefix or postfix increments.
–	The – operator acts just like the Java – (decrement) operator, returning the original integer decremented by one. The – operator can be used in both prefix or postfix increments.
-	The - or unary operator returns the negation of the original operand value.

An example that increments an index variable is shown in the following code snippet:

```
<c:expr value="$index++"/>
```

Logical Operators

The logical operators are used to compare Boolean values. The result of all logical comparisons is a Boolean value. All of the defined logical operators are described in Table 24.6.

Table 24.6 Logical Operators

OPERATOR	DESCRIPTION
&&	The logical AND operator returns true if both operands can be converted to the Boolean value true; otherwise, false is returned.
||	The logical OR operator returns true if either operand can be converted to the Boolean value true; otherwise, false is returned.
!	The logical NOT operator returns false if the operand can be converted to a Boolean true; otherwise, true is returned.

An example that tests either variable *a* or *b* for the Boolean value true is shown in the following code snippet:

```
<c:expr value="$a || b"/>
```

String Operators

There is only one string operator. This operator is the + operator, and it is used to concatenate two strings together. An example concatenating two strings together is shown in the following code snippet:

```
<c:expr value="$stringVar1 + ' ' + stringVar2"/>
```

Using the Expression Language Tags

In this section we are going to look at a simple example showing how ECMAScript and the EL tags can be leveraged in a JSP. Listing 24.1 contains this example.

```
<%@ taglib prefix="c" uri="http://java.sun.com/jstl/ea/core" %>

<html>
  <head>
    <title>EL Standard Tag Library Example</title>
  </head>

  <body>

  <!-- Use the set tag -->
  <c:set var="firstname" scope="page">
    <%=request.getParameter("firstname") %>
  </c:set>

  <!-- Use the set tag -->
  <c:set var="lastname" scope="page">
    <%=request.getParameter("lastname") %>
  </c:set>

  <!-- Use the declare tag -->
  <c:declare id="firstname" type="java.lang.String"/>
  <c:declare id="lastname" type="java.lang.String"/>

  <!-- output the stored variables -->
  <c:expr value="$username + ' ' + lastname"" />
  <br>
  <%=firstname + ' '' + lastname%>

  </body>
</html>
```

Listing 24.1 ELExample.jsp

Before we examine the actual source for this JSP, let's take a look at the output from the evaluation of the ELExample.jsp. To see this example running, make sure you have the JSTL tag library installed, copy this JSP to the <TOMCAT_HOME>/ webapps/*webappname*/ directory, and open your browser to the following URL:

```
http://localhost:8080/webappname/ELExample.jsp
  ?firstname=Bob&lastname=Roberts
```

If everything went according to plan, you should see a page that contains the string *Bob Roberts* two times.

NOTE Make sure that you substitute the string *webappname* in the preceding URL with the name of the Web application that you will be deploying this example to.

The ELExample.jsp begins by including the JSTL tag library, using the <taglib> directive. After the JSTL has been included in the JSP, the JSP then uses two instances of the expression language tag <c:set> to create and initialize the EL variables *firstname* and *lastname*. The value of each of these EL variables is set using their bodies as opposed to their value attributes. This is because we are using standard JSP expressions to retrieve the firstname and lastname parameters from the request, and, as stated earlier in the chapter, the attributes of the EL tags cannot be set using runtime expression.

```
<c:set var="firstname" scope="page">
  <%=request.getParameter("firstname") %>
</c:set>

<c:set var="lastname" scope="page">
  <%=request.getParameter("lastname") %>
</c:set>
```

After the two EL variables have been set, they are then made available as scripting variables, using the <c:declare> tag. This allows them to be accessed using standard JSP mechanisms.

```
<c:declare id="firstname" type="java.lang.String"/>
<c:declare id="lastname" type="java.lang.String"/>
```

Notice that the id attribute of the two <c:declare> tags matches the var attributes of the <c:set> tag. It is important to remember that the name of the id attribute of the <c:declare> tag must match the name of the EL variable that it intends to expose.

When the JSP has exposed its two scripting variables, it then prints out both the EL variables and the scripting variables. Following is the snippet that does this:

```
<c:expr value="$username + ' ' + lastname" />
<br>
<%=firstname + ' ' + lastname%>
```

As you examine this code snippet , you will see that we use two methods to print the contents of the variables to the JspWriter. The first method uses the <c:expr> tag, which simply evaluates the contents of the two EL variables, concatenates them using the + operator, and writes them to the client.

The second method listed prints the contents of the two scripting variables, using the standard JSP expression syntax. This method is included simply to show the results of the <c:declare> tags.

CHAPTER

25

Conditional Tags

In this chapter, we are going to look at conditional tags in the JSP Standard Tag Library. The current set of conditional tags provide tag replacements for two Java conditional statements: if and switch. The first of these replacements, which represents the if statement, is the <c:if> tag. The second replacement, which replaces a Java switch statement, is composed of three tags: the <c:choose> tag and two child tags; <c:when> and <c:otherwise>. All of these tags are discussed in the following sections.

<c:if />

The <c:if> tag evaluates its body if the condition named in the test attribute evaluates to true. The purpose of the <c:if> tag is to act as a replacement for scriptlet code similar to the following:

```
<%
  if (test == true) {

    out.println("Something prints upon positive test!");
  }
%>
```

The equivalent <c:if> representation looks similar to the following:

```
<c:if test="true">
  Something prints upon positive evaluation!
</c:if>
```

The actual syntax of the <c:if> tag is as follows:

```
<c:if test="boolean condition">
  Evaluated Body
</c:if>
```

This <c:if> has a body type of JSP and three attributes, all of which are described in Table 25.1.

Table 25.1 <c:if> Tag Attributes

ATTRIBUTE	DESCRIPTION
test	The *test* attribute represents the condition to be evaluated by the <c:if> tag. If the <c:if> tag is being included from the expression language tag library, the value represented by the test attribute must evaluate to a Boolean primitive or a java.lang.Boolean. If the <c:if> tag is being included from the runtime tag library, the value represented by the *test* attribute must evaluate to a java.lang.Boolean. (required)
var	The var attribute names the page-level variable used to store the result of the evaluated test condition. The resulting variable will be visible at the end of the <c:if> tag. (optional)

<c:choose />

The <c:choose> tag performs a conditional block execution similar to a Java switch statement. It works in conjunction with nested <c:when> and <c:otherwise> tags acting as a parent to *n* number of <c:when> tags and one <c:otherwise> tag.

When a <c:choose> tag is encountered, it tests each of its nested <c:when> tags, evaluating the body of the first <c:when> tag whose test attribute evaluates to true. If none of the <c:when> tags evaluates to true, the body of its <c:otherwise> tag is evaluated, if it is present. The syntax of the attributes tag is as follows:

```
<c:choose>
  <c:when test="first expression to evaluate">
    Evaluated Body, if the first test attribute evaluates to
    true
  </c:when>
  <c:when test="second expression to evaluate">
    Evaluated Body, if the first test attribute evaluates to
    true
  </c:when>
  <c:otherwise>
    Evaluated Body, if the no <c:when> tag evaluates to
    true
  </c:otherwise>
</c:choose>
```

The <c:choose> tag has a body type of JSP, but has no attributes.

<c:when />

The <c:when> tag is used within a <c:choose> tag, and must be nested immediately below a <c:choose> tag. If a <c:when> tag is encountered anywhere but nested directly below a <c:choose> tag, an exception is thrown..

A <c:when> tag's body is evaluated if it is the first <c:when> tag encountered with a test condition that evaluates to true. It represents the case in a switch statement. The syntax of the <c:when> tag is as follows:

```
<c:choose>
  <c:when test="first expression to evaluate">
    Evaluated Body, if the first test attribute evaluates to
    true
  </c:when>
  <c:when test="second expression to evaluate">
    Evaluated Body, if the first test attribute evaluates to
    true
  </c:when>
  <c:otherwise>
    Evaluated Body, if the no <c:when> tag evaluates to
    true
  </c:otherwise>
</c:choose>
```

NOTE **The <c:when> tag must be nested inside a <c:choose> tag.**

The <c:when> tag has a body type of JSP and a single attribute, which is described in Table 25.2.

Table 25.2 <c:when> Tag Attribute

ATTRIBUTE	DESCRIPTION
test	The test attribute represents the condition to be evaluated by the <c:when> tag. If the <c:when> tag is being included from the expression language tag library, the value represented by the test attribute must evaluate to a Boolean primitive or a java.lang.Boolean. If the <c:when> tag is being included from the runtime tag library, the value represented by the test attribute must evaluate to a java.lang.Boolean. (required)

<c:otherwise />

The <c:otherwise> tag is used as the final case within a <c:choose> tag. It acts like a default statement in a switch statement, rendering its body if none of the <c:when> tag's conditions evaluated to true. The immediate parent of a <c:otherwise> tag must be a <c:choose> tag; otherwise, an exception will be thrown. The <c:otherwise> tag is an optional tag and is not required to complete a <c:choose> tag. The following code snippet contains the syntax of a <c:otherwise> tag:

```
<c:choose>
  <c:when test="first expression to evaluate">
    Evaluated Body, if the first test attribute evaluates to
    true
  </c:when>
  <c:when test="second expression to evaluate">
    Evaluated Body, if the first test attribute evaluates to
    true
  </c:when>
  <c:otherwise>
    Evaluated Body, if the no <c:when> tag evaluates to
    true
  </c:otherwise>
</c:choose>
```

This tag has a body type of JSP.

NOTE **The <c:otherwise> tag must be nested inside a <c:choose> tag, and there can be only one <c:otherwise> tag for every <c:choose> tag.**

Using the Conditional Tags

In this section, we are going to provide an example of how each of the JSTL conditional tags can be leveraged in a working example. Listing 25.1 contains the source for this example. You should pay particularly close attention to the bolded areas.

```
<%@ taglib prefix="c" uri="http://java.sun.com/jstl/ea/core" %>

<html>
  <head>
    <title>Conditional Standard Tag Library Example</title>
  </head>

  <body>
  <!-- Use the set expression tag to add the username -->
  <!-- to the page. -->
  <c:set var="username">Bob</c:set>

  <!-- Test the value of the username variable -->
  <c:if test="$username == 'Bob'">
    <!-- Use the set expression tag to add the username -->
    <!-- to the page. -->
    <c:set var="role">guest</c:set>
```

Listing 25.1 ConditionalExample.jsp *(continues)*

```
  </c:if>

  <c:choose>
    <c:when test="$role == 'admin'">
      <c:expr value="$username" /> you have full access!
    </c:when>
    <c:when test="$role == 'user''"">
      <c:expr value="$username" /> you have limited access!
    </c:when>
    <c:otherwise>
      <c:expr value="$username" />
        you are not welcome, go away!.
    </c:otherwise>
  </c:choose>

  </body>
</html>
```

Listing 25.1 ConditionalExample.jsp *(continued)*

Before we examine the actual source for this JSP, let's take a look at the output from the evaluation of the ConditionalExample.jsp. To see this example running, make sure you have the JSTL tag library installed, copy this JSP to the <TOMCAT_HOME>/ webapps/*webappname*/ directory, and open your browser to the following URL:

```
http://localhost:8080/webappname/ConditionalExample.jsp
```

NOTE **Make sure that you substitute the string *webappname* in the preceding URL with name of the Web application that you will be deploying this example to.**

If everything went according to plan, you should see a page similar to Figure 25.1.

The ConditionalExample.jsp begins by first including the JSTL tag library, using the <taglib> directive. After the JSTL has been included in the JSP, the JSP then uses the expression language tag <c:set> to create and initialize the scripting variable *username* to the value *Bob*.

```
  <c:set var="username">Bob</c:set>
```

The JSP then goes on to test the *username* variable using the <c:if> statement. If the value tests positively, which it does in this case, we use another <c:set> tag to create and set a *role* scripting variable to the value *guest*.

```
<c:if test="$username == 'Bob'">
  <!— Use the set expression tag to add the username —>
  <!— to the page. —>
  <c:set var="role">guest</c:set>
</c:if>
```

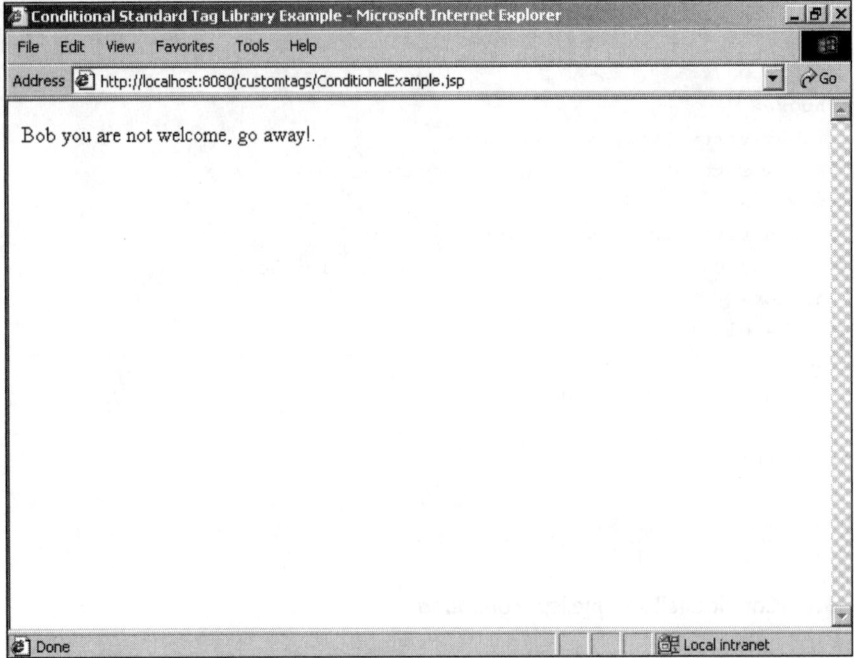

Figure 25.1 Output of the ConditionalExample.jsp.

After the ConditionalExample.jsp sets the *role* variable to the value *guest,* it then tests the role value using two <c:when> tags and a single <c:otherwise> tag.

```
<c:choose>
  <c:when test="$role == 'admin'">
    <c:expr value="$username" /> you have full access!
  </c:when>
  <c:when test="$role == 'user''">
    <c:expr value="$username" /> you have limited access!
  </c:when>
  <c:otherwise>
    <c:expr value="$username" />
      you are not welcome, go away!.
  </c:otherwise>
</c:choose>
```

The two <c:when> tags test the *role* variable against the strings admin and user, respectively. Neither of these cases tests true, which causes the <c:otherwise> tag's body to be evaluated. The evaluation of the <c:otherwise> tag's body results in the string *Bob you are not welcome, go away!*

CHAPTER

26

Iterator Tags

In this chapter, we are going to look at the JSTL iterator tags. There are two tags that belong in the Iterator grouping: <c:forEach> and <c:forTokens>. These two tags provide the functionality to iterate over the contents of Java collections and over tokens in a string, respectively.

<c:forEach />

The <c:forEach> tag is a very useful tag, allowing you to iterate over several different types of Java Collections. It will allow you to iterate over all standard java.util.Collections, arrays, java.util.Enumerators, java.util.Maps, java.sql.ResultSets, and comma-separated lists of strings. The collections can be iterated over from start to finish or by emulating a for loop using a begin and end attribute. The syntax of the <c:forEach> tag is as follows:

```
<c:forEach var="variable name"
  items="collection to iterate over"
  status="status variable name">
  Body being evaluated with each iteration
</c:forEach>
```

NOTE **The <c:forEach> tag has no required attributes; therefore, the preceding syntactical listing represents a common example as opposed to the required syntax.**

The <c:forEach> tag has a body type of JSP and supports six attributes, each of which are described in Table 26.1.

Table 26.1 forEach Tag Attributes

ATTRIBUTE	DESCRIPTION
items	The items attribute names the collection of objects to iterate over. If the items attribute is not included, the begin and end attributes are expected. (optional)
begin	The begin attribute names the index of the item to begin iterating when using a begin/end range similar to a for loop. The first item in the collection has an index of 0. (optional)
end	The end attribute names the index of the item to end iterating, when using a begin/end range similar to a for loop. (optional)
step	The step attribute indicates an incremental value used when iterating over a collection. An example of this would be a step value of 2. This would tell the <c:forEach> tag that we were interested in every other item in the collection. (optional)
var	The var attribute names the page-level variable used to store the object currently being iterated over. The exposed object is visible only within the opening and closing <c:forEach> tags. (optional)
status	The status attribute names the page-level variable that will be used to store the current status of the <c:forEach> tag. The exposed object is visible only within the opening and closing <c:forEach> tags. The properties exposed by the status object are described in Table 26.2. (optional)

The <c:forEach> tag exposes an expression language variable containing status information about the current state of the <c:forEach> tag and the elements being iterated over. This object is named by the status attribute described in Table 26.1. The information that it exposes is described in Table 26.2.

Table 26.2 status Object Properties

ATTRIBUTE	DESCRIPTION
current	The current property contains a reference to the current object in the collection.
index	The index property contains the zero-based index of the current item.
count	The count property contains the one-based index of the current item.
first	The first property contains a Boolean value indicating whether or not the current item is the first item in the collection.

Table 26.2 status Object Properties *(continued)*

ATTRIBUTE	DESCRIPTION
last	The last property contains a boolean value indicating whether or not the current item is the last item in the collection.

<c:forTokens />

The <c:forTokens> tag is essentially the same as <c:forEach>, except that it specializes in the tokenization of strings. Its main function is to take a java.lang.String object that is separated by known tokens and iterated over each substring separated by the known tokens. It shares the same attributes as the <c:forEach> tag with the addition of one extra attribute, delims, which is used to name the token delimiter. The syntax of the <c:forTokens> tag is as follows:

```
<c:forTokens
  items="string to tokenize"
  delims="the delimiter">
  Body being evaluated with each iteration
</c:forTokens>
```

This tag has a body type of JSP and supports seven attributes, which are described in Table 26.3.

Table 26.3 forTokens Tag Attributes

ATTRIBUTE	DESCRIPTION
items	The items attribute names the collection of objects to iterate over. If the items attribute is not included, the begin and end attributes are expected. (required)
delims	The delims attribute names the delimiter used when tokenizing the named string. (required)
begin	The begin attribute names the index of the item to begin iterating, when using a begin/end range similar to a for loop. The first item in the collection has an index of 0. (optional)
end	The end attribute names the index of the item to end iterating, when using a begin/end range similar to a for loop. (optional)
step	The step attribute indicates an incremental value used when iterating over a collection. An example of this would be a step value of 2. This would tell the <c:forTokens> tag that we were interested in every other item in the collection. (optional)
var	The var attribute names the page-level variable used to store the object currently being iterated over. The exposed object is visible only within the opening and closing <c:forTokens> tags. (optional)

Table 26.3 forTokens Tag Attributes *(continued)*

ATTRIBUTE	DESCRIPTION
status	The status attribute names the page-level variable that will be used to store the current status of the <c:forTokens> tag. The exposed object is visible only within the opening and closing <c:forTokens> tags. The properties exposed by the status object are described in Table 26.2. (optional)

Using the Iterator Tags

In this section we are going to look at an example of how each of the iterator tags functions. Listing 26.1 contains the source for this example. You should pay particularly close attention to the bolded areas.

```
<%@ taglib prefix="c" uri="http://java.sun.com/jstl/ea/core" %>

<html>
  <head>
    <title>Iterators Standard Tag Library Example</title>
  </head>

  <body>

  <jsp:useBean id="users" scope="page"
    class="java.util.Hashtable" />

  <%
    users.put("USER56", "Happy,Gilmore");
    users.put("USER99", "Austin,Powers");
    users.put("USER09", "Monty,Python");
  %>

  <table width="500" border="1">
  <tr>
    <th>Count</th>
    <th>Emp. Id</th>
    <th>First Name</th>
    <th>Last Name</th>
  </tr>
  <c:forEach var="user" items="$users" status="status">
    <tr>
      <td><c:expr value="$status.count" />.)</td>
```

Listing 26.1 IteratorExample.jsp *(continues)*

```
        <td><c:expr value="$user.key" /></td>

        <c:forTokens
          var="name"
          items="$user.value"
          delims=",">
          <td><c:expr value="$name"/></td>
        </c:forTokens>
      </tr>
    </c:forEach>

    </table>
    </body>
  </html>
```

Listing 26.1 IteratorExample.jsp *(continued)*

Before we examine the actual source for this JSP, let's take a look at the output from the evaluation of the IteratorExample.jsp. To see this example running, make sure you have the JSTL tag library installed, copy this JSP to the <TOMCAT_HOME>/ webapps/*webappname*/ directory, and open your browser to the following URL:

```
http://localhost:8080/webappname/IteratorExample.jsp
```

NOTE **Make sure that you substitute the string *webappname* in the preceding URL with the name of the Web application that you will be deploying this example to.**

If everything went according to plan, you should see a page similar to Figure 26.1.

The IteratorExample.jsp begins by first including the JSTL tag library, using the <taglib> directive. After the JSTL has been included in the JSP, the JSP then creates a java.util.Hashtable, and adds three key/value pairs to it. This is the collection that will be iterated over using the <c:forEach> tag.

```
<jsp:useBean id="users" scope="page"
  class="java.util.Hashtable" />

<%
  users.put("USER56", "Happy,Gilmore");
  users.put("USER99", "Austin,Powers");
  users.put("USER09", "Monty,Python");
%>
```

The next action performed by the IteratorExample.jsp is to start iterating over the elements in the Hashtable referenced by the scripting variable *users*. You should note that with each iteration we are exposing a variable named *user* and a status variable named *status*. The first section of the <c:forEach> tag follows:

```
<c:forEach var="user" items="$users" status="status">
  <tr>
```

```
    <td><c:expr value="$status.count" />.)</td>
    <td><c:expr value="$user.key" /></td>
```

As you look over the preceding snippet, notice that for each element in the collection we print the current count of the collection and the key referencing the bound to the current Hashtable element.

NOTE **When the collection being iterated over is a java.util.Map or java.util.RecordSet, each element in the collection exposes two properties: key and value. The key property represents a Map key or RecordSet column name, and the value property represents the value bound to the key or column name. If you were iterating over a collection of user-defined objects, you would reference the properties of the current object using the each data member's name.**

After the JSP prints the status.count and key of the current element, it then retrieves the value of the current element, which contains a first and last name separated by a comma, and passes it to the <c:forTokens> tag for tokenizing.

```
    <c:forTokens
      var="name"
      items="$user.value"
      delims=",">
      <td><c:expr value="$name"/></td>
    </c:forTokens>
  </tr>
</c:forEach>
```

As you can see, each string represented by a *$user.value* value is separated using a comma for a delimiter. This results in the first and last names being separated and printed to individual <td> elements. Now we have a <table> of users with each of their properties represented by unique <td> elements.

CHAPTER

27

Import Tags

In this chapter, we are going to look at the JSTL import tags. The import tags were created to resolve some of the shortcomings associated with the <jsp:include> standard action tag, including its inability to reference resources from different contexts and resources that exist on entirely different servers. There are currently three tags belonging to the import tag grouping: <c:import>, <c:urlEncode>, <param>.

<c:import />

The <c:import> tag provides a simple mechanism that can be used to access resources using a named url. The url name can be either fully qualified or relative. Some of the attributes that make this tag different from its predecessor, the <jsp:include> tag, are its ability to access a resource in the same context, in a different context on the same machine, or a resource that is running on a completely different server.

The syntax of the <c:import> tag is as follows:

```
<c:import url="relative or fully qualified url" />
```

The <c:import> tag has body content type of JSP and six attributes, each of which are described in Table 27.1.

Table 27.1 <c:import> Tag Attributes

ATTRIBUTE	DESCRIPTION
url	The url attribute represents the name of the resource to import using the <c:import> tag. This value can be either relative or fully qualified. (required)

Table 27.1 <c:import> Tag Attributes *(continued)*

ATTRIBUTE	DESCRIPTION
name	The name attribute represents the name of the PageContext attribute to retrieve. (optional)
var	The var attribute represents a variable name that, if present, will contain a java.lang.string representation of the results returned by the <c:import> tag. (optional)
scope	The scope attribute specifies the scope of the var or varReader objects. The default value is page scope. (optional)
varReader	The varReader attribute represents a variable name that, if present, will reference a java.io.Reader representation of the results returned by the <c:import> tag. (optional)
context	The context attribute specifies the name of a web running on the same server. This attribute allows the import tag to retrieve a resource from another ServletContext running on the same application server. If the context attribute is used, the url attribute must be relative to the named context. (optional)

<c:urlEncode />

The <c:urlEncode> tag is used to encode a string according to the encoding rules defined in RFC 1738, for use as the url of a <c:import> tag. The purpose of the <c:urlEncode> is to properly format request parameters so that it can be used when retrieving a named resource. The string being encoded can be specified using the value attribute or the tag's body content. The result of the encoding is, by default, written to the calling page using the JspWriter. The result can also be stored in the PageContext and can be retrieved using the named variable, using the var attribute.

The syntax of the <c:urlEncode> tag is as follows:

```
<c:urlEncode value="string to url encode" />
```

or

```
<c:urlEncode>
  string to url encode
</c:urlEncode>
```

This tag has a body type of JSP. The attributes of the <c:urlEncode> tag are described in Table 27.2.

Table 27.2 <urlEncode> Tag Attributes

ATTRIBUTE	DESCRIPTION
var	The var attribute represents a variable name that, if present, will contain a java.lang.string representation of the results returned by the <c:urlEncode> tag. (optional)

Table 27.2 <urlEncode> Tag Attributes *(continued)*

ATTRIBUTE	DESCRIPTION
scope	The scope attribute specifies the scope of the var or varReader objects. The default value is page scope. (optional)
value	The value attribute names the string to be encoded. If the value attribute is not specified, the encoding is performed on the tag's body. (optional)

<c:param />

The <c:param> tag is used when adding request parameters to a url resource being retrieved by a <c:import> tag. The value of the <c:param> is, by default, url encoded. If you do not want the value attribute to be encoded, add the encode attribute with a value of false. The syntax of the <c:param> tag is as follows:

```
<c:import url="relative or fully qualified url">
  <c:param name="parameter name" value="parameter value" />
</c:import>
```

NOTE The <c:param> tag, by default, encodes the parameter value prior to adding it to the <c:import> tag's url. By encoding and adding the parameter to the url, the <c:param> tag is a much easier-to-use replacement for the <c:urlEncode> tag.

The <c:param> tag has no body and three attributes. The attributes of the <c:param> tag are described in Table 27.3.

Table 27.3 <c:param> Tag Attributes

ATTRIBUTE	DESCRIPTION
name	The name attribute identifies the name of the request parameter to be added to the imported url. (required)
value	The value attribute specifies the value of the named request parameter. (required)
encode	The encode attribute is a Boolean attribute that signifies that the string, represented by the value attribute, should or should not be encoded. The default value is true. (optional)

Using the Import Tags

In this section, we are going to take a look at an example of how the import tags can be used in a JSP. Listing 27.1 contains the source for this example.

```
<%@ taglib prefix="c" uri="http://java.sun.com/jstl/ea/core" %>

<html>
  <head>
    <title>Import Standard Tag Library Example</title>
  </head>

  <body>

    <!-- Import resource from a context on the same server -->
    <c:import url="/jsp/dates/date.jsp" context="/examples"/>
    <hr>

    <!-- Import a resource from an external server -->
    <c:import var="avssearch"
  url="http://web.webcrawler.com/d/search/p/webcrawler/index.jhtml">
      <c:param name="c" value="web" />
      <c:param name="s" value="Colorado Avalanche"/>
    </c:import>

  <c:expr value="$avssearch"/>
  </body>
</html>
```

Listing 27.1 ImportExample.jsp

To see this example in action, make sure you have the page tag library installed, copy this JSP to the <TOMCAT_HOME>/webapps/*webappname*/ directory, and open your browser to the following URL:

```
http://localhost:8080/webappname/ImportExample.jsp
```

If everything went according to plan, you should see a page similar to Figure 27.1, with two imported resources separated by an HTML <hr> element.

This example begins by using the <c:import> tag to retrieve a resource from the /examples Web application. The resource that is being retrieved is a JSP named date.jsp that simply prints the current date.

```
<c:import url="/jsp/dates/date.jsp" context="/examples"/>
```

The important thing to note about this first statement is that it uses the context attribute to retrieve a resource on the same server, but existing in a different Web application. The retrieved resource is constructed from the context and the relative path named in the url. The complete resource for the preceding example is as follows:

```
http://servername:portnumber/examples/jsp/dates/date.jsp
```

The next step performed by the ImportExample.jsp is to retrieve a resource that exists on a completely different server, and store the results in an expression language variable. The resource being retrieved is a search engine on the webcrawler.com Web site. Because the webcrawler resource exists on a completely different server from our JSP, we must provide a fully qualified url in the <c:import> tag.

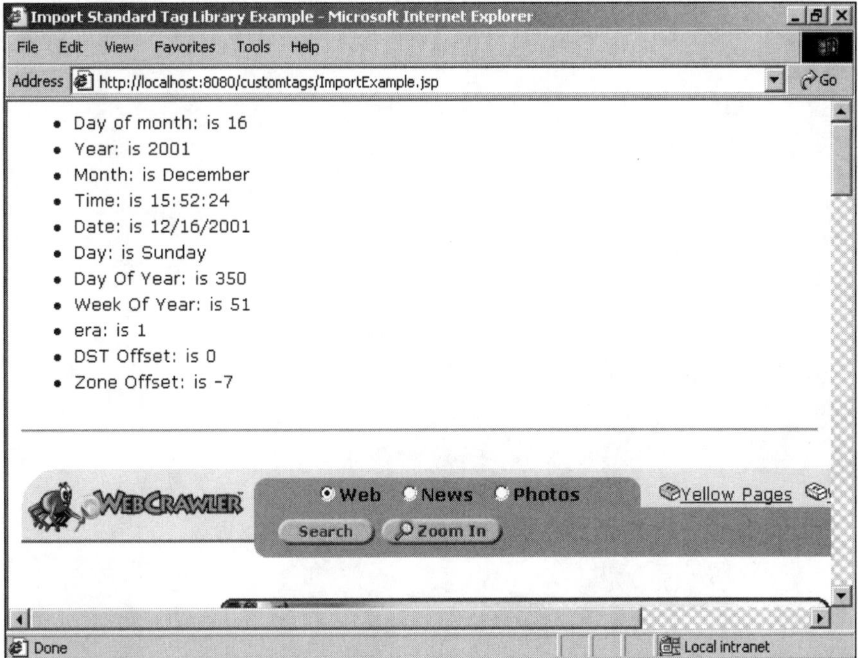

Figure 27.1 Output of the ImportExample.jsp.

```
<c:import var="avssearch"
 url="http://web.webcrawler.com/d/search/p/webcrawler/index.jhtml">
  <c:param name="c" value="web" />
  <c:param name="s" value="Colorado Avalanche"/>
</c:import>
```

To retrieve the webcrawler resource we name the url to the webcrawler resource and two request parameters. The first parameter tells webcrawler that we want to perform a Web search and the second states that we want to search for the string "Colorado Avalanche". It is important to note that the second <c:param> has a value that includes a space. This does not hinder the evaluation of this request because the <c:param> tag, by default, encodes the parameter value. This is the functionality that we spoke of earlier that makes the <c:param> tag easier to use than the <c:urlEncode> tag.

CHAPTER

28

SQL Tags

In this chapter, we are going to look at the JSTL SQL tags. The SQL tags were created to perform basic JDBC functions. There are currently five tags belonging to the SQL Tag Library: <sql:driver>, <sql:query>, <sql:update>, <sql:transaction>, and <sql:param>.

The SQL tags differ from the core tags that we described in the previous chapters, in that they are referenced using a separate TLD. The library itself is included in the JSTL archive, standard.jar, but does require the completion of the following steps before its use:

1. Copy the TLD packaged with the SQL Tag Library, sql.tld, to the <TOMCAT_HOME>/webapps/*webappname*/WEB-INF directory.
2. The SQL tags also rely upon the JDBC 2.0 extended package, which can be found at the http://java.sun.com site. You can also find the necessary JAR packaged with the JSTL Example WAR. Once you have this file, jdbc2_0-stdext.jar, copy it to the <TOMCAT_HOME>/webapps/*webappname*/WEB-INF/lib directory.
3. Add the following <taglib> subelement to the web.xml file of the Web application:

```
  <taglib>
  <taglib-uri>
    http://java.sun.com/jstl/ea/sql
  </taglib-uri>
  <taglib-location>
    /WEB-INF/sql.tld
  </taglib-location>
</taglib>
```

After the preceding steps are complete, add the following taglib directive to each JSP that will leverage the SQL Tag Library:

```
<%@ taglib
  uri=" http://java.sun.com/jstl/ea/sql"
  prefix="sql" %>
```

This directive identifies the URI defined in the previously listed <taglib> element, and states that all SQL tags should be prefixed with the string *sql*.

<sql:driver />

The <sql:driver> tag is used to create a JDBC DataSource that connects to the targeted database. According the JSTL documentation, the <sql:driver> tag is recommended for development only. When you actually deploy a solution using the SQL tags, it is recommended that you create a DataSource using logic that has been separated from your application's presentation layer. The syntax of the <sql:driver> tag is as follows:

```
<sql:driver
  var="EL variable that will reference the dataSource"
  driver="JDBC driver name"
  jdbcURL="JDBC URL to Database" />
```

The <sql:driver> tag has no body and four attributes. The attributes of the <sql:driver> tag are described in Table 28.1.

Table 28.1 <sql:driver> Tag Attributes

ATTRIBUTE	DESCRIPTION
var	The var attribute names an EL variable that will reference the created dataSource. (required)
driver	The driver attribute specifies the JDBC driver to use when connecting to the targeted database. If this attribute is not set, the driver must be set using a context parameter, as described following. (optional)
jdbcURL	The jdbcURL attribute specifies the URL pointing to the targeted database. If this attribute is not set, it must be set using a context parameter, as described following. (optional)
userName	The userName attribute specifies the name of the user to use when connecting to the targeted database. If the userName attribute is not set, it must be set using a context parameter, as described following. (optional)

The <sql:driver> tag also allows you to set its attributes using context parameters in the web.xml file. If an attribute is set using both a context parameter and a tag attribute, the tag attribute will take precedence. The following list contains the four context parameter names. Each parameter name should be self-explanatory.

- javax.servlet.jsp.jstl.sql.driver.driver
- javax.servlet.jsp.jstl.sql.driver.url
- javax.servlet.jsp.jstl.sql.driver.user
- javax.servlet.jsp.jstl.sql.driver.password

If you want to use any of these parameters, you need add an entry to the web.xml file similar to the following code snippet:

```
<context-param>
  <param-name>
    javax.servlet.jsp.jstl.sql.driver.user
  </param-name>
  <param-value>
    someusername
  </param-value>
</context-param>
```

NOTE **The <sql:driver> tag does not provide a password attribute. This is to prevent the use of a password in the clear text of a JSP. To set a password, you must use the javax.servlet.jsp.jstl.sql.driver.password context parameter, as shown previously.**

<sql:query />

The <sql:query> tag is used when performing SQL queries. The <sql:query> tag allows the user to specify query statements using either the tag's body or the sql attribute. If both methods are used, the sql attribute takes precedence. The results of the SQL query are returned in the format of a java.sql.ResultSet that is referenced by an EL variable named by the var attribute. The syntax of the <sql:query> tag is as follows:

```
<sql:query
  var="EL Variable to that will reference the returned results"
  dataSource="previously created DataSource EL variable">
  SQL query to perform
</sql:query>
```

The <sql:query> tag has a body content type of JSP and five possible attributes, each of which is described in Table 28.2.

Table 28.2 <sql:query> Tag Attributes

ATTRIBUTE	DESCRIPTION
var	The var attribute names an EL variable that will reference the ResultSet returned by the <sql:query> tag. (required)
sql	The sql attribute provides an optional method of specifying the SQL query to perform. (optional)

Table 28.2 <sql:query> Tag Attributes *(continued)*

ATTRIBUTE	DESCRIPTION
dataSource	The dataSource attribute names an EL variable that references a previously created DataSource. (optional)
startRow	The startRow attribute is an optional attribute used to specify the starting row for the returned ResultSet. (optional)
maxRow	The maxRow attribute is an optional attribute that restricts the number of rows returned in a ResultSet. (optional)

<sql:update />

The <sql:update> tag is used to perform SQL updates including INSERTS, UPDATES, and DELETES. The <sql:update> tag allows the user to specify update statements using either the tag's body or the sql attribute. If both methods are used, the sql attribute takes precedence. The results of the <sql:update> are optionally exposed using the var attribute. These results are returned in the form of a java.lang.Integer object that tells how many rows were affected by the update statement. The syntax of the <sql:update> tag is as follows:

```
<sql:update
  var="EL Variable to that will reference the returned results"
  dataSource="previously created DataSource EL variable">
  SQL UPDATE, INSERT, or DELETE to perform
</sql:update>
```

The <sql:update> tag has a body type of JSP and three possible attributes. The attributes of the <sql:update> tag are described in Table 28.3.

Table 28.3 <sql:update> Tag Attributes

ATTRIBUTE	DESCRIPTION
var	The var attribute names an EL variable that will reference a java.lang.Integer object that tells how many rows were affected by the update statement. (optional)
sql	The sql attribute provides an optional method of specifying the SQL update statement to perform. (optional)
dataSource	The dataSource attribute names an EL variable that references a previously created DataSource. (optional)

<sql:transaction />

The <sql:transaction> tag is used to create a transaction context for <sql:query> and <sql:update> tags. It allows the tag user to embed one or more SQL tags in its body, which will be performed as a single transaction. The syntax of the <sql:transaction> tag is as follows:

```
<sql:transaction
  dataSource="previously created DataSource EL variable">
  one or more SQL Tags
</sql:transaction>
```

NOTE **All SQL tags that are embedded in the body of the <sql:transaction> tags must use the DataSource of its parent <sql:transaction> tag.**

The <sql:transaction> tag has a body type of JSP and a single attribute. The attribute of the <sql:transaction> tag is described in Table 28.4.

Table 28.4 <sql:transaction> Tag Attributes

ATTRIBUTE	DESCRIPTION
dataSource	The dataSource attribute names an EL variable that references a previously created DataSource. (optional)
transactionIsolationLevel	The transactionIsolationLevel attribute is used to set JDBC transaction isolation levels. These levels are the same as the levels supported in JDBC by java.sql.Connection. (optional)

NOTE **As of Early Access 3 of the JSTL, the <sql:transaction> tag's documentation describes the transactionIsolationLevel attribute, but the attribute is not included in the TLD describing the SQL Tag Library, which renders the attribute unusable.**

<sql:param />

The <sql:param> tag used is used as a subtag of both <sql:query> and <sql:update>. It is used to set the values of parameter markers, represented by *?* characters, in its parent's SQL statement. The value that will replace the *?* character can be set using either the body of the <sql:param> tag or the value attribute. The syntax of the <sql:param> tag is as follows:

```
<sql:query
  url="relative or fully qualified url">
  select * from sometable where username = ?
  <sql:param value="parameter value" />
</sql:query>
```

NOTE **The values substituted by the <sql:param> tags are replaced in the order of the <sql:param> tags' appearance.**

The <sql:param> tag has a body type of JSP and a single attribute. The attribute of the <sql:param> tag is described in Table 28.5.

Table 28.5 <sql:param> Tag Attributes

ATTRIBUTE	DESCRIPTION
value	The value attribute specifies the value of the SQL parameter. (optional)

Using the Import Tags

In this section, we are going to take a look at an example of how the SQL tags can be used to perform basic JDBC functions. Listing 28.1 contains the source for this example.

```
<%@ taglib prefix="sql"
  uri="http://java.sun.com/jstl/ea/sql" %>
<%@ taglib prefix="c"
  uri="http://java.sun.com/jstl/ea/core" %>

<html>
  <head>
    <title>SQL Standard Tag Library Example</title>
  </head>

  <!-- Create a DataSource -->
  <sql:driver
    var="contactmanager"
    driver="sun.jdbc.odbc.JdbcOdbcDriver"
    jdbcURL="Jdbc:Odbc:contacts" />

  <!-- Use the update tag to add another contact -->
  <sql:update dataSource="$contactmanager">
    insert into contacts
    values ('broberts',
    'Bob',
    'Roberts',
    'Sales',
    '(303) 555-0909',
    'broberts@anywhere.com''')
  </sql:update>
```

Listing 28.1 SQLExample.jsp *(continues)*

```
    <!-- use the query tag to get all of the contacts -->
    <sql:query var="contacts" dataSource="$contactmanager">
      select * from contacts
    </sql:query>

  <!-- Iterate over the results using the forEach tag -->
  <table border="1">
    <tr>
      <th>username</th>
      <th>firstname</th>
      <th>lastname</th>
      <th>title</th>
      <th>phone</th>
      <th>email</th>
    </tr>
    <c:forEach var="rows" begin="1" items="$contacts.rows">
      <tr>
        <td><c:expr value="$rows.get('username')"/></td>
        <td><c:expr value="$rows.get('firstname')"/></td>
        <td><c:expr value="$rows.get('lastname')"/></td>
        <td><c:expr value="$rows.get('title')"/></td>
        <td><c:expr value="$rows.get('phone')"/></td>
        <td><c:expr value="$rows.get('email')"/></td>
      </tr>
    </c:forEach>
  </table>

    </body>
  </html>
```

Listing 28.1 SQLExample.jsp *(continued)*

To see this example in action, make sure you have the Page Tag Library installed, copy this JSP to the <TOMCAT_HOME>/webapps/*webappname*/ directory, and open your browser to the following URL:

```
http://localhost:8080/webappname/SQLExample.jsp
```

NOTE **This example used the contacts.mdb database configured in Chapter 2, "Configuring and Testing the Web Application Environment." Make sure you have this database configured prior to executing this JSP.**

If everything went according to plan, you should see a page similar to Figure 28.1.

The SQLExample.jsp begins by including the both JSTL Core and SQL tag libraries, using the <taglib> directive. After these libraries have been included in the JSP, the JSP then creates a DataSource using the <sql:driver> tag.

```
<sql:driver
  var="contactmanager"
  driver="sun.jdbc.odbc.JdbcOdbcDriver"
  jdbcURL="Jdbc:Odbc:contacts" />
```

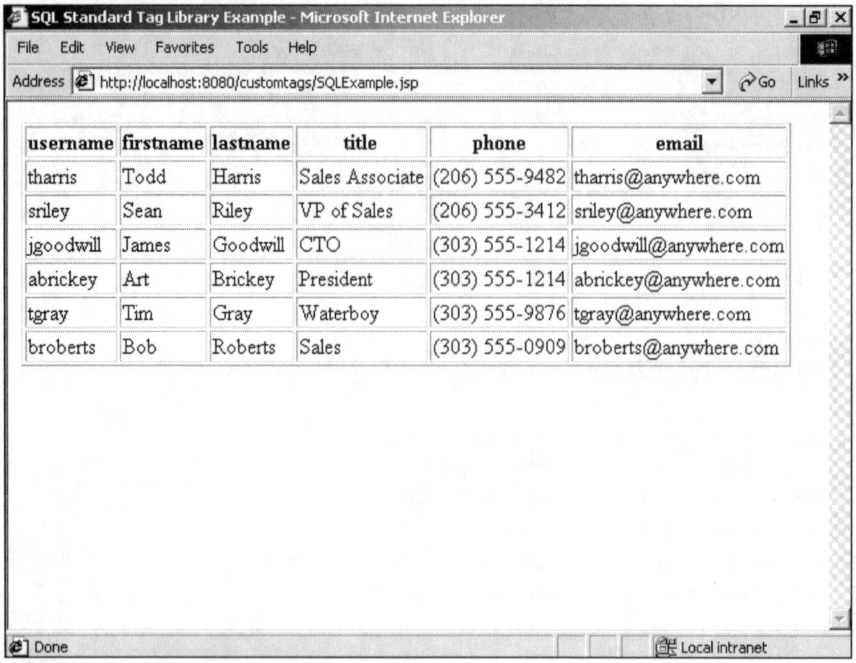

username	firstname	lastname	title	phone	email
tharris	Todd	Harris	Sales Associate	(206) 555-9482	tharris@anywhere.com
sriley	Sean	Riley	VP of Sales	(206) 555-3412	sriley@anywhere.com
jgoodwill	James	Goodwill	CTO	(303) 555-1214	jgoodwill@anywhere.com
abrickey	Art	Brickey	President	(303) 555-1214	abrickey@anywhere.com
tgray	Tim	Gray	Waterboy	(303) 555-9876	tgray@anywhere.com
broberts	Bob	Roberts	Sales	(303) 555-0909	broberts@anywhere.com

Figure 28.1 Output of the SQLExample.jsp.

This instance of the <sql:driver> tag creates a DataSource that references the contacts database and exposes this DataSource using the EL variable *contactmanager*. This variable will be used to perform all of the following SQL actions.

After the *contactmanager* DataSource is created, the JSP then performs a SQL INSERT using the <sql:update> tag. The instance of this tag inserts the contact *broberts* into the contacts table, referenced by the *contactmanager* DataSource.

```
<sql:update dataSource="$contactmanager">
  insert into contacts
  values ('broberts',
  'Bob',
  'Roberts',
  'Sales',
  '(303) 555-0909',
  'broberts@anywhere.com''')
</sql:update>
```

After the new contact is inserted, the JSP then performs a SQL query that retrieves all contacts from the contacts table. The results of this query are exposed using the EL variable *contacts*.

```
<sql:query var="contacts" dataSource="$contactmanager">
  select * from contacts
</sql:query>
```

The final action performed by this JSP is to take the results of the previously listed <sql:query> and iterate over them. This is done using the Core <c:forEach> tag, which we discussed in Chapter 26, "Iterator Tags." The result of this action is an HTML table containing the contacts in the contacts.mdb database.

```
<c:forEach var="rows" begin="1" items="$contacts.rows">
  <tr>
    <td><c:expr value="$rows.get('username')"/></td>
    <td><c:expr value="$rows.get('firstname')"/></td>
    <td><c:expr value="$rows.get('lastname')"/></td>
    <td><c:expr value="$rows.get('title')"/></td>
    <td><c:expr value="$rows.get('phone')"/></td>
    <td><c:expr value=""$rows.get('email'')"/></td>
  </tr>
</c:forEach>
```

The only thing that needs to be noted about this last section is how a ResultSet is iterated over, using the <c:forEach> tag. The collection that is being iterated over, in this instance, is the ResultSet exposed by the <sql:query> tag. This collection is referenced using the rows property of the EL variable *contacts*. Once the collection is named, each column of the current row is accessed using the *rows* EL variable.

APPENDIX

A

Tag Library APIs

In this appendix, we are going to look at the tag library APIs. These APIs are contained in the javax.servlet.jsp.tagext package. This package contains all of the classes and interfaces required to create a custom JSP tag library. These classes and interfaces are graphically depicted in Figure A.1.

We will describe each of the objects throughout this appendix.

NOTE **This appendix covers the classes and interfaces described by the JSP 1.2 specification.**

Interfaces

In this section, we are going to discuss the two custom tag interfaces defined by the JSP 1.2 specification.

Tag Interface

```
public interface Tag extends java.lang.Object
```

Actions in a tag library are defined through subclasses of the abstract class Tag. The class has 13 fields and 19 methods, as described in the following sections.

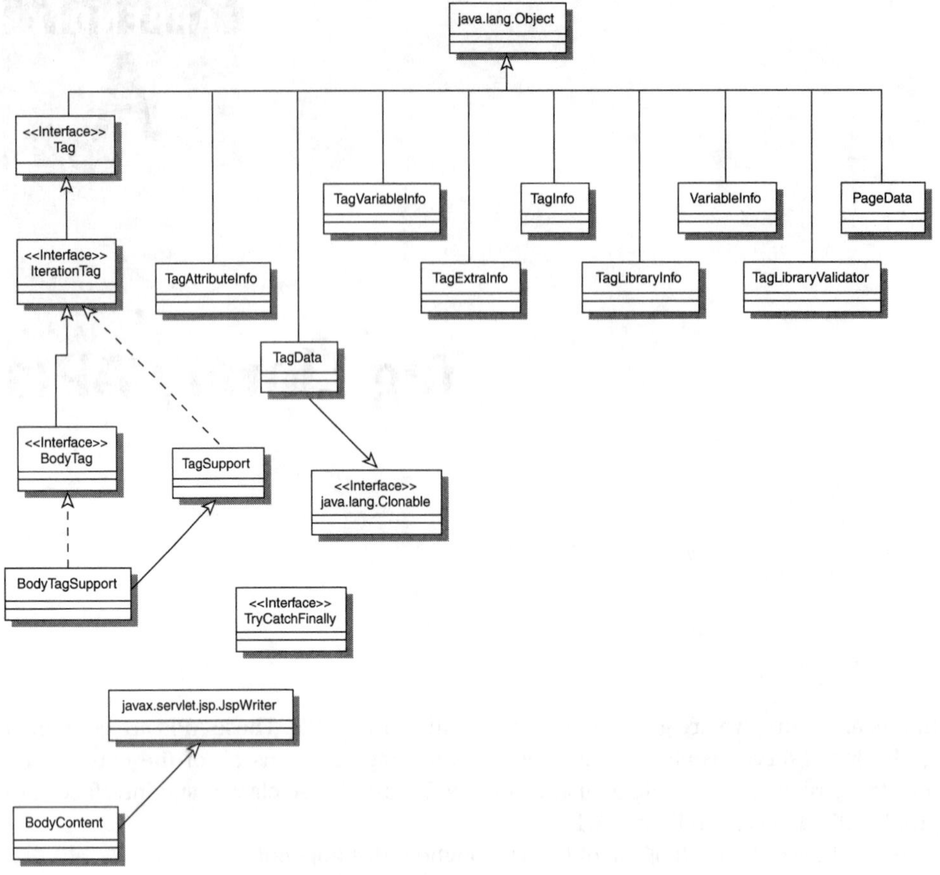

Figure A.1 Classes and interfaces of the javax.servlet.jsp.tagext package.

bodyOut Field

```
protected BodyJspWriter bodyOut
```

This field is used to hold the reference to the BodyJspWriter.

EVAL_BODY Field

```
public static final int EVAL_BODY
```

This field is used to hold the reference to the return value for doStartTag() and doAfterBody().

EVAL_PAGE Field

```
public static final int EVAL_PAGE
```

This field is used to hold the reference to the return value for doEndTag().

libraryPrefix Field

```
private java.lang.String libraryPrefix
```

This field is used to hold the prefix for the tag library of this tag.

pageContext Field

```
protected PageContext pageContext
```

This field is used to hold the reference to the current PageContext.

parent Field

```
private Tag parent
```

This field is a reference to the parent tag kept by each Tag instance, which effectively provides a runtime execution stack.

previousOut Field

```
private JspWriter previousOut
```

This field is a reference to the JspWriter, and is valid when the tag is reached.

SKIP_BODY Field

```
public static final int SKIP_BODY
```

This field indicates whether the body of the action should be evaluated.

SKIP_PAGE Field

```
public static final int SKIP_PAGE
```

This field indicates whether or not the action should continue to evaluate the rest of the page.

tagData Field

```
protected TagData tagData
```

This field contains the value information for a tag instance.

tagId Field

```
private java.lang.String tagId
```

This field contains the value information for a tag id.

tagName Field

```
private java.lang.String tagName
```

This field contains a reference to the tag's short name.

values Field

```
private java.util.Hashtable values
```

This field contains a reference to a Hashtable containing the tags and their associated values.

Tag() Method

```
public Tag(java.lang.String libraryPrefix, java.lang.String
  tagName)
```

In this default constructor, all subclasses must define a public constructor with the same signature, and call the constructor of the superclass. This constructor is called by the code generated by the JSP translator. Tag() returns no value and throws no exceptions.

Parameters

java.lang.String

java.lang.String

doAfterBody() Method

```
public int doAfterBody() throws JspError
```

This method is invoked after every body evaluation. doAfterBody() has no parameters.

Returns

int

Exceptions Thrown

JspError

doBeforeBody() Method

```
public int doBeforeBody() throws JspError
```

This method is invoked before every body evaluation. doBeforeBody() has no parameters.

Returns

int

Exceptions Thrown

JspError

doEndTag() Method

```
public int doEndTag() throws JspException
```

This method processes the end tag. This method will be called on all Tag objects. It returns an indication of whether the rest of the page should be evaluated or skipped. doEndTag() has no parameters.

Returns

int

Exceptions Thrown

JspException

doStartTag() Method

```
public int doStartTag() throws JspException
```

This method processes the start tag for this instance. The doStartTag() method assumes that initialize() has been invoked prior to its own execution. When this method is invoked, the body has not yet been invoked. doStartTag() has no parameters.

Returns

int

Exceptions Thrown

JspException

findAncestorWithClass() Method

```
public static final Tag findAncestorWithClass(Tag from,
  java.lang.Class class)
```

This method finds the instance of a given class type that is closest to a given instance. This method is used for coordination among cooperating tags. findAncestorWithClass() throws no exceptions.

Parameters

Tag

java.lang.Class

Returns

Tag

getBodyOut() Method

```
protected final BodyJspWriter getBodyOut()
```

This method returns the value of the current out JspWriter. getBodyOut() has no parameters and throws no exceptions.

Returns

BodyJspWriter

getLibraryPrefix() Method

```
public java.lang.String getLibraryPrefix()
```

This method returns the library prefix being used with this tag. getLibraryPrefix() has no parameters and throws no exceptions.

Returns

java.lang.String

getPageContext() Method

```
public PageContext getPageContext()
```

This method returns the PageContext for this tag. getPageContext() has no parameters and throws no exceptions.

Returns

PageContext

getParent() Method

```
public Tag getParent()
```

This method returns the parent extension tag instance or null. getParent() has no parameters and throws no exceptions.

Returns

Tag

getPreviousOut() Method

```
protected final JspWriter getPreviousOut()
```

This method returns the value of the out JspWriter prior to pushing a BodyJspWriter. getPreviousOut() has no parameters and throws no exceptions.

Returns

JspWriter

getTagData() Method

```
public TagData getTagData()
```

This method returns the immutable TagData for this tag. getTagData() has no parameters and throws no exceptions.

Returns

TagData

getTagId() Method

```
public java.lang.String getTagId()
```

This method returns the value of the id or null for the tag. getTagID() has no parameters and throws no exceptions.

Returns

java.lang.String

getTagName() Method

```
public java.lang.String getTagName()
```

This method returns the short name for the tag. getTagName() has no parameters and throws no exceptions.

Returns

java.lang.String

getValue() Method

```
public java.lang.Object getValue(java.lang.String key)
```

This method returns the value associated with the tag. getValue() throws no exceptions.

Parameters

java.lang.Object

Returns

java.lang.String

initialize() Method

```
public void initialize(Tag parent,
  TagData tagData,
  PageContext pc)
```

This method initializes a Tag instance so it can be used or reused. A newly created Tag instance has to be prepared by invoking this method before invoking doStartTag(). A Tag instance that has been used and released by invoking release() must be reinitialized by invoking this method. initialize() returns no value and throws no exceptions.

Parameters

Tag

TagData

PageContext

release() Method

```
public void release()
```

This method releases a Tag instance so it can be used or reused. release() has no parameters, returns no value, and throws no exceptions.

setBodyOut() Method

```
public void setBodyOut(BodyJspWriter b)
```

This method sets the BodyJspWriter. It will be invoked once per action invocation at most. It will not be invoked if there is no body evaluation. setBodyOut() returns no value and throws no exceptions.

Parameters

BodyJspWriter

setValue() Method

```
public void setValue(java.lang.String key,
  java.lang.Object value)
```

This method sets a user-defined value on the tag. setValue() returns no value and throws no exceptions.

Parameters

java.lang.String

java.lang.Object

IterationTag Interface

```
public interface IterationTag extends Tag
```

The IterationTag interface extends Tag by defining an additional method and data member that is used to reevaluate the body of a tag.

EVAL_BODY_AGAIN Field

```
public static final int EVAL_BODY_AGAIN
```

The EVAL_BODY_AGAIN data member is used to tell the JSP/servlet container that you want to evaluate the tag body again. This value should be returned from the doAfterBody() method.

doAfterBody() Method

```
public int doAfterBody() throws JspException
```

The doAfterBody() method is executed after the tag body has been evaluated. This method is not invoked in empty tags or in tags returning SKIP_BODY in doStartTag().This method should return EVAL_BODY_AGAIN if you want to evaluate the tag body again.

Exceptions

JspException

Returns

int

BodyTag Interface

```
public interface BodyTag extends IterationTag
```

The BodyTag interface extends IterationTag by defining additional methods that let a Tag handler access its body.

The interface provides two new methods. The first is to be invoked, to set the Body-Content for the evaluation of the body. The second is to be re-evaluated after every body evaluation.

EVAL_BODY_TAG Field

```
public static final int EVAL_BODY_TAG
```

Request the creation of new BodyContent on which to evaluate the body of this tag. Returned from doStartTag and doAfterBody. This is an illegal return value for doStart-Tag when the class does not implement BodyTag because BodyTag is needed to manipulate the new Writer.

EVAL_BODY_BUFFERED Field

```
public static final int EVAL_BODY_TAG
```

Request the creation of new BodyContent on which to evaluate the body of this tag. Returned from doStartTag and doAfterBody. This is an illegal return value for doStart-Tag when the class does not implement BodyTag because BodyTag is needed to manipulate the new Writer.

setBodyContent() Method

```
public void setBodyContent(BodyContent b)
```

The setBodyContent method is used by the JSP/servlet engine to set the body content of the tag.

Parameters

BodyContent

doInitBody() Method

```
public void doInitBody() throws JspException
```

The method will be invoked once per action invocation by the page implementation after a new BodyContent has been obtained and set on the tag handler via the setBody-Content() method and before the evaluation of the tag's body into that BodyContent.

Exceptions

JspException

TryCatchFinally Interface

```
public interface TryCatchFinally
```

The TryCatchFinally interface can be extended by a Tag, IterationTag, or BodyTag tag handler that wants additional hooks for managing resources. The TryCatchFinally interface defines two methods to handle exceptions thrown during tag execution: doCatch() and doFinally().

doCatch() Method

```
public int doCatch(Throwable t) throws JspException
```

The doCatch() method is invoked if a Throwable occurs while evaluating the Tag.doStartTag(), Tag.doEndTag(), Iteration-Tag.doAfterBody(), and BodyTag.doInit-Body() of a tag that implements the TryCatchFinally. This method can throw an exception that will be propagated further up the catching chain. If an exception is thrown, doFinally() will be invoked.

Parameters

Throwable

Exceptions

Throwable

doFinally() Method

```
public int doFinally()
```

The doFinally() method is invoked after the doEndTag() in all implementing classes. This method is invoked even if an exception has occurred while evaluating the body of the tag, or in any of the following methods: Tag.doStartTag(), Tag.doEndTag(), IterationTag.doAfterBody(), and BodyTag.doInitBody().

Classes

The classes defined to develop JavaServer Pages tag libraries are described in the following sections.

BodyContent Class

```
public abstract class BodyContent extends JspWriter
```

BodyContent is a JspWriter subclass that can be used to process body content so they can be re-extracted at a later time.

enclosingWriter Field

```
private JspWriter enclosingWriter
```

The enclosingWriter represents the JspWriter that is used to write output back to the tag body.

BodyContent() Method

```
protected BodyContent(JspWriter writer)
```

This method is used to construct a BodyJspWriter. It should be used only by a subclass. BodyJspWriter() returns no values and throws no exceptions.

Parameters

JspWriter

clearBody() Method

```
public void clearBody()
```

The clearBody() method is another implementation of the JspWriter method clear(). The only difference is that clearBody() is guaranteed not to throw an exception. clear-Body() has no parameters and returns no value.

getReader() Method

```
public abstract java.io.Reader getReader()
```

The getReader() method returns the value of this BodyJspWriter as a Reader after the BodyJspWriter has been processed. getReader() has no parameters and throws no exceptions.

Returns

java.io.Reader

getString() Method

```
public abstract java.lang.String getString()
```

The getString() method returns the value of this BodyJspWriter as a String after the BodyJspWriter has been processed. It has no parameters and throws no exceptions.

Returns

java.lang.String

writeOut() Method

```
public abstract void writeOut(java.io.Writerout)
```

The writeOut() method writes the contents of this BodyJspWriter into a Writer. It returns no value and throws no exceptions.

Parameters

java.io.Writer

getEnclosingWriter() Method

```
public JspWriter getEnclosingWriter()
```

The getEnclosingWriter() method returns a reference to the enclosing JspWriter used to write data back to the tag's body.

Returns

javax.servlet.jsp.JspWriter

BodyTagSupport Class

```
public class BodyTagSupport extends TagSupport implements
  BodyTag
```

The BodyTagSupport class acts as a helper class for custom tags that process body content. It provides default implementations for all of the methods defined by the BodyTag interface.

bodyContent Field

```
protected javax.servlet.jsp.tagext.BodyContent bodyContent
```

The bodyContent data member represents an encapsulation of the evaluation of the body of an action so it is available to a tag handler.

BodyTagSupport() Method

```
public BodyTagSupport()
```

This is the default constructor. BodyTagSupport() takes no parameters, returns no values, and throws no exceptions.

doAfterBody() Method

```
public int doAfterBody() throws JspException
```

This is the default implementation for the doAfterBody() method defined by the BodyTag interface. The doAfterBody() method takes no parameters.

Returns

int

Exceptions

JspException

doEndTag() Method

```
public int doEndTag() throws JspException
```

This is the default implementation for the doEndTag() method defined by the BodyTag interface. The doEndTag() method takes no parameters.

Returns

int

Exceptions

JspException

doInitBody() Method

```
public void doInitBody() throws JspException
```

This is the default implementation for the doInitBody() method defined by the BodyTag interface. The doInitBody() method takes no parameters and returns no values.

Exceptions

JspException

doStartTag() Method

```
public int doStartTag() throws JspException
```

This is the default implementation for the doStartTag() method defined by the BodyTag interface. The doStartTag() method takes no parameters.

Returns

int

Exceptions

JspException

getBodyContent() Method

```
public BodyContent getBodyContent()
```

This is the default implementation for the getBodyContent() method defined by the BodyTag interface. The getBodyContent() method takes no parameters and throws no exceptions.

Returns

BodyContent

getPreviousOut() Method

```
public int getPreviousOut()
```

This is the default implementation for the getPreviousOut() method defined by the BodyTag interface. The getPreviousOut() method takes no parameters and throws no exceptions.

Returns

JspWriter

release() Method

```
public void release()
```

This is the default implementation for the release() method defined by the BodyTag interface. The release() method takes no parameters, returns no values, and throws no exceptions.

setBodyContent() Method

```
public void setBodyContent(BodyContent b)
```

This is the default implementation for the setBodyContent() method defined by the BodyTag interface. The setBodyContent() method returns no values and throws no exceptions.

Parameters

BodyContent

TagSupport Class

```
public class TagSupport implements IterationTag, Serializable
```

The TagSupport class acts as a helper class for custom tags that do not process body content. It provides default implementations for all of the methods defined by the Tag interface.

id Field

```
protected java.lang.String id
```

This field is used to hold the id attribute for the defined tag.

pageContext Field

```
protected PageContext pageContext
```

This field is used to hold the reference to the tag PageContext object.

TagSupport() Method

```
public TagSupport()
```

This is the default constructor. TagSupport() takes no parameters, returns no values, and throws no exceptions.

doEndTag() Method

```
public int doEndTag() throws JspException
```

This is the default implementation for the doEndTag() method defined by the Tag interface. The doEndTag() method takes no parameters.

Returns

int

Exceptions

JspException

doStartTag() Method

```
public int doStartTag() throws JspException
```

This is the default implementation for the doStartTag() method defined by the Tag interface. The doStartTag() method takes no parameters.

Returns

int

Exceptions

JspException

findAncestorWithClass() Method

```
public static final Tag findAncestorWithClass(Tag from,
  java.lang.Class klass)
```

The findAncestorWithClass() method finds the instance of a given class type that is closest to a given instance. This class is used for coordination among cooperating tags. This method throws no exceptions.

Parameters

Tag

java.lang.Class

Returns

Tag

getId() Method

```
public java.lang.String getId()
```

The getId() method returns the value of the id attribute of this tag or null. This method takes no parameters and throws no exceptions.

Returns

java.lang.String

getParent() Method

```
public Tag getParent()
```

The getParent() method returns the Tag instance enclosing this tag instance. This method takes no parameters and throws no exceptions.

Returns

Tag

getValue() Method

```
public java.lang.Object getValue(java.lang.String k)
```

The getValue() method returns the value associated with named attribute. It throws no exceptions.

Parameters

java.lang.String

Returns

java.lang.Object

getValues() Method

```
public java.util.Enumeration getValues()
```

The getValues() method returns all the attribute values in an Enumeration. It takes no parameters and throws no exceptions.

Returns

java.util.Enumeration

release() Method

```
public void release()
```

This is the default implementation for the release() method defined by the Tag interface. The release() method takes no parameters, returns no values, and throws no exceptions.

removeValue() Method

```
public void removeValue(java.lang.String k)
```

The removeValue() method removes the value associated with named attribute. It throws no exceptions and has no return value.

Parameters

java.lang.String

setId() Method

```
public void setId(java.lang.String id)
```

The setId() method is the basic accessor for setting the tags id attribute. It throws no exceptions and has no return value.

Parameters

java.lang.String

setPageContext() Method

```
public void setPageContext(PageContext pageContext)
```

The setPageContext() method is the basic accessor for setting the tags PageContext. It throws no exceptions and has no return value.

Parameters

PageContext

setParent() Method

```
public void setParent(Tag t)
```

The setParent() method is the basic accessor for setting the tag's parent. It throws no exceptions and has no return value.

Parameters

Tag

setValue() Method

```
public void setValue(java.lang.String k, java.lang.Object o)
```

The setValue() method is the basic accessor for setting a tag's named attribute. It throws no exceptions and has no return value.

Parameters

java.lang.String

java.lang.Object

TagAttributeInfo Class

```
public class TagAttributeInfo extends java.lang.Object
```

This class encapsulates information about a Tag attribute. It is instantiated from the Tag Library Descriptor file (TLD).

ID Field

```
public static final java.lang.String ID
```

This field holds a reference to the tag's ID.

TagAttributeInfo() Method

```
public TagAttributeInfo(String name, boolean required,
  String type, boolean reqTime)
```

This is the default constructor. TagAttributeInfo() takes four parameters, returns no values, and throws no exceptions.

Parameters

java.lang.String

boolean

java.lang.String

boolean

setValue() Method

```
setValue(java.lang.String name,
  java.lang.String type,
  boolean reqTime)
```

This method is the constructor for TagAttributeInfo. There is no public constructor. This class is to be instantiated only from the tag library code under request from some JSP code that is parsing a TLD (Tag Library Descriptor). setValue() returns no value and throws no exceptions.

Parameters

java.lang.String

java.lang.String

boolean

getIdAttribute() Method

```
public static TagAttributeInfo
  getIdAttribute(TagAttributeInfo[] a)
```

This method is a convenience method that goes through an array of TagAttributeInfo objects and looks for an attribute with the name of id. getIdAttribute() throws no exceptions.

Parameters

TagAttributeInfo[]

Returns

TagAttributeInfo

getName() Method

```
public java.lang.String getName()
```

This method returns the name of the attribute for the tag. getName() has no parameters and throws no exceptions.

Returns

java.lang.String

getTypeName() Method

```
public java.lang.String getTypeName()
```

This method returns the type of the attribute for the tag. getTypeName() has no parameters and throws no exceptions.

Returns

java.lang.String

canBeRequestTime() Method

```
public boolean canBeRequestTime()
```

The canBeRequestTime() method returns true or false, depending on whether or not this attribute can hold a request-time value, respectively.

Returns

boolean

isRequired() Method

```
public boolean isRequired()
```

The isRequired() method returns true or false, depending on whether or not this attribute is required, respectively.

Returns

boolean

toString() Method

```
public java.lang.String toString()
```

The toString() method returns a String representation of the values of this instance of the TagAttributeInfo class.

Returns

java.lang.String

TagData Class

```
public class TagData implements java.lang.Cloneable
```

This class encapsulates Tag instance attributes and values. Often, this data is fully static in the case where none of the attributes have runtime expressions as their values. Thus, this class is intended to expose an immutable interface to a set of immutable attribute/value pairs. This class implements Cloneable, so that implementations can create a static instance and then just clone it before adding the request-time expressions. The TagData class has two fields and five methods, described in the following sections.

REQUEST_TIME_VALUE Field

```
public static final java.lang.Object REQUEST_TIME_VALUE
```

This field holds a reference to a distinguished value for an attribute. The value is a request-time expression, which is not yet available because this TagData instance is being used at translation-time.

TagData() Method

```
public TagData(java.lang.Object[][] atts)
```

This method is the constructor for a TagData object. It takes a single parameter, a two-dimensional array of static attributes and values. TagData() returns no values and throws no exceptions.

Parameters

java.lang.Object[][]

TagData() Method

```
public TagData(Hashtable atts)
```

This method is the constructor for a TagData object. It takes a single parameter, a Hashtable of static attributes and values. TagData() returns no values and throws no exceptions.

Parameters

java.util.Hashtable

getAttribute() Method

```
public java.lang.Object getAttribute(java.lang.String name)
```

This method returns the passed-in name's value. getAttribute() throws no exceptions.

Parameters

java.lang.String

Returns

java.lang.Object

getAttributeString() Method

```
public java.lang.String
  getAttributeString(java.lang.String name)
```

This method returns the value of an attribute as a java.lang.String. getAttributeString() throws no exceptions.

Parameters

java.lang.String

Returns

java.lang.String

getId() Method

```
public java.lang.String getId()
```

This method returns the value of the id attribute or null. getID() has no parameters and throws no exceptions.

Returns

java.lang.String

setAttribute() Method

```
public void setAttribute(java.lang.String name,
  java.lang.Object value)
```

This method sets the value of an attribute/value pair. setAttribute() returns no value and throws no exceptions.

Parameters

java.lang.String

java.lang.Object

getAttributes() Method

```
public java.util.Enumeration
  getAttributeString(java.lang.String name)
```

The getAttributes() method returns an Enumeration of the attributes associated with the current TagData instance.

Parameters

non

Returns

java.util.Enumeration

TagExtraInfo Class

```
public abstract class TagExtraInfo extends java.lang.Object
```

This class provides extra tag information for a custom tag. It is mentioned in the Tag Library Descriptor file (TLD). This class must be used if the tag defines any scripting variables, or if the tag wants to provide translation-time validation of the tag attributes.

getTagInfo() Method

```
public TagInfo getTagInfo()
```

This method returns the TagInfo object for this class. getTagInfo() has no parameters and throws no exceptions.

Returns

TagInfo

getVariableInfo() Method

```
public VariableInfo[] getVariableInfo(TagData data)
```

This method returns information on scripting variables defined by this tag. getVariableInfo() throws no exceptions.

Parameters

TagData

Returns

VariableInfo[]

isValid() Method

```
public boolean isValid(TagData data)
```

This method performs translation-time validation of the TagData attributes, returning a Boolean value indicating validity. isValid() throws no exceptions.

Parameters

TagData

Returns

boolean

setTagInfo() Method

```
public void setTagInfo(TagInfo info)
```

This method sets the TagInfo object for this class. setTagInfo() returns no value and throws no exceptions.

Parameters

TagInfo

TagInfo Class

```
public abstract class TagInfo extends java.lang.Object
```

This class provides Tag information for a tag in a tag library. It is instantiated from the Tag Library Descriptor file (TLD).

BODY_CONTENT_JSP Field

```
public static final java.lang.String BODY_CONTENT_JSP
```

This field holds a reference to a static constant for getBodyContent() when it is a JSP.

BODY_CONTENT_TAG_DEPENDENT Field

```
public static final java.lang.String BODY_CONTENT_TAG_DEPENDENT
```

This field holds a reference to a static constant for getBodyContent() when it is Tag dependent.

BODY_CONTENT_EMPTY Field

```
public static final java.lang.String BODY_CONTENT_ EMPTY
```

This field holds a reference to a static constant returned by getBodyContent() when the JSP's body is empty.

TagInfo() Method

```
public TagInfo(java.lang.String tagName,
  java.lang.String tagClassName,
  java.lang.String bodycontent,
  java.lang.String infoString,
  TagLibraryInfo tagLib,
  TagExtraInfo tagExtraInfo,
  TagAttributeInfo[] attribInfo)
```

This method is the constructor for TagInfo. There is no public constructor. This class is to be instantiated only from the tag library code under request from some JSP code that is parsing a TLD (Tag Library Descriptor). TagInfo() returns no value and throws no exceptions. This constructor is used for JSP 1.1 backward compatibility.

Parameters

java.lang.String

java.lang.String

java.lang.String

java.lang.String

TagLibraryInfo

TagExtraInfo

TagAttributeInfo[]

TagInfo() Method

```
public TagInfo(java.lang.String tagName,
  java.lang.String tagClassName,
  java.lang.String bodycontent,
  java.lang.String infoString,
  TagLibraryInfo tagLib,
  TagExtraInfo tagExtraInfo,
  TagAttributeInfo[] attribInfo,
  String displayName,
  String smallIcon,
  String largeIcon,
  TagVariableInfo[] tvi)
```

This method is the constructor for TagInfo. There is no public constructor. This class is to be instantiated only from the tag library code under request from some JSP code that is parsing a TLD (Tag Library Descriptor). TagInfo() returns no value and throws no exceptions. This constructor is used for JSP 1.2.

Parameters

java.lang.String

java.lang.String

java.lang.String

java.lang.String

TagLibraryInfo

TagExtraInfo

TagAttributeInfo[]

java.lang.String

java.lang.String

TagVariableInfo[]

getAttributes() Method

```
public TagAttributeInfo[] getAttributes()
```

This method returns a reference to an array of TagAttributeInfo objects. If a null is returned, then there is no attribute information. getAttributes() has no parameters and throws no exceptions.

Returns

TagAttributeInfo[]

getBodyContent() Method

```
public java.lang.String getBodyContent()
```

This method returns a reference to a java.lang.String containing information on the body content of these tags. getBodyContent() has no parameters and throws no exceptions.

Returns

java.lang.String

getInfoString() Method

```
public java.lang.String getInfoString()
```

This method returns a reference to a java.lang.String containing the optional string information for this tag. getInfoString() has no parameters and throws no exceptions.

Returns

java.lang.String

getTagClassName() Method

```
public java.lang.String getTagClassName()
```

This method returns a reference to a java.lang.String containing the name of the tag handler class. getTagClassName() has no parameters and throws no exceptions.

Returns

java.lang.String

getTagExtraInfo() Method

```
public TagExtraInfo getTagExtraInfo()
```

This method returns a reference the TagExtraInfo object. getTagExtraInfo() has no parameters and throws no exceptions.

Returns

TagExtraInfo

setTagExtraInfo() Method

```
public void setTagExtraInfo(TagExtraInfo tei)
```

This method is used to set a reference to a TagExtraInfo object.

Parameters

TagExtraInfo

setTagLibrary() Method

```
public void setTagLibrary()
```

This method sets a reference to a TagLibraryInfo object.

Parameters

TagLibraryInfo

getTagLibrary() Method

```
public TagLibraryInfo getTagLibrary()
```

This method returns a reference the TagLibraryInfo object. getTagLibrary() has no parameters and throws no exceptions.

Returns

TagLibraryInfo

getTagName() Method

```
public java.lang.String getTagName()
```

This method returns a reference to a java.lang.String containing the name of this tag. getTagName() has no parameters and throws no exceptions.

Returns

java.lang.String

getVariableInfo() Method

```
public VariableInfo[] getVariableInfo(TagData data)
```

This method returns information on the object created by this tag at runtime. If null is returned, then no such object was created. The default is null if the tag has no id attribute. getVariableInfo() throws no exceptions.

Parameters

TagData

Returns

VariableInfo[]

isValid() Method

```
public boolean isValid(TagData data)
```

This method performs translation-time validation of the TagData attributes. isValid() throws no exceptions.

Parameters

TagData

Returns

boolean

getDisplayName() Method

```
public java.lang.String getDisplayName()
```

This method returns a reference to a java.lang.String containing the display name of this tag. This method will most often be used by JSP tools.

Returns

java.lang.String

getSmallIcon() Method

```
public java.lang.String getSmallIcon()
```

This method returns a reference to a java.lang.String representing the path to a small icon to be used by JSP tools.

Returns

java.lang.String

getLargeIcon() Method

```
public java.lang.String getLargeIcon()
```

This method returns a reference to a java.lang.String representing the path to a large icon to be used by JSP tools.

Returns

java.lang.String

toString() Method

```
public java.lang.String toString()
```

The toString() method returns a String representation of the values of this instance of the TagInfo class.

Returns

java.lang.String

getTagVariableInfos() Method

```
public TagVariableInfo[] getTagVariableInfos()
```

This method returns a reference to an array of TagVariableInfo objects. If a null is returned, then there is no attribute information. getTagVariableInfos() has no parameters and throws no exceptions.

Returns

TagVariableInfo[]

TagLibraryInfo Class

```
public abstract class TagLibraryInfo extends java.lang.Object
```

This class provides information on the tag library. It is instantiated from the Tag Library Descriptor file (TLD). TagLibraryInfo class has eight fields and nine methods.

prefix Field

```
protected java.lang.String prefix
```

This field holds a reference to the prefix used by the taglib directive.

uri Field

```
protected java.lang.String uri
```

This field holds a reference to the URI used by the taglib directive to identify the tag library.

tags Field

```
protected TagInfo[] uri
```

This field holds an array of TagInfo objects for the tags defined in this tag library.

tlibversion Field

```
protected java.lang.String tlibversion
```

This field holds a reference to the URI actually used by the taglib directive.

jspversion Field

```
protected java.lang.String jspversion
```

This field holds a reference to the required JSP version for this taglib.

shortname Field

```
protected java.lang.String shortname
```

This field holds a reference to the preferred short name, as identified by the TLD, for this taglib.

urn Field

```
protected java.lang.String urn
```

This field holds a reference to a URN referencing the tag library's TLD.

info Field

```
protected java.lang.String info
```

This field holds a reference to the information string, defined in the TLD, for this tag library.

TagLibraryInfo() Method

```
public TagLibraryInfo(java.lang.String prefix,
  java.net.URL uri)
```

This method is the constructor for the TagLibraryInfo class. It will invoke the constructors for TagInfo and TagAttributeInfo after parsing the TLD file. TagLibraryInfo() returns no value and throws no exceptions.

Parameters

java.lang.String

java.net.URL

getInfoString() Method

```
public java.lang.String getInfoString()
```

This method returns the information string for this tag library. getInfoString() has no parameters and throws no exceptions.

Returns

java.lang.String

getPrefixString() Method

```
public java.lang.String getPrefixString()
```

This method returns the prefix assigned to this taglib from the taglib directive. getPrefixString() has no parameters and throws no exceptions.

Returns

java.lang.String

getReliableURN() Method

```
public java.lang.String getReliableURN()
```

This method returns a reliable URN to a TLD. getReliableURN() has no parameters and throws no exceptions.

Returns

java.lang.String

getRequiredVersion() Method

```
public java.lang.String getRequiredVersion()
```

This method returns the required JSP version for this taglib. getRequiredVersion() has no parameters and throws no exceptions.

Returns

java.lang.String

getShortName() Method

```
public java.lang.String getShortName()
```

This method returns the preferred short name for the taglib. getShortName() has no parameters and throws no exceptions.

Returns

java.lang.String

getTag() Method

```
public TagInfo getTag(java.lang.String name)
```

This method returns the TagInfo for a given tag short name. getTag() throws no exceptions.

Parameters

java.lang.String

Returns

TagInfo

getTags() Method

```
public TagInfo[] getTags()
```

This method returns an array of TagInfo objects for the tags defined in this tag library. getTags() has no parameters and throws no exceptions.

Returns

TagInfo[]

getURI() Method

```
public java.net.URL getURI()
```

This method returns the URI from the taglib directive for this library. getURI() has no parameters and throws no exceptions.

Returns

java.net.URL

VariableInfo Class

```
public class VariableInfo extends java.lang.Object
```

This class provides information on the scripting variables that are created and modified by a tag at runtime. This information is provided by TagExtraInfo classes, and it is used by the translation phase of JSP.

AT_BEGIN Field

```
public static final int AT_BEGIN
```

This field states that the visibility of a variable begins after the start tag.

AT_END Field

```
public static final int AT_END
```

This field states that the visibility of a variable begins after the end tag.

NESTED Field

```
public static final int NESTED
```

This field states that the visibility of a variable is between the start and end tags.

VariableInfo() Method

```
public VariableInfo(java.lang.String varName,
  java.lang.String className,
```

```
boolean declare,
int scope)
```

This method is the VariableInfo constructor. These objects can be created at translation time by the TagExtraInfo instances. VariableInfo() returns no value and throws no exceptions.

Parameters

java.lang.String

java.lang.String

boolean

int

getClassName() Method

```
public java.lang.String getClassName()
```

This method returns to the class name of the scripting variable. getClassName() has no parameters and throws no exceptions.

Returns

java.lang.String

getDeclare() Method

```
public boolean getDeclare()
```

This method returns a Boolean that indicates whether the variable is a new variable. getDeclare() has no parameters and throws no exceptions.

Returns

boolean

getScope() Method

```
public int getScope()
```

This method returns an integer indicating the lexical scope of the variable. getScope() has no parameters and throws no exceptions.

Returns

int

getVarName() Method

```
public java.lang.String getVarName()
```

This method returns to the class name of the scripting variable. getVarName() has no parameters and throws no exceptions.

Returns

java.lang.String

TagVariableInfo Class

```
public class VariableInfo extends java.lang.Object
```

The TagVariableInfo class contains variable information for a tag in a given tag library. This class is instantiated from the Tag Library Descriptor file (TLD) and is available only at translation time.

TagVariableInfo() Method

```
public TagVariableInfo(java.lang.String nameGiven,
  java.lang.String nameFromAttribute,
  java.lang.String className,
  boolean declare,
  int scope)
```

This method is the TagVariableInfo constructor.

Parameters

java.lang.String

java.lang.String

java.lang.String

boolean

int

getClassName() Method

```
public java.lang.String getClassName()
```

This method returns to the class name of the tag variable. getClassName() has no parameters and throws no exceptions.

Returns

java.lang.String

getNameFromAttribute() Method

```
public java.lang.String getNameFromAttribute()
```

This method returns the name of an attribute whose translation-time value will contain the name of the variable. getNameFromAttribute() has no parameters and throws no exceptions.

Returns

java.lang.String

getDeclare() Method

```
public boolean getDeclare()
```

This method returns a Boolean that indicates whether the variable is to be declared or not. getDeclare() has no parameters and throws no exceptions.

Returns

boolean

getScope() Method

```
public int getScope()
```

This method returns an integer indicating the lexical scope of the variable. getScope() has no parameters and throws no exceptions.

Returns

int

getNameGiven() Method

```
public java.lang.String getNameGiven()
```

This method returns to the name of the tag variable as a constant. getNameGiven() has no parameters and throws no exceptions.

Returns

java.lang.String

TagLibraryValidator Class

```
public abstract class TagLibraryValidator extends
  java.lang.Object
```

The TagLibraryValidator class is an abstract class that provides a mechanism for implementing translation-time validators for JSP pages. A validator operates on the XML document associated with the JSP page.

TagLibraryValidator() Method

```
public TagLibraryValidator ()
```

This method is the TagVariableInfo constructor. This method takes no parameters and throws no exceptions.

getInitParameters() Method

```
public java.util.Map getInitParameters()
```

This method returns a Map containing the init parameters found in the tag library's TLD as an immutable Map. The parameter names are keys, and parameter values are the values. getInitParameters() has no parameters and throws no exceptions.

Returns

java.util.Map

setInitParameters() Method

```
public void getInitParameters(java.util.Map map)
```

This method sets the Map containing the init parameters found in the tag library's

TLD. The parameter names are keys, and parameter values are the values. getInitParameters() has no return value and throws no exceptions.

Parameters

java.util.Map

release() Method

```
public void release()
```

This method releases all data, reserved by this TagLibraryValidator instance, being used for validation purposes. release() has no parameters and throws no exceptions.

Returns

java.lang.String

validate() Method

```
public java.lang.String validate(java.lang.String prefix,
  java.lang.String uri,
  PageData page)
```

The validate() method validates a JSP based upon the implementation of this method. This method is invoked once per directive in the JSP page. This method will return a null String if the page passed through is valid. If the page fails validation, an error message will be returned. The validate() method takes three parameters and throws no exceptions.

Parameters

java.lang.String

java.lang.String

javax.servlet.jsp.tagext.PageData

Returns

java.lang.String

PageData Class

```
public abstract class PageData extends
  java.lang.Object
```

The PageData class contains translation-time information on a JSP page. The information corresponds to the XML view of the JSP page.

PageData() Method

```
public PageData()
```

This method is the PageData constructor. This method takes no parameters and throws no exceptions.

getInputStream() Method

```
public abstract java.io.InputStream getInputStream()
```

This getInputStream() method returns an input stream containing an XML view of the current JSP page.

Returns

java.io.InputStream

Index

E

L

M

N-O

P

T

U-V

W